THE ESSENTIAL
LAW OF ATTRACTION
COLLECTION

THE ESSENTIAL
LAW OF ATTRACTION
COLLECTION

Includes the all-time international bestsellers:
THE LAW OF ATTRACTION
MONEY, AND THE LAW OF ATTRACTION
THE VORTEX

ESTHER AND JERRY HICKS

The Teachings of Abraham®

HAY HOUSE, INC.
Carlsbad, California • New York City
London • Sydney • Johannesburg
Vancouver • Hong Kong • New Delhi

Published and distributed in the United States by: Hay House, Inc.: www.hay house.com® • *Published and distributed in Australia by:* Hay House Australia Pty. Ltd.: www.hayhouse.com.au • *Published and distributed in the United Kingdom by:* Hay House UK, Ltd.: www.hayhouse.co.uk • *Published and distributed in the Republic of South Africa by:* Hay House SA (Pty), Ltd.: www.hayhouse.co.za • *Distributed in Canada by:* Raincoast: www.raincoast.com • *Published in India by:* Hay House Publishers India: www.hayhouse.co.in

Cover design: Aeshna Roy
Interior design of <u>The Law of Attraction</u> *and*
    <u>Money, and the Law of Attraction</u>*:* Tricia Breidenthal
Interior design of <u>The Vortex</u>*:* Nick C. Welch

The Law of Attraction, The Teachings of Abraham, The Art of Allowing, Segment Intending, and *The Science of Deliberate Creation* are registered trademarks of Esther and Jerry Hicks.

Library of Congress Control Number: 2013942839

Hardcover ISBN: 978-1-4019-4420-9

16 15 14 13   4 3 2 1
1st edition, September 2013

Printed in the United States of America

CONTENTS

BOOK 1

The Law of Attraction

The Basics of the Teachings of Abraham®

*This book is dedicated to all of you who, in your
desire for enlightenment and Well-Being, have asked
the questions this book has answered; and to the four
delightful children of our children, who are examples
of what the book teaches: Laurel (8); Kevin (5);
Kate (4); and Luke (1), who are not yet asking
because they have not yet forgotten.*

*And these teachings are especially dedicated to Louise Hay,
whose desire to ask and learn—and disseminate around
this planet—the principles of Well-Being, has led her to create
the Hay House publishing company, which has enabled
the distribution of so much joy throughout the world.*

Foreword

by Neale Donald Walsch, the best-selling author of
The Conversations with God series and
Home with God in a Life That Never Ends

This is it. Here they are. You don't have to go any further. Put all the other books down, un-enroll from all the workshops and seminars, and tell your life coach you won't need to be calling anymore.

Because this is it: everything you need to know about life and how to make it work. Here they are: all the rules of the road for this extraordinary journey. All the tools with which to create the experiences you've always wanted. You don't have to go any further than where you are right now.

Indeed, look at what you've done already.

Just look.

I mean, *right now,* look at what you're holding in your hands.

You did that. You put this book right here, right where it is, right in front of your eyes. You manifested it, out of the clear blue sky. That alone is all the evidence you need that *this book works.*

Do you understand? No, no, don't jump over this. It's important that you really hear this. I'm telling you that you are holding in your hands the best proof you could ever give yourself that the *Law of Attraction* is real, is effective, and produces *physical outcomes in the real world.*

Let me explain.

Somewhere in the deep reaches of your consciousness, somewhere in an important place in your mind, you set an intention to receive this message, or this book would never have found its way to you.

This is no small thing here. This is a big deal. Believe me, it's a big deal. Because *you are about to create exactly what you set your intention to create:* a major change in your life.

That *was* your intention, wasn't it? Of course it was. What is occurring as you read these words wouldn't be happening if you hadn't placed your attention on a deep desire to lift your day-to-day experience to a new level. You've wanted to do this for a long time. Your only questions have been: *How? What are the rules? What are the tools?*

Well, here they are. You asked for them, you got 'em. And that's the very first rule, by the way. What you ask for, you get. But there's more to it than that—lots more. And that's what this extraordinary book is about. Here, you're not only going to be given some pretty amazing tools, but *instructions on how to use them.*

Have you ever wished that life came with an instruction book?

Hey, good wishing. Now it does.

We have Esther and Jerry Hicks to thank for that. And, of course, Abraham. (They will tell you all about who *that* is in the fascinating, exhilarating text to follow.) Esther and Jerry are devoting their lives to the joy of sharing the wondrous messages that Abraham has given them. I admire and love them so much for this; and I am so, so grateful, for they are truly extraordinary people on a glorious mission to bring glory to the mission upon which we have *all* embarked: the living and the experiencing of the glory of Life itself, and of Who We Really Are.

I know that you will be so impressed, and so blessed, by what you find here. I know that reading this book will produce a turning point in your life. Here is not only a description of the most important law of the universe (the only one you'll ever need to know about, really), but an easy-to-understand explanation of the *mechanics of life.* This is breathtaking information. This is monumental data. This is brilliant, flashing insight.

There are very few books about which I would say what I am going to say next. *Read every word here, and do everything this book says.* It answers all the questions you have so earnestly asked in your heart. So—may I be this direct?—pay attention.

This book is about *how* to pay attention, and if you pay attention to *how* to pay attention, your every intention can be made manifest in your reality—and that will change your life forever.

ᴥᴥᴥ ᴥᴥᴥ

Preface

by Jerry Hicks

T he groundbreaking philosophy of practical spirituality that you are about to discover in this book was first revealed to Esther and me in 1986, in response to the very long list of questions that I had been without answer for, for many years.

Within these pages you'll find the basics of the *Teachings of Abraham*™ as they were lovingly spoken to us in the very first days of our interactions with them (please note that the singular name "Abraham" is a *group* of loving entities, which is why they're referred to in the plural).

The recordings from which this book evolved were first formally published in 1988 as part of an album of ten *Special Subjects* cassette recordings. But since that time, many aspects of Abraham's basic teachings regarding the *Universal Law of Attraction* have been published in varied forms of books, CDs, DVDs, card decks, calendars, articles, radio and television shows, and workshops, as well as by the many other best-selling authors who have incorporated the teachings of Abraham into their teachings. However, never before this book, *The Law of Attraction,* have these original teachings been published in their entirety in a single volume.

(Should you like to hear one of the original recordings from the series, you can find our free *Introduction to Abraham* as a 70-minute download at our Website: **www.abraham-hicks.com**.)

This book was created by transcribing our original *"Abraham Basics" Starter Set* of five CDs and then asking Abraham to edit them slightly to enhance the readability of the spoken word. Abraham has also added several new passages for the sake of clarity and continuity.

Millions of readers, listeners, and viewers have been enjoying the value they've received from these teachings. And Esther and I are thrilled to offer to you, in this *Law of Attraction* format, the original basic teachings of Abraham.

But how does this book compare to Abraham's *Ask and It Is Given?* Well, consider *The Law of Attraction* the basic primer from which all of the other teachings have flowed. And consider *Ask and It Is Given* to be the most comprehensive volume of the first 20 years of Abraham's teachings.

Revisiting this life-changing material in the preparation of the publication of this book has been a wonderful experience for Esther and me, for we've been reminded of these basic and simple *Laws* that Abraham effectively explained to us so many years ago.

Since originally receiving this material, Esther and I have done our best to apply to our own lives what we have learned about these *Laws*, and the marvelous progression of our joyous lives is astounding. We took Abraham at their word because everything they told us made so much sense to us, but the application of these teachings has now been proven in our day-to-day experience. And it is with extraordinary joy that we can tell you—from our own personal experience: *This works!*

⋖⋖⋖ ⋗⋗⋗

(**Editor's Note:** Please note that since there aren't always physical English words to perfectly express the Non-Physical thoughts that Esther receives, she sometimes forms new combinations of words, as well as using standard words in new ways—for example, capitalizing or italicizing them when normally they wouldn't be—in order to express new ways of looking at life.)

Our Path to the Abraham Experience

INTRODUCTION

by Jerry Hicks

We've written this book to introduce you to *Universal Laws* and practical processes that will guide you clearly and precisely to the realization of your natural state of Well-Being. Your reading of this book will give you the unique and beneficial experience of hearing precise, powerful answers to questions that I've accumulated from a lifetime of asking. And your successful utilization of this joy-based philosophy of practical spirituality will also help you guide others to living whatever they would consider to be the perfect life.

Many have indicated to me that my questions, in many ways, have mirrored their own. And so, as you experience the clarity and brilliance of Abraham's answers, not only will you likely begin to feel a true satisfaction that long-asked questions have been answered, but you'll discover, as we (Esther and I) have, a renewed enthusiasm for your own life experience. And as you, from your fresh new outlook on life, begin to apply the practical processes that are offered here, you'll discover that you can deliberately create for yourself anything that you want to do, be, or have.

It seems to me that my life, from as far back as I can remember, produced a stream of seemingly never-ending questions to which I wasn't able to find satisfactory answers, for I had strongly wanted to discover a philosophy of life that was based on absolute truth. But once Abraham came into our experience—revealing to Esther and me their explanation of the powerful *Laws* of the Universe, coupled with effective processes that helped us to turn ideology and theory into practical results—I came to realize that the steady stream of books, teachers, and life experiences that I *did* encounter on my path were the perfect steps along the way to the discovery of Abraham.

I like thinking about the opportunity that you now have as you read this book to discover for yourself the value of what Abraham offers, because I know how these teachings have enhanced our life experience. I'm also aware that you would not now be holding this book in your hands if your life experience had not prepared you (as my life has prepared me) for receiving this information.

I feel an eagerness for you to dive into this book to discover the simple and powerful *Laws* and practical processes that Abraham offers so that you may begin to *deliberately* attract into *your* experience everything that *you* desire, and so that you may release anything from your experience that you don't want.

A Steady Stream of Religious Groups

My parents weren't religious people, so I don't really understand why it was that I felt such a powerful compulsion to find a church and become involved in the tenets of its religion, but it was a powerful force within me as I was growing up. Maybe it was an attempt to fill the very real void that I felt deep inside, or maybe it was because so many others around me were demonstrating their religious fervor and their certainty that they had discovered *truth*.

During my first 14 years, I lived in 18 homes in six states, so I had the opportunity to evaluate a wide variety of philosophies. In any case, I systematically marched myself into church after church, each time hoping with all my heart that inside *these* doors I would find what I was looking for. But as I moved from one religious or philosophical group to another, my disappointment grew as they each exclaimed *their* rightness, at the same time declaring all of the others *wrong*. And in this environment, with my heart sinking again and again, I knew that I hadn't found the answers I was looking for. (It was only after discovering the teachings of Abraham that I've been able to come to understand, and to no longer feel negative emotion about, those apparent philosophical contradictions.) And so, my search for answers continued.

A Ouija Board Spells the Alphabet

Even though I'd never had any personal experience with a Ouija board, I did, nevertheless, have strong negative opinions about it. I believed that it was, at best, only a game, and at worst, an absolute hoax. So in 1959 when friends in Spokane, Washington, presented me with the idea of playing with the board, I immediately dismissed it as ridiculous. But as my friends persisted, and subsequently presented me with my first actual experience with it, I saw for myself that a real phenomenon was occurring.

Therefore, since I was still searching for answers to my lifelong list of questions, I asked the board, "How can I become truly good?" At first, and with dramatic speed, it spelled the alphabet, and then the planchette pointed to **R-E-A-D.**

"Read what?" I asked. It spelled **B-O-O-K-S.** And then when I asked, "What books?" it spelled (again with that first dramatic speed): **A N Y A N D A L L B Y A L B E R T S C H W E I T Z E R.** My friends had not heard of Albert Schweitzer, and while I knew very little about him, my curiosity was piqued, to say the least, and I decided to do some research to find out about this man who had just come into my conscious awareness in this truly extraordinary way.

In the first library I could find, I discovered a very large selection of books written by Albert Schweitzer, and I systematically read them all. And while I cannot say that I discovered any specific answers to my long list of questions, Schweitzer's book *The Quest of the Historical Jesus* especially opened my mind to the awareness that there are many more ways of looking at things than I had been willing to consider.

My enthusiasm for what I had hoped was to be a window into powerful enlightenment and answers to all of my questions was eventually dashed as I found neither powerful enlightenment from the Ouija board nor answers to all of my questions, but it had certainly awakened within me the realization that there was an avenue of intelligent communication available that I had never believed was possible before I had experienced it myself.

The Ouija board wouldn't work for me at all when I used it on my own, but I tried it on hundreds of people in my travels as an entertainer, and I found three people who had success with it. With some friends in Portland, Oregon (whom the board *did* work for), we "talked" for hundreds of hours with what we thought to be Non-Physical Beings. What an entertaining parade of pirates, priests, politicians, and rabbis conversed with us! It was much like the kind of fascinating conversations you might engage in at parties, with individuals offering a wide variety of agendas, attitudes, and intellects.

I have to say that I learned nothing of value from that board that I could use in my own life—or that I wanted to teach anybody else—so one day I just threw it away, and that was the end of that stage of my interest or activity with the Ouija board. However, this remarkable experience—especially with the Intelligence that encouraged my reading of books—not only awakened within me an understanding that there is much more "out there" than I currently understood, but it provoked within me an even more powerful desire to find answers. I came to believe that it was possible to tap into an Intelligence that had practical answers to questions about how the Universe works, why we are all here, how we can live more joyous lives, and how we can fulfill our reasons for being here.

Think and Grow Rich

Perhaps the first experience of actually finding practical answers to my growing list of questions came to me in the discovery of a fascinating book while I was doing concerts in a series of colleges and universities in 1965. The book was lying on a coffee table in the lobby of a small motel somewhere in Montana, and I remember a contradiction formulating within me as I held it and looked at the words on the front cover: *Think and Grow Rich!* by Napoleon Hill.

This title was off-putting to me, for I, like so many others, had been taught to shore up my negative impression of rich people as justification for my own lack of easily acquired resources. There was something undeniably compelling about this book, though, and after I'd gotten only about 12 pages into it, the hair was standing up all over my body, and thrill bumps were rippling up and down my spine.

We've now come to understand that these physical, visceral sensations are confirming evidence that we're currently on the path to something of extreme value, but even then I felt that this book awakened within me the knowledge that my thoughts are important, and that my life experience somehow reflects the contents of my thoughts. The book was compelling and interesting, and it inspired a desire within me to attempt to follow the suggestions that were offered—and I did.

Utilizing the teachings worked so well for me, in fact, that in a very brief amount of time I was able to build a multinational business, giving me the opportunity to touch the lives of thousands of people in a meaningful way. I even began teaching the principles that I was learning. But although I had personally received incredible value from Napoleon Hill's life-changing book, many of the lives of those I was teaching weren't as dramatically improved as mine had been no matter how many courses they took, so my search for more specific answers continued.

Seth Speaks about Creating Your Reality

While my lifelong quest to discover meaningful answers to my questions still persisted, and my desire to find a way to help others more effectively achieve their goals loomed larger than ever before, I was temporarily distracted from all of that by the new life that Esther and I were making together in Phoenix, Arizona. We were married in 1980 after knowing each other for a few years, and we found ourselves to be inexplicably compatible. We were experiencing joy, day after wonderful day, exploring our new city, making our new home, and discovering our new life together. And while Esther didn't exactly share my thirst for knowledge or my hunger for answers, she was eager about life, always happy, and very nice to be with.

One day while passing time in a library, I spotted a book entitled *Seth Speaks* by Jane Roberts, and it seemed that before I could extract the book from the shelf, I felt my hairs standing on end again, and my body was again covered in thrill bumps. I leafed through the pages of this book, wondering what it could possibly contain that could be responsible for my emotional response.

During the time that Esther and I had been together, I had discovered only one point of contention between us: She didn't want to hear about my Ouija-board experiences. Whenever I would launch into (what I considered to be) an extremely entertaining account, Esther would leave the room. She'd been taught during her childhood to have tremendous fear of anything that wasn't physical, and since I didn't want to disturb her, I stopped telling those stories, at least while she was around. And so, it wasn't really a surprise to me that Esther didn't want to hear about the book *Seth Speaks* either. . . .

Author Jane Roberts would go into a sort of trance and allow Seth, a Non-Physical personality, to speak through her in order to dictate the series of highly influential *Seth* books. I found the works to be stimulating and fascinating, and I began to see an avenue to some of the answers to my long list of questions. But Esther was frightened by the book. Her discomfort surfaced immediately upon hearing of the manner in which the book had been written, and was powerfully compounded when she viewed the strange-looking picture on the back of the book of Jane, in trance, speaking for Seth.

"You can read the book if you want to," Esther told me, "but please don't bring it into our bedroom."

I've always believed in judging the tree by its fruits, so everything that I consider, I do from the standpoint of how *I* feel about it . . . and there was so much of the Seth material that just felt right to me. So it didn't make any difference to me *where* it came from or *how* it was presented. In essence, I felt that I had found valuable information that *I* could use—and that I could pass on to other people whom I believed could use it. I was excited!

-⊲❖⊳-

My Fears Were Resolved

by Esther Hicks

I thought it was both very wise and very kind of Jerry not to push the *Seth* books at me, because I really did feel a strong aversion to them. The whole idea of a person being in contact with a Non-Physical Being made me extremely uncomfortable, so, since Jerry didn't want to disturb me, he would get up early in the morning, and while I was still sleeping, he'd read those books to himself. Gradually, when he'd find something that was particularly interesting to him, he would gently slip it into the conversation, and in my less resistant state, I could often hear the value of the idea. Bit by bit, Jerry introduced another concept and another, until I began to feel true interest in those amazing works. Eventually, it became our morning ritual. We would sit together, and Jerry would read to me from the *Seth* books.

My fears weren't grounded in any negative personal experience, but from hearsay that I'd picked up, probably from others who had also picked it up from hearsay. Looking back, it now seems utterly illogical that I had those fears. In any event, I experienced a real change in attitude once I realized that as far as my personal experience was concerned . . . it all felt good.

As time passed, and as my fear of Jane's process in the receiving of the information from Seth subsided, I began to feel immense

17

appreciation for these wonderful books. In fact, we were so happily involved in what we were reading that we thought we would take a trip to New York to meet Jane and her husband, Robert—and even Seth! How far I had come, in that now I actually wanted to meet this Non-Physical Being. But the authors' phone number was unpublished, so we didn't know exactly what to do next to accomplish this meeting.

One day we were eating lunch in a little café next to a bookstore in Scottsdale, Arizona, and Jerry was leafing through a new book he'd just purchased, when a stranger who was sitting nearby asked us, "Have you read any of the *Seth* books?"

We could hardly believe what we were hearing, because we hadn't told a single person that we were reading those books. Then the man asked, "Did you know that Jane Roberts is dead?"

I remember my eyes filling with tears as the impact of these words washed over me. It was as if someone had told me my sister was dead and I hadn't known about it. It was shocking. We felt such disappointment, as we realized that now there would be no possible way for us to meet Jane and Rob . . . or Seth.

Sheila "Channels" Theo

Within a day or so of our hearing about Jane's death, our friends and business associates, Nancy and her husband, Wes, met us for dinner. "We have a tape we want you to hear," Nancy said, pushing a cassette into my hand. Our friends' behavior seemed awkward to me; there was just something odd about it. In fact, I felt the same feeling coming from them that I'd felt from Jerry upon his discovery of the *Seth* books. It was as if they had a secret that they wanted to share but were worried about how we'd respond once it *was* shared.

"What is it?" we asked.

"It's channeled," Nancy whispered.

I don't believe that either Jerry or I had ever heard the word *channeled* offered in that context. "What do you mean, 'channeled'?" I asked.

As Nancy and Wes offered their brief and somewhat disjointed explanation, both Jerry and I realized that they were describing the same process by which the *Seth* books had been written. "Her name is Sheila," they continued, "and she speaks for an entity named Theo. She's coming to Phoenix, and you can make an appointment to talk with her if you want to."

We decided to make an appointment, and I can still remember how excited we were. We met in a beautiful (Frank Lloyd Wright–designed) home in Phoenix. It was broad daylight, and to my relief, nothing even remotely spooky happened. Everything was very comfortable and pleasant. As we sat and "visited" with Theo (well, I should say, as *Jerry* visited with Theo—I don't think I said a word during that meeting), I was absolutely amazed!

Jerry had a notebook full of questions, ones he said he'd saved up since he was six years old. He was so excited, asking question after question, sometimes interrupting in the middle of an answer so that he could get one more question in before our time was up. The half hour passed so quickly, and we felt wonderful!

"Can we come back tomorrow?" I asked, because now I was developing a list of questions that *I* wanted to ask Theo.

Should I Meditate?

When we went back the next day, I asked Theo (through Sheila) what we could do to move faster toward our goals. Theo said: *Affirmations,* and then gave me a wonderful one: *I, Esther Hicks, see and draw to me, through Divine Love, those Beings who seek enlightenment through my process. The sharing will elevate us both, now.*

Jerry and I knew about affirmations; we were already using them. And then I asked, "What else?" Theo replied: *Meditate.* Well, I didn't personally know anybody who was meditating, but the whole idea of it just felt strange to me. It wasn't something that I could see myself doing. Jerry said he associated it with people seeing how bad their lives could become—how much pain or poverty they could take—and still exist. In my mind, meditation belonged in the same weird category as walking on hot coals or lying on beds of nails or standing on one foot all day, holding your hand out asking for a donation.

But then I asked Theo, "Well, what do you mean by 'meditate'?"

Theo responded, *For 15 minutes each day, sit in a quiet room, wear comfortable clothing, and focus on your breathing. And as your mind wanders, and it will, just release the thought and focus back on your breathing.* I thought, *Well, that doesn't sound so weird.*

I asked if I should bring our 14-year-old daughter, Tracy, to meet Theo, and the response was: *If it is her asking, but it is not necessary—for you, too, are channels.* I remember how implausible it seemed that something as strange as being a channel—or as significant as being one—could have not been known by us before now. And then the tape recorder clicked off, indicating that, once again, our time was up.

I couldn't believe how fast the time had passed. And so, as I looked down at my list of still-unanswered questions, Stevie, the friend of Sheila's who was operating the tape recorder and taking notes during our conversation with Theo, perhaps noticed my mild frustration, because she asked, "Do you have one last question? Would you like to know the name of *your* spiritual guide?"

That was not a question that would have occurred to me, because I had never heard the term *spiritual guide.* But I liked the sound of such a thing, so I said, "Yes, who is my spiritual guide?"

Theo said: *We are told it will be given to you directly. You will have a clairaudient experience, and you will know.*

We left that beautiful house that day feeling better than we ever remembered. Theo had encouraged us to meditate together. *Because you are compatible, it will be more powerful.* And so, following Theo's suggestions, we went directly home, put on our bathrobes (our most comfortable clothing), closed the drapes in the living room, and sat with the intention of meditating (whatever that meant). I remember thinking, *I'm going to meditate every day for 15 minutes, and I'm going to find out the name of my spiritual guide.* It felt odd for Jerry and me to be doing this strange thing together, so we sat in large wingback chairs with an étagère between us so we couldn't see each other.

Something Began "Breathing" Me

Theo's instructions on the process of meditation had been very brief: *For 15 minutes each day, sit in a quiet room, wear comfortable clothing, and focus on your breathing. And as your mind wanders, and it will, just release the thought and focus back on your breathing.*

So we set a timer for 15 minutes, and I settled back into my large comfortable chair and focused on my breathing. I began counting my breaths, in and out. Almost immediately I began to feel a sort of numbness come over me. It was an extremely pleasant sensation. I liked it.

The timer sounded its alarm and startled me. As I regained my awareness of Jerry and the room, I exclaimed, "Let's do it again!" We set the timer for another 15 minutes, and again I felt that wonderful feeling of detachment, or numbness. This time I couldn't feel the chair beneath me. It was as if I were suspended there in the room and nothing else was there.

So we set the timer for another 15 minutes, and again I settled into this new delicious feeling of detachment—and then I felt the incredible sensation of being "breathed." It was as if something powerful and loving was breathing the air into my lungs and then drawing the air back out again. I realize now that this was my first powerful contact with Abraham, but at that time, all I knew was that something more loving than anything I'd ever experienced before was flowing throughout my entire body. Jerry said that as he heard the difference in the sound of my breathing, he had looked around the étagère at me, and it appeared to him that I was in a state of ecstasy.

When the timer sounded and I began to regain my conscious awareness of my surroundings, there was the feeling of an Energy moving through me unlike anything that I'd ever felt before. It was the most extraordinary experience of my lifetime, and my teeth buzzed (not chattered) for several minutes.

What an amazing sequence of events had led to this still rather unbelievable meeting with Abraham: Irrational fears that I had carried with me my entire life, which had no actual basis in my own life experience, had been released, and were replaced with a most loving and personal encounter with *Source Energy*. I'd never read anything that had given me any real understanding of what or who God was, but I knew that what I had experienced must surely be just that.

My Nose Spells the Alphabet

Because of the powerful and emotional experience of our very first attempt, we made a decision to set aside 15 or 20 minutes every day to meditate. And so, for approximately nine months, Jerry and I sat in our wingback chairs, silently breathing and feeling Well-Being. And then, right before Thanksgiving of 1985, during a period of meditation, I experienced something new: My head began moving very gently. It was a very pleasant sensation, in my state of detachment, to feel the sensation of that subtle movement. It was almost a feeling of flying.

I didn't really think anything of it, except that I knew *I* wasn't doing it and that it was an extremely pleasant experience. My head moved like that for two or three days whenever we were meditating, and on the third day or so, I realized that my head wasn't just meaninglessly moving around—I was actually spelling letters with my nose as if it were writing on a chalkboard. I exclaimed in amazement, "Jerry, I'm spelling the alphabet with my nose!"

With the conscious realization that something remarkable was happening, and that someone was offering communication to me, intense waves of thrill bumps began moving all through my body. Never before that moment or since have I experienced the intensity of such wonderfully thrilling sensations rippling through my body. And then they spelled: *I am Abraham. I am your spiritual guide. I love you. I am here to work with you.*

Jerry got his notebook and began recording everything that I was awkwardly translating with my nose. Letter by letter, Abraham began answering Jerry's questions, sometimes for hours at a time. We were so excited to have made contact with Abraham in this way!

Abraham Begins to Type the Alphabet

It was a somewhat slow and awkward means of communication, but Jerry was getting answers to his questions, and the experience was absolutely exhilarating for both of us. So, for about two months, Jerry asked questions, Abraham answered by spelling out words by guiding the movements of my nose, and Jerry wrote everything down. Then one night we were lying in bed, and my hand began to softly thump on Jerry's chest. It surprised me, and I explained to him, "That's not me. It must be them." And then I felt a strong impulse to type.

I went to my typewriter and held my hands over the keyboard, and in the same way that my head had been involuntarily moving to spell out the letters in the air with my nose, my hands began to move across the keyboard of my typewriter. They were moving so rapidly and with such power that it was somewhat alarming to Jerry. He stood by ready to grab my hands if necessary because he didn't want my fingers to be hurt. He said they were moving so fast that he could barely see them. But there was nothing to be alarmed about.

My fingers touched every key, many, many times, before they began spelling the letters of the alphabet, and then they proceeded to write nearly a page of: **i w a n t o t y p e i w a n t t o t y p e i w a n t t o t y p e**, with no capitalization and no spaces between the words. Then my fingers began typing a message, slowly and methodically, asking that I go to the typewriter every day for 15 minutes. And so that's the way we communicated for the next two months.

The Typist Becomes the Speaker

One day we were driving on the freeway in our small Cadillac Seville, and on either side of us was a large 18-wheeler truck and trailer. This section of the freeway didn't seem to be banked properly, and as all three of us began making this sweeping turn at the same time, both trucks seemed to be crossing over into our lane. It appeared to us that we were about to be crushed by these large vehicles. In the midst of that intensity of emotion, Abraham began to speak. I felt my jaw tighten (not so different from the sensation of yawning), and then my mouth began to involuntarily form these words: *Take the next exit.* And we did. We sat by that underpass, and Jerry talked to Abraham for many hours that day. It was very exciting!

Although I grew more comfortable every day as the process of my translation of Abraham evolved, I asked Jerry if we could just let this be our secret, because I was afraid of how others might respond if they found out what was happening to me. In time, however, a handful of close friends began gathering to dialogue with Abraham, and it was about a year later that we decided to open these teachings to the public, as we are still continuing to do.

The evolution of my experience in translating the vibration of Abraham continues every day. Every seminar leaves Jerry and me feeling amazement at their (Abraham's) clarity, wisdom, and love.

One day I laughed so hard at this realization: "I was so afraid of the idea of the Ouija board, and now I *am* one."

The Delicious Abraham Experiences Evolve

We're never able to find adequate words to express what we feel for this work with Abraham. Jerry seems to have always known what he wanted most, and he'd found ways to achieve much of it before meeting Abraham. But what he has said is that Abraham has brought to his understanding an awareness of our purpose here, and an absolute clarity of *how* we're getting or not getting, and with that, the knowledge that we have complete control. There are no bad "breaks," no "unlucky" days, and no need to move with the tides that have been moved by someone else. Also, we are free . . . we are the absolute creators of our experience—and we love it!

Abraham has explained that my husband and I were a perfect combination for presenting these teachings because Jerry's powerful desire to find answers to his questions summoned Abraham to us, and I was able to quiet my mind and release resistance in order to allow the answers to come forth.

24

It takes very little time for me to allow Abraham to begin speaking through me. From my point of view, I just set forth the intention: *Abraham, I want to clearly speak your words,* and then I focus on my breathing. Within a few seconds, I can feel the clarity, love, and power of Abraham rising within me, and then off we go. . . .

I Have a Conversation with Abraham

by Jerry Hicks

So, this adventure with Abraham, through Esther, continues to excite me, for I've discovered an unending resource for answers to the seemingly unending questions that my own life experience continues to give birth to.

For the first several months after meeting Abraham, Esther and I set aside time in every day to talk with Abraham as I began making my way through my evolving list of questions. In time, as Esther relaxed more into the idea of being someone who could quiet her mind and allow this Infinite Intelligence to flow through her, we began to gradually widen the circle of friends and associates who would gather to discuss the details of their lives with Abraham.

It was very early in our experience when I presented Abraham with my list of burning questions. It's my hope that their answers to *my* early questions may also be satisfying to you. Of course, since that defining moment of plying Abraham with *my* questions, we've met thousands of people who have taken these questions even deeper, and who have added their own important questions to the list, to which Abraham has offered their love and brilliance. But here's where I began with Abraham.

(I have no real way of understanding how it is that Esther is able to allow Abraham to speak through her. From my point of view,

Esther closes her eyes and breathes a few very deep, soft breaths. Her head gently nods for a few moments, and then her eyes open and Abraham addresses me directly, as follows.)

We (Abraham) Describe Ourselves as Teachers

Abraham: Good morning! It is nice to have an opportunity to visit. We extend our appreciation to Esther for allowing this communication, and to you for soliciting it. We have been considering the immense value of this interaction, as it will provide an introduction of that which we are to our physical friends. But even more than a mere introduction of Abraham to your physical world, this book will provide an introduction of the role of the Non-Physical in your physical world, for these worlds are inextricably tied together, you know. There is no way of separating one from the other.

Also, in the writing of this book, we are all fulfilling an agreement that we set forth long before you came into your physical bodies. We, Abraham, agreed that we would remain here focused in the broader, clearer, and therefore more powerful Non-Physical perspective, while you, Jerry and Esther, agreed to go forth into your magnificent physical bodies and into the Leading Edge of thought and creation. And once your life experiences had stimulated within you clear and powerful desire, it was our agreement to rendezvous for the purpose of powerful co-creation.

Jerry, we are eager to answer your long list of questions (so deliberately prepared and honed from the contrast of your life experience), for there is much that we want to convey to our physical friends. We want you to understand the magnificence of your Being, and we want you to understand who-you-really-are and why you have come forth into this physical dimension.

It is always an interesting experience to explain to our physical friends those things that are of a Non-Physical nature, because everything that we offer to you must then be translated through the lens of your physical world. In other words, Esther receives our thoughts, like radio signals, at an unconscious level of her Being, and then translates them into physical words and concepts. It is a perfect blending of the physical and Non-Physical that is occurring here.

As we are able to help you understand the existence of the Non-Physical realm from which we are speaking, we will thereby assist you in understanding more clearly who-you-are. For you are, indeed, an extension of that which we are.

There are many of us here, and we are gathered together because of our current matching intentions and desires. In your physical environment, we are called *Abraham,* and we are known as *Teachers,* meaning those who are currently broader in understanding, who may lead others to that broader understanding. We know that words do not teach, that only life experience teaches, but the combination of life experience coupled with words that define and explain can enhance the experience of learning—and it is in that spirit that we offer these words.

There are *Universal Laws* that affect everything in the Universe—everything that is Non-Physical and everything that is physical. These *Laws* are absolute, they are Eternal, and they are omnipresent (or everywhere). When you have a conscious awareness of these *Laws,* and a working understanding of them, your life experience is tremendously enhanced. In fact, only when you have a conscious working knowledge of these *Laws* are you able to be the Deliberate Creator of your own life experience.

You Have an *Inner Being*

While you certainly are the physical Being that you see here in your physical setting, you are much more than that which you see with your physical eyes. You are actually an extension of Non-Physical *Source Energy.* In other words, that broader, older, wiser Non-Physical you is now also focused into the physical Being that you know as you. We refer to the Non-Physical part of you as your *Inner Being.*

Physical Beings often think of themselves as either dead or alive, and in that line of thinking they sometimes acknowledge that they existed in the Non-Physical realm before coming forth into their physical body, and that, following their physical death, they will return to that Non-Physical realm. But few people actually understand that the Non-Physical part of them remains currently, powerfully, and predominantly focused in the Non-Physical realm while a *part* of that perspective flows into this physical perspective and their *now* physical body.

An understanding of both of these perspectives and their relationship to each other is essential for a true understanding of who-you-are and of how to understand what you have intended as you came forth into this physical body. Some call that Non-Physical part the "Higher Self" or "Soul." It matters not what you call it, but it is of great value for you to acknowledge that your *Inner Being* exists, for only when you consciously understand the relationship between you and your *Inner Being* do you have true guidance.

We Do Not Want to Alter Your Beliefs

We come forth not to alter your beliefs, but to reacquaint you with the *Eternal Laws of the Universe* so that you may *intentionally* be the creator that you have come forth to be, for there is not another who attracts into your experience that which you are getting—you are doing it all.

We come forth not to get you to believe anything, for there is nothing that you believe that we do not want you to believe. And as we are viewing this wondrous physical Earth plane, we see great diversity in that which you believe—and in all of that diversity, there is perfect balance.

We will present these *Universal Laws* to you in a simple format. And we will also offer practical processes whereby you may deliberately access the *Laws* for the achievement of whatever is important to you. And although we know that you will revel in the creative control that you will discover over your own life experience, we know that the greatest value of all will be the freedom that you will discover as you learn to apply the *Art of Allowing*.

Since the larger part of you already knows all of this, we see our work as reminding you of what, at some level, you already know. It is our expectation that as you read these words, if it is your desire you will be guided step-by-step to an Awakening—to a recognition of the *Total You.*

You Are Valuable to *All-That-Is*

It is our desire that you return to the understanding of the immense value that you are to *All-That-Is,* for you are truly on the Leading Edge of thought, adding unto the Universe with your every thought, word, and deed. You are not inferior Beings here trying to catch up, but instead, Leading-Edge creators with all of the resources of the Universe at your disposal.

We want you to know your value, for in the absence of that understanding, you do not attract the legacy that truly belongs to you. In your lack of self-appreciation, you deny yourself your natural inheritance of continuous joy. And while the Universe still benefits from everything that you experience, it is our desire that *you* begin to reap the fruits of your labor here and now, also.

It is our absolute knowing that you will find the keys that will lead you to the life experience that you intended even before you emerged into this body. We will assist you in fulfilling your life's purpose, and we know that this is important to you, for we hear you ask: *Why am I here? What can I do to make my life better? How do I know what is right?* And we are here to answer all of that in detail.

We are ready for your questions.

-◄▨►-

An Introduction to Being Well-Being

Jerry: What I would like, Abraham, is an introductory book, written especially for those people who want to have conscious control over their own life experiences. I would like for there to be enough information and guidance in this one book so that each reader could begin immediately using these ideas, and therefore immediately experience an increase in their state of happiness, or their state of Well-Being . . . understanding that they will probably want further clarification on some specific points later on.

Abraham: Everyone will begin from right where they are, and it is our expectation that those who are seeking will find the answers they are looking for here in this book. None of us can offer everything that we know, or want to convey, at any one point in time. And so, we will offer a clear basis of understanding the *Laws of the Universe* here, knowing that some will be interested in going beyond what is written, and some will not. Our work is continually evolving through the questions that are being asked as a result of the stimulation of what has been discussed before. There is no end to the evolution of that which we all are.

The *Universal Laws:* Defined

There are three *Eternal Universal Laws* that we want to assist you in understanding more clearly so that you may apply them intentionally, effectively, and satisfactorily through your physical expression of life. The *Law of Attraction* is the first of the *Laws* that we will offer, for if you do not understand, and are not able to effectively apply, the *Law of Attraction,* then the second *Law,* the *Science of Deliberate Creation,* and the third, the *Art of Allowing,* cannot be utilized. You must first understand and effectively utilize the first *Law* in order to understand and utilize the second. And you must be able to understand and utilize the second *Law* before you will be able to understand and utilize the third.

The first *Law,* the *Law of Attraction,* says: *That which is like unto itself, is drawn.* While this may seem like a rather simple statement, it defines the most powerful *Law* in the Universe—a *Law* that affects all things at all times. Nothing exists that is unaffected by this powerful *Law.*

The second *Law,* the *Science of Deliberate Creation,* says: *That which I give thought to and that which I believe or expect—is.* In short, you get what you are thinking about, whether you want it or not. A *deliberate* application of thought is really what the *Science of Deliberate Creation* is about, for if you do not understand these *Laws,* and deliberately apply them, then you may very well be creating by default.

The third *Law,* the *Art of Allowing,* says: *I am that which I am, and I am willing to allow all others to be that which they are.* When you are willing to allow others to be as they are, even in their not allowing of you, then you will be an *Allower,* but it is not likely that you will reach that point until you first come to understand *how* it is you get what you get.

Only when you understand that another cannot be a part of your experience unless you invite them in through your thoughts (or through your attention to them), and that circumstances cannot be a part of your experience unless you invite them to you through your thought (or through your observation of them), will you be the *Allower* that you wanted to be when you came forth into this expression of life.

An understanding of these three powerful *Universal Laws,* and a deliberate application of them, will lead you to the joyous freedom of being able to create your own life experience exactly as you want it to be. Once you understand that all people, circumstances, and events are invited into your experience by you, through your thought, you will begin to live your life as you intended when you made the decision to come forth into this physical body. And so, an understanding of the powerful *Law of Attraction,* coupled with an intention to *Deliberately Create* your own life experience, will ultimately lead you to the unparalleled freedom that can only come from a complete understanding and application of the *Art of Allowing.*

ᴥᵹ ᴥᵹ ᴥᵹ ᵹᴥ ᵹᴥ ᵹᴥ

PART II

The *Law* of
Attraction

The Universal *Law of Attraction:* Defined

Jerry: Well, Abraham, I assume that the first subject that you will discuss with us in detail is the *Law of Attraction.* I know you've said that this is the most powerful *Law.*

Abraham: Not only is the *Law of Attraction* the most powerful *Law* in the Universe, but you must understand it before anything else that we offer will be of value. And you must understand it before anything you are living, or anything you observe anyone else living, will make any sense. Everything in your life and the lives of those around you is affected by the *Law of Attraction.* It is the basis of everything that you see manifesting. It is the basis of everything that comes into your experience. An awareness of the *Law of Attraction* and an understanding of how it works is essential to living life on purpose. In fact, it is essential to living the life of joy that you came forth to live.

The *Law of Attraction* says: *That which is like unto itself, is drawn.* When you say, "Birds of a feather flock together," you are actually talking about the *Law of Attraction.* You see it evidenced when you wake up feeling unhappy, and then throughout the day things get worse and worse, and at the end of the day you say, "I shouldn't have gotten out of bed." You see the *Law of Attraction* evidenced in your society when you see that the one who speaks most about illness has illness; when you see that the one who speaks most about prosperity has prosperity. The *Law of Attraction* is evident when you set your radio dial on 630AM and you *expect* to receive the broadcast from the transmitting tower of 630AM, because you understand that the radio signals between the transmitting tower and your receiver must *match.*

As you begin to understand—or better stated, as you begin to remember—this powerful *Law of Attraction,* the evidence of it that surrounds you will be easily apparent, for you will begin to recognize the exact correlation between what you have been thinking about and what is actually coming into your experience. Nothing merely shows up in your experience. *You attract it—all of it. No exceptions.*

Because the *Law of Attraction* is responding to the thoughts that you hold at all times, it is accurate to say that *you are creating your own reality.* Everything that you experience is attracted to you because the *Law of Attraction* is responding to the thoughts that you are offering. Whether you are remembering something from the past, observing something in your present, or imagining something about your future, the thought that you are focused upon in your powerful now has activated a vibration within you—and the *Law of Attraction* is responding to it now.

People often explain, in the midst of unwanted things occurring in their experience, that they are certain *they* did not create such a thing. "I wouldn't have done this unwanted thing to myself!" they explain. And while we know that you did not deliberately bring this unwanted thing into your experience, we must still explain that only *you* could have caused it, for no one else has the power to attract what comes to you but you. By focusing upon this unwanted thing, or the essence of it, you have created it by *default.* Because you did not understand the *Laws of the Universe,* or the rules of the game, so to speak, you have invited unwanted things into your experience through your attention to them.

To better understand the Law of Attraction, *see yourself as a magnet attracting unto you the essence of that which you are thinking and feeling. And so, if you are feeling fat, you cannot attract thin. If you feel poor, you cannot attract prosperity, and so on. It defies* Law.

Giving Thought to It Is Inviting It

The more you come to understand the power of the Law of Attraction, *the more interest you will have in deliberately directing your thoughts—for you get what you think about, whether you want it or not.*

Without exception, that which you give thought to is that which you begin to invite into your experience. When you think a little thought of something that you want, through the *Law of Attraction,* that thought grows larger and larger, and more and more powerful. When you think a thought of something you do not want, the *Law of Attraction* draws unto it, and it grows larger and larger, also. And so, the larger the thought grows, the more power it draws unto it, and then the more certain you are to receive the experience.

When you see something you would like to experience and you say, "Yes, I would like to have that," through your *attention* to it you invite it into your experience. However, when you see something that you do not want to experience and you shout, "No, no, I do not want that!" through your *attention* to it you invite that into your experience. In this attraction-based Universe, there is no such thing as exclusion. Your attention to it includes it in your vibration, and if you hold it in your attention or awareness long enough, the *Law of Attraction* will bring it into your experience, for there is no such thing as "No." To clarify, when you look at something and shout, "No, I don't want to experience that; go away!" then what you are actually doing is calling it into your experience, for there is no such thing as "No" in an attraction-based Universe. Your attention to it says, "Yes, come to me, this thing I do *not* want!"

Fortunately, here in your physical time-space reality, things do not manifest into your experience instantaneously. There is a wonderful *buffer of time* between when you begin to think about something and the time it manifests. That *buffer of time* gives you the opportunity to redirect your attention more and more in the direction of the things that you actually do want to manifest in your experience. And long before it manifests (actually, when you first begin to give thought to it), you can tell by the way you *feel* whether it is something you want to manifest or not. If you continue to give your attention to it—whether it is something you want or something you do not want—it will come into your experience.

These *Laws,* even if you do not understand that they do, affect your experience even in your ignorance of them. And while you may not be aware of having heard of the *Law of Attraction*, its powerful effect is evident in every aspect of your life experience.

As you consider what you read here and begin to notice the correlation between what you are thinking and speaking and what you are getting, you will begin to understand the powerful *Law of Attraction.* And as you deliberately direct your thoughts and focus upon the things that you do want to draw into your experience, you will begin to receive the life experience that you desire on all subjects.

Your physical world is a vast and diverse place full of an amazing variety of events and circumstances, some of which you approve of (and would like to experience), and some of which you disapprove of (and would not like to experience). It was not your intention as you came forth into this physical experience to ask the world to change in order to accommodate your opinions of the way things should be, by eliminating all things that you do not approve of and adding to the things you *do* approve of.

You are here to <u>create</u> the world around you that <u>you</u> choose, while you <u>allow</u> the world—as <u>others</u> choose it to be—to exist, also. And while their choices in no way hinder your own choices, your attention to what they are choosing does affect your vibration, and therefore your own <u>point of attraction</u>.

My Thoughts Have Magnetic Power

The *Law of Attraction* and its magnetic power reaches out into the Universe and attracts other thoughts that are vibrationally like it . . . and brings that to you: Your attention to subjects, your activation of thoughts, and the *Law of Attraction's* response to those thoughts is responsible for every person, every event, and every circumstance that comes into your experience. All of these things are brought into your experience through a sort of powerful magnetic funnel as they are vibrational matches to your own thoughts.

You get the essence of what you are thinking about, whether it is something you want or something you do not want. That may be unsettling to you at first, but in time, it is our expectation that you will come to appreciate the fairness, the consistency, and the absoluteness of this powerful *Law of Attraction*. Once you understand this *Law* and begin to pay attention to what you are giving your attention to, you will regain control of your own life experience. And with that control you will again remember that there is nothing that you desire that you cannot *achieve*, and there is nothing that you do not want that you cannot release from your experience.

Understanding the *Law of Attraction* and recognizing the absolute correlation between what you have been thinking and feeling—and what is manifesting in your life experience—will cause you to be more aware of the stimulation of your own thoughts. You will begin to notice that your own thoughts may be stimulated from something you read or watch on television or hear or observe from someone else's experience. And once you see the effect that the *Law of Attraction* has upon these thoughts that begin small and grow larger and more powerful with your attention to them, you will feel a desire within you to begin to direct your thoughts to more of the things that you do want to experience. For whatever you are pondering, and no matter what the source of stimulation of that thought . . . as you ponder that thought, the *Law of Attraction* goes to work and begins to offer you other thoughts, conversations, and experiences that are of a similar nature.

Whether you are remembering the past, observing the present, or imagining the future, you are doing it right *now*, and whatever you are focusing upon is causing an activation of a vibration that the *Law of Attraction* is responding to. At first you may be privately pondering a particular subject, but if you think about it long enough, you will start to notice other people beginning to discuss it with you as the *Law of Attraction* finds others who are offering a similar vibration and brings them right to you. The longer you focus upon something, the more powerful it becomes; and the stronger that your *point of attraction* is to it, the more evidence of it appears in your life experience. *Whether you are focusing upon things you want or things you do not want, the evidence of your thoughts continually flows toward you.*

My *Inner Being* Communicates Through Emotion

You are much more than you see here in your physical body, for while you are, indeed, a wondrous *physical* creator, you exist, simultaneously, in another dimension. There is a part of you, a *Non-Physical* part of you—we call it your *Inner Being*—that exists right now while you are here in this physical body.

Your emotions are your physical indication of your relationship with your Inner Being. In other words, as you are focused upon a subject and have your specific perspective and opinion about it, your *Inner Being* is also focused upon it and has a perspective and opinion about it. The *emotions* that you feel are your indication of the match or mismatch of those opinions. For example, something may have happened and your current opinion of yourself is that you should have done better or that you are not smart, or that you are unworthy. Since the current opinion of your *Inner Being* is that you are doing fine, and that you are smart and eternally worthy, there is a definite mismatch in these opinions, and you would feel this mismatch in the form of *negative emotion.* On the other hand, when you feel proud of yourself or love yourself or someone else, your current opinion is a much closer match to what your *Inner Being* is feeling in the moment; and in that case, you would feel the *positive emotions* of pride, love, or appreciation.

Your *Inner Being,* or *Source Energy,* always offers a perspective that is to your greatest advantage, and when your perspective matches that, then positive attraction is occurring. In other words, the better you feel, the better your *point of attraction,* and the better things are turning out for you. The comparative vibrations of your

42

perspective and that of your *Inner Being* are responsible for this magnificent *Guidance* that is always available to you.

Since the *Law of Attraction* is always responding to and acting on whatever vibration you are offering, it is extremely helpful to understand that your emotions are letting you know whether you are in the process of creating something you want or something you do not want.

Often, when our physical friends learn of the powerful *Law of Attraction* and begin to understand that they are attracting things to themselves by virtue of what they are thinking, they try to monitor each thought, often feeling guarded about their thoughts. But the monitoring of thoughts is a difficult thing because there are so many things that you might think about, and the *Law of Attraction* is continually bringing more.

Rather than trying to monitor your thoughts, we encourage you to simply pay attention to how you are feeling. For if you should choose a thought that is not in harmony with the way the broader, older, wiser, loving *Inner Being* part of you sees it, you will feel the discord, and then you can easily redirect your thought to something that feels better and which therefore serves you better.

You knew, when you made the decision to come forth into this physical body, that you would have access to this wonderful *Emotional Guidance System,* for you knew then that through your wonderful, ever-present emotions, you would be able to know if you were straying from your broader knowing or flowing with it.

When you are giving thought in a direction of something that you want, you will feel positive emotion. When you are giving thought in the direction of what you do not want, you will feel negative emotion. And so, simply by paying attention to the way you are feeling, you will know, at all times, the direction from which your powerful magnetic Being is attracting the subject of whatever you are giving thought to.

My Omnipresent *Emotional Guidance System*

Your wonderful *Emotional Guidance System* is a great advantage to you because the *Law of Attraction* is always working whether you know that it is or not. And so, whenever you are giving thought to something that you do *not* want, and you stay focused upon that thought, by *Law* you are attracting more and more and more and more, until eventually you will attract matching events or circumstances right into your experience.

However, if you are aware of your *Emotional Guidance System* and are sensitive to the way you feel, then you will notice, in the early, subtle stages, that you are focused upon something that you do *not* want, and you can easily change the thought to begin attracting something that you *do* want. If you are not sensitive to the way you are feeling, then you will not consciously notice that you are thinking in the direction of what you do not want, and you may very well attract something very large and powerful that you do not want that will be more difficult to deal with later.

When an idea occurs to you and you feel eagerness about it, that means that your *Inner Being* is a *vibrational match* to the idea, and your positive emotion is an indication that the vibration of your thought in this moment matches that of your *Inner Being*. That is, in fact, what *inspiration* is: You are, in the moment, a perfect vibrational match to the broader perspective of your *Inner Being*, and because of that alignment, you are now receiving clear communication, or *Guidance*, from your *Inner Being*.

What If I Want It to Happen More Quickly?

Because of the *Law of Attraction,* matching thoughts are drawn together, and as they do so, they become more powerful. And as they become more powerful—and therefore closer to manifestation—the emotion that you feel also becomes proportionately larger. When you are focused upon something that you desire, then through the *Law of Attraction,* more and more thoughts about what you desire will be drawn, and you will feel greater positive emotion. *You can speed the creation of something simply by giving it more attention—the Law of Attraction takes care of the rest and brings to you the essence of the subject of your thought.*

We would define the words *want* or *desire* as follows: *To focus attention, or give thought toward a subject, while at the same time experiencing positive emotion.* When you give your attention to a subject and you feel only positive emotion about it as you do so, it will come very quickly into your experience. Sometimes we hear our physical friends speaking the words *want* or *desire* while at the same time feeling *doubt* or *fear* that their desire cannot be achieved. From our point of view, it is not possible to purely desire something while feeling negative emotion.

Pure desire is always accompanied by positive emotion. Perhaps that is why people disagree with our use of the words *want* or *desire*. They often argue that "wanting" implies a sort of lack and contradicts its own meaning, and we agree. But the problem is not with the word or label itself, but instead, with the state of emotion expressed while using the word.

It is our desire to help you understand that you can get to wherever you want to be from wherever you are, no matter where you are or what your current state of Being. The most important thing to understand is that your mental state of Being, or your attitude, in the moment is the basis from which you will attract more. So, the powerful and consistent *Law of Attraction* is responding to everything in this vibrational Universe—bringing people with matching vibrations together, bringing situations with matching vibrations together, and bringing thoughts with matching vibrations together. Indeed, everything in your life, from the way thoughts roll across your mind, to the people you rendezvous with in traffic, is the way that it is, due to the *Law of Attraction.*

How Do I Want to See Myself?

For most of you, many things in your life are going well and you want a continuation of those things, but there are also things that you wish to be different. In order for things to change, you have to see them as you want them to be rather than continuing to observe them as they are. The majority of the thoughts that you probably think are about the things that you are observing, which means that *what-is* dominates your focus, attention, vibration, and therefore your *point of attraction*. That is further compounded as those around you also observe you.

And so, as a result of the overwhelming amount of attention that most of you give to your current situation *(what-is)*, change comes very slowly or not at all. A steady stream of different people flows into your life, but the essence or theme of those experiences does not change very much.

In order to effect true positive change in your experience, you must disregard how things are—as well as how others are seeing you—and give more of your attention to the way you prefer things to be. With practice, you will change your *point of attraction* and will experience a substantial change in your life experience. Sickness can become wellness, lack of abundance can become abundance, bad relationships can be replaced with good relationships, confusion can be replaced with clarity, and so on.

By deliberately directing your thoughts—rather than merely observing what is happening around you—you will begin to change the vibrational patterns to which the *Law of Attraction* is responding. And in time, with far less effort than you may currently believe, you will no longer—by responding to what others perceive you to be—be creating a future that is so similar to your past and present. Instead, you will be the powerful deliberate creator of your own experience.

You would not likely see a sculptor throwing his large wad of clay down onto his worktable exclaiming, "Oh, it didn't turn out right!" He knows that he must put his hands into his clay and work with it to mold it so that the vision in his mind matches the clay on his table. The variety of your life experience gives you the clay from which you will mold your life experience, and merely observing it as it is, without getting ahold of it and deliberately molding it to match your desires, is not satisfying—and is not what you had in mind when you made the decision to come into this time-space reality. We want you to understand that your "clay," no matter how it may look right now, is moldable. No exceptions.

Welcome, Little One, to Planet Earth

You may be feeling that it would be easier to be hearing these words if they had come to you on the first day of your experience upon this planet Earth. And if we were talking to you on your first day of physical life experience, this is what we would be saying:

Welcome, little one, to planet Earth. . . . There is nothing that you cannot be, do, or have. You are a magnificent creator, and you are here by virtue of your powerful and deliberate wanting to be here. You have specifically applied the wondrous Science of Deliberate Creation, and by your ability to do that, you are here.

Go forth, giving thought to what you want, attracting life experiences to help you decide what you want, and once you have decided, giving thought only unto that.

Most of your time will be spent collecting data—data that will help you decide what it is you want. . . . Your real work is to decide what you want and then focus upon it, for it is through focusing upon what you want that you will attract it. That is the process of creating: giving thought to what you want, so much thought, and such clear thought, that your Inner Being offers forth emotion. And as you are giving thought, with emotion, you become the most powerful of all magnets. That is the process by which you will attract what you want into your experience.

Many of the thoughts that you will be thinking will not be powerful in their attracting, not in the beginning—not unless you stay focused upon them long enough that they become more. For as they become more in quantity, they become more in power. And as they are becoming more in quantity and more in power, the emotion that you will be feeling from your Inner Being will be greater.

When you think thoughts that bring forth emotion, you are accessing the power of the Universe. Go forth (we would say) *on this first day of life experience, knowing that your work is to decide what you want—and then to focus upon that.*

But we are not talking to you on the first day of your life experience. You have been here for a while. Most of you have been seeing yourself, not only through your own eyes (in fact, not even primarily through your own eyes), but through the eyes of others; therefore, *many of you are not now currently in the state of Being that you want to be.*

Is My "Reality" Really All That Real?

We intend to offer you a process whereby you can achieve the state of Being that is of your choosing so that you can access the power of the Universe and begin attracting the subject of your *wanting,* rather than the subject of what you feel is your actual state of Being. For, from our perspective, *there is a very great difference between that which now exists—which you call your "reality"—and that which your reality really is.*

Even if you sit in a body that is not healthy or in one that is not of the size, shape, or vitality that you choose; in a lifestyle that does not please you; driving an automobile that embarrasses you; interacting with others who do not bring you pleasure . . . we want to assist you in understanding that while that may seem to be your state of Being, it need not be. *Your state of Being is the way you feel about yourself at any point in time.*

How Can I Increase My Magnetic Power?

The thoughts that you think without bringing forth the feeling of strong emotion are not of great magnetic power. In other words, while every thought that you think has creative potential, or magnetic attracting potential, the thoughts that are thought in combination with the feeling of strong emotion are the most powerful. Certainly, the majority of your thoughts, then, have no great attracting power. They are more or less maintaining what you have already attracted.

And so, can you not see the value of spending 10 or 15 minutes every day deliberately setting forth powerful thoughts that evoke great, powerful, passionate, positive emotion in order to attract circumstances and events into your life experience that are to your wanting? (We see great value in that.)

Here we will offer a process by which you may spend a little bit of time every day intentionally attracting into your experience the health, vitality, prosperity, positive interaction with others . . . all the things that make up your vision of what the perfect life experience would be for you. And that will be a changing thing, friends. For as you intend and receive, you will not only receive the benefit of that which you have created, but you will also receive a new perspective from which your intentions will be different. That is what evolution and growth are about.

Abraham's *Creative Workshop Process*

Here is the process: You are going to go to a kind of *Creative Workshop* every day—not for a long period of time—15 minutes is a good amount of time; 20 minutes at most. This *Workshop* need not occur in the same place in every day, but it is good if it is a place where you will not be distracted or interrupted. This is not a place where you will enter an altered state of consciousness; it is not a meditative state. It is a state of giving thought to what you want with such clarity that your *Inner Being* responds by offering confirming emotion.

Before you begin this process, it is important that you be happy, for if you go there unhappy or feeling no emotion, then your work will not be of great value, for your attracting power will not be there. When we say "happy," we are not speaking of that jumping-up-and-down sort of excitement. We mean an uplifted, lighthearted feeling, that sort of sensation where all is well. And so, we recommend that you do whatever it takes to get happy. For each of you it is a different process. . . . For Esther, hearing music is a very fast way to get that uplifted, joyous feeling—but not all music accomplishes this, and not even the same music every time. For some of you it is interacting with animals or being near moving water, but once you bring yourself to that good feeling, then sit—and now your *Workshop* has begun.

Your job here in this *Workshop* is to assimilate data that you have been collecting from your real-life experiences (as you have been interacting with others and moving in and out of your physical environment). Your work here is to bring the data together in a sort of picture of yourself, one that satisfies and pleases you.

Your life experience outside of your *Workshop* will be of great value, for as you are moving around through your day, no matter what you are doing—going to work; working around your home; interacting with your mate or your friends or your children or your parents—*if you will use your time, with one of your intentions being to collect data and look for things that you like that you may bring into your Workshop—then you will find that every day is one of fun.*

Have you ever gone on a shopping spree where you had some money in your pocket and your intent was to find something to buy? And as you were looking around, although there were many things that you did not want, your intent was to find something that you *did* want to exchange for the money. Well, that is the way we would like you to look at every day of your life experience . . . as if you have a pocketful of something that you are exchanging for this data that you are collecting.

For example, you may see someone who has a joyful personality. Collect that data, intending to bring it into your *Workshop* later. You may see someone driving a vehicle that you would like; collect that data. You may see an occupation that pleases you. . . . Whatever it is that you are seeing that pleases you, remember it. (You could even write it down.) As you see anything that you think you would like to be in your life experience, see yourself collecting that data in a sort of mental bank. And then when you go into your *Workshop,* you can begin assimilating the data, and as you do so, *you will prepare a picture of yourself from which you will begin attracting into your experience the essence of that which has been pleasing you.*

If you are able to grasp the knowledge that your *real* work—no matter what other activities you are performing—is to look around for things that you want with the intent of bringing them into your *Workshop* in order to create your vision of yourself from which you will attract—then you will come to know that there is nothing that you cannot be, do, or have.

I Am Now in My *Creative Workshop*

And so now you are feeling happy, and you are sitting someplace in your *Workshop.* Here is an example of the work you may do in your *Creative Workshop:*

I like being here; I recognize the value and power of this time. I feel very good to be here.

I see myself in a sort of total package, one that I know is of my own creating, and certainly a package of my choosing. I am full of energy in this picture of myself—tireless, and really moving through life experience without resistance. As I see myself gliding about, moving in and out of my car, in and out of buildings, in and out of rooms, in and out of conversations, and in and out of life experiences, I see myself flowing effortlessly, comfortably, and happily.

I see myself attracting only those who are in harmony with my current intent. And I am clearer and clearer in every moment about what it is I want. When I get into my automobile and I am moving to a place, I see myself arriving healthy and refreshed and on time, and prepared for whatever it is that I am about to do there. I see myself dressed to perfection in just the manner that I choose for myself. And it is nice to know that it matters not what others are choosing, or what others are even <u>thinking</u> about what I am choosing.

What is important is that I am pleased with me, and as I see myself, I certainly am.

I recognize that I am unlimited in all facets of my life. . . . I have a bank account balance that is unlimited, and as I see myself moving through life experiences, it is exhilarating to know that there is nothing that I am choosing that is limited by money. I am making all of my decisions based upon whether I want the experience or not—not based upon whether or not I can <u>afford</u> the experience. For I know I am a magnet who attracts, at any point, whatever prosperity, health, and relationships I choose.

I choose absolute and continuing abundance, for I understand that there is no limit to the abundance in the Universe, and that by my attracting abundance to myself I am not limiting another. . . . There is enough for everyone. The key is for each of us to see it and want it—and then we will each attract it. And so, I have chosen "unlimited," not necessarily putting a big stash away—for I understand that I have the power to attract it as I want it for whatever I want it for. And as I think of something else that I want, the money flows to me easily, so I have an unlimited supply of abundance and prosperity.

There are abundant aspects in every area of my life. . . . I see myself surrounded by others who, like me, want growth; and who are drawn to me by my willingness to allow them to be, do, or have whatever they want while I do not need to draw into my experience those things that they may be choosing that I do not like. I see myself interacting with others; and talking, laughing, and enjoying that which is perfect in them while they enjoy that which is perfect in me. All of us are appreciating one another, and none of us is criticizing or noticing those things that we do not like.

I see myself in perfect health. I see myself in absolute prosperity. I see myself invigorated with life, again appreciating this physical life experience that I wanted so very much as I decided to be a physical Being. It is glorious to be here as a physical Being, making decisions with my physical brain but accessing the power of the Universe through the power of the <u>Law of Attraction</u>. And it is from this marvelous state of Being that I now attract more of the same. It is good. It is fun. I like it very much.

I will leave this <u>Workshop</u>, and I will set out—during the remainder of this day—to look for more things that I like. It is nice to know that if I see one who is prosperous, but sick, I do not need to bring the whole package into my <u>Workshop</u>, just the part that I like. So I will bring the example of prosperity, and I will leave out the example of sickness. My work, for now, is done.

Are Not All *Laws* Universal *Laws?*

Jerry: Abraham, you spoke to us of three major *Universal Laws.* Are there some *Laws* that are not *Universal?*

Abraham: There are many that you may call *Laws.* We reserve our definition of *Law* for those things that are *Universal.* In other words, as you enter into this physical dimension, you have the agreement of time, the agreement of gravity, and the agreement of this perception of space; but those agreements are not *Universal,* for there are other dimensions that do not share those experiences. In many cases, where you may use the word *Law,* we would use the word *agreement,* instead. There are no other *Universal Laws* that we are waiting to divulge to you later.

How Do I Best Utilize the *Law of Attraction?*

Jerry: Are there many different ways that we can consciously or deliberately use this *Law of Attraction?*

Abraham: We will begin by saying that you are *always* utilizing it, whether you know that you are or not. You cannot stop using it, for it is inherent in everything that you do. But we appreciate your question, for you want to understand how to *deliberately* use it for the achievement of that which you *intentionally* desire.

Being aware that the *Law of Attraction* exists is the most important part of utilizing it deliberately. Since the *Law of Attraction* is always responding to your thoughts, a deliberate focusing of your thought is important.

Choose subjects that are of interest to you, and think about them in a way that benefits you. In other words, look for the *positive aspects* of the subjects that are important to you. As you choose a thought, the *Law of Attraction* will act upon it, attracting more thoughts like it, thus making that thought more powerful.

By staying focused on a subject of your choosing, your <u>point of attraction</u> on that topic will become much more powerful than if your mind moves from subject to subject. There is tremendous power in focusing.

As you make deliberate choices about the thoughts you think, the things you do, and even the people you spend time with, you will feel the benefit of the *Law of Attraction.* When you spend time with others who appreciate you, it stimulates your own thoughts of appreciation. When you spend time with those who see your flaws, then their perception of your flaws often becomes your *point of attraction.*

As you come to realize that whatever you are giving your attention to is getting larger (because the *Law of Attraction* says that it must), you may become more particular about those things that you give your initial attention to. It is much easier to change the direction of your thoughts in the early stages of the thought before the thought has gathered much momentum. But it is possible to change the direction of your thought at any time.

Can I Instantly Reverse My Creative Momentum?

Jerry: Let's say there are those who already have something going on, from their previous thoughts, and now they decide they want to suddenly change the direction of their creation. Isn't there a momentum factor? Don't they have to first slow down what's already in the process of being created? Or can they instantly create in a different direction?

Abraham: There is a momentum factor caused by the *Law of Attraction*. The *Law of Attraction* says: *That which is like unto itself, is drawn.* So whatever thought you have activated by your attention to it is getting bigger. But we want you to realize that the gathering of momentum is a gradual thing. And so, rather than trying to turn that thought around, consider focusing upon another thought.

Let us say you have been thinking about something that you do not want, and you have been doing that for a while, so you have a rather strong negative momentum going. It would not be possible for you to suddenly begin thinking the opposite thought. In fact, from where you are standing, you would not even have access to those kinds of thoughts—*but you could choose a thought that feels slightly better than the thoughts you have been thinking, and then another, and then another, until gradually you could change the direction of your thoughts.*

Another effective process for changing the direction of your thought is to change the subject altogether, deliberately looking for the positive aspect of something. If you are able to do that, and if you are willing to try to stay focused upon that better-feeling thought for a while, then, since the *Law of Attraction* is now responding to that thought, the balance of your thoughts is now improved. Now when you go back to revisit your previous negative thought, since you are now in a different mode of vibration, that thought will be slightly affected by your vibrational improvement. Little by little you will improve the vibrational content of the subject that you choose to think about, and as that happens, everything in your life begins to shift in a more positive direction.

How Can a Person Overcome Disappointment?

Jerry: For the individual who is trying to make a severe switch in the positive direction of their prosperity, or of their health, if they already had a momentum factor going the other way, how much faith or belief would it require for them to overcome their disappointment and say, "Well, I know this is going to work out for me," even though it hasn't worked yet?

Abraham: You see, from your point of disappointment, you are attracting more to be disappointed about. . . . An understanding of the process of creation is really the best way. That is the value of the *Creative Workshop,* of getting happy, and then going to a place where you *see* it as you are wanting it to be; seeing it until you are believing it so clearly that it is already bringing forth emotion—and from *that* state of Being, you will attract it as you want it to be.

Disappointment *is communication from your Inner Being letting you know that that which you are focused upon is not what you want. If you are sensitive to the way that you are feeling, then the disappointment itself will let you know that what you are thinking about is not what you want to experience.*

What Causes Worldwide Waves of Unwanted Events?

Jerry: Over the years, I've seen TV newscasts, or whatever, that report the hijacking of an airplane or a terrorist act or a severe case of child abuse or a mass murder or something negative like that—and then I'll see an almost worldwide wave of those events beginning to occur. Is that brought on by the same process?

Abraham: Attention to any subject amplifies it because attention to the subject activates the vibration of it and the *Law of Attraction* responds to the activated vibration.

Those who may be planning the hijacking of an airplane are adding power to that thought, but those who are *frightened* by the prospect of a hijacking are also adding power to the thought—for you add power to those things you do not want through your attention to them. Those who have a clear intent to not draw any sort of negative information into their experience are probably not watching the broadcast to begin with, you see.

There are so many different intentions and combinations of intentions that it is very difficult for us to point out, in general, how one would bring it about. . . . Certainly, these newscasts add to these situations. For as more and more people are focused upon what they are not wanting, they are adding to the creation of what they do not want. Their emotional power is adding great influence to the overall events of your world. That is what mass consciousness is about.

Can Attention to Medical Procedures Attract More?

Jerry: Currently, there's a wide range of televised surgery going on. Do you see that sort of thing as increasing the amount of surgery that will actually occur per capita? In other words, when individuals observe televised medical procedures, can they automatically become more of a vibrational match to the essence of medical procedures?

Abraham: When you give your attention to something, your potential for attracting it is increased. The more vivid the details, the more attention you will give it, and the more likely you are to attract it into your experience. And any negative emotion that you feel as you watch such a thing is your indication that you are negatively attracting.

Of course, the illness does not come upon you immediately, so you often do not make the correlation between your thoughts, your subsequent negative emotion, and the resulting illness, but they are absolutely linked together. *Your attention to anything is drawing it closer to you.*

Fortunately, because of the *buffer of time,* your thoughts do not become reality instantaneously, so you have ample opportunity to evaluate the direction of your thought (by the way you are feeling) and to change the direction of your thought whenever you find yourself feeling negative emotion.

The steady offering of details of illness is very influential in the increasing of sickness in your society. If you allow yourself to focus upon the constant barrage of unpleasant statistics regarding the never-ending stream of possible physical maladies, it cannot help but affect your personal *point of attraction.*

You might, instead, find a way of focusing your attention on those things that you *do* want to draw into your experience, for whatever you are consistently looking at, you are attracting. . . . *The more you think about illness and worry about illness—the more you attract illness.*

Should I Seek the Cause of My Negative Emotions?

Jerry: Suppose you are using the *Creative Workshop Process* of focusing on the things that you want, but then later, if you are out of the *Workshop* and you feel a negative emotion, would you suggest trying to find out what thought caused the negative emotion? Or would you suggest just thinking of one of the things that you'd been thinking about in the *Workshop* that you want?

Abraham: The power of the *Creative Workshop Process* is that the more attention you give to a subject, the more powerful it becomes, the easier it is to think about it, and the more of it begins to appear in your experience. Whenever you are aware that you are feeling negative emotion, it is important to understand that while you may not be aware of it, you have been conducting a negative *Workshop.*

Whenever you catch yourself feeling negative emotion, we would suggest that you try to gently pull your thoughts around to something that you *do* want to experience, and little by little you will change your habit of thought regarding those things. Whenever you are able to identify something that you do *not* want, you can always then identify what is it that you *do* want. And as you do that again and again, your pattern of thought—on every subject that is important to you—will shift more in the direction of what you do want. In other words, you will gradually build bridges from any current beliefs that are about things you do *not* want over to beliefs about things you *do* want.

An Example of Bridging an Unwanted Belief

Jerry: Can you provide an example of what you mean by "bridging a belief"?

Abraham: Your *Emotional Guidance System* works best when you are setting forth continual, deliberate intentions of what you desire. So let us say that you have intended, in your *Workshop,* perfect health; you've visualized yourself as a healthy, vital Being. And now you are moving through your day, and while having lunch you are sitting with a friend who is discussing her own illness. As she speaks about her illness, you find yourself feeling very uncomfortable and uneasy in the conversation. . . . Now, what is happening is, your *Guidance System* is indicating to you that *that which you are hearing and that which you are thinking—that which your friend is speaking—is not in harmony with your intent.* And then you make a very clear decision to stop this conversation from going any further in the direction of illness. And so you attempt to change the subject, but your friend is very excited and emotionally drawn to this topic, and she brings the conversation back to her illness. Again, your *Guidance System's* warning bells begin to ring.

The reason why you are feeling negative emotion is not only because your friend is talking about something that you do not want. *Your negative emotion is your indication that you hold beliefs that are contrary to your own desire.* Your friend's conversation merely activated beliefs within you that challenge your desire for wellness. So walking away from your friend and from this conversation will not change those beliefs. It is necessary that you start, right where you are, in the midst of that belief, and move it gradually, building a bridge, so to speak, to a belief that is more in harmony with your desire for wellness.

It is helpful, whenever you feel negative emotion, to stop and acknowledge what you were thinking about when the negative emotion surfaced. Whenever you feel negative emotion, it is always telling you that whatever you are thinking about is important, and that you are thinking about the opposite of what you really desire. So questions such as "What was I thinking about when this negative emotion surfaced?" and "What is it that I do want regarding this?" will help you realize that you are, in this moment, focused in direct opposition to what you really do want to attract into your experience.

For example: "What was I thinking about when this negative emotion surfaced? I was thinking about this being the flu season, and I was remembering how very sick I have been in the past with the flu. Not only did I miss work, and many other things that I wanted to do, but I felt miserable for so many days. What is it that I *do* want? I want to remain healthy this year."

But merely saying "I want to remain healthy" is usually not sufficient under these conditions because your memory of having the flu and therefore your belief about the probability of getting the flu are much stronger than your desire to remain well.

We would attempt to bridge our belief in this way:

This is usually the time of year that I get the flu.
I don't want to get the flu this year.
I hope I don't get the flu this year.
It seems like everyone gets it.
That may be an exaggeration. Everyone doesn't get the flu.
In fact, there have been many flu seasons when I didn't get the flu.
I don't always get the flu.

It's possible that this flu season could come and go without touching me at all.

I like the idea of being healthy.

Those past flu experiences came before I realized that I can control my experience.

Now that I understand the power of my own thoughts, things have changed.

Now that I understand the power of the Law of Attraction, things have changed.

It isn't necessary for me to experience the flu this year.

It isn't necessary for me to experience anything that I don't want.

It's possible for me to direct my thoughts toward things I do want to experience.

I like the idea of guiding my life to things that I do want to experience.

Now you have bridged the belief. If the negative thought returns— and it may continue to do so for a while—just guide your thoughts more deliberately, and eventually it will not come up again.

Are My Thoughts in My Dreams, Creating?

Jerry: I would like to understand the dream world. Are we creating in our dreams? Are we attracting anything through the thoughts that we're having or experiencing in our dreams?

Abraham: You are not. While you sleep, you have withdrawn your consciousness from your physical time-space reality, and you are temporarily not attracting while you are sleeping.

Whatever you are thinking (and therefore feeling) and that which you are attracting is always a match. Also, what you are thinking and feeling in the dream state and what is manifesting in your life experience is always a match. *Your dreams give you a glimpse into what you have created or what you are in the process of creating— but you are not in the process of creating while you are dreaming.*

Often you are unaware of the pattern of your thoughts until they actually manifest in your experience because you have developed your habit of thought gradually over a long period of time. And while it is possible, even after something unwanted has manifested, to focus and change it to something you do want, it is more difficult to do that after it has manifested. An understanding of what your dream state really is can help you recognize the direction of your thoughts before they actually materialize in your experience. *It is much easier to correct the direction of your thoughts when your dream is your indication than it is when a real-life manifestation is your indication.*

Must I Take Their Good and Their Bad?

Jerry: To what degree are we a part of what someone whom we're associated with has attracted (wanted or unwanted)? In other words, how much does another person whom we're associated with bring into our life what they've attracted—the things that we want or the things that we don't want?

Abraham: Nothing can come into your life without your attention to it. Most people, however, are not very selective about the aspects of others to which they give their attention. In other words, if you notice *everything* about someone else, then you are inviting *all* of those aspects into your experience. If you give your attention only to the things you like most about them, you will invite into your experience only those things.

If someone is in your life, you have attracted them. And while it is sometimes difficult to believe, you also attract everything about your experience with them—for nothing can come into your experience without your personal attraction of it.

Should I "Resist Not, Evil"?

Jerry: So we don't really need to repel any negatives? We only have to attract what we want?

Abraham: It is not possible to push things that you do not want away from you, because in your pushing against them you are actually activating the vibration of them and therefore attracting them. Everything in this Universe is attraction based. In other words, there is no such thing as exclusion. When you shout "No!" at those things you do not want, you are actually inviting those unwanted things into your experience. When you shout "Yes!" at those things you do want, you are actually inviting those wanted things into your experience.

Jerry: That's where that saying "Resist ye not evil" probably came from.

Abraham: *If you are resisting anything, you are focused upon it, pushing against it, and activating the vibration of it—and therefore attracting it.* And so, it would not be a good idea to do that with anything that you do not want. "Resist ye not evil" would also be spoken by someone wise enough to understand that what humans call "evil" does not exist.

Jerry: Abraham, what would be your definition of the word *evil?*

Abraham: There would be no reason for the word *evil* to be in our vocabulary because there is nothing that we are aware of that we would label with the word. When humans use the word, they usually mean "that which opposes good." We have noticed that when humans use the word *evil,* they mean something that opposes *their* idea of what is good, or what is God. *Evil* is that which one believes is not in harmony with what they want.

Jerry: And *good?*

Abraham: *Good* is that which one believes they do want. You see, good and evil are only ways of defining *wanted* and *unwanted*. And *wanted* and *unwanted* only apply to the individual doing the wanting. It gets tricky when humans get involved in the wanting of others, and even trickier when they attempt to *control* the desires of others.

How Do I Find Out What I Really Want?

Jerry: One of the most common concerns I've heard over the years is people saying, "Well, I just don't know what I want." How *do* we know what we want?

Abraham: You have come forth into this physical life experience with the intention of experiencing the variety and contrast for the very purpose of determining your own personal preferences and desires.

Jerry: Could you give us an idea of a process we could use to find out what we want?

Abraham: Your life experience is continually helping you identify what you want. Even as you are keenly aware of something that you *do not* want, in that moment you are becoming more clear about that which you *do* want. And it is helpful to make the statement "I want to know what I want," because in your conscious awareness of that intention, the attraction process is intensified.

Jerry: So the person who's telling me "I want to know what I want," is, at that moment, beginning to find out what they want?

Abraham: Through the experience of life, you cannot help but identify, from your perspective, your personal opinions and preferences: "I prefer that to this, I like that more than this, I want to experience this, I don't want to experience that." You cannot help but come to your own conclusions as you sift through the details of your own life experience.

We do not believe that people are having such a difficult time deciding what they want as much as they do not believe that they can receive what they want. . . . Because they have not understood the powerful *Law of Attraction,* and because they have not been consciously aware of their own vibrational offering, they have not experienced any conscious control over the things that have come into their own experience. Many have experienced the discomfort of really wanting something and working very hard to try to achieve it, only to continue to hold it away because they were offering thoughts of the lack of it more predominantly than thoughts of the receiving of it. So, over time, they begin to associate the receiving of wanted things with hard work, struggle, and disappointment.

So when they say, "I don't know what I want," what they really mean is, "I don't know how to get what I want," or "I'm not willing to do what I think I need to do to try to get what I want," and "I really don't want to work so hard again only to have the discomfort of still not getting what I want!"

To make the statement "I want to know what I want!" is a first and powerful step in *Deliberate Creation.* But then, a deliberate directing of your attention to the things you want to attract into your experience must come next.

Most people have not been deliberately directing their thoughts toward the things that they really want, but instead, are simply observing whatever is going on around them. So when they see something that pleases them, they feel positive emotion, but when they see something that displeases them, they feel negative emotion. *Few realize that they can control the way they feel and positively affect the things that come into their life experience by deliberately directing their thoughts. But because they are not accustomed to doing that, it takes practice.* That is the reason why we encourage the *Creative Workshop Process.* By deliberately directing your thoughts and by creating pleasing mental scenarios in your own mind that induce good-feeling emotions within you, you begin to change your own *point of attraction.*

The Universe, which is responding to the thoughts that you are thinking, does not distinguish between a thought brought about by your observation of some reality you have witnessed and a thought brought about by your imagination. In either case, the thought equals your <u>point of attraction</u>—and if you focus upon it long enough, it will become your reality.

I Wanted Blue and Yellow but Got Green

When you are clear about *everything* that you want, you will get *all* of the results that you want. But often you are not completely clear. You say, for example, "I want the color yellow, and I want the color blue." But what you end up with is green. And then you say, "How did I get green? I did not intend that at all." But, it came forth as a blending of other intentions, you see. (Of course, blending the color yellow with the color blue creates the color green.)

And so, in a similar manner (at an unconscious level), there is a blending of intentions that is continually occurring within you, but it is so complex that your conscious thinking mechanism cannot sort it all out. But your *Inner Being can* sort it out—and can offer you guiding emotions. All that is required is that you pay attention to the way you feel, and that you let yourself be drawn to those things that feel good or right to you while you let yourself be moved away from those things that do not.

When you have practiced clarifying your intentions a bit, you will find yourself, in the very early stages of interacting with others, knowing whether what they are offering is of value or not. You will know whether you want to invite them into your experience or not.

How Does the Victim Attract the Robber?

Jerry: I can understand robbers being attracted to those they're robbing, but it's difficult to see innocent victims (as they're called) *attracting* the robbery, or the person being discriminated against *attracting* the prejudice.

Abraham: But they are, just the same. The assaulted and the assaulter are co-creators of the event.

Jerry: So, one of them is thinking about what they *don't* want and getting *it,* and the other is thinking about what they *do* want and getting (the vibrational essence of) that. In other words, they are, what you call, a vibrational match?

Abraham: It makes no difference whether you want the specifics of it or not; it is the vibrational essence of the subject of your attention that is attracted. *That which you really, really want, you get—and that which you really, really do not want, you get.*

The only way to avoid developing a powerful emotional thought about something is by not thinking the first not-so-powerful thought that is then added to by the *Law of Attraction.*

Let us say you read in the paper that someone has been robbed. Unless you read a detailed account that brings forth great emotion within you, reading the account or hearing about it will not necessarily put you in the attracting mode. But if you read about it or see it on television or discuss it with another until you begin to feel an emotional response about it, then you begin to draw a similar experience closer to you.

As you hear the statistics of what percentage of your population will be robbed this year, you must understand that the numbers are so high and getting higher because so many people are being stimulated by the thought. Those *warnings* do not protect you from robberies, but instead make them more likely. They do such a good job of making you aware of the prevalence of robberies, bringing that awareness to your attention again and again, that you not only think of it with emotion—but you expect it. *It is no wonder that you get so many of the things you do not want—you give so much of your* <u>attention</u> *to the things you do not want. . . .*

We would recommend that if you hear of an assault, you say, "That is their experience. I do not choose that." And then release the thought of what you *do not* want, and think of what you *do* want, because *you get what you think about, whether you want it or not.*

You came into this environment with so many others because you wanted the wonderful experience of co-creating. You can attract from your population those people with whom you would like to positively create, and you can attract from the people in your life the experiences you would like to create. *It is not necessary, or possible, to hide from or avoid unwanted people or experiences—but it is possible to attract only the people and experiences that please you.*

I Decided to Improve My Life

Jerry: I recall that, as a kid, I had extremely poor health and my body was very weak; and then as a teenager, I decided to, and did, build up my body strength, and I learned how to defend myself. I practiced martial arts and got very good at self-defense.

From the time I was a teenager until I was 33 years old, there was seldom a week that went by that I didn't have what we used to call a "fistfight," that I didn't hit somebody in the head. Then, in my 33rd year, after reading (in *The Talmudic Anthology*) about the counterproductivity of taking revenge, I made some major decisions, and one of them was that I was going to stop taking revenge—and since then I have not had to hit one person. In other words, all those people that I believed were picking on others and starting fights with me—from the day that I stopped practicing fighting (physically and mentally), those fight-provoking people stopped coming into my experience.

Abraham: So in your 33rd year you changed the direction of your attraction. You see, through the process of living your life and having those fights, week in and week out, you were coming to many conclusions about what you wanted and what you did not want. And while you may not have been consciously aware, with every fight you experienced you were getting clearer about not wanting that experience.

You did not like being hurt; you did not like hurting others; and even though you always felt completely justified in your reason for fighting, clear preferences were being born within you. The attraction of the book you mentioned came about because of those intentions. And as you read the book, it answered the questions that had been formulating within you at many levels of your Being. And as those answers came, a new intention was clarified, and a new *point of attraction* was born within you.

What's Behind Our Religious and Racial Prejudices?

Jerry: Why is there prejudice?

Abraham: It is often felt that there are those who do not like certain characteristics about other Beings, so in their dislike of those characteristics, they are responsible for the prejudice. We want to point out that it is not only the doing of the one who is accused of being prejudiced. More often, the one who *feels* discriminated against is the most powerful creator in that experience.

The Being who feels that others do not like him—for whatever reason—whether it is religion, race, gender, or social status . . . no matter what the reason is that he feels that he is being discriminated against—it is his attention to the subject of the prejudice that attracts his trouble.

Do "Likes Attract," or Do "Opposites Attract"?

Jerry: Abraham, there's a statement that doesn't seem to blend with what we've heard from you. And that statement is "Opposites attract." That seems different from what you teach, as far as "like attracting like." For instance, opposites do seem to attract, like an outgoing man will marry a shy woman, or an outgoing woman will be attracted to a shy man.

Abraham: Everything you see and everyone you know is offering vibrational signals, and those signals must match before attraction can take place. So even in a situation where people seem to be different, there must be a dominant basis of vibrational similarity for them to be together. It is *Law*. Within all people there are vibrations of that which is wanted and vibrations of the lack of what is wanted, and everything that comes into their experience always matches the vibrations that are dominant. No exceptions.

Let us introduce the word *harmony*. When two are exactly the same, then their intentions cannot be fulfilled. In other words, one who wants to sell does not do well to attract another seller. But the attracting of a buyer brings forth the *harmony*.

The shy man attracts an outgoing woman because his *intention* is to be more outgoing, so he is actually attracting the *subject* of his intention.

The magnetized skillet, whose essence is of iron, will attract to itself another object whose essence is of iron (that is, a bolt or a nail or another iron skillet) but it will not attract a skillet that is made of copper or aluminum.

When you set your radio receiver to the frequency of 98.7FM, you cannot pick up the signal of 630AM being broadcast from a radio tower. Those frequencies must match.

There is no vibrational evidence, anywhere in the Universe, that supports the idea that opposites attract. They do not.

What about When What Felt Good Now Feels Bad?

Jerry: How is it that some people seem to eventually attract something they've really, really wanted, but then when it comes, they find that it turns out to be a very negative situation? It brings them pain.

Abraham: Often, from a place that is very far from what is wanted, people will decide what they do want. But instead of focusing upon that desire, and practicing the vibration of it until they have achieved vibrational alignment with their true desire—and allowing the *Law of Attraction* to then reach out into the Universe and bring them perfect matching results—they become impatient and try to *make* it happen by jumping into action. But when they take action before they have improved the content of their vibration, what they get is something that matches their current vibration instead of something that matches their desire.

Until you practice your vibration, there is often a big gap between the vibration of what you actually want and the vibration that you are offering. However, without exception, what comes to you matches the vibration that you are offering.

For example, let us say that a woman has recently come from a bad relationship where her partner has verbally and physically abused her. She did not want that or like that. In fact she hated the life that she lived with that person. So, from her place of really knowing what she does *not* want, she makes a clear statement of what she *does* want. She wants a partner who loves her and treats her with kindness and respect. But she feels very insecure without a partner, and she wants a new partner immediately. And so, she goes someplace where she is accustomed to going and meets a new person who seems nice enough. But what she may not realize is that the *Law of Attraction* is still matching her up with whatever is dominant within her. And right now, what is still dominant within her is the vibration of what she does not want because the unwanted parts of her last relationship are much more active within her thoughts than the new intentions that have been established. In her eagerness to soothe her feelings of insecurity, she takes action and jumps into this new relationship—and gets *more* of what is dominant within her vibration.

It would be our encouragement that she take things more slowly and spend more time thinking about what she wants until those thoughts are the basis for the dominant vibration within her. And then, let the *Law of Attraction* bring her wonderful new partner to her.

Jerry: Okay, that makes sense. It's sort of like we used to say: "They got some things they hadn't bargained for."

Abraham: That is the value of the *Creative Workshop Process.* When you get into your *Workshop,* visualizing *all* of the wonderful possibilities, letting your emotion come forth when you are touching upon that which you are really wanting, and then working upon staying focused where it feels good, then you will not have so much of that. You will discover how to make what you *do* want your most dominant vibration, and then when the *Law of Attraction* matches those thoughts that you have been practicing, you will not be surprised. In fact, you will begin to recognize (the manifestation of) the wonderful things that you have been practicing in your mind.

Is Everything Composed of Thought?

Jerry: Is everything and everyone composed *of* thought or *by* thought? Or neither?

Abraham: Both. Thought can be attracted by other thoughts through the power of the *Law of Attraction.* Thought is the vibration that the *Law of Attraction* is acting upon. Thought is the stuff, or the manifestation, and it is also the vehicle through which all things are attracted or created.

See your world as a sort of well-stocked kitchen where every possible ingredient that has ever been pondered, considered, thought of, or wanted exists in an abundant, never-ending quantity; and see yourself as the chef, soliciting forth from the shelves of your kitchen whatever ingredients, in whatever quantity, you desire, and you are mixing it all together for the creation of your cake, which currently pleases you.

I Want More Joy, Happiness, and Harmony

Jerry: What if someone would say to you, "Abraham, I want to be more joyful. How can I use what you're teaching to attract more joy, happiness, and harmony into my life?"

Abraham: First, we would compliment the person on discovering the most important desire of all: *the seeking of joy.* For in seeking and finding joy, you not only find perfect alignment with your *Inner Being* and with who-you-really-are, but you also find vibrational alignment with all things that you desire.

When joy is really important to you, you do not allow yourself to focus upon things that do not feel good—and the result of thinking only thoughts that feel good would cause you to create a wonderful life filled with all things that you desire.

When you hold the desire to be joyful and you are sensitive to the way you feel, and therefore guide your thoughts in the direction of things that feel better and better, you improve your vibration, and your *point of attraction* becomes one that will only attract—through the *Law of Attraction*—things that you desire.

Deliberately guiding your thoughts is the key to a joyful life, but a desire to feel joy is the best plan of all . . . because in the reaching for joy, you find the thoughts that attract the wonderful life you desire.

Isn't it Selfish to Want More Joy?

Jerry: Some would say that for a person to want to be joyous all the time would be a very selfish way to want to be, as though desiring joy is a negative.

Abraham: *We are often accused of teaching selfishness, and we always agree that we certainly do teach selfishness, for you cannot perceive life from any perspective other than from that of yourself. Selfishness is the sense of self. It is the picture that you hold of yourself.* Whether you are focusing upon yourself or another, you are doing it all from your selfish vibrational viewpoint, and whatever you are feeling is your *point of attraction.*

So, if from your perspective of self you are focused in a way that you are feeling good, then your *point of attraction* is such that the things that you are attracting—through the *Law of Attraction*—will please you when they get there.

If, however, you are not selfish enough to insist upon focusing in a way that feels good, and you are focused upon something that feels bad, then your *point of attraction* is such that you are negatively attracting—and you will not like what is coming when it gets there.

Unless you are selfish enough to care about how you feel, and there-fore direct your thoughts in such a way that you are allowing a true con-nection to your <u>Inner Being</u>, you have nothing to give another anyway. Everyone is selfish. It is not possible to be otherwise.

Which Is More Moral, Giving or Receiving?

Jerry: So, you would seem to see as much that is right and joyful in *giving* as in *receiving*. In other words, you don't see one as morally superior to the other?

Abraham: Because of the powerful *Law of Attraction*, what-ever you are giving—by way of your vibrational offering—you are receiving. . . . The *<u>Law of Attraction</u> always accurately sorts things out and brings to everyone the matching product of their thoughts.* So when you give a thought of Well-Being, you always receive the matching equivalent. When you offer thoughts of hatred, the *Law of Attraction* cannot bring you loving results. That defies the *Law.*

Often when people speak of giving and receiving, they are referring to gifts of action, or material things, but the *Law of Attraction* is not responding to your words or actions, but instead to the vibration that is at the basis of those words and actions.

Let us say that you see those who are in need of something. Perhaps they have no money, transportation, or food. And as you see them, you feel sad (because you are focused on their lack and activating that within your own vibration), and from your place of sadness you offer them the action of money or food. The vibration that you are transmitting is actually saying to them, *I do this for you because I see that you cannot do this for yourself.* Your vibration is actually focused upon their *lack* of Well-Being and therefore, even though you have offered money or food through your action, *your dominant offering is perpetuating their lack.*

It is our encouragement that you take the time to imagine those people in a better situation. Practice the thought of their success and happiness in your own mind, and once that is the dominant vibration that you hold about them, then offer whatever inspired action you now feel. In that case, because of the dominant vibration of your Being, as you are holding them as your object of attention, you will attract a matching vibration of Well-Being from them. In other words, you will uplift them. You will assist them in finding the vibration that matches their desire for Well-Being instead of the vibration that matches their current situation. In our view, that is the only kind of *giving* that has value.

So the question is not "Which is superior, giving or receiving?" The question is "Which is superior, focusing upon what is *wanted* or upon what is *unwanted?*" "Which is superior, uplifting another by believing in their success, or adding to their discouragement by noticing where they are?" "Which is superior, being in alignment with my *Inner Being* and then taking action, or being out of alignment and taking action?" "Which is superior, adding to one's success or adding to one's failure?"

The greatest gift that you could ever give another is the gift of your expectation of their success.

There are as many different worlds as there are perceivers, Beings, or individuals. You are not here to create one world where everyone is the same, wanting and getting the same. You are here to be that which you want to be, while you allow all others to be that which *they* want to be.

What If Everyone Got Everything They Wanted?

Jerry: Let me play the part of devil's advocate here. If each of the selfish Beings on the planet were getting everything they individually want, what kind of mess would this world be in?

Abraham: It would not be, and is not, a "mess" at all. For, through the *Law of Attraction*, they would attract unto them those who are in harmony with *their* intent. You see, this is a very well-balanced place in which you live. There is some of everything here, in enough proportion, abundance, and difference, to give you all of the ingredients for this vast and marvelous "kitchen" that you have come to participate in.

How Can I Assist Those Who Are Feeling Pain?

Jerry: I live a joyous and glorious life, but I am often aware that there is much agony being experienced in the world around me. What could I do to make this life experience painless for *everyone?*

Abraham: You cannot create in the experience of another because you cannot think their thoughts. . . . It is the thoughts they are thinking, the words they are speaking, or the acts they are doing that is bringing forth the emotional response (agony) from their *Inner Being. They are creating their own agony by giving thought to that which they do not want.*

Now, what you *can* do for them is to set the example of joy. Become a Being who *thinks* only of that which he is wanting; who *speaks* of only that which he is wanting; who *does* only that which he is wanting—and therefore brings forth only joyful emotion.

Jerry: I can do that. I can focus on what I want, on that joy, and I can learn to allow them to have whatever experience they create. So would it be accurate to say that if I focus on their painful experience, that I will now create pain in my own experience? And then I'll be setting *that* example—the example of a painful experience.

Abraham: Let us say that someone in pain comes into your experience and as you see them in their painful situation, a desire wells up inside of you that they find the way out of their painful situation, so their pain only brushed you slightly as you quickly identified your desire for their joyful solution. *If you then turn your undivided attention to their successful resolution of their painful situation, you would feel no real pain, and you could be a catalyst to inspire an actual solution for them. That is an example of what true upliftment is. However, if you only focus upon their pain, or upon the situation that has caused it, you will activate within yourself the vibration that matches that, and you will also begin to feel pain as you then begin the attraction of that which you do not want.*

Is Setting a Joyous Example the Key?

Jerry: Is the key to just continue to seek joy myself? To set that example and allow the others—*really allow them*—to have whatever experience they're choosing (in whatever way they are choosing it) for themselves?

Abraham: You really have no other choice but to allow them to have whatever experience they are attracting, because you cannot think for them or vibrate for them—and therefore you cannot attract for them.

True *Allowing* is maintaining your own balance, your own joy, no matter what they are doing. So the advantage that you offer them is that as you remain in balance, connected to your own *Inner Being*, aligned with the wonderful life-giving resources of the Universe, and you hold them as your object of attention, they benefit. The more you feel good as you hold others as your object of attention, the greater the power of your positive influence.

You will know when you have reached the point of *Allowing* them to be, do, or have whatever they want (or do not want), when, as you are aware that they are doing it, you are not feeling negative emotion about it. *When you are an <u>Allower</u>, you are feeling joy as you are observing the experience of all.*

You have come full circle with your questions in helping us explain the three *Laws* that are so very important.

The *Law of Attraction* is responding to the vibration of your thoughts.

As you deliberately offer your thoughts by choosing thoughts that feel good, you allow your connection to your *Inner Being*, to who-you-really-are. When you are connected to who-you-really-are, anyone you hold as your object of attention benefits. And, of course, in all of that, you feel joy!

In time, you will be so aware of how you feel, and you will become so adept at *deliberately* offering your thoughts, that you will predominantly be in the state of positive attraction. And then (really, *only* then) will you be comfortable in letting others create as they choose. *When you understand that unwanted things cannot assert themselves into your experience, but that everything is invited to you and by you through thought, you never again feel threatened by what others may be choosing to live, even if they are very close by—for they cannot be a part of your experience.*

Can I Think Negative Yet Feel Positive?

Jerry: So how can we give our attention to, or have a thought about, something that's negative and not have a negative emotional response to it?

Abraham: You cannot. And we would not suggest that you try. In other words, to say *never* have negative emotion would be the same as saying, "Do not have a *Guidance System*. Pay no attention to your *Emotional Guidance System*." And that is the opposite of what we are saying. We want you to be aware of your emotions and then guide your thoughts until you feel relief.

As you are focused upon a little (negative) thought, you will feel a little (unwanted) negative emotion. And if you are sensitive to the way you feel and want to feel better, you will change the thought. It is easy to change it when it is a small thought and a small emotion. It is much harder to change when it is a big thought and therefore a big emotion. The emotion will be proportionate, in intensity, to the amount of thought that you have amassed by the *Law of Attraction*. The longer you stay focused upon what you do not want, the greater and more powerful that thought will become. But if you are sensitive to your emotions and you withdraw your attention from the unwanted subject very quickly, you will begin to feel better, and you will stop the attraction of this unwanted thing.

What Are Some Words to Enhance Being Well-Being?

Jerry: Could you give us some words that we could use to help attract a variety of things, like perfect health . . . ?

77

Abraham: *I want perfect health! I like feeling good. I enjoy my good-feeling body. I have many positive memories of feeling good in my body. I see many people who are clearly in a state of good health, and it is easy to see how much they are enjoying their good-feeling bodies. When I think thoughts like these, I feel good. These thoughts are in harmony with a healthy body.*

Jerry: What about perfect financial prosperity?

Abraham: *I want financial prosperity! There are so many wonderful things that are readily available in this wonderful world, and financial prosperity opens the door to so many of those things. Since the Law of Attraction responds to my thoughts, I have decided to focus predominantly upon the abundance that is possible, understanding that it is only a matter of time before my thoughts of prosperity will be matched by the flow of financial prosperity. Since the Law of Attraction will bring me the object of my attention, I choose abundance.*

Jerry: And great relationships?

Abraham: *I want great relationships. I so enjoy nice, clever, funny, energetic, stimulating people, and I love knowing that this planet is abundant with them. I have met so many interesting people, and I love the discovery of fascinating characteristics in the people I meet. It seems that the more I enjoy people, the more people whom I enjoy come into my experience. I love this time of spectacular co-creation.*

Jerry: What about positive Non-Physical experiences?

Abraham: *I want to attract those who are in harmony with me, physical and Non-Physical. I'm fascinated by the Law of Attraction and am comforted by the knowledge that when I'm feeling good, I can only attract that which feels good. I love understanding that the basis of that which is Non-Physical is pure, positive Energy. I enjoy utilizing my Emotional Guidance System so that I can rendezvous with that Source.*

Jerry: And continual, joyous growth?

Abraham: *I am a growth-seeking Being, and it is exhilarating to remember that expansion is not only natural but inevitable. I love knowing that joy is simply a choice. So, since my expansion is inevitable, I choose to have all of it—in joy.*

Jerry: And that will attract these things?

Abraham: Your *words* will not bring you immediate manifestations of what you are asking for, but the more often you say them, and the better you feel while you are saying them, the purer or less contradicted your vibration will be. And soon your world will be filled with these things you have spoken about. . . . *Words alone do not attract, but when you feel emotion when you speak, that means your vibration is strong—and the <u>Law of Attraction</u> must answer those vibrations.*

What Is the Measure of Our Success?

Jerry: What do you see as success? What would you say is the mark of *success?*

Abraham: The achievement of anything that you desire must be considered success, whether it is a trophy, money, relationships, or things. But if you will let your standard of success be your achievement of joy, everything else will fall easily into place. For in the finding of joy, you are finding vibrational alignment with the resources of the Universe.

You cannot feel joy while you are focusing upon something not wanted, or the lack of something wanted; therefore, while you are feeling joy, you will never be in the state of contradicted vibration. And only the contradiction in your own thoughts and vibration can keep you from the things you desire.

We are amused as we watch the majority spending most of their life seeking a set of rules against which they can measure their life experience, looking outside of self for those who will tell them what is right or wrong, when all along they have within themselves a

Guidance System that is so sophisticated, so intricate, so precise, and so readily available.

By paying attention to this *Emotional Guidance System,* and by reaching for the best-feeling thought that you can find right now from wherever you are, you will allow your broader perspective to help you move in the direction of the things that you truly want.

As you sift through the magnificent contrast of your physical time-space reality, consciously aware of the way you feel, and deliberately guiding your thoughts toward those that feel better and better, in time you begin to see your life through the eyes of your broader *Inner Being.* And as you do so, you feel the satisfaction of being upon the path that you chose from your Non-Physical perspective when you made the decision to come forth into this wonderful body. For, from your Non-Physical vantage point, you understood the eternally evolving nature of your Being and the promise that this Leading Edge contrasting environment held. You understood the nature of your magnificent guidance system and how, with practice, you could see this world as your *Inner Being* sees it. You understood the powerful *Law of Attraction* and the fairness and accuracy with which it responds to the free will of all creators.

By reaching for the best-feeling thought you can find, you reconnect with that perspective, and you will shiver with exhilaration as you reconnect with your purpose, with your zest for life, and with *you!*

PART III

The *Science* *of* *Deliberate* *Creation*

The *Science of Deliberate Creation:* Defined

Jerry: Abraham, you have spoken to us of *Deliberate Creation.* Would you discuss the value of that to us and clarify what you mean by *Deliberate Creation?*

Abraham: We have called it the *Science of Deliberate Creation* because we are assuming that you want to create on purpose. But actually, it is more aptly called the *Law of Creation,* for it works whether you are thinking of what you want, or of what you do not want. Whether you are thinking of what you do want, or whether you are thinking of the lack of what you want (the direction of your thought is your choice), the *Law of Creation* goes to work upon whatever you are thinking about.

From your physical perspective, this equation of creation has two important parts: the launching of the thought and the expectation of the thought—the *desire* for the creation and the *allowing* of the creation. From our Non-Physical perspective, we experience both parts of that equation simultaneously, for there is no gap between what we desire and what we fully expect.

Most humans are unaware of the power of their thoughts, the vibrational nature of their Being, or the powerful *Law of Attraction,* so they look to their *action* to make everything happen. And while we agree that action is an important component in the physical world in which you are focused, it is not through your action that you are creating your physical experience.

When you understand the power of thought and practice your deliberate offering of it, you will discover the powerful leverage (in creating) that only comes from *desiring* and *allowing.* When you prepave, or positively anticipate with your thoughts, the amount of action required is far less, and the action is much more satisfying. If you do not take the time to align your thoughts, far more action is required, without the satisfying results.

Your hospitals are filled to the brim with those who are now taking action to compensate for inappropriate thoughts. They did not create the illness on purpose, but they did create it—through thought and through expectation—and then they went to the hospital to take physical action to compensate. We see many people spending their days exchanging their action for money, because the money is essential to the freedom of life in this society. And yet, in most cases, the action is not action in joy. It is an attempt to compensate for misaligned thought.

You have intended action; that is part of the deliciousness of this physical world in which you live. But you did not intend to do your creating through physical action—you intended to use your body to enjoy that which you have created through your thought.

As you set forth your thought in advance, feeling positive emotion, you have then launched your creation, and when you walk through space and time toward that manifestation in the future, expecting that it will be there . . . then, *from that joyful creation that you have launched into the future, you will be inspired to the action that is action in joy.*

When you are taking action in your now, and it is not action in joy, it is our absolute promise to you that it will not lead to a happy ending. It cannot; it defies the *Law.*

Rather than being so ready to jump into action to get the things that you want, we say *think* them into being; *see* them, *visualize* them, and *expect* them—and *they will be.* And you will be guided, inspired, or led to the perfect action that will bring about the process that will lead you to that which you seek . . . and there is a great difference between that which we have spoken and the way most of the world is going about it.

I Invited It by Giving It Thought

Often, as we begin to impart our knowledge to our physical friends regarding the *Deliberate Creative Process,* we meet with resistance, for there are those who have things in their life experience that they do not want. And as they hear us say, "All things are invited by you," they protest, saying, "Abraham, I wouldn't have invited this because I don't want it!"

So we eagerly offer this information to you to help you understand *how* you are getting what you are getting so that you may be more deliberate in your attracting of it, and so you may *consciously* attract those things that you *do* want—while you may avoid attracting those things that you do *not* want.

We know that you are not inviting, attracting, or creating it—on purpose. But we will say to you that you are the inviter, the attractor, and the creator of it . . . because you are doing it by giving thought to it. By *default,* you are offering your thought, and then the *Laws* that you do not understand are responding to your thought, causing results that you do not understand. And so, that is why we have come forth: to speak to you of the *Universal Laws* so that you may understand *how* you are getting what you are getting, so that you may understand how to gain *deliberate* control of your life.

Most physical Beings are so completely integrated into their physical world that they have very little conscious awareness of their relationship with the Non-Physical world. For example, you want light in your bedroom, so you go to the lamp by your bedside, turn a little switch, and watch the light flood the room. Then you would explain to others, "This switch causes the light." But you understand, without our explaining, that there is much more to the story of where the light comes from. And so it is with all things that you are experiencing in your physical setting. You are explaining only a little bit of what makes things happen. We are here to explain the rest of it to you.

You have emerged into your physical dimension from your broader, Non-Physical perspective with great intent and purpose. You have come forth because you wanted this physical experience very much. This is not the first of such experiences for you. You have had many physical, as well as Non-Physical, life experiences. And you have emerged into this one because you want to add to that continuing evolving Being that you-really-are—that Being that through this body and through these physical senses you may not now know, but that Being, indeed . . . that broader, expansive, growth-seeking, joy-seeking, evolving part of *you.*

My *Inner Being* Is Communicating with Me

We want to help you remember that you are the creator of your experience and that there is such joy in being deliberate about that. We want to help you remember your relationship with the Non-Physical part of you, your *Inner Being,* who is aware of you and involved with you in everything that you do.

You do not remember the details of what you have lived before you came into this physical body, but your *Inner Being* is fully aware of all that you have become, and is continually offering you information to assist you in living in the most joyous way possible, in all moments in time.

As you emerged into this life experience, you did not bring with you the memory of that which you have lived before, for those details would only serve to distract you from the power of your *now.* However, because of your relationship with your *Inner Being,* you do have access to the knowledge of that broader perspective, or *Total You. Your broader Non-Physical part of you communicates with you, and has done so from the day you emerged into this physical body. That communication comes in many varieties—but all of you are receiving the basic communication that comes forth, in the form of your emotion.*

Every Emotion Feels Good . . . or Feels Bad

Every emotion that you feel is, without exception, communication from your *Inner Being* letting you know, in the moment, the appropriateness of whatever you are thinking, speaking, or acting. In other words, as you *think* a thought that is not in vibrational harmony with your overall intent, your *Inner Being* will offer you negative emotion. As you *do* or *say* something that is not in vibrational harmony with who-you-are and what you want, your *Inner Being* will offer you negative emotion. And, in like manner, when you are speaking, thinking, or acting in the direction of that which *is* in harmony with your intentions, your *Inner Being* will offer you *positive* emotion.

There are only two emotions: One of them feels good, and the other feels bad. You call them all sorts of different things, depending upon the situation that brought them forth. But as you recognize that this *Guidance System* (which comes forth from within you in the form of emotion) speaks to you from your broader, all-inclusive perspective, you will be able to understand that you have the benefit of all the intentions that you hold here today and all of the intentions that you emerged into this physical body with—and that you have the ability to factor in all of the details of *all* your desires and your beliefs, in order to be able to make the absolute appropriate decisions at every point in time.

I Can Trust My Guidance from Within

Many people have set their own intuitive guidance aside, replacing it with the opinions of parents, teachers, experts, or leaders in a variety of disciplines. But the more you look to others for their guidance, the more removed you become from your own wise counsel. So often as we begin to remind our physical friends of who-they-really-are, helping them to reconnect with the *Guidance System* that is within them, they feel hesitation. They have often become convinced of their unworthiness and of their incorrectness, so they are afraid to move forward, trusting their own guidance or their own conscience, because they believe that there may be someone else who knows more clearly than they do what is appropriate for them.

But we want to help you remember the worthy, powerful Being that you are, and your reason for coming into this time-space reality. We want you to remember your intent to explore the contrast of this wonderful environment, knowing that it would give birth to a continual stream of new intentions; and we want you to remember that who-you-really-are—your *Inner Being*, or *Total You*, or *Source*—is joyous in the expansion that you are about. We want you to remember that you can feel, by the power of your emotions in every moment, whether you are seeing your current situation through the eyes of that broader perspective or whether you are cutting yourself off from that *Source* by choosing thoughts that are of a different nature. In other words, when you feel love, that means that the way you are seeing the object of your attention matches the way the *Inner You* sees it. When you feel hate, you are seeing it without that *Inner Connection*.

You intuitively knew all of this, especially when you were younger, but gradually most of you were worn down by the insistence of those older and self-described "wiser" others who surrounded you as they worked hard to convince you that you could not trust your own impulses.

And so, *most of you physical Beings do not trust yourselves, which is amazing to us, for that which comes forth from within you is all that you may trust.* But instead, you are spending most of your physical lifetimes seeking a set of rules or a group of people (a religious or political group, if you will) who will tell you what is right and wrong. And then you spend the rest of your physical experience trying to hammer your "square peg" into someone else's "round hole," trying to make those *old* rules—usually those that were written thousands of years before your time—fit into this *new* life experience. And, as a result, what we see, for the most part, is your frustration, and at best, your confusion. And, we also have noticed that every year there are many of you who are dying, as you are arguing about whose set of rules is most appropriate. We say to you: *That overall, all-inclusive, never-changing set of rules does not exist—for you are ever-changing, growth-seeking Beings.*

If your house were on fire and the firefighters came with their truck—that marvelous equipment with the big, long hoses and all of the water surging through—and sprayed their hoses into your house and extinguished the flame, you would say, "Indeed, that is most appropriate behavior." But if, on a day when there was no fire, those same firefighters and the same hoses were to enter your house spraying water around, you would say, "Indeed, that is *not* appropriate!"

And so it is with the laws that you are passing relative to one another: *Most of your past laws and rules are not appropriate to that which you are now living. If you had not intended growth, you would not be here in this physical life experience. For you are here as an expanding, ever-changing, growth-seeking Being because you want to add unto that which you understand. And, you want to add unto <u>All-That-Is</u>. . . . If that which was figured out long ago was the ultimate, then there would be no reason for your existence today.*

How Am I Getting What I'm Getting?

At first, our insistence that you are the creator of your own reality is met with a joyful acceptance, because most people long for the control of their own experience. But as you come to understand that everything that is coming to you is being attracted by your own thought *(you get what you think about whether you want it or not),* some of you feel uncomfortable with what seems like the overwhelming task of monitoring thoughts, sorting them out, and offering only those that will yield things that you *do* want.

We do not encourage a monitoring of thoughts, for we agree that would be incredibly time-consuming and cumbersome, but instead we recommend a conscious utilization of your *Emotional Guidance System.*

If you will pay attention to the way that you are feeling, then a monitoring of your thoughts is not so necessary. Whenever you are feeling good, know that you are, in that moment, speaking, thinking, or acting in accordance with your intentions—and know that whenever you are feeling bad, you are not aligned with your intentions. In short, whenever there is negative emotion present within you, you are, in that moment, miscreating, either through your thought, your word, or your action.

And so, the combination of being more deliberate about what you want, more clear about what you intend, and more sensitive to the way you feel is, in essence, what the Deliberate Creative Process is all about.

I Am the Sole Creator of My Experience

The big question that usually comes up at this point of our discussion is, "Abraham, how do I know that what comes forth from within me may be trusted? Isn't there someone greater than I who makes all of the rules and wants me to be or do specific things?" And we say, you are the creator of your experience, and you have emerged forth into this physical body through the power of your desire. You are not here to prove yourself worthy of something else; you are not here because you seek greater salvation on some other plane. You are here because you have a specific purpose in being here. You want to be a *Deliberate Creator,* and you have chosen this physical dimension, where there is time and space, so that you may finely tune your understanding and then see the benefits of whatever you have created in thought by allowing it to come into your physical experience. You are adding to the expansion of the Universe, and *All-That-Is* benefits from your existence, by your exposure to this experience and by your expansion.

All that you do pleases that which you seek to please. There is not a list of things that are right and a list of things that are wrong—there is only that which aligns with your true intent and purpose, and that which does not. You may trust your Guidance that comes forth from within you to help you know when you are in alignment with your state of natural Well-Being.

Magnetically, I Attract Thoughts in Vibrational Harmony

The *Law of Attraction* is responsible for much that is obvious in your life experience. You have coined many phrases because of your partial understanding of this *Law.* You say, "Birds of a feather flock together." You say, "The better it gets, the better it gets; and the worse it gets, the worse it gets." You say, "This day started out bad and ended up much, much worse." But even as you are saying these things, most of you do not truly understand how powerful the *Law of Attraction* really is. People are drawn together because of it. Every circumstance and event is a result of it. . . . Thoughts that are vibrationally similar to one another are drawn magnetically to one another through the powerful *Law of Attraction;* people who feel a certain way are drawn to one another, magnetically, through this *Law;* indeed, the very thoughts that you think are drawn one unto the other until what was once a very small or insignificant and not-so-powerful thought may—because of your focus upon it—grow to be very powerful.

Because of the <u>Law of Attraction</u>, each of you is like a powerful magnet, attracting unto you more of the way that you feel at any point in time.

As We're Thinking and Speaking, We're Creating

No other creates in your experience. You are doing it all; you get all of the credit. As you observe your own life experience and the experiences of those around you, we want you to understand that there is not a shred of evidence that is contrary to these powerful *Laws* that we are expressing. As you begin to notice the absolute correlation between what you are thinking and speaking—and what you are getting—your understanding of the *Law of Attraction* will continue and your desire to utilize your *Guidance System* to deliberately direct your thoughts will increase. And, of course, you will have a much greater understanding of the lives of those around you as well. (In fact, it is sometimes easier for you to see it with others.)

Have you noticed that those who speak most of illness have more and more illness? Have you noticed that those who speak of poverty live more of it, while those who speak of prosperity have more of it? As you understand that your thoughts are magnetic and your attention to them causes them to grow in power until eventually the subject of the thought becomes the subject of your experience, your willingness to pay attention to the way you feel will help you more deliberately choose the direction of your thought.

It is easy to see the *Law of Attraction* at work as you are involved in a conversation with another. For example, imagine that your friend is speaking of something she is experiencing and you want to be a good friend, so you are focusing upon her words and listening to the examples she is offering about what is happening to her. As you stay focused there longer, your own examples of similar situations come into your mind. As you then join her in conversation by adding the matching stories of your experience, the thought vibration grows stronger still. Enough attention to these subjects and enough conversations about things you have experienced will bring more of the same kinds of experiences to you. And as more and more thoughts are brought forth related to what you do *not* want, you will eventually find yourself absolutely surrounded by thoughts, words, and experiences that are in the direction of that which you do *not* want. (You and your friend will now have even more unpleasant situations to discuss with one another.)

Now if you had been sensitive to the way you were *feeling* as the conversation first began leaning in the direction of what you do not want, you would have been aware of the sick feeling in the pit of your stomach. You would have recognized your *Guidance,* which is essentially saying, *You are thinking and speaking about that which you do __not__ want.* And the reason for that warning signal, that "warning bell," was the discord between who-you-really-are and what you desire, and what you are focusing upon in this moment. Your emotions indicate your misalignment. Your *Guidance* is alerting you to the fact that while you are thinking and speaking of those unwanted things, you are a magnet attracting circumstances, events, and other Beings unto you, and soon you will have in your experience the essence of the very thing that you have been speaking about that you do *not* want.

In like manner, if you are speaking about that which you *do* want, your thoughts will be drawn more unto *that.* You will draw more people to you who will want to talk about what you *do* want. And all the while that you are speaking of what you *do* want, your

Inner Being will be offering you a positive emotion to let you know that you are in harmony with—and that that which you are attracting to yourself is in vibrational harmony with—the essence of the balance of intentions that you hold.

The Delicate Balance Between *Wanting* and *Allowing*

The *Science of Deliberate Creation* is a delicately balanced *Law;* it has two parts: On the one hand, there is the thought of what you want. On the other hand, there is the expectation or belief—or the allowing into your experience—of what you are creating through your thought.

And so, if you say, "I want a new red car," you have literally, through your thought, set forth the beginning of the creation of that new red car into your experience. And now, the more attention you give to that thought, and the more you are able to purely imagine that red car within your experience, the more excited about it you will become. And the more excited you become, or the more positive emotion that comes forth as you think about your red car, then the faster your red car is coming into your experience. Once you have created it through thought, and once you have felt powerful positive emotion while thinking of it, the car moves rapidly into your experience. It has been created, it now exists, and in order to now have it in your experience, you have only to *allow* it. And you allow it by expecting it, by believing it, and by letting it be.

When you doubt your ability to have the new red car, you stifle your creation. If you say, "I want a new red car," you begin the creation of it, but if then you add, *"but* it is too expensive," you hold yourself apart from your creation. In other words, you have done the first part of the creating by your wanting, but you have now hindered the creation of that which you want by not believing, by not expecting, and by not *allowing*—for in order to bring your creations into your physical experience, both parts of the process are necessary.

Just because you are talking about the subject of your creation does not necessarily mean that you are allowing it. When you think

about your new red car and you feel excitement about it, you are allowing it, but when you are thinking about your new red car from a place of worrying that you cannot achieve it (or frustration that it has not yet come), you are actually focused upon the *absence* of the car, and you are not allowing it into your experience.

Sometimes in the early stages of the creation of something you want, you are right on track for receiving it as you are feeling excited about it and are positively expecting it, but then you express your desire to another, who begins to tell you all of the reasons why it *cannot* be, or why it *should not* be. Your friend's negative influence would not be serving you, for when you were focused upon the *essence of your desire*, you were attracting it, but now that you are focused upon the *lack of your desire*, you are pushing what you want away.

How Does It Feel, Good or Bad?

And so, as you say, "I want a new red car, and I know it is coming to me," it is. But as you are saying, *"But where is it? I have wanted it for a very long time. I believed Abraham, but the things that I want are not coming,"* now you are not focused upon what you want. Now you are focused upon the *lack* of what you want, and you are getting, through the *Law of Attraction,* what you are focused upon.

If you focus upon whatever you want, you will attract whatever you want. If you focus upon the lack of whatever you want, you will attract more of the lack. (Every subject is really two subjects: what you want and the lack, or absence, of what you want.) If you are paying attention to the way you are feeling, you will always know whether you are focused upon what you want or upon the lack of it—for when you are thinking of what you want, you are feeling good, and when you are thinking of the lack of what you want, you are feeling bad.

As you say, "I want money to support my lifestyle," you are attracting the money, but as you focus upon the things that you want that you do not have, noticing the lack—you are pushing your abundance away.

An Exercise to Assist in *Deliberate Creation*

Here is an exercise that will assist you in your *Deliberate Creating:*

Take three separate pieces of paper, and at the top of each page write one thing that you want. Now take the first page, and beneath the subject of what you have written, write: "<u>These are the reasons that I want this</u>. . . ." Write whatever comes to your mind—write whatever flows forth naturally; do not try to force it. And when nothing more comes, you are complete for now.

Now, turn your paper over and write at the top of the second side of the page: "<u>These are the reasons that I believe that I will have this</u>. . . ."

The first side of your page enhances what you want (the first side of the equation of *Deliberate Creation*). The second side of the page enhances your belief that you will have it (the second side of the equation of *Deliberate Creation*). And now that you have focused upon and activated within your vibration both sides of the equation, you are now in the state of receiving the manifestation of your desire, for you have successfully accomplished both sides of the *Creative Process*. All that is necessary now is that you want it—and continue to expect it until you have it—and it will be yours.

There is no limit to the number of things that you can simultaneously create, for it is not difficult to hold a desire and at the same time hold an expectation of achieving it. But in the beginning, while you are still learning to focus your thoughts, it may be helpful to deliberately concentrate upon only two or three desires at a time, for the longer the list of things you are working on, the greater the potential for doubt to creep in as you look at all the things that you have not yet accomplished. The more you play the game, the better you become at focusing your thoughts, and eventually there will be no reason to limit your list in any way.

Before you can experience something in your physical life experience, you must first give thought to it. Your thought is the invitation, and without it, it will not come. We are encouraging

an *intentional* deciding of what is wanted, and then an *intentional* giving of thought to those things that you *want* while you are *intentionally* not giving thought to those things that you do not want. And, in suggesting this, we encourage that you set some time aside every day when you sit and *intentionally* bring your thoughts together into a sort of vision of what you want to experience in your life, and we have been referring to this time as your *Workshop for Deliberate Creating.*

As you are moving through your daily experience, set forth the intention to notice things that you like: *Today, no matter what I'm doing and no matter whom I'm doing it with, it is my dominant intention to look for things that I like.* And as you deliberately gather this data, you will have the available resources to effectively create when you go to your *Creative Workshop.*

Thoughts Evoking Great Emotion Manifest Quickly

We have told you that your thoughts are magnetic. But we want to add a point of clarification here: *Although every thought has creative potential, the thoughts that do not bring great emotion with them are not bringing the subject of your thought into your experience with any sort of speed. When it comes to thoughts that you feel strong emotion about—whether it is positive emotion or negative emotion—the essence of those thoughts is being quickly manifested into your physical experience. And that emotion that you are feeling is communication from your <u>Inner Being</u>, letting you know that you are now accessing the power of the Universe.*

If you go to a horror movie, and as you are sitting there in the theater with a friend, looking at the screen and all of the frightening detail that is being offered with the color and the sound, you are, at that time, in a *negative Workshop.* For as you are envisioning all that you do *not* want to see, the emotion that you are feeling is your *Inner Being* saying to you, *You are seeing something that is so vivid that the Universe is now offering power unto it.*

But when you leave the theater, fortunately, you usually say, "It was only a movie," so you do not *expect* it. You do not *believe* it will happen to you, so you do not complete the second part of the equation. You have given thought to it with emotion, so you have created it, but you do not allow it into your experience because you do not really *expect* it. However, as you are walking out of the theater, if your friend says to you, "It may only be a movie, but it once happened to *me*," then you may begin pondering *that* thought, and in doing so, you may bring yourself to the *belief* or *expectation* that that could also happen to *you*—and then it will. *Giving thought, on the one hand, and expecting or believing, on the other hand, is the balance that brings to you that which you receive.*

If you want it and expect it, it will be yours very soon. However, it is not often that you have achieved a balance where your wanting and your expecting are equal. Sometimes your wanting is very high, but your belief is not there at all. For example, in the story of the mother whose child is trapped beneath the automobile, she does not *believe* that she can lift that heavy vehicle off of her child, but her *wanting* is so extreme that she does. On the other hand, there are many examples where your belief is high, but your wanting is not. The creation of an illness, such as cancer, is that sort of example where your *belief* in it is very keen, while your *wanting* of it is not.

Many of you find yourselves in what we would term a negative *Workshop* many times a day. As you are sitting at your desk with your stack of bills beside you, feeling tension or even fear because there is not enough money to pay them, you are in a negative *Workshop*. For as you sit there giving thought to not having enough money, you are in the perfect position for the creating of more of what you do *not* want. The way you are *feeling* about that is the signal from your *Inner Being* saying to you that what you are thinking is not in harmony with what you want.

A Summary of the *Deliberate Creation Process*

Now let us summarize all that we have offered here so that you may have a clear and definite plan for the deliberate control of your life experience: First, recognize that you are more than you see here in this physical body; and that there is a broader, wiser, certainly older part of you that remembers all that you have lived, and, more important, knows that which you now are. And, from that all-encompassing perspective, this part of you can offer you clear and absolute information as to the appropriateness of that which you are doing, speaking, or thinking, or of that which you are *about* to do or *about* to speak.

Now if you will clearly set forth the intentions that are yours at this time, then your *Guidance System* can work even more effectively, for it has the ability to include all of the data—gathered from *all* of your experiences (all of your desires, all of your intentions, and all of your beliefs)—and compare it with what you are doing, or about to do, in order to give you absolute guidance.

Then, as you are moving through your day, be sensitive to the way you are feeling. And whenever you find yourself feeling negative emotion, stop whatever it is you are doing that is bringing the emotion forth, for the negative emotion means that, in this moment, you are negatively creating. *Negative emotion exists only when you are miscreating. And so, when you recognize that you are feeling negative emotion—no matter why, no matter how it got there, no matter what the situation is—stop doing whatever it is that you are doing and focus your thoughts on something that feels better.*

Practice the *Deliberate Creating Process* for 15 or 20 minutes every day by sitting quietly, undisturbed and undistracted by that which is around you, daydreaming about your life, seeing yourself as you want to be, and envisioning yourself surrounded by that which pleases you.

Attention to *What-Is* Only Creates More *What-Is*

The *Law of Attraction* is responding to *you*, to your *point of attraction*—and your *point of attraction* is caused by your thoughts. The way you *feel* is caused by the thoughts that you are thinking. So the way you *feel* about yourself is your strong and powerful magnetic *point of attraction*. When you *feel* poor, you cannot attract prosperity. When you *feel* fat, you cannot attract thin. When you *feel* lonely, you cannot attract companionship—it defies the *Law*. Many around you want to point out "reality" to you. They say, "Face the facts. Look at *what-is*." And we say to you, if you are able to see only *what-is*—then, by the *Law of Attraction*, you will create only more of *what-is*. . . . You must be able to put your thoughts beyond *what-is* in order to attract something different or something more.

Your emotional attention to *what-is* will root you like a tree to this spot, but an emotional (happy) vision of what you would like to begin attracting into your experience will bring you those changes. *Much of what you are now living, you want to continue, so keep giving your attention to those things, and you will continue to hold those things in your experience. But anything that you do not want, you must take your attention from.*

Appreciation of It Attracts It to Me

Thoughts that evoke your emotions are those that most quickly effect change in your life. Thoughts that you think while feeling no emotion will maintain what is already there. And so, those things that you have already created and appreciate can be kept in your life by continuing to appreciate them. But those things that you do not yet have that you want very soon (and very much), you must give clear, conscious, deliberate, emotion-evoking thought.

An extremely effective use of the *Creative Workshop* is to ponder the aspects you appreciate regarding the subjects that are most important to you. Each time you revisit a subject, your attention to detail will grow stronger, and with more time and more detail, your emotion about the subject will increase, also. Utilizing the *Creative*

Workshop in this way accomplishes everything that is required for *Deliberate Creation,* for you are thinking about something that you want, and in your emotion of appreciation, you are allowing that which you desire to manifest into your experience. As you often go to your *Creative Workshop,* you will begin to notice an obvious correlation between the things you are contemplating inside your *Workshop* and the manifestations that are showing up in your life experience.

Will *Universal Laws* Work Without My Belief?

Jerry: Abraham, tell me, these *Laws* that you speak of, these *Universal Laws,* do they work even if we don't believe that they work?

Abraham: They do, indeed. You are offering vibration even when you do not know you are doing it; that is why there is creating by *default.* You cannot turn your *Creative Mechanism* off; it is always functioning, and the *Laws* are always responding. That is why there is such value in understanding the *Laws.* Not understanding them is a little bit like coming into a game where you do not know the rules. And so, as you are playing the game, you do not understand *why* you are getting what you are getting. And that sort of game becomes frustrating, and most want to leave it.

How Do I Not Get What I Don't Want?

Jerry: Abraham, how would you tell people how to *not* get what they *don't* want?

Abraham: Do not think about what you do not want. Do not give thought to that which you do not want—for your attention to it attracts it. The more you think about it, the more powerful your thought becomes, and the more emotion comes forth. However, when you say, "I'm not going to think about that subject anymore," in that moment you are still thinking about that subject. So the key is to think about something else—something that you *do* want. With practice you will be able to tell by the way you feel if you are thinking about something wanted or unwanted.

This Civilized Society Seems Short on Joy

Jerry: We live in what I call a very civilized society, and in economical and material aspects we are doing relatively well, yet I don't see much joy in the people around me on the streets and in the businesses, and so on and so forth. Is that because of those factors that you speak about . . . that they have very little desire but a strong belief?

Abraham: Most people offer the majority of their vibration in response to what they are observing. And so, when they observe something that makes them feel good, they feel joy, but when they observe something that makes them feel bad, they simply do not feel joy. And most people do not believe that they have any control over the way they feel because they cannot manage to gain control over the conditions to which they are having these feeling responses. It is their belief in the lack of control of their own experience that is most responsible for the absence of joy that you are noticing. And we must remind you that if you continue to notice their lack of joy—yours will be gone as well.

I Want to Want with More Passion

Jerry: You've also said that if our *wanting* is passionate, our *belief* doesn't need to be so strong. So how would we go about building a passionate desire into the *Workshop* that you speak of?

Abraham: There must be a beginning place for all things. In other words, many who are interacting with us say, "Abraham, I hear what you're saying, but I don't know what I want." And so we say, begin by stating: *I want to know what I want.* For in setting forth that statement, you will become a magnet that will attract all sorts of data from which you can make your decisions. *Begin somewhere, and let the Law of Attraction deliver unto you examples and choices; and then the more you think about those choices, the more passionate you will be.*

Attention to any subject will cause it to grow stronger, and the emotion will therefore increase as well. When you think about what you want and you continue to add details to the picture, those thoughts grow stronger. But when you think about something that you desire but then think about it not yet coming . . . and then you think about how much fun it will be to have it, but then remember that it costs a great deal of money and you cannot yet afford it . . . that back-and-forth thinking dilutes your passion and slows the power of your thoughts.

Could I Release Counterproductive Beliefs?

Jerry: Could people create in one particular desired direction even though they've been led to believe (by others) that they're *destined* to create in a different direction?

Abraham: If their wanting is enough, they could. In other words, the mother we mentioned in the story earlier was taught by her society and by her own life experience to believe that she could not pick up an automobile that weighed so much, yet when her wanting was keen enough (when her child was in jeopardy), she was able to do it. And so, if the wanting is great enough, beliefs can be overridden.

Beliefs are very powerful, and they are slow to change, but they *can* be changed. As you continue to reach for better and better-feeling thoughts, you will find them and activate them, and the *Law of Attraction* will respond to them, and in time, your new life will reflect those changes in thought. If you hold to the idea that you can only believe the things that are currently based in "factual evidence," then nothing can change for you, but when you understand that the refocusing of thought, and the response of the

Law of Attraction to the new thought, will bring new evidence, then you understand the power of *Deliberate Creation.*

Can Past-Life Beliefs Affect My Current Life?

Jerry: Are there any thoughts (or beliefs) from any of our past lives that are still creating, or capable of creating, circumstances in our current physical experience?

Abraham: You are a continually expanding Being, and your *Inner Being* is the culmination of all that you have lived. Your *Inner Being* not only believes, but knows, the worthiness and value of your Being, so as you choose thoughts that are in agreement with those of your *Inner Being,* you feel the clarity of that knowledge.

However, the details of any past physical experience do not affect you in this physical experience. There is much confusion about that, and it comes largely because there are those who do not want to accept that they are the creator of their own experience. They say, "I'm fat in this life experience because I starved to death in the last." And we say: *There is nothing from past-life experience that is influencing that which you are doing now, unless, in some way, you have become aware of it and are now giving it your attention.*

Can My Negative Expectations
Affect the Well-Being of Others?

Jerry: If, in our concern for the welfare of those we really care about, we find our thoughts drifting toward some negative expectation regarding them, can we, just by pondering a problem occurring in *their* lives, actually cause them damage?

Abraham: *You cannot create in the experience of another because you cannot offer their vibration—which is their <u>point of attraction</u>—for them.* But when you focus upon something long enough that your thought becomes strong, and you are feeling strong emotion about it, you can *influence* the thoughts that they are thinking about a subject.

Remember, most people offer most of their vibration in response to what they are observing, so if they are observing you and see that look of concern on your face, or are observing the concerned comments you are making, they may very well lean in the direction of what is not wanted.

If you want to be of greatest value to others, see them as you know they want to be. That is the influence that you want to offer.

Can I Undo Past Programming by Others?

Jerry: If one's mind has been "programmed" by others into some belief, and this person finds that this belief is no longer desirable in their life, how can this person undo those beliefs?

Abraham: *You are negatively influenced by two major hindrances: One is the influence of others; the other is the influence of your own old habits. . . .* You have developed patterns of thinking, so you can easily fall into those old habitual patterns rather than think the new thought that is in harmony with the new desire. It is a matter of deliberately utilizing a little strength, or as you say, willpower, and refocusing your attention in a new direction.

The "programming" that you are referring to is only the result of your having focused upon something and then upon *Law of Attraction*'s response to that focus, so anything that you focus upon will grow stronger. Some of what you may be calling "programming" is merely a healthy integration into your current society, but some of it actually hinders your personal expansion. In time, and with practice, you will be able to tell the difference, and guide your thoughts in the direction of *your* personal choices. And that is really what *Deliberate Creation* is all about.

My Point of Power Is Right Now?

Jerry: Abraham, there's a phrase from the *Seth* books that says: *Your point of power is in the present.* What does that mean to you?

Abraham: Whether you are thinking about something that is occurring right now or about something that has happened in your past, or about something that you would like to occur in your future—you are doing the thinking right now. You are offering your vibration of thought in your present, and it is this present-thought vibration that the *Law of Attraction* is always responding to; therefore, your power to create is *now.*

It is also helpful to acknowledge that your emotion is coming forth in response to your *current* thought, whether it concerns your *past, present,* or *future.* The greater the emotion you are feeling, the more powerful your thought is, and the faster you are attracting into your experience things that match the essence of that thought.

You could be recalling an argument you had with someone many years earlier, or with someone who may have died ten years ago, but as you are recalling the argument *now,* you are activating the vibration of it *now,* and your current *point of attraction* is being affected by it *now.*

How Did the First Negative Thing Occur?

Jerry: I've often wondered how the first disease, or the first negative thing, occurred. Is it true that the first of almost everything occurred through the thought of it? In other words, like the first electric light, the thought came first and then the electric light followed, so our advancement into more diseases or into good or exciting things is only one step, or one thought, beyond something that has been previously thought?

Abraham: *All things—whether you determine that they are good or bad—are just the next logical steps from where you are currently standing.*

You are correct when you understand that the thought comes first. First there is thought, then thought-form, then manifestation. Your current situation is a platform of experience that inspires the next thought and the next.

When you realize that you can choose to positively expect, or negatively expect, but in either case, the *Law of Attraction* will add power to the thought until it will eventually manifest, you may wish to become more deliberate in the direction of your thoughts. Nothing ever manifests from your first, subtle attention to it. It takes time and attention to a subject to draw enough power to it to cause its manifestation. That is why all kinds of things, both wanted and unwanted, increase. In other words, diseases increase and become more plentiful as humans focus more and more upon diseases.

Is Imagination Not the Same as Visualization?

Jerry: Abraham, how would you describe the term *imagination?* What does it mean to you?

Abraham: *Imagination* is the mixing and massaging of thoughts into various combinations. It is similar to observing a situation. However, in imagination, you are creating the images rather than watching something in your current reality. Some use the word *visualization,* but we want to offer this subtle distinction: *Visualization* is often only a memory of something that you have once observed. By *imagination,* we mean deliberately bringing desired components together in your mind to create a desired scenario. In other words, focusing with the intention of inducing positive emotion. When we use the term *imagination,* we are really talking about *Deliberately Creating* your own reality.

Jerry: But how could a person visualize or imagine something that they haven't seen yet, like a mate they would like to have, a child they would like to give birth to, or a vocation that they've never considered?

Abraham: As you observe the world around you, deliberately gather and ponder the aspects of life that are appealing to you. Notice the beautiful smile that someone offers you or the beautiful home that someone lives in. Make mental or written notes about the things you enjoy in your world, and then mix those components together in your own mind, creating scenarios and versions of life that please you. Do not look for perfect role models, for you are unique and the creator of your own unique reality.

In time, you will discover, or remember, that this art of imagination will cause pleasing results to make their way into your experience, but the art of imagination is also very entertaining and fun. As you begin saying, "I want to know what I want," you will begin to attract, by *Law,* all sorts of examples. And as you are collecting the data that comes to you, let your dominant intent, in each day, be to look for things that you want. Then you can look around you and see in others those traits or characteristics that you would like to have in your own mate or companion or work. *Truly, the perfect role model for you, regarding any subject, does not exist—you are the creator of that.*

Sometimes we hear it said, "I wanted to be wealthy, and then I met a man who was wealthy, but he had bad health and a rotten marriage, so then I associated prosperity with rotten marriages and bad health, so I no longer wanted prosperity." And we say, collect the prosperity data if you want it—and leave out the bad health and the bad marriage.

Jerry: So we can visualize piecing together all of the desired characteristics of the mate or the child or the work that we've wanted?

Abraham: Yes. And that is really the point of the *Workshop.* It is a place where you can go, undistracted, and where you begin to formulate pictures in your mind.

Jerry: So it doesn't have to be something that's already existed, ever; it has to be just what you now feel you want to experience?

Abraham: And as you are working in your *Workshop,* you will find that, in most cases, it will not come to you instantly. You will know when you are clear because you will feel excited. . . . Have you ever been working on a project and you thought about it, you thought about it quite a lot, and suddenly you say, "I have a good idea!"? That feeling of *I have a good idea!* is your point of launching your creation. In other words, you have been mulling the thoughts over in your mind until you have become specific enough that when you hit upon the perfect combination of thoughts, your *Inner Being* offered you emotion saying, *Yes, that is it! Now you have it!* And so, the point of the *Workshop* is to think about all sorts of things until you feel that sensation of a good idea.

Jerry: When a strong intention that we've been visualizing hasn't yet materialized, what's the most common cause for that?

Abraham: *If you have been <u>purely</u> visualizing your intention, then it must come, and come quickly.* The purity of the visualization is the key, and by that we mean purely offering thoughts only in the direction of what you want. When you say, "I want it, *but . . .*" as you add your *but,* you cancel it or defeat it at birth. Often you are offering as many or more thoughts about the absence of your desire as you are about the presence of your desire. *If something you want is slow to come to you, it can be for only one reason: You are spending more time focused upon its absence than you are about its presence.*

If you could identify what you want and then *deliberately* think clearly upon what you want until you get it, the essence of all things that you want would be yours very quickly. If you could spend your time purely envisioning what you want, rather than giving your attention to the reality of *what-is,* you would be attracting more of what you want instead of more of *what-is.* It is a matter of changing your magnetic *point of attraction.*

Get your eyes, words, and thoughts off of <u>what-is,</u> and put them purely on what you now want. The more you think and speak of what you want, the faster what you want will be yours.

Is Being Patient Not a Positive Virtue?

Jerry: Abraham, how do you feel about telling someone, "Just be patient"?

Abraham: When you understand the *Law of Attraction,* and when you begin to deliberately direct your own thoughts, the things you desire will flow quickly and steadily into your experience—and patience will not be necessary.

We are not excited about anyone learning patience, for it implies that things naturally take a long time, and that is not true. They only take a long time in coming when your thoughts are contradicted. If you move forward then backward, then forward then backward, you could potentially never get to where you want to go. But when you stop moving backward and only move forward, you will get there quickly. And that does not require patience.

I Want to Take a Quantum Leap

Jerry: Well, it's easy to take a small step beyond where we are and just *do* a little more than what we've been doing, *be* a little more of what we are, and *have* slightly more than what we now have, but how about what we call a "quantum leap"? In other words, achieving something almost beyond anything that we've ever seen before. How would one go about creating something like that?

Abraham: Good. Now you have hit upon the key. The reason it is easier for you to take those small steps forward is because it is easy for you to acknowledge the beliefs that you now hold and stretch those beliefs just a little bit. You are not completely changing your beliefs; you are just expanding them a little bit. "Quantum leap" often means you must release your current belief and adopt a new one.

Quantum leaps are not achieved by enhancing the belief part or the allowing part of the equation. Quantum leaps are achieved by enhancing the wanting part.

Would you not agree that the mother who (in the story we offered) lifted the automobile from her child experienced a "quantum leap"? If she had been in a gymnasium, it would have taken a very long time, little by little, to convince herself she could pick up something that heavy. But her powerful desire caused the "quantum leap" in the moment.

We are not proponents of "quantum leaps" because they require exaggerated contrast, which causes a dramatic propulsion of your desire and can produce a startling result. But that result is almost always temporary, for the balance of your beliefs will eventually bring you back to where you were before. A gradual bridging of beliefs in the direction of your desires is a much more satisfying way to create.

Jerry: And tell me one more time: How can we fan our desire? How can we make ourselves want more?

Abraham: Put your thoughts upon what you believe you want, and the *Law of Attraction* will draw more information, more data, and more circumstances to your creation.

You see, it is a natural process that when you look at what you want, you will feel powerful, positive emotion. So it is a matter of holding your thoughts upon what you want. If possible, go to the places where the things that you want are so that you deliberately put yourself in that position of feeling wonderful. And as you are feeling good, all things that (by your estimation) are good will begin coming into your experience.

When you focus upon something, the *Law of Attraction* will do the "fanning." So if it seems that it is requiring a great deal of work for your desires to increase and the positive emotion to be more, it is because you are thinking about what you want and then about its opposite, so you are not allowing steady, forward motion.

Aren't the Grander Things Harder to Manifest?

Jerry: Then what would you say is the reason why almost everyone feels that they can create or manifest little things, but they feel like they can't create the larger things?

Abraham: It is because they are not understanding the *Law*, and they are hinging what-can-be upon what-has-been. . . . *When you understand the <u>Laws</u>, then you understand that it is not more difficult to create a castle than it is a button. They are equal. It is not more difficult to create $10 million than $100,000. It is the same application of the same <u>Law</u> to two different intentions.*

Can I Prove These Principles to Others?

Jerry: When a person wants to test these *Laws* or principles in order to try to prove their validity to someone else and they're saying, "Let me show you what I can do with this," does that have any bearing on the effectiveness of the *Law of Attraction?*

Abraham: The problem with trying to prove something is that it often causes you to push against something that you do *not* want. And as you do that, you activate *that very thing* in your vibration, which makes it more difficult to accomplish what you *do* want. It also can be discouraging, for if *they* have strong doubt, they may influence *you* to have some doubt.

There is not a need to prove anything to anyone with your words. Let that which you are—that which you are living—be your clear example to uplift others.

Why Is There a Need to Justify One's Worthiness?

Jerry: Abraham, why do you feel that so many of us, in physical form, seem to have a need to justify the good that comes to us?

Abraham: Part of the reason is that humans incorrectly believe in the limitation of resources, so they feel they must explain to others why they should receive it instead of *them.* Belief in "unworthiness" is another factor. There is a very powerful thought here in your physical dimension that says, "You are not worthy, so you are here to *prove* yourselves as worthy."

You are not here to prove your worthiness. *You are worthy!* You are here for the experience of joyful expansion. It was by the power of your desire, and by the power of your allowing—indeed, by your application of the very *Laws* that we are discussing here—that you have emerged into this time-space reality. And so, your physical existence here is proof of your worthiness, or deservedness, to be, do, or have whatever you desire, you see.

If you could realize that the reason your thought about your "unworthiness" feels so bad is because that thought is in utter disagreement with the way your *Inner Being* feels, you might then seek to improve the direction of your thought. But if you do not understand that, then often you flounder around, trying to please others, but because there is no consistency in what they ask of you, eventually you lose your way.

When you are in the mode of justifying, you are in a negative mode, for you are not focused upon what you want. Instead, you are trying to convince others that it is all right for you to desire, and you need not do this. It *is* all right.

How Does *Action,* or *Work,* Fit into Abraham's Recipe?

Jerry: So many of those I've seen who've had tremendous results in their life—people to whom joyous things happen materially, with relationships, and healthwise—don't seem to put out very much physical energy to receive these things. They seem to work a lot less than a lot of the other folks who seem to work much harder but who then receive so much less. So where does the *physical work,* or *action* part, fit into your recipe for creating what we want?

Abraham: You did not come into this environment to create through *action*. Instead, your *action* is meant to be a way in which you enjoy what you have created through *thought*. When you take the time to deliberately offer your thought, discovering the power of aligning the thoughts of your desires with matching beliefs and expectations, the *Law of Attraction* will yield to you the results you are seeking. However, if you do not take the time to line up your thoughts, there is not enough *action* in the world to compensate for that misalignment.

Action that is inspired from aligned thought is joyful action. Action that is offered from a place of contradicted thought is hard work that is not satisfying and does not yield good results. When you really feel like jumping into action, that is a clear sign that your vibration is pure and you are not offering contradictory thoughts to your own desire. When you are having a hard time making yourself do something, or when the action you offer does not produce the results you are seeking, it is always because you are offering thoughts in opposition to your desire.

You are mostly physical-action Beings at this time because you do not yet understand the power of your thought. When you are better at applying your deliberate thought, there will not be so much action for you to tend to.

I Am Prepaving My Future Circumstances

Often people will say to us, "Well, Abraham, I have to offer action—I can't just sit around and think today." And we agree that your lives are under way, and that they do require action. But if we were standing in your physical shoes, we would, today, begin to offer as much deliberate thought about the things that are important to us as we could. And when we found ourselves thinking about things we do not want (thoughts which are always accompanied by negative emotion), we would stop and make an effort to find a better-feeling way of thinking about that. And in time, things would begin to improve on all subjects.

Let us say that you are walking down a street and you find a big bully (by your estimation) beating up a smaller person. Some sort of action is required right now! Your options, at this stage of this manifestation, are either to walk away and let the smaller person be hurt, or to get involved and perhaps risk getting hurt yourself. Neither option is satisfying.

So, take whichever action you choose, but do not leave your thought where it is right now. Gather positive images from life experience of people living more harmoniously, and take *them* to your *Workshop,* and make *those* kinds of thoughts the most active vibrations within you. And, in time, the *Law of Attraction* will not bring you into situations where there seem to be no positive choices.

One who sees himself as a "savior," saving little ones from the big ones, will find himself often coming across people who need to be saved. . . . And if it is your desire to have these kinds of experiences, then continue the thought of those kinds of experiences—and the *Law of Attraction* will continue to bring them to you. But if you prefer something different, think about that—and the *Law of Attraction* will bring *that* to you. *The subjects of your thoughts are prepaving your future experiences.*

How the Universe Fulfills Our Diverse Desires

Jerry: I used to tell people that my observation had been that those who worked the hardest through life had the least, and those who worked the least had the most. And yet, somebody had to dig the potatoes, milk the cows, drill the holes for the oil, and do what we call the *hard work.* So explain to me, Abraham, how can it all work out so that each of us can still have, do, and be what we want, no matter what kind of work needs to be done.

Abraham: You are living in what we see as a perfectly balanced Universe. You are like chefs in a well-stocked kitchen, and all of the ingredients that have ever been imagined are here in abundant proportion to allow you to create whatever sort of recipe you want. When you really *do not* want to do a thing, it is hard for you to imagine that there are others who may *want* to do it, or who do not mind doing it.

114

It is our absolute knowing that if your society decided that they did not want to do a certain task, by the power of your wanting, you would come forth with another way of doing it, or of doing without it. It is a common thing for a society to reach the point where there is no longer a desire for a thing, and so it ceases to be, while it is replaced with a new and improved intention.

How Does Physical Life Differ from the Non-Physical?

Jerry: What are the chief differences in *our* life, here in our physical experience, and *your* life, in your Non-Physical dimension? What do *we* have here on Earth that *you* don't have?

Abraham: Since you are a physical extension of that which we are, much of what you experience, we do as well. We do not allow ourselves, however, to focus upon the things that bring *you* discomfort. We are more keenly focused upon what *is* wanted, and therefore we do not experience the negative emotion that you experience.

You have the ability to feel as we feel, and in fact, when you are in the mode of *appreciation*, for example, or *love*, the very emotion that you feel is your indication that you are looking at your current situation in the same way that we see it.

There is no separation between what you know as the physical world and what you see as our Non-Physical world; however, in the Non-Physical world, our thoughts are purer. We do not push against what is not wanted. We do not think about the lack of what is wanted. *We give our undivided attention to continually evolving desires.*

Your physical world, Earth, is a nice environment for fine-tuning your knowledge, for here your thoughts do not translate into an instant equivalent—you have a <u>buffer of time</u>. As you set forth your thoughts of what you want, you must become very clear (clear enough that emotion comes forth) before you begin the attracting process. And even then, you must *allow* it and *expect* it into your experience before it manifests. That *buffer of time* provides you with much opportunity to be very clear about how desirable the thought *feels* to you.

If you were in a dimension where you were instantly manifesting, you would be spending more of your time trying to get rid of your mistakes (as many of you are now doing anyway) than you would in creating the things you want.

What Prevents Every Unwanted Thought from Manifesting?

Jerry: What is it—in that *buffer of time* zone—that culls out the unwanted from our thoughts before they physically manifest?

Abraham: In most cases, it is not "culled" out. Most people have a little bit of the things they like, and a little bit of the things they don't like. *Most are creating almost everything in their lives by default because they do not understand the rules of the game. They do not yet understand the Laws.*

But there are those who are coming to understand these *Eternal Universal Laws* (and by that we mean that they exist even in your ignorance of them, and they exist in all dimensions). For those people, then, their awareness of the way they are *feeling* is what makes the difference as to which of their thoughts manifest.

Shouldn't I Visualize the Means of Manifestations?

Jerry: Abraham, when we're visualizing or thinking about something that we want, should we be looking at the *means* (or the *how*) of obtaining it as well as *whatever* we want to obtain? Or would it be smarter to just visualize the final result only, and let the *how*, more or less, take care of itself?

Abraham: If you have already identified that you want to participate in the specific *means*, then it is all right to give your attention to that.

The simple key to knowing whether you are not specific enough or too specific is by the way you *feel*. In other words, as you are in your *Workshop*, the specifics of your thought will bring forth the enthusiasm, or the positive emotion; but if you become too specific before you've collected enough data, then you will feel doubtful or worried. *And so, recognizing the balance of your intentions is a matter of paying attention to the way you feel. . . . Be specific enough that you feel positive emotion, but not so specific that you begin feeling negative emotion.*

When you speak of _what_ you want and _why_ you want it, you usually feel better. However, when you speak of _what_ you want and _how_ it will come to you, if you do not right now see a way that it will unfold, then that specific thought will feel worse. If you speak of _who_ will help it to come, _when_ it will come, or _where_ it will come from, and you don't have any of those answers, then those specifics are hindering more than they are helping. _It really is a matter of being as specific as you can be, while still continuing to feel good._

Am I Too Specific in My Desires?

Jerry: Let's say that I'd like to be a teacher in a very joyous situation. Would it be any advantage to say, "Well, then, I should decide whether I want to teach history, math, or philosophy, or whether I want to teach high school or something else"?

Abraham: As you think about the *reason* that you want to be a teacher: *I want to uplift others to the joy that I have discovered in this specific knowledge,* your positive emotion indicates that your thought is helping your creation. But then if you were to think, *But I'm not well versed in this subject* or *There is no freedom for students in this current school system* or *I remember how stifled I felt as a student* or *I never had a teacher I liked,* these thoughts do not feel good, and the *specifics* of them are hindering your joyful creation.

The question is not about whether you should be specific or general. The question is about the direction of the thought. What you are reaching for are good-feeling thoughts. So reach for good-feeling thoughts, and realize that you will usually find them faster as you stay general in your approach; but then from that place of feeling good, continue to gently add more and more good-feeling specifics to them until you can easily be very specific and feel good at the same time. This is the best way to create.

Jerry: Would we be better off to just envision the essence of the end result and let the specific details take care of themselves completely?

Abraham: That is a good way of going about it. Fast-forward to the happy end results that you are seeking. Imagine already having achieved whatever it is that you desire. And from that place of feeling good, you will attract the specific thoughts, people, circumstances, and events to bring all of that about.

Jerry: Then how detailed would you recommend our thoughts be about the end result of what we want?

Abraham: *Be as detailed in your thoughts about your desire as you can be—and still feel good.*

Can I Erase Any Disadvantageous Past Thoughts?

Jerry: Is there any way a person could erase the slate of all past experiences, thoughts, and beliefs that aren't of any advantage to our joyous creating in this moment?

Abraham: You cannot look at an unwanted experience and announce that you will no longer think about *that,* because even in that moment you *are* thinking about *that.* But you can think about something else. And in giving your attention to something else, that unwanted subject from your past will lose power and, in time, you will no longer think about it, at all. *Rather than trying so hard to erase the past, focus on the present. Give thought to what you now want.*

How Could One Reverse a Downward Spiral?

Jerry: If you were to find yourself in a downward spiral where all the things that were important to you seemed to be falling away or depreciating, how could you stop the negative downward motion and turn it in a positive upward direction?

Abraham: It is an excellent question. That "downward spiral" is the *Law of Attraction* at work. In other words, it started with a little negative thought. Then more thoughts were drawn unto it, more people were drawn unto it, more conversation was drawn unto it, until it became a very powerful, as you say, downward spiral. It takes a very strong Being to take your thought from what is not wanted when it is that intense. In other words, when your toe is really throbbing, it is difficult to put your thought upon a healthy foot. *In extremely negative situations, we would suggest distraction rather than trying to change the thought. In other words, go to sleep or go to a movie; listen to music; pet your cat . . . do something that will change your thought.*

Even when you are in what you are calling "a downward spiral," some things in your life are better than others. As you focus on the best of what you have, even if it is a small part of what is happening, the *Law of Attraction* will now bring you more of that. *You can replace a fast-moving "downward spiral" with a fast-moving "upward spiral" just by directing your thoughts to more and more things that you do want.*

How about When Two Compete for the Same Trophy?

Jerry: Since, in a competitive situation, when one person *wins* the trophy it means that the other person *loses* it, how can each person get what they want?

Abraham: By recognizing that there are unlimited "trophies." When you *put* yourself in a competition where there *is* only one trophy, you are putting yourself automatically in a situation of knowing that only one will win the trophy. The one who is clearest, the one with the strongest desire and the greatest expectancy of winning, will win it. . . .

Competition can serve you because it stimulates your desire, but it can be a disadvantage if it hampers your belief in succeeding. Find a way to have fun in the competition. Look for the advantages it brings you, even if you do not bring home the trophy. And as you feel good, no matter what, you win what we consider to be the greatest trophy of all. You win *Connection*. You win clarity. You win vitality. You win alignment with your *Inner Being*. And in that attitude, you will bring home more trophies.

In this unlimited Universe, there need be no <u>competition</u> *for resources, for the resources are unlimited. You may deprive yourself of receiving them, and therefore* <u>perceive</u> *a shortage, but it is really of your own making.*

If I Can Imagine It, It's Realistic

Jerry: Is there anything that we might want that you would consider to be unrealistic?

Abraham: *If you are able to imagine it, it is not "unrealistic." If, from this time-space reality, you have been able to create the desire, this time-space reality has the resources to fulfill it. All that is required is your vibrational alignment with your desire.*

Jerry: Well, if I can *envision* it in any way, does that mean that I have *imagined* it?

Abraham: As you are *envisioning* yourself within that which you are *imagining,* you are attracting the circumstances whereby you will find the means to create it.

Could We Use These Principles for "Evil"?

Jerry: Could a person use the same process of creation that you're teaching to create what some would see as "evil," like taking the lives of others, or taking things from others, against their will?

Abraham: Is it possible for someone to create what *they* want, even though *you* do not want them to want it?

Jerry: Yes.

Abraham: Indeed. For whatever *they* want . . . they may attract.

Is There More Power in Group Co-creating?

Jerry: Can we compound our power, or our ability to create something, by coming together as a group of people?

Abraham: The *advantage* to coming together to create something is that you may stimulate and enhance the desire. The *disadvantage* is that as there are more of you, it becomes more difficult to stay focused only upon what is wanted by you. . . . *Individually, you hold enough power to create anything that you can imagine. Therefore, you do not need to come together with others. It can, however, be fun!*

What If They Don't Want Me to Succeed?

Jerry: Is it possible to create effectively when we're in the company of people who strongly oppose what we want?

Abraham: By focusing upon what *you* desire, you could ignore their opposition. If you oppose their opposition, however, then you would not be focused upon what you want, and your creation would be affected. It is easier to walk away where you no longer need to focus on the opposition in order to stay focused upon your desire. But if you need to walk away from someone because of the potential for opposition, then you need to get out of town, too, for most certainly there are those there who are not in total agreement with your ideas; and out of this country; and off of the face of this planet. *Removing yourself from opposition is not necessary. Just focus upon what you want, and by the power of your own clarity, you will be able to positively create under any circumstances.*

Jerry: Are you saying that we will be receiving the essence of everything we are thinking about—whether it's something we do want or something we don't want—as long as it has emotion connected to it?

Abraham: If you are thinking a thought and you remain focused upon it long enough, the *Law of Attraction* will deliver more thoughts unto it until it becomes clear enough that emotion will be evoked. *Every thought that you think, if you keep thinking it, will eventually become powerful enough to attract the essence of itself into your experience.*

How Do I Use My Momentum's Flow for Growth?

Jerry: Abraham, how can we get into a state of flow where the momentum that we've created is now adding to our growth—that is, to our forward motion?

Abraham: By finding one small thing that makes you happy when you think about it, and then focusing upon it until the *Law of Attraction* brings more and more and more. The more you think of what you want, the more positive emotion will come forth . . . and the more positive emotion that comes forth, the more you will know that you are thinking about what you want. And so, it is a matter of you—deliberately and consciously—making the decision of which direction of flow you want.

Everyone, without exception, is attracting everything that comes into their experience, but when you deliberately choose the direction of your thought, gently guiding your attention to better-feeling thoughts, you will no longer create unwanted things by default. Your conscious awareness of the powerful *Law of Attraction,* coupled with your determination to pay attention to your emotions and your desire to feel good, will cause you to experience the joy of *Deliberate Creation.*

PART IV

The *Art* of
Allowing

The *Art of Allowing:* Defined

Jerry: Abraham, this next subject, I would say, has had the most impact in the way of new understanding for me because I'd never thought of it from the perspective and with the clarity that you have, and that's the *Art of Allowing.* Would you speak about it?

Abraham: We are most eager to help you remember your role in the *Art of Allowing* because a deliberate understanding and application of this *Law* brings everything together for you. In other words, the *Law of Attraction* just *is,* whether you understand that it is or not. It is always responding to you and giving you accurate results, which always match what you are thinking about. But a deliberate application of the *Art of Allowing* requires that you be consciously aware of the way you feel so that you choose the direction of your thoughts. An understanding of this *Law* is what determines whether you create *intentionally* or by *default.*

We have put the *Art of Allowing* in this order, following the *Law of Attraction,* first; and the *Science of Deliberate Creation,* second, because the *Art of Allowing* cannot begin to be understood until the first two are.

What we mean by the *Art of Allowing* is: *I am that which I am, and I am pleased with it, joyful in it. And you are that which you are, and while it is different perhaps from that which I am, it is also good. . . . Because I am able to focus upon that which I want, even if there are those differences between us that are dramatic, I do not suffer negative emotion because I am wise enough not to focus upon that which brings me discomfort. I have come to understand, as I am one who is applying the <u>Art of Allowing</u>, that I have not come forth into this physical world to get everyone to follow the "truth" that I think is the truth. I have not come forth to encourage conformity or sameness—for I am wise enough to understand that in sameness, in conformity, there is not the diversity that stimulates creativity. In focusing upon bringing about conformity, I am pointed toward an ending rather than to a continuing of creation.*

And so, the *Art of Allowing* is absolutely essential to the continuation or the survival of this species, of this planet, and of this Universe, and that continuation is powerfully allowed from the broader perspective of Source. You, from your physical perspective, may not be allowing your own expansion, and when you do not, you feel rotten. And when you do not *allow* another, you feel rotten.

When you see a situation that bothers you and you decide that you will do nothing to try to stop it or change it, you are *tolerating* the situation. That is very different from what we mean by *allowing*. *Allowing* is the art of finding a way of looking at things that still allows your connection to your *Inner Being* at the same time. It is achieved by selectively sifting through the data of your time-space reality and focusing upon things that feel good. It is about using your *Emotional Guidance System* to help you determine the direction of your thoughts.

Shouldn't I Protect Myself from Others' Thoughts?

Jerry: The question that was difficult for me in the beginning of this was: How do we protect ourselves from others who are thinking differently from us, differently enough that they might invade our space, so to speak, in some way?

Abraham: Good. That is why we said that before you can understand and accept the *Art of Allowing,* you must first understand the *Law of Attraction* and the *Science of Deliberate Creation.* For, certainly, if you do not understand how something is coming unto you, then you are fearful of it. If you do not understand that others cannot come into your experience unless you invite them through thought, then of course you would worry about what others are doing. But when you understand that nothing will come into your experience unless you invite it through your thought—with emotional thought and great expectation—then unless you actually accomplish this delicate creative balance, you will not receive it.

When you understand these powerful *Universal Laws,* you no longer feel a need for walls, barricades, armies, wars, or jails; for you understand that you are free to create your world as you want it to be, while others are creating their world as they choose it to be, and their choices don't threaten you. You cannot enjoy your absolute freedom without this knowledge.

In this physical world, there are those things that you are in absolute *harmony* with, and there are those things that you are in absolute *disharmony* with—and there is some of everything in between. But you have not come forth to destroy or contain that which you do not agree with, for that is a continually changing thing. Instead, you have come forth to identify, moment by moment, segment by segment, day by day, and year by year, what it is *you* want, and to use the power of your thought to focus upon it and to allow the power of the *Law of Attraction* to draw it unto you.

We Are Not Vulnerable to the Behaviors of Others

The reason most are not willing to allow what some others are doing is because, in their lack of understanding of the *Law of Attraction,* they incorrectly believe that the unwanted experience can seep or jump into their experience. As they live unwanted experiences, or see others doing so, they assume that since no one would deliberately choose these bad experiences, the threat must be real. They fear that if others are allowed to behave in that way, it will spread into their own experience. In their lack of understanding of the *Law of Attraction,* they feel defensive and vulnerable, so walls are constructed, and armies are assembled from this place of vulnerability, but to no avail. For pushing against these unwanted things only produces more of them.

We are not offering these words so that you may free your world from all of its contrast, for the very contrast you would like to eliminate is responsible for the expansion of *All-That-Is.* We offer these words because we understand that it is possible for you to live joyful lives amidst the enormous variety that exists. These words are being offered to assist you in finding the personal freedom that you will experience only when you understand and apply the *Laws of the Universe.*

Until the first two *Laws* are understood and applied, the *Art of Allowing* cannot be understood or applied, for it is not possible for you to be willing to *allow* others until you understand that what they do and what they say need not affect you. Because your feeling—one that comes from the very core of your Being—is so very powerful that, because you want to preserve your own self, you cannot and will not *allow* one who threatens that.

These Laws that we are presenting to you are Eternal, which means that they are forever. These Laws are Universal, which means that they are everywhere. They are Absolute, whether you know that they are or not; they exist, whether you accept that they exist or not—and they influence your life, whether you know that they do or not.

The Rules of the Game of Life

When we use the word *Law,* we are not referring to the Earthly agreements that many of you term *law.* You have the law of gravity, and you have the law of time and space, and you have many laws, even laws regarding the controlling of your traffic and the behavior of your citizens. But when *we* use the word *Law,* we are speaking of those everlasting, ever-present *Universal Laws.* And there are not as many of them as you might believe there are.

If you will come to understand and apply these three basic *Laws,* you will have an understanding of how your Universe functions.

You will have an understanding of how everything that comes into your experience comes. You will recognize that you are the inviter, the creator, and the attractor of all things that come to you; and you will, indeed, then have deliberate control of your own life experience. And, in all of that, you will then, and only then, feel free—for freedom comes from an understanding of *how* you get what you get.

Here, we will express the rules of your game of physical experience, and we do so enthusiastically, because they are the same rules of the game of all life, whether it is physical life experience or Non-Physical life experience.

The most powerful *Law* in the *Universe*—the *Law of Attraction*—simply says that that which is like unto itself is drawn. You may have noticed that when bad things begin to happen in your life, it seems that everything starts to go wrong. But when you wake up in the morning feeling good, you have a happier day. However, when you begin the day with a fight with someone, you find that the rest of your day is negative in many regards—that is your awareness of the *Law of Attraction*. And, indeed, everything that you are experiencing—from the most obvious to the most subtle—is influenced by this powerful *Law*. . . . When you think about something that pleases you, by the *Law of Attraction,* other thoughts that are similar to it will begin to come forth. When you think of something that displeases you, by the *Law of Attraction,* other thoughts that are like that will begin to come forth until you find yourself reaching into your past for similar thoughts; and you will find yourself discussing them with others until you are surrounded by a larger and larger, ever-growing larger, thought. And as this thought is growing larger and larger, it is gaining momentum; it is gaining power . . . attraction power. An understanding of this *Law* will put you in a position where you may decide to focus your thoughts *only* in the direction of what you *want* to attract into your experience, while you may decide to take your attention from those thoughts that you do not want to draw into your experience.

Now, the *Law of Deliberate Creation* is described in this way: *That which I give thought to, I begin to attract. That which I give thought to that brings forth strong emotion, I attract more quickly. And once I have launched it powerfully by giving thought that evokes emotion, then, as I expect that which I have thought about—I get it.*

The balance of *Deliberate Creation* is two-sided, so to speak. On the one hand is the thought, and on the other hand is the expectancy or the belief, or the *Allowing*. And so, when you have given thought to something and are now expecting it or believing that it will be, now you are in the perfect position to receive the subject of your thought. That is why you get what you think about, whether you want it or not. Your thoughts are powerful, attractive magnets—attracting one to another. *Thoughts attract to themselves, and you attract thoughts by giving your attention to them.*

It is usually easier to see these *Laws* at work when you look into others' experiences: You will notice that those who speak most of prosperity, have it. Those who speak most of health, have it. Those who speak most of sickness, have it. Those who speak most of poverty, have it. It is *Law*. It can be no other way. *The way you feel is your point of attraction, and so, the Law of Attraction is most understood when you see yourself as a magnet, getting more and more of the way you feel.* When you *feel* lonely, you attract more loneliness. When you *feel* poor, you attract more poverty. When you *feel* sick, you attract more sickness. When you *feel* unhappy, you attract more unhappiness. When you *feel* healthy and vital and alive and prosperous—you attract more of all of those things.

Life Experiences, Not Words, Bring about Our Knowing

We are teachers, and in all of our experiences of teaching, we have learned this most important fact: *Words do not teach. It is life experience that brings you your knowing.* And so, we encourage you to reflect into your own life experience to remember those things that you have experienced before, and to begin watching, from this point forward, for the absolute correlation between the words that you are reading here in this book and the life experience that you are living. And so, when you begin to notice that you are getting what you are thinking about, then, and only then, will you want to pay attention to (in fact, to deliberately control) your thoughts.

Controlling your thoughts will become easier when you make the decision that you will do it. You think about things you do not want, mostly because you have not understood how detrimental it is to your experience. For those of you who *do not* want those negative experiences, and for those of you who *do* want those positive experiences, *once you have recognized that thinking of what you do not want only attracts more of what you do not want into your experience, controlling your thoughts will not be a difficult thing, because your desire to do so will be very strong.*

Rather Than Monitor Thoughts, I'll Feel Feelings

Monitoring your thoughts is not an easy thing to do, for while you are monitoring your thoughts, you are not having time to think them. And so, rather than monitoring your thoughts, we are going to offer to you an alternative, an effective alternative. There are very few who understand that while you are a physical Being, focused through this physical apparatus, that simultaneously there is a part of you—a broader, wiser, and certainly an older part of you—that exists at the same time, and that part of you (we refer to it as your *Inner Being*) communicates with you. The communication takes many different forms. It may come in the form of clear, vivid thought—even an audible spoken word at times—but in all cases, it comes to you in the form of emotion.

You set forth, before you emerged, an agreement that communication with your <u>Inner Being</u> would exist. And it was agreed that it would be a feeling, one that could not be missed, rather than a stimulation of thought or an offering of words that could be missed. For, as you are thinking your thoughts, you might not always receive a different thought that is being offered in that same moment. Just as when you are thinking, or deep in thought, you sometimes do not hear what someone who is standing in the same room with you is saying to you. And so, the process of feeling, as in emotion, is a very good process for communication.

There are two emotions: One feels good and one feels bad. And it was agreed that the feeling that feels good would be offered when you are thinking, speaking, or doing that which is in harmony with what you want; while it was agreed that a feeling that feels bad would be offered when you are speaking, thinking, or acting in a direction that is not in harmony with your intentions. So, it is not necessary for you to monitor your thoughts. Simply be sensitive to the way you are feeling, and anytime you feel negative emotion, recognize that you are—in the moment of that feeling—miscreating. In the moment of that negative feeling, you are thinking a thought of something you do not want, thereby attracting the essence of it into your experience. Creation is the process of attraction; when you think a thought, you attract the subject of your thought.

When I'm Tolerating Others, I'm Not *Allowing*

And so, this essay has been prepared that you might understand that there is not another who is, or offers, any threat to you. For you are the controller of your own experience. The *Art of Allowing,* which says, *I am that which I am, and I am willing to allow all others to be that which they are,* is the *Law* that will lead you to total freedom—freedom from any experience that you do not want, and freedom from any negative response to any experience that you do not approve of.

When we say it is good to be an *Allower,* many of you misunderstand what we mean by that, for you think that *Allowing* means that you will *tolerate.* You will be that which you are (which by your standards is that which is appropriate), and you will let everyone else be that which they want to be, even if you do not like it. You will feel negative about it; you will feel sorry for them; you may even feel fearful for yourself, but, nevertheless, you will let them be—but in a tolerant fashion.

When you are *tolerating,* you are not *Allowing.* They are two different things. One who *tolerates* is feeling negative emotion. One who is an *Allower* does not feel negative emotion. And that is a very great difference, for it is the absence of negative emotion that is freedom, you see. You cannot experience freedom when you have negative emotion.

Tolerance may seem to be an advantage for others because you are not hindering them from what they want to do. But tolerance is not an advantage to *you*, because while you are being tolerant, you are still feeling negative emotion, and therefore, you are still negatively attracting. Once you become an *Allower*, you will no longer attract into your experience those unwanted things, and you will experience absolute freedom and joy.

Am I Seeking Solutions or Observing Problems?

Many would say, "Abraham, do you mean that I should put my head in the sand? I should not look and see those who are having trouble? I should not look for an opportunity where I may be of assistance to them?" And we say, if you intend to be of assistance, your eye is not upon the *trouble* but upon the *assistance,* and that is quite different. *When you are looking for a solution, you are feeling positive emotion—but when you are looking at a problem, you are feeling negative emotion.*

You can be of great assistance to others as you see what they want to be, and as you uplift them to what they want to have, through your words and through your attention to that. But, as you see one who is down on his luck, as you see one who has great poverty or great illness, and as you speak with him in pity and sympathy about that which he does not want, you will feel the negative emotion of it, because you are a contributor to that. As you talk to others about what you know they do not want, you assist them in their miscreating, because you amplify the vibration of attracting what is not wanted.

If you see friends who are experiencing illness, try to imagine them well. Notice that when you focus upon their illness, you feel bad; but when you focus upon their possible recovery, you feel good. By focusing upon their Well-Being, you *allow* your connection to your *Inner Being,* who also sees them well, and you may then influence your friend to improvement. When you are in connection with your *Inner Being,* your power of influence is much greater. Of course, your friends may still choose to focus more upon the illness than the wellness, and in doing so, may remain sick. If you let your friends influence you to thoughts that cause negative emotion within you, then their influence toward the unwanted is now stronger than your influence toward the wanted.

I Uplift Through My Example of Well-Being

You will not uplift others through your words of sorrow. You will not uplift others through your recognition that what they have is not what they want. You will uplift them by being something different yourself. You will uplift them through the power and clarity of your own personal example. As you are healthy, you may stimulate their desire for health. As you are prosperous, you may stimulate their desire for prosperity. Let your example uplift them. Let what is in your heart uplift them. You will uplift others when your thought feels good to you. . . . You will depress others, or add unto their negative creating, when your thought makes you feel bad. That is how you know whether or not you are uplifting.

You will know that you have achieved the state of *Allowing* when you are willing to allow another, even in their not allowing of you; when you are able to be that which you are, even when the others do not approve of what you are; when yet you are able to still be that which you are, and not feel negative emotion toward their thoughts about you. When you can look into this world and feel joy all of the time, you are an *Allower*. When you are able to know which experiences contain joy and which ones do not—and you have the discipline to participate only where there is joy—you will have achieved *Allowing*.

The Subtle Difference Between *Wanting* and *Needing*

Just as the difference between positive emotion and negative emotion can sometimes be very subtle—*the difference between wanting and needing can be very subtle.*

When you are focusing upon what you *want,* your *Inner Being* offers you positive emotion. When you are focusing upon what you *need,* your *Inner Being* offers you negative emotion because you are not focused upon what you want. You are focused upon the *lack* of what you want—and your *Inner Being* knows that that which you give thought to is that which you attract. Your *Inner Being* knows that you do not want the lack; your *Inner Being* knows you want what you want, and your *Inner Being* is offering you guidance so that you will know the difference.

Focusing upon a <u>solution</u> makes you feel positive emotion. Focusing upon a <u>problem</u> makes you feel negative emotion, and while the differences are subtle, they are very important, for when you are feeling positive emotion, you are attracting into your experience that which you want. When you are feeling negative emotion, you are attracting into your experience that which you do not want.

I Can Create Deliberately, Intentionally, and Joyfully

So, we might say, an *Allower* is one who has learned the *Law of Deliberate Creation* and has reached the position where he does not miscreate. He creates deliberately, intentionally, and joyfully. You see, *contentment* comes from only one place. Contentment comes only from wanting, then allowing, and then receiving. And so, as you are moving through this experience of physical life, holding your thoughts in the direction of what is wanted, letting the powerful *Law of Attraction* work for you, bringing more and more of the events and circumstances and other Beings who are compatible with you into your experience—then you will find your life spiraling upward to joy and freedom.

You have some questions for us regarding the *Art of Allowing?*

I Am Living the *Art of Allowing*

Jerry: I do have questions, Abraham. To me, the *Art of Allowing* is the most exciting topic of them all.

Abraham: *Allowing* is that which you have come forth into this experience to teach. But before you can teach, you must know.

Ordinarily, this subject comes up more in the line of, "Someone is doing something I do not like; how can I get them to do something I do like instead?" And what you will come to understand is: *Rather than trying to get the world to all do the same thing, or to do the things that you like, it is a much better plan to put yourself in the position of accepting that everyone has the right to be, do, or have whatever they want; and that you, through the power of your thoughts, will attract unto you only that which is in harmony with you.*

How Can I Know Right from Wrong?

Jerry: I didn't know about the *Art of Allowing* before meeting you, so the way I used to decide what was right or wrong for me was, if I was considering some particular action, I'd try to imagine what the whole world would be like if everyone did it. And then if it looked like it would be really a joyous or comfortable world, then I'd go ahead with the action. And if it looked like a world that I wouldn't want to live in if *everybody* was doing it, then I'd decline to perform the action, so to speak.

I'll give you an example. I used to like to stream-fish for trout, and at first I fished like everyone else did. I caught every fish that I could possibly catch. But I guess I became a little uncomfortable regarding the rightness or wrongness of doing that, and I thought, *What would it be like if the whole world did that?* And in my imagination, I realized that if everyone caught fish the way I did, we'd fish all these streams empty and there wouldn't be any fish left for others to have this spectacular pleasure that I was having. So with that, then my new decision was that I wouldn't *kill* any of the fish. I would catch them (on barbless lures), but I would turn them loose. In other words, I'd use a lure without a barb on it, and I'd only take the fish out of the water that someone had asked me to bring back for them to eat.

Abraham: Good. *That which any of us has to offer of greatest value is the example of that which we are. Our words can add to that example, our thoughts can add to that example, and certainly, our actions add* *to that example. But the key for any of us—in our desire to uplift this world—is to make more clear decisions about what we want to be at any point in time—and then to be that.*

That which you were doing, in your example, is in harmony with that which we are teaching now, in that once you decided what you wanted, then your *Inner Being* offered you emotion to help you know the appropriateness of what you were about to do. In other words, once you had decided that you wanted to uplift this world, once you had decided that you wanted to add unto it and not take from it disproportionately, then any action that you began to make, or that you anticipated making, that was not in harmony with that intention would have felt uncomfortable to you.

You had exaggerated your desire for the world to be a better place by imagining that everyone in the world did whatever it was you were thinking about doing—which brought forth exaggerated guidance from within. It is a good way of going about it. You were not trying to get them all to do it; you were only using that *idea* of them all doing it to help you be clear about whether it was a good thing for *you* to do or not. And it was a good plan.

But What about When I Observe Others Committing Wrongs?

Jerry: It worked for me, so my fishing days were ones of absolute, spectacular joy. But I still felt uncomfortable when I saw other people wasting fish and killing them just for the fun of it . . . or whatever their reason.

Abraham: Good. Now we have come upon a very important point. As *your* actions were in harmony with *your* intentions, you felt joy. But as *others'* actions were not in harmony with *your* intentions, you did not feel joy. And so, what is required is that you set forth another set of intentions regarding the others. A very good set of intentions regarding others is this: *They are that which they are, creators of their own life experience, attracting unto themselves, while I am creator of my experience, attracting unto me. That is the <u>Art</u>*

of Allowing. . . . And as you state that to yourself again and again, soon you will come to recognize that they are not really messing up your world in the way that you might think that they are. They are creating their own world. And to them, it may not be a world that is messed up.

What is difficult is when you are looking at your world as one that is not abundant . . . when you begin thinking in terms of how many fish there are, or when you begin thinking in terms of how much prosperity and abundance is present. For then you begin to worry about someone else wasting it or squandering it, leaving not enough for the rest, or not enough for you.

When you come to understand that this Universe . . . indeed, this physical experience in which you are participating, is abundant—and that there is not an ending to that abundance—then you do not worry. You let them create and attract to *them*, while you create and attract to *you*.

Will Ignoring the *Unwanted* Allow the *Wanted?*

Jerry: Well, the way I resolved that dilemma, in essence, was that back in 1970, and for the following nine years, I completely turned off my input from what I'll call the outside world. I turned off my television and my radio, I didn't read newspapers anymore, and I also turned off a lot of people who were talking about things I didn't want to hear. Again, that decision worked for me. It worked so well that during that nine-year period I achieved what I felt were magnificent results in the areas of the meaningful relationships that evolved with many other people, the regaining and maintaining of perfect physical health, and the development of significant financial resources. It was fulfilling, like nothing that had happened before in my life. But by my shutting out that negative input in that way and keeping my attention upon my intentions, it was really more like just sticking my head in the sand than it was what you're calling *Allowing*.

Abraham: There is great value to giving your attention to what is important to you. As you put your head in the sand, so to speak, closing out much of the outside influences, you were able to focus upon that which was important to you. As you give thought to anything, you draw power, clarity, and results to it, you see. And as you do that, you receive contentment—the contentment that comes only from wanting, allowing, and achieving.

As far as being one who was ignoring, or putting your head in the sand, not paying attention, rather than being an *Allower,* perhaps those fit together better than you think. . . . *Giving your attention to what is important to you is the process by which you will allow others to be that which they want to be. To give your attention to yourself, while you allow them to give their own attention to themselves, is a very important process in the art of becoming an Allower.*

Jerry: In other words, because I was expecting (although I'd never heard the words before) the *Law of Attraction* and the *Deliberate Creation Process* to work for me, I had automatically shifted into the stage of *Allowing,* in a sense of the word?

Abraham: That is correct. You were giving your attention to what was important to you, therefore attracting more of that, which made watching television not interesting and reading newspapers not important. *It was not that you were depriving yourself of something that you wanted; instead, by the Law of Attraction, you were drawn more to what you most wanted.* As you observe things on the television or in the newspaper that, because you do not want them, make you feel negative emotion—you hinder your allowance of what you *do* want.

Do We All Want to Allow Joyousness?

Jerry: Are most of us, in physical form, seeking to understand this *Art of Allowing?* Or are you saying that only those of us who are speaking to you want that understanding?

Abraham: All of you who exist upon Earth today, in physical bodies, intended, before your emergence into these bodies, to understand and be an *Allower*. But most of you, from your physical perspective, are far from understanding it or wanting it; you would rather try to *control* one another than *allow* one another. It is not difficult to learn to control the direction of your thoughts, but it is utterly impossible to control one another.

But What about When Others Are Having Negative Experiences?

Jerry: So, is this state of *Allowing* that we are, from some level, seeking, one in which we can still see and be aware of the negatives around us (or what feels negative from our perspective) and still remain joyous? Or will we not be able to see it at all? Or, won't we see it as negative?

Abraham: All of that. When you were focused upon the things that were important to you, you were not watching the television and you were not reading the newspapers—you were enjoying what you were doing. You were giving your attention to what was important to you, and the *Law of Attraction* brought more and more and more power and clarity to that. And so, the other was simply not drawn into your experience because it did not fit with your intentions of growth and achievement.

When you are clear about what you want, you do not have to force-fully keep yourself upon the track, for, by the Law of Attraction, it occurs. And so, it is not difficult to be an Allower. It comes easily and simply because you will not be so interested in all of those things that have nothing to do with what you are about.

Your television, while it offers you much information that is of value, offers much, much more information that has very little to do with what any of you want in your life experience. Many of you sit and watch the television simply because it is there, because no other decision has been made, and so watching the television is not so much, usually, a *deliberate* act as it is an action by *default*. And in that state of not-deliberateness, in that state of no-decision, you are opening yourself to being influenced by whatever is thrown at you. And so, as you are being bombarded, literally, with the stimulation of thoughts of unwanted things that occur all around your world, and because you have made no decision about what you *do want* to think about, you find yourself accepting into your experience, through thought, many things that you would not have chosen.

This is what creating by default is: giving thought to something without being deliberate about it . . . thinking about it, and thereby attracting it—whether you want it or not.

I'll Only Look for What I Want

Jerry: Abraham, how would you tell me to achieve and maintain this state of *Allowing* that I want, in spite of the fact that I'm aware that there are many around me who, from their perspective, are experiencing pain, or what I call *negatives?*

Abraham: *We would suggest to you that you make a decision—a decision that no matter what you are doing in this day, no matter who you are interacting with, no matter where you are, that your dominant intent will be to look for those things that you want to see. And as that is your dominant intent, by the <u>Law of Attraction</u>, you will attract only those things that you want to attract, and you will see only those things that you want to see.*

A *Selective Sifter* as a Selective Attractor

As your dominant intent is to attract only that which you desire, you will become a more *selective sifter.* You will become a more selective attractor. You will become a more selective noticer. In the beginning, you will still notice that you are attracting some of that which is not to your liking because you will have set forth some momentum from thoughts and beliefs that have been before this time. But, in time, once Well-Being has been your dominant intention at the beginning of every day for 30 to 60 days, you will begin to notice that there is very little that is in your life experience that is not to your liking—for your momentum, your thought, will have carried you beyond what is now occurring.

It is difficult to be an *Allower* when you see someone very close to you doing that which you feel threatens you, or doing that which threatens someone else. And so, you say, "Abraham, I don't understand what you mean when you say I can think it away, that through my thoughts I can deal with it, and that no action need be taken." And we say, it is through your thoughts that you invite, but what you are living today is a result of thoughts that you have thought before this time, just as the thoughts that you are thinking today, you are projecting into your future. Your thoughts today are now prepaving your future, and there will be a point in time when you will move to *that* future place, and you will *then* live the results of the thoughts that you are thinking *now*, just as today you are living the results of the thoughts that you have thought before.

Our Past, Present, and Future as One

You are always thinking, and you cannot disconnect your past, present, and future, for they are all one; they're all tied together with the continuum of thought. And so, let us say you are walking down the street and you come across a fight—there is a very big bully beating up on a much smaller man—and as you walk closer, you are filled with negative emotion. When you think, *I'm going to turn my eyes away; I'm going to walk away and pretend like this has not happened,* you feel terrible negative emotion because you do not want this little one to be hurt. And so, then you think, *Well, I will go in and I will help.* But now you also feel negative emotion because you do not want your own face to be broken or your own life to be taken away. And so you say, "Abraham, now what do I do?" And we say, we agree. In this example, there is not an option that seems to be the perfect one—because you are, in this moment, having to do so much work because of your lack of prepaving in your past.

If, in your past, as you began each day, you had intended safety, you had intended harmony, and you had intended interacting with those who were in harmony with your intentions, it is our absolute promise to you that you would not now be in this uncomfortable position. And so, we say deal with it now in whatever way you choose, but today if you will begin to set forth your thoughts of what you want in the future, you will not find yourself walking into another sort of uncomfortable ambush where no matter which way you go it is not comfortable.

Must I Allow the Injustices I Witness?

Until you understand *how* it is you get what you get, it is going to be very difficult for you to accept the idea of *Allowing*, because there are so many things that you see in this world that you do not like, and you say, "How can I allow this injustice?" And we say, you allow it by recognizing that it is not part of your experience. And that, in most cases, it is truly not any of your business. It is not your work. It is the creation; it is the attraction; it is the experience of the others.

Rather than trying to control the experiences of all others (which you cannot do no matter how hard you try), instead, intend to control your own participation within those experiences. And by setting forth your clear image of the life you want to live, you will prepave a smooth and pleasant path for yourself.

My Attention to *Unwanted* Creates More of *Unwanted*

You attract through your thought. You get what you think about, whether you want it or not. And so, as you give attention to the drivers who are not courteous, you will attract more of them into your experience. As you give your attention to those who are not giving you good service as you are going from business to business, you will begin attracting more of those sorts of experiences unto you. *That which you give your attention to—particularly your emotional attention to—is that which you draw into your experience.*

Does the *Art of Allowing* Affect My Health?

Jerry: Abraham, I would like to cover a series of, what I call, everyday, real-life experiences, and have you, if you would, tell me a little bit about how you see the *Art of Allowing* applying to these particular conditions. First, as far as physical health is concerned, I recall having had many years of an extreme physical illness during my childhood. And then I reached a stage in my life when I wanted out of that, so I've had extremely good physical health, in essence, ever since then. How does the *Art of Allowing* fit into those two situations, from extreme illness to extreme health?

Abraham: When you have made a decision about something you want, you have accomplished one-half of the equation for the *Deliberate Creation* of it. You have given thought with emotion, which is what *wanting* is. On the other side of the equation for the *Deliberate Creation* is the *Allowing,* or the expecting, the letting it be. . . . And so, when you say *I want, and I allow, therefore it is,* you will be very fast in your creation of whatever it is that you want. You are literally *allowing* yourself to have it by not resisting it, by not pushing it away with other thoughts.

You have heard us say that when you are in the state of *Allowing,* you do not have negative emotion. The state of *Allowing* is freedom from negativity; therefore, when you have set forth your deliberate intent to have something and you are feeling only positive emotion about it, then you are in the state of *Allowing* it to be. And then you will have it, you see.

To have health instead of illness, you must think about health. When your body is sick, it is easier to notice the sickness, so it requires desire, focus, and a willingness to look beyond what is happening right now. By imagining a healthier body in the future, or by remembering a time when you were healthier, your thought, in the moment, will match your desire, and you will *then* be allowing an improvement in your condition. The key is to reach for thoughts that feel better.

Allowing, from Extreme Poverty to Financial Well-Being

Jerry: The next subject I would like to discuss would be the area of wealth and prosperity. During my childhood, I lived at the poverty end of it, like living in chicken houses and tents and caves, and so on and so forth. And then, in 1965 I found the book *Think and Grow Rich!,* which gave me a different perspective of how to look at things, and from that day forward, my financial life spiraled upward. From living in my Volkswagen bus, I moved on to creating six-figure, and then seven-figure, annual incomes.

Abraham: What do you think took place in that changing of your perspective from the reading of that book?

Jerry: Well, what I remember the most is, I began, for the first time in my adult life, to focus only on what I wanted, more or less exclusively. But I'd like to hear your perspective on that phenomenon.

Abraham: You achieved an understanding that you *could* have what you wanted. The desire was already in place from the living of life, but in reading that book you came to *believe* that it was possible. The book caused you to begin to *allow* your desire to be realized.

Allowing, Relationships, and the Art of Selfishness

Jerry: Another area, a big one that I'd like to talk about, is the area of relationships. There were times when I found it difficult for me to allow friends to have their own thoughts and beliefs, and their own "inappropriate" activities.

Abraham: When you are using the word *allow* in this sense, what do you mean?

Jerry: I felt as if they should *think* and *act* the way I wanted them to think and act. And when they didn't, it made me extremely, and often angrily, uncomfortable.

Abraham: And so, as you were observing what they were doing or what they were speaking, you felt negative emotion—your signal that you were not in the state of *Allowing*.

Is the Art of Selfishness Not Immoral?

Jerry: And I, at that time, thought of myself as very selfless and very giving. In other words, I would not have been considered a selfish person, so I expected them to be less selfish and more giving, also. And the fact that they weren't was very disturbing to me. Then I found David Seabury's book *The Art of Selfishness,* and that made me look at *selfishness* from another perspective, so I was able to understand a lot of my negativity because of that new perspective.

Abraham: It is important that you allow yourself to pay attention to what you want. And there are those who call that *selfishness,* and they do so in a judging or disapproving way. And we say to you that unless you have a healthy view of self, unless you are allowing yourself to want, and expecting to receive that which you want, you will never be deliberate in your creating, and you will never have a very satisfying experience.

The not allowing of self is usually where the not allowing of others comes forth. Usually the one who is most disapproving of a quality in himself notices that same quality in others, and disapproves of it there as well. And so, an accepting, an approving, an appreciating, and an allowing of oneself is the first step in the appreciating, approving, or allowing of others. And that does not mean that you must wait until you are, by your standards, perfect, or that they are, by their standards, perfect, for there will never be that perfect ending place—for you are all ever-changing, ever-growing Beings. It means looking and intending to see in you what you want to see, or intending to see in others what you want to see.

We are often accused of teaching *selfishness,* and we agree that we do. Everything that you perceive is from the perspective of *self;* and if you are not selfish enough to insist on your connection or alignment with your broader, wiser *Inner Being,* then you have nothing to offer to others. By being selfish enough to care how you feel, you can then utilize your *Guidance System* to align with the powerful Energy of *Source,* and then anyone who is fortunate enough to be *your* object of attention, benefits.

Their Disapproval of Me Is Their Lack

If there are others who see something in you that they do not approve of, most often you see their disapproval reflected back through their eyes, and you feel that you have gone wrong in some way. And we say unto you, it is not *your* lack, it is *theirs.* It is *their* inability to be the *Allower* that brings forth their negative emotion; it is not *your* imperfection. And, in like fashion, when you feel negative emotion because you have seen something in others that you do not want to see, it is not *their* lack, it is *your own.*

And so, when you make the decision that you want to see only that which pleases you, then you will begin to see only that which pleases you, and all of your experiences will bring forth positive emotion, because, by the *Law of Attraction,* you will attract unto you only that which is in harmony with what you want. By understanding the power of your emotions, you can then direct your thoughts, and then you will no longer need others to behave differently in order for you to feel good.

But What about When One Is Violating Another's Rights?

Jerry: Here's another area that's given me much discomfort in the past, and that is regarding the rights of one or another: property rights, territorial rights, or rights to our own peace. In other words, I used to be extremely disturbed when a person's rights were violated by violence on a person, or by someone forcefully taking someone else's property. Also, I was torn over territorial rights, and who should be allowed into our country and who should not be allowed into our country. Why should one person be allowed in and another person not? But then, after meeting you, I got to the point that I see all those things they're doing with each other as "games" that they're playing—more or less "agreements" that they have between one another, spoken or unspoken. I've gotten somewhat better at not feeling their pain. But can I get to the point that I don't feel anything negative when I see someone violating the rights of another? Can I just look at whatever they're doing to one another out there, and think, *You're all doing to one another what you have somehow chosen to do?*

Abraham: You can. As you understand that they are each attracting through their thought, then you will be exuberant rather than feeling pain for them, for you will understand that they are reaping the negative or positive emotion, depending upon their choice of thoughts. Of course, most of them do not understand how they are getting what they are getting. And that is the reason why there are so many who believe that they are victims. They believe that they are victims because they do not understand how they get what they get. They do not understand that they invite through their thought or through their attention. It may help you to realize that each experience causes a clarification of desire.

There Is Not a Shortage of Anything

Now you have mentioned *territorial rights*. We have a rather different view of "territory" than those of you who are in physical form, because in your physical world you continue to see limitation. You feel that there is only so much space, which will eventually all be taken up, so you feel that there is not enough.

In your attitude of limitedness; in your feeling of lack rather than abundance; in your notice of not enough space or not enough money or not enough health, you feel a reason to guard. From our perspective, there is not a limitation of anything, but an ever-flowing abundance of all subjects. There is enough of everything for all of you. And so, as you come to understand that, then any feeling of limitation, of lack, of a need for protection, or of defending territorial rights will not be an issue.

By the *Law of Attraction* we are drawn together. Here in our Non-Physical perspective, this "Family of Abraham" is together because we are, in essence, the same—and in our sameness we are attracted to one another. And so, there is not a keeper of the gate. There are not guards to keep the unharmonious out, for they are not drawn to us because we are not giving our attention to them. It is the same in your environment. While you do not see it as clearly as we do, the *Laws* are working as perfectly for you as they are for us. It is that you have so many physical explanations for things, physical explanations that may be right, in part, but are not the complete explanation. In other words, as you describe how the water gets into your glass by pointing to the faucet and the knob, we say there is much, much more to the story. And so, as you explain to us that you have aggressors who live upon your Earth who would like to take from you everything that you have, we say to you that they cannot. Unless you invite them through your thought, aggressors will not be part of your experience. That is *Law*, in your physical setting or in our Non-Physical setting.

Is There Value in Losing One's Life?

Jerry: Haven't you said that through having these life experiences, that's how we learn our lessons? But when a person loses their physical life in the process of some violent experience, have they learned any lesson?

Abraham: It is not that you are being offered "lessons." We do not like that word very much, for that sounds as if there is some order of that which you should, or must, learn, and there is none of that. It is that your life experience brings you knowing, and you become wiser and broader through that knowing.

What must be understood before you can appreciate the value, even in the loss, of physical life, is that you are adding unto a greater, broader experience than the one you know as your collective experience here in this physical body. Everything that you are now living adds unto that broader knowing. And so, even when you are removed from your focus through this body, all that you have experienced here will be part of that greater knowing that you hold. And so, yes, there is even value in having an experience that removes you from this physical body. It is not for nothing.

I Am the Culmination of Many Lifetimes

Jerry: Are you saying that losing my life is an experience that somehow adds to all of the experience of that broader Being?

Abraham: It is, indeed. You have lost your physical life on many occasions. You have lived thousands of lifetimes. That is the reason why your zest for life is so great. We could not express to you in words the number of lifetimes that you have lived, let alone much detail from each of them; you have had so much experience that memory of all that experience would confuse and hinder you here. And so, as you are born into this body, you come forth not remembering that which has been before because you do not want the distraction of all that memory. You have something much better than that: You have an *Inner Being* that is the culmination of all of those lifetimes of experience.

Just as now you are that which you are as a culmination of all that you have lived, there is little value for you to sit here and talk about the things you did when you were 3 or 10 or 12. Of course, you are that which you now are *because* of all of that . . . but to continue to look back into your past and regurgitate those experiences does not add much unto that which you now are.

And so, as you accept that you are this magnificent, highly evolved Being, and as you are sensitive to the way you feel, then you have the benefit of your *Emotional Guidance System*—as to the appropriateness of anything that you are about to do—based upon the way you feel.

You are physical Beings, and you are knowing you, the physical you, while most of you are not knowing yourself from your broader perspective. The physical you is a magnificent and important you, but it is also an extension of a broader, greater, wiser, certainly older, you. And that *Inner You* made the decision to come forth to be focused in this body because it wanted the experience of this lifetime to add unto the knowing of the greater, broader *Inner You*.

Why Don't I Remember My Past Lives?

It was agreed, before you came, that you would not have memory—muddling, confusing, hindering memory—of all that you have lived before, but that you would have a sense, a *Guidance*, that comes forth from within. And it was agreed that the *Guidance* would be in the form of emotion, which would be manifested to you in the form of feeling. Your *Inner Being* cannot respond in thought at the same time that you are transmitting a thought, and so, your *Inner Being* has agreed to offer you a *feeling* so that you can know the appropriateness of what you are feeling, speaking, or doing in the context of your greater or broader intentions.

Every time you set forth a conscious intention of something you want, your *Inner Being* factors all of that in. And so, as you are more *deliberate* in that which you offer, in the form of *intent:* "I want, I intend, I expect," your *Inner Being* is able to factor all of that in to give you clearer, more specific, more appropriate *Guidance*.

Many physical Beings, because they do not understand that they are the creator of their own experience, do not set forth <u>deliberate intentions.</u> They resign themselves to taking what comes, not understanding that they are the *attractor* of what comes. But under those conditions, it is more difficult to *allow*, because you feel that you are a victim. You feel that you are vulnerable; you feel that you are not in control of what comes, so you feel you must guard yourself from what may come, not understanding that you are the inviter of what comes. That is why we say that *an understanding of how you are getting what you are getting is essential before you will be in a position of being willing to allow yourself, or to allow any other.*

What about When Sexuality
Becomes a Violent Experience?

Jerry: Another area that I've felt some discomfort with would be morality relating to sexual practices. I've now reached the point of allowing others to have their sexual choices, but I still feel uncomfortable when someone uses force against another person in *any* area. Is there a point, again, that I can get to so that whatever they do, whether one uses force or not, it won't affect my thinking?

Abraham: No matter what the subject is, it is important to understand that there are no victims. There are only co-creators.

You are all, as magnets, attracting unto you the subject of your thought. And so, if there is one who gives much thought to, or one who speaks much about, rape, then it is very likely that they will be the "victim," by their words, of such an experience. Because, by *Law, you attract unto you the essence of that which you give thought to.*

As you give *thought,* feeling emotion, you launch your creation, and then as you *expect,* it is your experience. And so, there are many who launch creations that they do not actually receive in their experience because they only do half of the equation. They launch it by giving thought, even emotional thought, but then they do not *expect,* and so they do not receive. This is true of the things you *do* want, as well as the things that you *do not* want.

What Is My *Expectancy* Around This Issue?

We've offered the example of going to the horror movie where you are stimulated to much clear, vivid thought through the sound and picture that is coming forth from the movie. Now you have launched the creation of this scenario as you have given thought, usually with great emotion, but as you leave the theater, you say, "It was only a movie; that would not happen to me." And so, you do not complete the *expectancy* part.

Notice, in your society, that the more that is offered regarding any topic, the greater the public *expectancy* of it. In the same way the greater the *expectancy* of the individuals, the greater the likelihood is that they will attract it.

Do not give thought to those things that you do not want, and you will not have them in your experience. Do not speak of that which you do not want, and you will not attract it into your experience. And so, when you understand that, then, as one who is observing others having experiences that they do not want, you are not so filled with negative emotion, because you understand that they are now in the process of receiving an understanding of how all things come to them.

Now, true, none of us feel joy in watching another being raped or watching another being robbed or murdered. Those are not pleasant experiences. But when you come to the point of understanding how you attract these events into your experience, you will no longer give thought to that—*and then you will no longer be one who is even seeing any of that.*

You draw into your experience that which you give thought to. Your television confuses it, because you turn on your television, intending to have entertainment, and then newscasters bring to you those sudden news bulletins where you are told of some horrible event happening. But when it is your intent to see—no matter what you are doing—only that which you want to see . . . you will be drawn away from the television before such a bulletin is offered.

I Am Prepaving My Future Right Now

When you see something in a newspaper or magazine that begins to bring forth a little negative emotion, you can immediately set it aside rather than continuing with it and receiving more negative emotion as the *Law of Attraction* is adding to the subject. But even beyond that, in this moment, as you are intending to attract unto you only that which you want, you will begin prepaving so that your future action will not need to be so definite. You will not be drawn to the television. You will not be drawn to the newspapers. Instead, you will be drawn, by the *Law of Attraction,* to the subject of your deliberate intent.

The reason so many of you are drawn to subjects of indeliberate intent is because you do not have deliberate intent. You are not saying often enough what you *do* want, and so you are attracting *some* of all of it. The more deliberate you are in what you want, the more pre-paving you will be doing, so that less action will be needed to get unwanted things out of your experience. You will not be ambushed by your television, so to speak, or ambushed by the predators of your society—for the Universe will have prepaved something different for you.

But What about the Innocent Little Child?

Jerry: Many people will accept your basic premise about creating through thought, Abraham, but the point where I see a number of people stub their toe, so to speak, or find difficulty with your teachings is when thinking about innocent children. They'll ask, "But what about the little children? How could little children have thoughts that would bring them physical deformities, ill health, or a violent invasion of their bodies of some sort?"

Abraham: It is because the babies have been surrounded by those who are having those thoughts, and so they have been receiving (the essence of) those thoughts.

Jerry: Something like telepathy?

Abraham: That is correct. You see, long before the child is speaking, the child is thinking. But you cannot know how clear in thought that little child is, because he has not yet learned to verbally communicate with you. He is not yet communicating his thoughts.

Jerry: The child is not thinking in *words*. That is, I can sense that a child is having thoughts long before he or she is speaking words.

Abraham: The child *is* thinking, and receiving vibrational thought from you on the day that he enters your environment. That is the reason why beliefs are transmitted so easily from parent to child, from parent to child, from parent to child. The child is vibrationally receiving your fears and your beliefs, even without your spoken word. *If you want to do that which is of greatest value for your child, give thought only to that which you want, and your child will receive only those wanted thoughts.*

Shouldn't Others Fulfill Their Agreements with Me?

Jerry: Abraham, regarding *Allowing*, I still have, creeping into my mind, an old saying: *One has a right to swing their arms as much as they want* (which to me was "Allowing"), *as long as they don't interfere with my right to swing my arms, or as long as they don't hit my nose.*

In other words, as I go through life and I'm allowing other people to be, do, and have whatever they want, if that interferes with something we have previously agreed to in business, sometimes it's a little difficult not to, at least, call for a sticking to our agreement or to the fulfilling of their responsibilities as we had previously agreed.

Abraham: As long as you have concern that another can interfere in your experience, or that another can swing his arms into your face, then you do not yet really understand how it is that you get what you get. You can begin, today, to think only of what you want; and then begin, today, to attract only what you want. Your question comes forth because yesterday, or somewhere in your past, you did not understand this, and you were inviting—through your thought—those who swing their arms into your face. And so, now, in this moment, you ask, "What do I do about it?"

If there are those in your experience who are swinging their arms in an uncomfortable way, take your attention from them and they will go away, and in their place will come those who feel comfortable to you, who are in harmony with you. But what usually happens is, as they swing their arms, as they do the things you do not want them to do, you give your attention to that. You get angrier about it, you get more upset about it, and by the *Law of Attraction,* you attract more of the essence of that, until soon you have more than one in your experience. There are two, or three, or many. . . . Take your attention from that which does *not* please you, put your attention upon that which *does* please you, and you will then change the momentum. Not instantly, but it will begin to change.

If, every morning for the next 30 days, you begin your day by saying: *I intend to see; I want to see; I expect to see, no matter who I am working with, no matter who I am talking with, no matter where I am, no matter what I am doing . . . I intend to see that which I want to see,* you will change the momentum of your life experience. And all things that now displease you will be gone from your experience and will be replaced by things that *do* please you. It is absolute. It is *Law.*

I Will Never Get It Wrong . . . or Done

When we say that from your Non-Physical Perspective, from the perspective of that which you were even before you became focused in this physical body, that it was your intent to become an *Allower* and to understand the *Art of Allowing*—it is so. *What we want you to understand is that you never get it completed. You are not like a table that is imagined, then created, and then is finished. You are continually in the state of becoming. You are in the process of growth, eternally. But you are always that which you are in this moment.*

You want to understand the *Laws of the Universe* so well that you become at one with them. You want to understand how it is that things come to you so that you do not feel like a victim, or vulnerable to the whims of others swinging their arms.

It is hard for you to understand these things when you are in the middle of what seems to be two worlds: the world that you created before you understood these things that we have talked about here, and the world that you are in the process of creating now that you are understanding more clearly. And so, some of the things that are in your experience because of the prepaving or the prethinking of your past do not fit very well with what you *now* want. And so, we know there is a little bit of discomfort as you are in this transitional stage, but there will be less and less and less discomfort as you are clearer and clearer and clearer about what you want. Much of the clutter of past momentum is now moving from your experience.

When you are in the state of positive emotion and considering only what *you* are doing or thinking or speaking, you are *Allowing yourself.* When you are in the state of positive emotion regarding your view into *another's* experience, you are *Allowing another.* It is that simple. . . . And so, you cannot have negative emotion about yourself and be in the state of *Allowing* yourself.

To be an *Allower* is to be one who feels positive emotion, which means that you must control what you are giving your attention to. It does not mean that you get everything in your world whipped into shape so that everything and everyone is just the way you want it to be. It means that you are able to see, and therefore solicit forth, from the Universe, from your world, and from your friends, that which is in harmony with you, while you let the other parts go unnoticed by you—therefore unattracted by you, and therefore not invited by you. That is *Allowing,* you see.

And we will tell you, friends, *Allowing* is the most glorious state of Being you will ever achieve on a long, ongoing basis. For once you are an *Allower,* you are spiraling upward and upward, for there is no negative emotion to balance you out and bring you down. There is no backward swing of the pendulum. You are forever and gloriously moving forward and upward!

PART V

Segment Intending

The Magical Process of *Segment Intending*

Jerry: Abraham, my feeling is that the combination of the ingredients of the *Law of Attraction*, the *Science of Deliberate Creation*, and the *Art of Allowing* . . . and then added to that, this next one, the *Segment Intending Process*, seems to comprise the total recipe for making things happen in general. Would you speak to us about the *Segment Intending Process*.

Abraham: Once you understand that you are the creator of your experience, then you will want to identify more clearly what you desire so that you may allow it into your experience. Because until you have stopped to identify what you really want, there is not a possibility of *Deliberate Creation*.

You do not want the same thing in every segment of your life experience. In fact, in every day, there are many segments that carry many different intentions. And so, the point of this *Segment Intending* essay is to help you understand the value of stopping many times during your day to identify what it is you want most so that you may add emphasis, and therefore power, unto that.

There is very little that you are actually living in this day that is a result of only what you are thinking in this day. But whenever you are stopping, segment by segment, and identifying what it is you want in this segment, you are setting forth thoughts that begin to prepave your future experience whenever you are entering segments that are similar.

In other words, let us say that you are getting into your vehicle and you are alone, so intending communication with someone else, or clarity of listening to what another is saying, is not a very important intention. But intending safety and smooth-flowing traffic, and arriving refreshed and on time are intentions that are very well placed in this segment as you are traversing from one place to another. The identification of your *intention* as you are entering this segment of driving not only affects *this* segment, but it sets forth a prepaving into your future so that at future times when you are getting into your vehicle, you will have, in fact, prepaved or created circumstances and events that will be to your liking.

It is possible that, in the beginning, even though you are identifying, segment by segment, what you want, there will still be some momentum from past thoughts that you have set forth. But in time, as you are setting forth, segment by segment, what you want, you will have prepaved a path before you that is very much to your liking. And then you will not have to take so much action in the moment to get things to be the way you want them.

I Can *Segment-Intend* My Success

Technically, all of your creative power is in this moment. But you are projecting it not only into this moment, but also into the future that exists for you. And so, the more you are willing to stop and identify what you want in *this* segment, then the greater, clearer, and more magnificent your future path will be. And each of your moments will be better and better and better, also.

The purpose of this essay is to offer, to those who want it, a practical process with which to put into immediate practice the primary *Laws of the Universe*, in order to give you absolute and deliberate control of your life experience. And while to some, this may seem to be a very broad overstatement, for it seems to most that you cannot control the experiences of your life, we want you to know that you can.

We have come forth to assist those of you who are here, now focused in physical bodies, to understand specifically how you attract everything you are attracting—and to assist you in understanding that nothing comes to you unless you invite it through your thought. And that once *you* begin looking into *your* life experience and begin to see the absolute correlation between what *you* are speaking, what *you* are thinking, and what *you* are getting, then you will clearly understand that, indeed, you are the inviter, you are the attractor, and you are the creator of your physical experience.

These Times Are the Best of Times

You are living in a wonderful time, in a highly technologically advanced society where you have access to stimulation of thought from all around your world. Your access to that information is of great benefit, for it provides you with the opportunity for expansion, but it can also be a source of immense confusion.

Your ability to focus upon a narrower subject brings forth more clarity, while your ability to focus upon many things at once more often brings confusion. You are receptive Beings; your thought processes are very fast, and as you are considering only one subject, you have the ability, by the power of the *Law of Attraction,* to bring forth more and more clarity upon that subject until you can literally accomplish anything regarding it. But because of the availability in your society of so much stimulation of thought, very few of you remain focused upon any one subject long enough to take it forward very far. Most of you find yourselves so distracted that you do not have an opportunity to develop any one thought to any great degree.

The Purpose and Value of *Segment Intending*

And so, *Segment Intending* is the process of deliberate identification of what is specifically wanted for this moment in time. It is done with the intent of bringing forth from all of the confusion of what is considered to be your total life experience, your awareness of what you most want in this particular moment. And as you take a moment to identify what that *intention* is, you bring forth tremendous power from the Universe, and all of it is funneled into this very specific moment in which you now stand.

Think of your thoughts as magnetic. (Indeed, everything within your Universe is magnetic, drawn unto that which is like unto itself.) And so, whenever you are contemplating or focusing upon even a small negative thought, by the power of the *Law of Attraction*—it will grow larger. If you are feeling particularly disappointed or sad, you will find yourself attracting others who are not feeling much different, for the way you *feel* is your *point of attraction*. And so, if you are *unhappy,* you will attract more of that which makes you unhappy. Whereas if you *feel good,* you will attract more that you consider to be good.

Since you attract or invite into your experiences the others with whom you interact; the people who surround you in traffic; the people you rendezvous with while shopping; the people you meet while you're walking; the subjects that people discuss with you; the way you are treated by your waiter at the restaurant; the waiter assigned to you at the restaurant; the money that flows into your experience; the way your physical body looks and feels; the people you date (this list could go on to include everything in your experience)—it is of value to understand the power of your *now* moment in time. The point of the *Segment Intending Process* is to clearly direct your thought to those things that you want to experience by identifying the elements of life that are most important to you in this particular segment of your life.

When we say to you that *you are the creator of your experience,* and *there is nothing in your experience that you have not invited,* sometimes we are met with resistance. The resistance comes because many of you have things in your life that you do not want. And so, you say, "Abraham, I would not have created this thing that I do not want." We agree, you would not have done it on purpose, but we will not agree that you have not done it. For it is through your thought—and only through and by *your* thought—that you are getting the things that you are getting. But until you are ready to accept that you are the creator of your experience, then there is not much that will be offered here that will be of value to you.

The *Law of Attraction* affects you, whether you are consciously aware of it or not; and *Segment Intending* will help you be more aware of the power of your thoughts because the more you deliberately apply it, the more the details of your life will reflect your *Deliberate Intent*.

Your Society Offers Much Stimulation of Thought

You live in a society that offers much stimulation of thought, and as you are open and receptive to that, you may very well be attracting more thoughts, and thereby more circumstances and events and people than you have the time or desire to deal with.

In just one hour of your exposure to your media, there is tremendous stimulation that is offered to you, and it is not a wonder that you often find yourself absolutely overwhelmed and that many of you have shut down completely, closed to all things, because there is so much coming to you so fast.

This *Segment Intending Process* will offer you the solution, for as you are reading the words that are offered here, your confusion will be replaced with absolute clarity; your feeling of being out of control will be replaced by a feeling of being in control; and for many of you, a feeling of stagnation will be replaced with a glorious, invigorating feeling of fast-forward motion.

Confusion comes forth when you are considering too many things at one time, while clarity comes forth while you are more singular in thought—and it all hinges upon the Law of Attraction. As you set forth a thought regarding any subject, the *Law of Attraction* immediately goes to work to deliver more stimulation of thought regarding that subject. As you are moving from thought to thought to thought to thought, the *Law of Attraction* is offering you more thought regarding the thought, the thought, and the thought. And that is the reason you often find yourself feeling overwhelmed, for by the *Law of Attraction,* you have now summoned information upon a great many subjects.

In many cases, that information will come forth from your past; in many cases, it will come forth from those who are closest to you, but the end result is all the same: You are considering so many things that you are moving forward in no one specific direction—and the result, of course, is a feeling of frustration or confusion.

From Confusion to Clarity to *Deliberate Creation*

As you choose any one primary subject that you want to ponder, the *Law,* the *Universe,* will deliver unto you more regarding that specific thought. But instead of many thoughts coming from many directions—even conflicting, opposing directions—the thoughts and the events that *now* come forth will all be in harmony with the primary thought that you have set forth. And thus, there will be a feeling of clarity, and even more important than the feeling of clarity will be the understanding that you are moving forward in your creation. *When you consider many subjects at the same time, you generally do not move forward strongly toward any of them, for your focus and your power is diffused, whereas if you are focusing upon that which is most important in any point in time, you move forward more powerfully toward that.*

Dividing My Days into *Segments of Intentions*

The point at which you now stand, the point from which you are now consciously perceiving—that point is a *segment.* Your day may be divided into many segments, and there are not two of you who would have precisely the same segments. On one day your segments may be different from the next, and all of that is fine. It is not necessary to have a rigid schedule of segments. It *is* important that you identify when you are moving from one segment, and therefore from one set of intentions—into another.

For example, when you wake up in the morning—you are now entering a new segment. That time that you are awake before you get out of bed—that is a segment. . . . That time that you are preparing yourself for your next activity—that is a segment. . . . When you get into your vehicle—that is another segment, and so on.

Whenever you realize that you are moving into a new segment of life experience, if you will pause for a moment and set forth aloud, or in your own mind, what you most want as you are moving into that segment, you will begin, by the powerful *Law of Attraction,* to solicit thoughts, circumstances, events, and even conversation or action from others that will harmonize with your intent.

As you take the time to recognize that you are moving into a new segment and you go even further by identifing what your dominant intentions are within it, you will avoid the confusion of being swept up by the influence of others or even the confusion of being carried by your own less than deliberate habit of thought.

I Operate and Create on Many Levels

In every segment of your life experience, you are operating on many levels. There are those things that you are *doing* in the segment. (Doing is powerful creating.) There are those things that you are *speaking* about in the segment. (Speaking is powerful creating.) And there are those things that you are *thinking* in the segment. (Thinking is powerful creating.) Also, within each segment, you may be considering what is happening in your *present;* you may be considering what has already happened in your *past;* or you may be considering what is about to happen in your *future.*

When you are thinking about what you want in your future, you begin attracting the essence of that which you want for your future. But because your present has not yet been prepared for it, it will not likely come into your present—but it will begin its motion forward. And as you are moving forward toward that future place, so are those events and circumstances to which you have given thought.

The Thoughts I Think Today Are Prepaving My Future

Here is the process that we refer to as *Prepaving:* In your present, you give thought to your future so that when you get to that future time, your future has been *prepaved,* or prepared, for you by you. And so, much that you are experiencing today is as a result of your thoughts about today that you thought yesterday and the day before and the year before and the year before. . . .

Every thought that you think that is directed <u>toward what you want</u> for your future is of great benefit to you. Every thought that you are thinking about your future that <u>you do not want</u> is a disadvantage to you.

As you think of vitality and health—and want it and expect it in your future—you are prepaving and preparing that for yourself. But as you fear or worry about decline or disease, you are also preparing or prepaving *that* for your future.

Segment Intending will assist you whether you are in your *now,* thinking about your *now;* or are in your *now,* thinking about your future. For, in each of these cases, you will now be deliberate in your creating. And that is the point of the *Segment Intending Process.* Whether you are specifically intending something to do or say in this moment, or whether you are prepaving your future in this moment, it is of great value for you to do it on purpose.

When you get into your vehicle, if you will set forth your deliberate intent for safety on this journey, you will literally attract the circumstances that will bring that about. Now, of course, if you had intended that as you were beginning many previous journeys . . . if, in your past, as you viewed your future, you had wanted and expected safety, then those intentions set forth in advance would have already begun to prepave your future, and your *Segment Intending* would now be adding unto that intent . . . strengthening it, indeed.

I Can Prepave Life or Live by Default

If you have not prepaved and you are not deliberately intending in this segment, then you are living life by default, and so, the possibility of being swept up in the confusion or intentions of someone else is likely.

Two Beings who are in two separate vehicles, arriving at the same point at the same time and experiencing a collision . . . are two Beings who have not intended safety. They were living life by default, and they now find themselves, in their confusion, attracting one another, you see.

If you want and expect to receive the subject of your intent, it will be. But if you do not take the time to establish what you want, then you are attracting, by the influence of others or by the influence of your own old habits, all sorts of things that you may or may not want. We agree that there are some things that you attract accidentally or by default that you *do* like, just as there are some things that you attract, not intentionally, but by default, that you do *not* want, but there is not much satisfaction in attracting by default. The true joy of life is in *Deliberate Creation.*

As I Am Feeling, I Am Attracting

Now, this is the key to your *Deliberate Creating:* See yourself as this magnet, attracting unto you the way you *feel* at any point in time. When you *feel* clear and in control, you will attract circumstances of clarity. When you *feel* happy, you will attract circumstances of happiness. When you *feel* healthy, you will attract circumstances of health. When you *feel* prosperous, you will attract circumstances of prosperity. When you *feel* loved, you will attract circumstances of love. *Literally, the way you feel is your point of attraction.* And so, the value of *Segment Intending* here is that you pause many times during your day to say, *This is what I want from this segment of my life experience. I want it and I expect it.* And as you set forth those powerful words, you become what we call a *Selective Sifter,* and you will attract into your experience what you want.

You see, the Universe—indeed, the very world in which you live—is filled with all sorts of things. There are things that you like very much, just as there are things that you do not like very much. But all of that comes into your experience only by your invitation through thought. And so, if you are taking the time, many times in a day, to identify what you want, and setting forth your statement of desire and expectation, you will gain the magnetic control of your own experience. No more will you be the "victim" (there is not really such a thing), and no more will you be the indeliberate attractor or the default attractor. Once you begin to segment your day, to identify many times in the day what it is you do want, now you are a *Deliberate Attractor.* And that is a joyful experience.

What Is It That I Now Want?

The reason that *Segment Intending* is so effective is because there are so many subjects you could consider, but when you try to do so all at the same time, you become overwhelmed and confused. The value of intending, segment by segment, is that as you focus more precisely on the fewer details of this moment, you allow the *Law of Attraction* to more powerfully respond; and you are less likely to confuse the issue further with your contradictory thoughts of doubt, worry, or an awareness of lack.

For example, when your telephone rings, you might pick it up and say, "Good morning." And when you hear who it is, you say, "Hello, there, hold just a second please," and then you say to yourself, *What is it that I most want to achieve in this conversation? I want to uplift the other person. I want to be understood. I want the other person to understand me, and I want the other to be positively influenced in the direction of my desire. I want the other to be stimulated and excited by my words. Indeed, I want this to be a successful conversation.* Then, when you come back on the line, you have *prepaved.* And now, that other one will respond to you much more in accordance with your desire than if you had not taken that time.

When another person has initiated the telephone call, they know what *they* want. And so, you must take a moment to identify what *you* want. Otherwise, by the power of their influence, they may achieve what they want—but you may not.

If you want many things all at the same time, it adds confusion. But when you focus upon the most important *specifics* of what you want in any particular moment, you bring about clarity, power, and speed. And that is the point of the *Segment Intending Process:* to stop as you are entering a new segment and to identify what it is you most want so that you may give it your attention and, therefore, draw power unto that.

Some of you are focused during some segments of your day's experience, but there are very few of you who are focused during very much of your day. And so, for most of you, an identification of segments, and an intent to identify what is most important within those segments, will put you in the position of being a deliberate magnetic attractor, or creator, in each of your segments through-out your day. And not only will you now find that you are more productive, but you will find that you are happier. For as you are deliberately intending, and then allowing and receiving, you will find great contentment.

You are growth-seeking Beings, and as you are moving forward, you are at your happiest; while, when you have that feeling of stagnation, you are not at your happiest.

An Example of a Day of *Segment Intending*

Here is an example of a day in which you are not only aware of each new segment that you are moving into, but you are also setting forth your intentions for each segment.

Let us say that you are beginning this process at the end of this day before you go to sleep. Recognize that entering into the sleep state will be a new segment of life experience. And so, as you are lying there with your head on the pillow, getting ready to go to sleep, set forth your intention for that time: *It is my intention for my body to completely relax. It is my intention to awaken rested, refreshed, and eager to begin my day.*

The next morning as you open your eyes, recognize that you have now entered into a new segment of life experience, and that the time you remain in bed until the time you remove yourself from the bed is a segment. Set forth your intent for that time: *While I'm lying here in my bed, I'm intending to have a clear picture of this day. I'm intending to become exhilarated and excited about this day.* And then, as you are lying there in the bed, you will feel that refreshment and that exuberance for the day coming upon you.

As you get out of bed, you have entered into another new segment of life experience. This may be the segment in which you are preparing yourself for the day. And so, as you are entering the segment of brushing your teeth and taking your bath, let your intent be: *I intend to acknowledge my wonderful body and to feel appreciation for the magnificent way it functions. I intend to be efficient in my grooming and to bring myself to looking my best.*

As you are preparing your breakfast, let your intent for this segment be: *I will select and prepare this wonderful, nutritious food efficiently. I will relax and eat it in joy, allowing my wonderful body to digest and process it perfectly. I will choose the food that is best for my physical body at this point in time. I will be replenished and refreshed by this food.* And as you set forth this intention, you will notice that as you are eating, you are feeling yourself more rejuvenated, replenished, and refreshed. And you will enjoy the food more than if you had not set forth that intent to do so.

As you get into your automobile and are traveling to your destination, let your intent in this segment be to travel from one place to another in safety, to feel invigorated and happy as you are moving forth, and to be aware of what the other drivers are intending or not intending so that you may move through traffic in a state of flow—safe and efficient.

When you get out of your automobile, you have now entered into a new segment. And so, pause for a moment and imagine yourself walking from where you are to where you intend to go. See yourself feeling good as you walk; intend that you will move efficiently and safely from point to point. Intend to breathe deeply as you feel the vitality of your body, and intend to feel the clarity of your thinking mechanism. . . . Set forth your vision or your intention for the next segment you are about to enter. Imagine your greeting of the staff or of the employer. . . . See yourself as one who uplifts others, having a smile ready. Recognize that everyone you meet is not deliberate in their intending, but know that by your deliberate intending, you will be in control of your life experience; and you will not be swept up by their confusion, or by their intent or influence.

As you are moving through a day of Segment Intending, you will feel the power and the momentum of your intentions building, and you will find yourself feeling gloriously invincible. And as you are seeing yourself again and again in creative control of your own life experience, you will feel as if there is nothing that you cannot be, do, or have.

For *Segment Intending*, Carry a Small Notebook

Of course, your segments will not be just as we have offered, and they will not be the same from day to day. In only a few days, you will find it very easy to identify each new segment and to identify what you most want from it, until very soon you will be able to clearly expect good results from every segment of your day.

Some of you may find it more efficient and effective to carry a small notebook and to physically stop to identify the segment while you write a list of your intentions in your notebook. Since writing something down onto paper is your strongest point of focus, in the beginning of your application of this *Segment Intending Process* you may find your notebook to be of great value.

You have gathered some questions for us upon this topic of *Segment Intending?*

Isn't There Some Goal to Be Achieved?

Jerry: Abraham, to me, *Segment Intending* appears to be the ideal vehicle for an instant practical application (and realization) of the *Law of Attraction*, the *Science of Deliberate Creation*, and the *Art of Allowing*. In other words, by immediately coupling our now-conscious awareness of these *Laws* (which your teachings have clarified for us) with this *Segment Intending Process,* we can each immediately discover for ourselves how our thoughts can affect our manifestations.

I have been equating *Segment Intending* with the equivalent of intending a series of small goals (or intentions) of which we can, almost instantly and consciously, experience their manifestations. This brings me to my next question: Is there not a basic overall goal (or intention) for us to complete in this physical life?

Abraham: There is. And just as *Segment Intending* is the intent that is closest to this moment in which you are now living, your intent as you emerged into physical expression is on the other end of that, so to speak. In other words, here you are now, intending what you most want from this moment, yet this moment is being affected by thoughts you have had about this moment even before your birth into this physical body. As you emerged into this physical body from that inner, broader perspective, you did have intentions, indeed, but your intentions from this physical conscious perspective are dominant now.

You are not a puppet acting out that which has been intended before. You have the choice, in every moment, to decide what is most appropriate from your ever-evolving perspective, *for you have grown beyond that which you were as you emerged into this body—for this life experience has already added unto that perspective.*

Can the Goal of Happiness Be Important Enough?

Jerry: So, since I don't consciously know what these specific, individual, overall goals are, would there be anything more important than having a goal to just be happy?

Abraham: You have hit upon the way to know what it is you have intended as you have come forth from your inner perspective. In other words, you said, "Since I don't consciously know what these specific, individual, overall goals are." The reason you do not consciously know what the specific goals are is because there were no specific goals. *You had, before your physical birth, general intentions, such as being happy, being an uplifter, having continuing growth . . . but the specific processes or vehicles through which you will achieve any of those things is up to you to decide here and now. In this time, you are the creator.*

How Can We Recognize That We're Having Growth?

Jerry: Let's take the intention that you mentioned: *growth.* How can we recognize when we're having growth?

Abraham: Since you are a growth-seeking Being, you will have positive emotion whenever you are recognizing your growth, and you will have negative emotion whenever you are feeling stagnation. You see, you do not necessarily have conscious recognition of the thoughts or intentions of your inner or broader perspective—but you do have communication. *All physical Beings have communication from their <u>Inner Being</u> in the form of emotion, and so, whenever your emotion is positive, you can know that you are in harmony with your inner intentions.*

What's a Valid Measure of Our Success?

Jerry: Then, what do you see, Abraham, from your Non-Physical perspective, as a valid measure of our being successful at what we're doing here?

Abraham: You have many ways of measuring your success. In your society, your dollars are a measure of success; your trophies are a measure of success—but from our perspective, the existence within you of positive emotion is your greatest measure of success.

Can *Segment Intending* Speed Up Our Manifestations?

Jerry: So, this process of *Segment Intending* can not only speed up our getting whatever we want, but then it can also make this experience that we're having more pleasurable, and more within our conscious control (and therefore more successful). Is that what it's about?

Abraham: It is absolutely "more within your conscious control" as you are consciously setting forth your intentions. The alternative is to not make a decision about what you want, and therefore, in your confusion, to attract a little bit of everything; and, in attracting a little bit of everything, there is some that you like and some that you do not like. The point of the *Segment Intending Process* is that you will always be attracting that which you deliberately want. No more creating by default; no more attracting what you do not want.

You are right when you say that it can speed up the process, for it is your clarity that speeds. Of course, you are physically creating as you move piles of dirt from one place to another (or whatever it is you are doing), but you have not accessed the power of the Universe unless your thoughts have brought forth emotion. When emotion is present—whether it is positive or negative—you have now accessed the power of the Universe.

When you really, really want something, it comes to you very fast. When you really, really do not want something, it comes to you very fast. The idea of <u>Segment Intending</u> is to set forth your thought of what you want, focusing upon it clearly enough, in this moment, that you bring forth emotion about it. Your clarity brings the speed.

Meditations, Workshops, and the *Segment Intending* Processes

Jerry: Let me clarify some terminology with you, please. There are three different Processes. One you call *Segment Intending*. One you call having a *Workshop*. And the other one you speak of sometimes, in terms of other people's words, is *Meditation*. Would you clarify what the differences and purposes of these three processes are?

Abraham: Each of these processes is for a different intention. And so, your question fits in perfectly with our subject of *Segment Intending,* for as you are about to enter into any of these three processes, it is a good idea to know *why* you are entering into them, and what you *expect* to receive.

A time of *Meditation,* by your terms, is a segment in which you are intending to quiet your conscious thinking mechanism in order to sense the *Inner World.* It is a time of physical distraction, or detachment from the physical, so that you may sense that which goes beyond the physical. There are different reasons for this detachment, and it is important that, as you are entering this segment, you identify what your reason is. Your reason in this segment of *Meditation* may be that you simply want a detachment from the world that is confusing or troubling you. You want some time of refreshment. When *we* encourage *Meditation,* it is with the intent of allowing the opening of your passageway so that you may blend the *Inner You* that exists in the *Inner Dimension* with the conscious physical you that is here in this physical body. *Meditation is a withdrawing of your focus from the physical conscious world, and an allowing of your focus to align with the <u>Inner World.</u>*

Now, the *Workshop Process* is a segment where you are intending to give specific and precise thought to the details of what you want, and to bring forth, by the *Law of Attraction,* clarity. In other words, you want to ponder your desire so specifically that you bring forth the power of the Universe to speed your creation. The *Workshop* is the time in which you guide your thoughts in the direction of your specific desire, aligning your thoughts, in this moment, with the desires that your life has helped you identify. *In your physical world, you cannot have a physical experience until you have created it first in thought. And so, the <u>Workshop</u> is that place where you give deliberate thought to, and where you begin the deliberate attraction of, the thing, or things, that you want.*

The process of <u>Segment Intending</u> is to simply recognize that you are moving into a segment where what you are intending is different from the last, and then to stop and identify what you are <u>now</u> wanting. Segment Intending is the process by which you eliminate the predominant hindrances to your *Deliberate Creation:* influence of others who may have different intentions than you do, or the influence of your own old habits.

How Can I Consciously Begin Feeling Happy?

Jerry: I've heard you suggest that we get to the point of feeling happy before we begin intending something. Would you give us some different ways of consciously generating the feeling of joy, or of bringing forth the feeling of positive emotion?

Abraham: Before we do that, we want to point out the great value in your being happy. You are like magnets, and the way you *feel* is your *point of attraction.* And so, if you are feeling unhappy, if you are giving thought to that which you do not want (which is what would be bringing forth the *feeling* of unhappiness), then you are attracting more of what you do not want. *There is great value in being happy, because only from the point of being happy can you attract that which you want, but it is also your most natural state of being. If you are not allowing yourself to be happy, you are holding yourself away from who-you-really-are.*

As you notice that you are, in this moment, happy, take the time to identify what things are present that may be affecting your happiness. For many of you it can be listening to music that is in harmony with you in the moment. For some it will be petting their cat or taking a walk or making love—or playing with a child. For some it will be reading a passage in a book. For some it will be calling a friend who is uplifting. There are many ways of doing it.

It is of value to find many touchstones to use to uplift yourself so that you may always use another approach to bring forth that feeling of happiness. *Take notice of that which uplifts you and remember it, and then, when you specifically want to feel uplifted, use that as a touchstone to your happiness.*

But What about When Those Around Me Are Unhappy?

Jerry: You have said that we can be happy under almost all conditions. But how can that be accomplished when we are observing someone who is experiencing extremely negative conditions?

Abraham: *You can be happy only under the condition of giving thought to what you want. And so, you can be happy under all conditions if you are clear enough and strong enough in your wanting to give your attention only to what you want.*

Jerry: But what if there are those you feel obligated to occasionally be with who do or say things that make you feel very uncomfortable, and yet you still want to try to please them because you feel guilty whenever you don't do or be what they want? How would you suggest we be happy in a situation like that?

Abraham: It is true. It is more difficult to remain happy or positive when surrounded by others who are unhappy, or when you are surrounded by or involved with those who want something different from you than you want to give them. But what we have noticed as we have been interacting with physical Beings is that while you may have an experience that only lasts five or ten minutes, and while that experience may be unpleasant and uncomfortable, the majority of your negative emotion comes forth not *during* the minutes of that negative experience, but they come forth in all the hours that you ponder and chew upon it *after* the experience. *Usually, there is much more of your time spent in thought of the negative thing that has happened than in the actuality of what is happening.*

The majority of your negative emotion could be eliminated if, in those times when you are alone, you would focus upon what you now want to think about. And then, in those briefer encounters, in those smaller parts of your life experience where you are actually being harassed by another, you will grow stronger in your ability to not notice the harassment so much and, in time, the *Law of Attraction* will not bring you to those experiences because those thoughts will no longer be active within you.

Can I *Segment-Intend* Around Unplanned Interruptions?

Jerry: So, let's take a situation in which people truly want to have a feeling of an orderly progression forward, but their intentions are quite often diverted by what I call *unplanned interruptions*. What sort of *Segment Intention* would you suggest in a situation like that?

Abraham: Of course, as your *Segment Intending* becomes more defined, and as you get better at it, you will automatically have far fewer interruptions. You have been encouraging the interruptions because of your lack of *Segment Intending* in the past.

As you begin your day envisioning free-flowing, smooth-flowing life experiences, you will have eliminated some of those interruptions already. And, for those interruptions that do come forth, you can deal with those segment by segment, simply by saying at the beginning of the interruption, *This will be brief, and I will not lose my train of thought. I will not lose the momentum that I have set forth. I will deal with this quickly and efficiently, and I will get on with what I was doing.*

Could *Segment Intending* Expand My Usable Time?

Jerry: I've said throughout the years, *I wish that there was a lot more of me so I could experience all of the wonderful things that I want to experience.* Is there a way that we can use *Segment Intending* so we can experience more experiences—that is, so we can do more of the things we want to do?

Abraham: You will find, as you become efficient with your *Segment Intending,* that you will have many more hours in your day to do those things you want to do.

Many of the things that you want have not been coming forth to you because you have not given clarity of thought to them and attracted them. And so, the *Segment Intending* itself will give you that which you are seeking in this question. *By being clear about what you want and no longer contradicting it with opposing thoughts, you will* *enable the <u>Laws of the Universe</u> to do their work, and you will not feel a need to offer so much action to compensate for inappropriate thought. By offering deliberate thought, you will harness the power of the Universe, and it will require far less time for you to accomplish much, much more.*

Why Isn't Everyone Creating Life on Purpose?

Jerry: Since we each have the choice of creating what we really want—on purpose—or creating by default and receiving indiscriminately both the wanted and the unwanted, then why does it seem like the majority of people choose by default?

Abraham: Most are creating their experiences by default because they do not understand the *Laws;* they really do not understand that they have those choices. They have come to believe in fate or luck. They say, "This is reality; this is just the way it is." They do not understand that they have control of their experience through their thought. It is like playing a game where they do not know the rules, and soon they grow tired of the game because they believe that they have no control over it.

It is of great value for you to give your conscious attention to what you specifically want, otherwise you can be swept up by the influence of that which surrounds you. You are bombarded by the stimulation of thought. And so, unless you <u>are</u> setting forth the thought that is important to you, you can be stimulated by <u>another's</u> thought that may or may not be important to you.

If you do not know what you want, then it is good for you to set forth the intent: *I want to know what I want.* And as you set forth that desire, you will begin attracting data; you will begin attracting opportunity; you will begin attracting many things to select from—and from the steady parade of ideas that will flow to you, you will get a better idea of what you specifically desire.

Because of the *Law of Attraction,* it is easier to just observe things as they are than it is to choose a different thought. And as people observe things as they are, the *Law of Attraction* brings them more of the same, and in time, people come to believe that they do not have control.

Many are taught that they are not allowed to choose, that they are not worthy of choice, or that they are not capable of knowing what is appropriate for them to choose. In time, and with practice, you will come to understand that you can tell, by the way you are feeling, the appropriateness of your choice, for when you choose the direction of thought that agrees with your broader perspective, your joy is your confirmation of the appropriateness of your thought.

How Important to Our Experience Is *Wanting?*

Jerry: Now the person who doesn't even say, "I want to know what I want," but just says, "As far as I know, I don't want anything," or "I've been taught that it is wrong to have desire," and is in some kind of a flat, listless state, would you have anything to say to this person?

Abraham: *Is the desire to have no desire—in order to achieve a greater state of worthiness—not also a desire? Wanting is the beginning of all Deliberate Creating. And so, if you refuse to allow yourself to want, then you are really refusing the deliberate control of your life experience.*

You are physical Beings, indeed, but you have a Life Force; an Energy Force; a God Force, a Creative Energy Force, that flows into you from the Inner Dimension. Your doctors, in all of their notice of it, do not know much about it. They know that some have it and some do not. They will say, "This one is dead; he has no Life Force." *Creative Life Force flows into you for the extension outward toward whatever you are giving your attention. In other words, it is the process by which your thought brings to you whatever desire you are giving thought to.*

The more you give thought to that which you desire, the more the *Law of Attraction* sets those things into motion, and you can feel the momentum of your thoughts. When you do not think about what you desire, or when you think about what you want and then immediately think about the lack of it, you hinder the natural momentum of thought.

That "flat, listless state" you are describing is caused by your constant slowing of the momentum of thought with your contradictory statements.

Why Do Most Settle for So Little?

Jerry: Abraham, we live in a nation where almost everyone is able to eat every day, and has a place to live and has clothing. Almost everyone at least gets by in some way. I meet people who say, "You know, I have enough to get by, but somehow I can't build up my desires strong enough to bring anything major or special into my life." What would you say to a person in that situation?

Abraham: It is not that you do not desire more, but you have somehow convinced yourself that you cannot *have* more. And so, you want to avoid the disappointment of wanting something and not getting it. It is not because you do not want it that you are not receiving what you want—it is because you are focusing upon the *lack* of it. And, by the *Law of Attraction*, you are attracting the subject of your thought (the lack of it).

Whenever you want something and then you say, "*But* I have wanted it and I did not get it," now your attention is upon the lack of what you want, and so, by *Law*, you are attracting the lack. Whenever you are thinking about what you want, you are feeling exhilarated, you are feeling excited, and you are feeling positive emotion; but as you are thinking about the lack of what you want, you are feeling negative emotion; you are feeling disappointment. The disappointment that you are feeling is your *Emotional Guidance System* saying to you, "What you're giving thought to is not what you want." And so, we would say, allow yourself to want a little, put your thought upon what you want, feel the positive emotion that comes forth from wanting, and let the disappointment go away. And, in your giving thought to what you want, you will attract it.

Speak to Us about *Prioritizing Our Intentions*

Jerry: You've given Esther and me a process that we've had great results with, and I'd like it if you would elaborate a little bit on it. It is the process you refer to as *Prioritizing Our Intentions*.

Abraham: Although you do not hold all of your intentions at any one point in time, you often have many intentions that do all relate to this point in time. For example, you are interacting with your mate, you want clear communication, you want to uplift yourself, you want to uplift your mate . . . and you may want to influence your mate to want the same. In other words, you want harmony.

It is important for you to identify which intentions you want most to fulfill, because as you <u>prioritize</u>, you give your singular attention to what is most important; and as you give it your singular attention—you attract power unto the intention that is most important to you.

So, let us say that you have begun your day, but you have not clearly identified your segments. You have blundered into the day, as most do, moving from one thing to another, buffeted about by the impulses and desires of others, or by your old habits. The telephone is ringing, your children are asking for this and that; your mate is asking you questions, and you find yourself not clear about anything, but you are moving about in a day that, for most, is rather normal.

Now, you find yourself involved in a discussion where you have not taken the time to identify what you want, and, let us say, you find yourself in a disagreement with either your children or your mate or with anyone—it matters not who it is. You feel "warning bells" coming forth from your *Inner Being.* The negative emotion is mounting in you for a number of reasons: You are a little bit mad at yourself for getting into this muddle because you have not intended clearly, but even beyond that, you are upset because you are in disagreement with what the other person is intending, what the other is stating, or what the other is wanting.

If you catch yourself in that segment and you say, *What do I most want right now in this situation?* you may recognize that *feeling harmony* really is your dominant intent—getting along with your wife or your child or whatever. That is, having a harmonious relationship is far more important than this insignificant issue. And as you recognize that harmony is what you want most, suddenly you are clear; your negative emotion goes away, and you make a statement such as, *Wait, let's talk. I don't want to argue, for you are my best friend. I want us to have harmony. I want us to be happy together.* And as you make that statement, you will disarm the other. You will remind the other that that is the dominant intent of him or her, also. And now, from your new and focused *prioritized intention,* which is harmony, you may take a fresh view of this less important subject at hand.

Here we will give you a statement that, if you will set it forth at the beginning of all segments of your life experience, will serve you very well: *As I'm entering this segment of life experience, it is my intent to see that which I want to see.* And what that will do—when you are interacting with others—it will help you to see that you want harmony; that you want to uplift them; that you want to put across your idea effectively, and that you want to stimulate their desire to one that harmonizes with your desire. That statement will serve you very well.

How Detailed Must My Creative Intentions Be?

Jerry: As we intend forward motion, how detailed should we be in the ways or the means, and how specific should we be in the outcome or the manifestations, of our intentions?

Abraham: You want to be detailed enough in your thought of what you want that you bring forth positive emotion about it, but not so detailed that the thought of what you want brings forth negative emotion. As you vaguely intend something, your thought will not be specific enough—and therefore not powerful enough—to bring forth the power of the Universe. But on the other hand, you can become too specific before you have collected enough data to support your belief. In other words, as you become specific, but it challenges your beliefs about the subject, you may find yourself feeling negative emotion. *And so, become specific enough in your intentions that you bring forth positive emotion, but not so specific that you bring forth negative emotion.*

Must I Regularly Repeat My *Segment Intentions?*

Jerry: Abraham, let's speak more in terms of *Segment Intending.* Since it would be very tedious to give our attention to every small detail involved in every moment, could we not just intend safety, say, the first thing in the morning? And then wouldn't that keep us safe for the rest of the day?

Abraham: It is not necessary that you intend it again and again and again, although there is value in reiterating what is most important to you at any point in time. *Once you have set forth your intent for safety and you begin feeling safe, now you are at the point of always attracting safety. At any time that you may feel unsafe, that is the time, again, to set forth your reinforcement of safety.*

Could This *Segment Intending Process* Hinder My Spontaneous Reactions?

Jerry: Could *Segment Intending* hinder our spontaneity, or our ability to react to a situation in the moment, in any way?

Abraham: *Segment Intending* would hinder your ability to react by *default*—but it would strengthen your ability to react *deliberately.* Spontaneity is wonderful as long as you are spontaneously attracting what you want. It is not so wonderful when you are spontaneously attracting that which you do not want. We would not replace deliberate creating with spontaneous-creation-by-default, at any cost.

The Delicate Balance Between Belief and Desire

Jerry: Abraham, would you take a moment here and speak to us about what you have called *the delicate balance of creating—between wanting and believing?*

Abraham: The two sides in this balance of creation are *want it* and *allow it*. You could also say *want it* and *expect it*. You could also say *think about it* and *expect it*.

The best scenario is to desire something and to bring yourself into the belief or expectation of achieving it. That is creation at its best. If you have a slight desire for something and you believe you can achieve it, the balance is complete and it becomes yours. If you have a strong desire for something but you doubt your ability to achieve it, it cannot come, at least not right now, for you must bring your thought of desire and your thought of belief into alignment.

Maybe you have been stimulated to a thought of something that you do not desire, but because you have often heard reports of this thing happening to others, you believe in the possibility of it. So your slight thought of this unwanted thing and your belief in its possibility make you a candidate for the achievement of that experience.

The more you think of what you want, the more the *Law of Attraction* will bring the evidence of it to you, until you *will* believe it. And when you understand the *Law of Attraction* (and it is easy to come to know it because it is always consistent) and you begin to deliberately direct your thoughts, your belief in your ability to be, do, or have anything will come into place.

When Does *Segment Intending* Lead to Work?

Jerry: We are physical Beings, and we're taught to believe that in order to get a financial return, our hard work is important. But you don't mention much about the physical action. How does *hard work* or *physical action* fit into your creative equation?

Abraham: The more attention you give to an idea through thought, the more the *Law of Attraction* responds—and the more powerful the thought becomes. By prepaving, *Segment Intending,* and imagining in your *Creative Workshop,* you will then begin to feel inspiration to act. *Action that comes from the feeling of inspiration is action that will produce good results, for you are allowing the <u>Laws</u>*

of the Universe to carry you. If you take action without deliberately prepaving, though, often your action feels like hard work because you are attempting to make more happen in this moment than your action alone can accomplish.

If you will think your creation into being and then follow through with inspired action, you will find your future ready and waiting for you to arrive, and then you can offer your action in order to enjoy the fruit of your true creative power instead of incorrectly trying to use your action to create.

Which Is the Best Choice of Action?

Jerry: So, when there are a lot of different actions that we _could_ be taking in order to accomplish something specific, how can we finally decide, in the last moment, which of these different possible actions would be the most effective for us to use?

Abraham: By imagining yourself taking the potential act, and then noting how you feel while you are imagining that action. If you have two choices, envision yourself taking one choice and note how you feel about it. And then envision yourself taking the other choice and see how you feel about that. The way you feel about the potential action will not be clear to you, however, unless you have taken the time to first identify your intentions and put them in an order of priority. And once you have done that, then making the decision of what is the most appropriate action will be a very simple process. You will be using your _Emotional Guidance System._

How Long Should I Wait for the Manifestation?

Jerry: Let's say there are those who are waiting for something to manifest right now and they find themselves getting a little discouraged because what they've been intending isn't there yet. How long should they wait before there are any visible signs of success? And what would be some signs that it _is_ going to happen?

Abraham: As you have set forth your intent to have something and you are looking expectantly for it, it is now on its way to you, and you will begin to see many signs of it: You will see others who have achieved something like it, which will stimulate your wanting; you will take more notice of aspects of it in many different directions; you will find yourself thinking about it and feeling excited about it often; and you will be feeling very good about that which you want—those will be some of the signs that what you want is on the way.

When you understand that the majority of your creative effort is spent in defining what you want and then aligning your thoughts to that desire, you may then realize that the majority of the creative process is taking place on a vibrational level. Therefore, your creation can be nearly complete, as much as 99 percent complete, before you see physical evidence of it.

If you will remember that the positive emotion you are feeling in anticipation of your creation is also evidence of its progress, then you will be able to move steadily and quickly toward the outcomes you desire.

Can I Use *Segment Intending* to Co-create?

Jerry: Abraham, how can we use this *Segment Intending Process* in order to mutually accomplish a goal with another person?

Abraham: The better the job you have done in your own *Segment Intending,* the more powerful your thoughts will be about *your* desire—and then your power of influence will be stronger. And so, as you interact with others, it will be easier for them to catch the spirit of your idea.

It is also extremely helpful for you to use the *Segment Intending Process* to evoke the best from others. If you expect them to be unhelpful or unfocused, you will attract that from them; while if you expect them to be brilliant and helpful, you will attract *that* from them. If you have spent some time bringing your thoughts to a powerful place before your physical meeting, you will have a much more satisfying co-creation for yourself, and for them.

How Can I Convey My Intent More Precisely?

Jerry: I recall, throughout the past years, that quite often I would go into a situation that I felt was very important, but the other person and I would talk back and forth, and then after I left, I would think, *Gee, I could have said* and *I should have said* and *I wanted to say,* but I didn't. So instead of feeling a sense of accomplishment when the interaction was over, I often felt a sense of frustration. How could I have avoided that?

Abraham: By thinking about your desired outcome *before* you enter into the conversation, you will get a momentum going that will help you more clearly convey your meaning. It is also of value to recognize that in this combining of thoughts, ideas, and experiences, together you have the potential of creating something even greater than you could create on your own. So prepaving your positive expectation of their contribution will put you in a position of rendezvousing with their clarity, power, and value. In this good-feeling alignment, your mind will be clear, you will evoke clarity from the other, and, together, you will have a wonderful co-creation.

Jerry: What if a person doesn't want to upset others, or hurt their feelings, or anger them when the subject of the interaction might be a controversial thing? In other words, if you're interacting with someone who has some *conflicting* desires, and yet you can see there could be some mutually *beneficial* goals that could be achieved if a potential controversy could be avoided, how can a situation like that work out for all persons involved?

Abraham: By intending—as you are moving into the segment—to focus upon those things that you *do* have in common; to focus upon your points of harmony; to give very little attention to what you are *not* agreeing upon, and to give your great attention to the things you *do* agree upon. That is the resolution in all relationships. *The trouble with most relationships is that you pick out the one little thing that you do not like and then give that most of your* *attention. And then, by the Law of Attraction, you solicit more of what you do not want.*

Can One Have Prosperity Without Working for It?

Jerry: You've told us many times that we can have it *all*. Let's take a situation where people want prosperity, but they don't want to go to work or find a job. How would you suggest they bridge that quandary?

Abraham: By considering the intentions separately. If they want prosperity, but it is their belief that prosperity comes only through working, then they will not be able to have prosperity because they do not want to do the only thing that they believe will bring it forth. But as they consider prosperity, singularly, then by not coupling it with the work that they are resisting, they will be able to attract prosperity.

You have come upon something very important; it is what we call conflicting intentions, or conflicting beliefs. *The solution is simply a matter of taking your eye off of what is conflicting, and putting it upon the essence of what you want.*

If you want prosperity and you believe that it requires hard work and you are willing to offer the hard work, there is no contradiction, and you will achieve a level of prosperity.

If you want prosperity and you believe that it requires hard work and you are averse to hard work, there is a contradiction in your thinking, and you will not only have a difficult time offering the action, but any action you offer will not be productive.

If you want prosperity and you believe that you deserve it, and you expect it to come to you just because you want it to, there is no contradiction in your thinking—and the prosperity will flow. . . . Pay attention to how you are feeling as you are offering your thoughts so you can sort out the contradictory thoughts, and as you eliminate the contradictions regarding anything that you desire, it must come to you. The *Law of Attraction* must bring it.

When the Job Offers Rained, They Poured!

Jerry: So let's say that there's a person who hasn't been able to find a job after months and months of wanting and trying, and then as soon as they *do* receive a job that they want, four or five other good offers come in all at once, say, in that same week. What would be the cause of that?

Abraham: The reason why the job was so long in coming was because, rather than focusing upon what they *wanted,* which was the job, they were focusing upon the *lack* of the job—pushing it away. Once they broke through and received a job, then the focus was no longer on the *lack* of it—*the focus was on what was wanted, so now, they began receiving more of what had been prepaved.* In your example, the desire grew stronger even though the belief was weak, so in time, the *Law of Attraction* yielded what this person was feeling the strongest. They tortured themselves unnecessarily, however, by not taking the time to clean up their thoughts.

Why Are Adoptions Often Followed by Pregnancies?

Jerry: Is that why if a couple who hasn't been able to get pregnant for years adopts a child, then, suddenly, the wife often becomes pregnant?

Abraham: It is the same story, indeed.

Where Does Competition Fit into the Intentions Picture?

Jerry: Another question: How does *competition* fit into the picture?

Abraham: From our perspective, in this vast Universe in which we are all creating, there truly is no *competition,* for there is enough abundance on all subjects to satisfy all of us. You put yourselves in a position of competition by saying that there is only one prize. And that can bring forth a little discomfort, for you want to win; you do not want to lose, but often the attention is upon losing rather than on winning.

When you put yourself in the position of competition, the one who wins is always the one who is clearest about his wanting, and most expectant of it. It is _Law._ If there is any value in competition, it is this: It stimulates desire.

Would Strengthening My Willpower Be an Advantage?

Jerry: Is there any way people could strengthen their will so that they could get more of what they want and less of what they don't want?

Abraham: Utilizing the process of *Segment Intending* certainly could accomplish that. But it is not so much "a strengthening of the will" as it is thinking thoughts that the *Law of Attraction* then adds to. *Willpower* can mean "determination." And *determination* can mean "deliberately thinking." But all of that sounds like harder work than is really required. *Simply give thought to what is preferred, consistently throughout the day, and the _Law of Attraction_ will take care of everything else.*

Why Do Most Beings Stop Experiencing Growth?

Jerry: It seems to me that most people in our society, by the time they've reached the age of 25 to 35, have gone about as far as they're going to go as far as their development and growth. They have the home they're going to have; the lifestyle they're going to have; the job they're going to have; the beliefs, politics, and religious convictions they're going to have; and even the variety of personal experiences that most of them are going to have. Do you have any idea what the cause of that is?

195

Abraham: It is not so much that they have had *all* of the experiences that they are going to have, it is that they are no longer attracting *new* experiences. In the new experience, there is excitement and more desire, but many of them are no longer deliberately setting forth their desire; they are more or less resigned to *what-is*.

Giving attention to *what-is* only attracts more of *what-is*. While giving attention to what is wanted attracts change. And so, there is a sort of complacency that comes about, simply because the *Laws* are not understood.

Most people stop deliberately reaching for expansion because they have not understood the *Laws of the Universe,* and so, they have been unintentionally offering contradictory thoughts resulting in not getting what they want. When your belief of what you can accomplish contradicts your desire of what you would like to accomplish, even hard work does not yield good results, and over time you just get tired.

Coming into conscious awareness of the *Laws of the Universe* and then beginning to gently guide your own thoughts to that which you prefer will begin to produce positive results immediately.

Jerry: So, let's say that a person has reached a particular point in life where they find themselves in what I would call a downward or negative spiral. How could they use *Segment Intending* to start that spiral moving back up again?

Abraham: Your *now* is powerful. In fact, all of your power is right here, right now. So if you will focus upon where you are right now and stop to think about what you most want from this segment only, you will find clarity. *You cannot, right now, sort out everything that you want about every subject, but you can, right now, define what you prefer from here. And as you do that, segment after segment, you will find a newfound clarity—and your downward spiral will turn upward.*

How Do We Avoid Influence from Old Beliefs and Habits?

Jerry: Abraham, it seems to be particularly difficult for most of us to discard our old ideas, beliefs, and habits. Would you be willing to give us an affirmation that would assist us in avoiding any influence from our past experiences and beliefs?

Abraham: *I am powerful in my <u>now</u>.* We are not encouraging a discarding of old ideas, for in trying to get rid of them you actually only think about them more. And, some of your old ideas are worth keeping. Just be more aware of how you are directing your thoughts, and make a decision that you want to feel good. *Today, no matter where I am going, no matter what I am doing, it is my dominant intent to see that which I want to see. Nothing is more important than that I feel good.*

Jerry: So, if people are witnessing the negatives being broadcast through the media, or even listening to the problems that they might hear presented by their friends, how could they keep that negativity from offsetting them?

Abraham: By setting forth the intent, in every segment of their life experience, to see that which they want to see. And then, even from the most negative presentations, they could see something that they do *want*.

Is It Ever Okay to State What Isn't Wanted?

Jerry: Is it *ever* okay for us to state the things we *don't* want?

Abraham: Stating what you do not want can sometimes bring you to a clearer picture of what you *do* want. But it is good to quickly get off the subject of what you do *not* want, and onto the subject of what you *do* want.

Is There Any Value in Researching
Our Negative Thoughts?

Jerry: Abraham, do you ever see any value in trying to identify the specific thought that may have brought forth some negative emotion?

Abraham: There can be value in it for this reason: *What is most important when you recognize that you are thinking a negative thought is to, in whatever way you can, stop thinking the negative thought.* If there is a belief within you that is very powerful, then you may find that this negative thought will come up again and again and again. And so, you continually have to divert your thought from that negative thought onto something else. In that case, it is of value to recognize the troublesome thought and modify it by applying a new perspective to it. In other words, mold the conflicting belief into one that is not so conflicting—and then it will not keep coming up and haunting you.

What about When Others Don't
Consider My Desires Realistic?

Jerry: If there's someone who knows what we want to accomplish (and it's something really far beyond the average), and this person tells us that our desires are "not realistic," how can we avoid being influenced by that?

Abraham: You can avoid others' influence by having given thought, even before your interaction with them, to what is important to you. *Segment Intending* will be of great value here. *As others insist that you look at "reality," they are influencing you to be rooted to this spot like a tree. As long as you are seeing only <u>what-is,</u> you cannot grow beyond it. You must be allowed to see what you want to see if you will ever attract what you want to see. Attention to <u>what-is</u> only creates more of <u>what-is.</u>*

How Is It Possible to "Have It All in 60 Days"?

Jerry: You've essentially said, that within 60 days, we could have everything be the way we want it to be in our lives. How would you suggest that we go about doing that?

Abraham: First, you must recognize that everything that you are now living is a result of the thoughts that have been offered by you in the past. Those thoughts have literally invited, or set up, the circumstances that you are now living. And so, today, as you begin setting forth your thought of your future and seeing yourself as you want to be, you begin the alignment of *those* future events and circumstances that will please you.

As you give thought to your future—your future that may be 10 years; your future that may be 5 years; or your future that may be 60 days away—you literally begin prepaving. And then, as you move into those prepaved moments, and as that future becomes your present, you fine-tune it by saying, *This is what I now want.* And all of those thoughts that you have put forth about your future, right down to this moment when you are now intending what action you want to take, will all fit together to bring you precisely that which you now want to live.

And so, it is a simple process of recognizing day by day that there are many segments. And as you are entering into a new segment, you need to stop and identify what is most important to you so that by the *Law of Attraction,* you may attract that unto you for your consideration. The more thought you give to something, the clearer you become; the clearer you become, the more positive emotion you feel and the more power you attract. And so, this business of *Segment Intending* is the key to swift and *Deliberate Creation.*

We have enjoyed interacting with you very much on this most important subject. There is great love here for you.

Now You Understand

Now that you understand the *rules,* so to speak, of this marvelous game of *Eternal Life* that you are playing, you are now destined to have a wonderful experience, for now you are in creative control of your own physical experience.

Now that you understand the powerful *Law of Attraction,* you will no longer misunderstand how it is that things are happening to you or to any other you may be observing. And as you practice and become proficient at directing your own thoughts toward those things that you desire, your understanding of the *Science of Deliberate Creation* will take you anywhere you decide to go.

Segment by segment, you will prepave your life experience, sending powerful thoughts into your future to make it ready for your joyful arrival. And by paying attention to the way you feel, you will learn to guide your thoughts into alignment with your *Inner Being* and who-you-really-are as you become the *Allower* you were born to be—destined to a life of fulfillment and never-ending joy.

We have enjoyed this interaction immensely.

And, for now, we are complete.

— **Abraham**

ఆఖఆఖఆఖ ఖఆఖఆఖఆ

BOOK 2

Money, and the Law of Attraction

Learning to Attract Wealth, Health, and Happiness

We have had the pleasure of meeting with some of the
most influential people of our time, and we know of no
one person who is more of a fountainhead for the outpouring
of positive upliftment than Louise Hay (Lulu), the founder of
Hay House—for guided by Lulu's vision, Hay House, Inc.,
has now become the world's largest disseminator
of spiritual and self-improvement materials.

And so, to Louise Hay—and to each person she has attracted to her
vision—we lovingly and with much appreciation dedicate this book.

Preface

by Jerry Hicks

What do you believe attracted you to this book? Why do you suppose you're reading these words? Which part of the title got your attention? Was it *Money? Health? Happiness? Learning to Attract?* Or was it the *Law of Attraction* perhaps?

Whatever the obvious reason may have been for your attention to this book, the information contained here has come to you in answer to something for which you have been somehow asking.

What is this book about? It teaches that life is supposed to feel good and that our overall Well-Being is what is natural. It teaches that no matter how good your life is now, it can always get better, and that the choice and the power to improve your life experience is within your personal control. And it offers practical philosophical tools that—when put into consistent use—will enable you to allow yourself to experience more of the wealth, health, and happiness that is your natural birthright. (And I know, because it keeps happening to me. As I move forward from each desire-clarifying experience of contrast to a new desire and then to a new manifestation —my life overall gets better and better.)

Life is good! It is New Year's Day of 2008, and I'm beginning this Preface while seated at the dining-room table of our new Del Mar, California, "haven."

From the time Esther and I were married (1980), we've been making it a point to visit this "Garden of Eden" area as often as has been practical. And now, after all those years as appreciative San Diego visitors, we will be actually living here as appreciative part-time residents.

And what's not to appreciate? There was our friend who led us to find the property. (We told him we were looking for a piece of property near Del Mar where we could park our 45-foot tour bus.) There were the landscape architects, engineers, designers, carpenters, electricians, plumbers, tile roofers, and copper gutterers. There were those talented, skilled tradespeople: tile layers; stuccoers; painters; and fence, gate, and ironworks creators. There were floor installers and custom-lift, slide-doors, arched-wooden-windows-and-doors, and stained-glass-window folks. There were the "high end" high-tech people who installed the Lutron master-controlled lighting system, the audio/video/computer networking system, the new Trane multiple-zone master-controlled (silent) air-conditioning system, and the Snaidero/Miele/Bosch/Viking kitchen and laundry equipment. There were those who placed our new furniture, and placed it again, and again—as we discovered what felt best. There were those teams of hardworking diggers, trenchers, haulers, cement pourers, stoneworkers, and transplanters of full-grown trees. . . . And then there were the thousands of people who had a hand in—and also earned money from—the invention, creation, and distribution of the thousands of products involved. . . . Well, that's a lot to appreciate.

And that was just the tip of the iceberg of what's to appreciate. There was the discovery of a new "favorite" restaurant—and owners and staff—only a couple of minutes away, and then there were those incredibly delightful eclectic, positive neighbors who welcomed us here in a style that we have never previously experienced.

There's more, too. There's the breathtaking view to the south into the primitive Torrey Pines State Reserve, across the Carmel Valley Creek and waterbird sanctuary and the lagoon, and down into the crashing, foaming waves of the Pacific Ocean as it untiringly washes up onto Torrey Pines Beach. Yes. Life is good!

(Esther and I just finished a brief walk on the beach, and we're now settling down for the evening to put some finishing touches on Abraham's newest book—*Money, and the Law of Attraction: Learning to Attract Wealth, Health, and Happiness.*)

It was over 40 years ago, while performing a series of concerts in colleges across the nation, that I "accidentally" noticed a book lying on a coffee table in a motel in a small town in Montana. That book, Napoleon Hill's *Think and Grow Rich,* changed my beliefs about money so dramatically that my use of its principles attracted financial success to me in a way I hadn't previously imagined.

Thinking or growing rich hadn't been something I had much interest in. But shortly before discovering that book, I *had* decided that I wanted to modify the way I earned money—and increase the amount I received. And so, it turned out that my attraction to Hill's book was a direct answer to what I had been "asking" for.

Soon after encountering *Think and Grow Rich* in that Montana motel, I met a man in a motel in Minnesota who offered me a business opportunity that was so compatible with Hill's teachings that for nine joyous years I focused my attention on building that business. During those nine years, the business grew into a multimillion-dollar international enterprise. And in that relatively short time, my finances grew from just getting by (which was all I'd previously really wanted) to reaching all of my newly inspired financial goals.

What I learned from Hill's book worked so grandly for me that I began using that work as a "textbook" to share his success principles with my business associates. But, looking back, even though the teachings had worked extremely well for me, I became aware that only a couple of my associates had received the huge financial success that I had wanted all of them to have. And so, I began to search for another level of answers that might be more effective for a broader range of people.

As a result of my personal *Think and Grow Rich* experience, I became convinced that the achievement of success was something that could be *learned.* We didn't have to be born into a family who had already discovered how to make money. We didn't have to get good grades in school or know the right people or live in the right country or be the right size, color, gender, religion, and so on. . . . We simply had to learn a few simple principles and then consistently put them into practice.

However, not everyone gets the same message from the same words—or the same results from the same books. And so, as soon as I began "asking" for more understanding, Richard Bach's enlightening book *Illusions* happened to come into my awareness. And although *Illusions* brought me to one of the most thrilling "Aha!" days of my life and brought some concepts that began to open my mind for the phenomenon that I was about to experience, it contained no additional principles that I could consciously utilize in my business.

The next "accidental" discovery of an ultimately valuable book for me came while I was just killing some time in a Phoenix library. I wasn't "looking for" anything, but I happened to notice a book, high on a shelf, entitled *Seth Speaks*, by Jane Roberts and Robert F. Butts. Seth, "a Non-Physical Entity," had "dictated" through Jane a series of books, and I read them all. And as strange as that form of communication may have seemed to most (Esther was extremely uncomfortable with it at first), I had always tended to judge the trees by their fruits. And so, I looked beyond the "strange" aspects and focused on what to me were the positive, practical parts of the Seth material that I felt I could utilize to help others improve their life experience.

Seth had a different perspective on life than what I had heard previously expressed, and I was particularly interested in two of Seth's terms: "You Create Your Own Reality" and "Your Point of Power Is in the Present." Although as much as I read, I never felt that I truly understood those principles, I somehow knew that there were, within them, answers to my questions. However, Jane was no longer in physical form, so "Seth" was unavailable for any further clarification.

Through a series of fortuitous events—in a manner similar to the Seth-and-Jane experiences—Esther, my wife, began receiving the material that is now known as the *Teachings of Abraham*®. (Should you like to hear one of the original recordings detailing our introduction to Abraham, you can find our free *Introduction to*

Abraham recording as a 70-minute download at our Website: **www. abraham-hicks.com**, or from our office as a free CD.)

In 1985 when this phenomenon began with Esther, I could sense that this would bring the answers to my desire to better understand the *Laws of the Universe* and how we might be able to naturally, deliberately work in harmony with them in order to fulfill our purpose for being in physical form. And so, about 20 years ago, I sat with Esther and a small cassette tape recorder and plied Abraham with hundreds of questions on primarily 20 different subjects, mostly regarding practical spirituality. And then, as other people began hearing about Abraham and wanting to interact with us, we produced those 20 recordings and published them as two special-subjects albums.

Over the course of two decades, millions of people have become aware of the Teachings of Abraham as a result of our many books, tapes, CDs, videos, DVDs, group workshops, and radio and television appearances. Also, other best-selling authors soon began to use Abraham's teachings in their books and radio, television, and workshop appearances . . . and then, about two years ago, an Australian television producer approached us requesting permission to build a TV series around our work with Abraham. She joined us with her film crew on one of our Alaskan cruises, filmed the show, and then went in search of other students of our teachings whom she could incorporate into the (pilot) film—and the rest is (as they say) history.

The producer called her movie *The Secret,* and it featured the basic tenet of the Teachings of Abraham: the *Law of Attraction.* And although it wasn't picked up by the Australian network (Nine) as a series, the documentary went straight to the DVD format and was transcribed into a book . . . and now because of *The Secret,* the concept of the *Law of Attraction* has reached many more millions of people who have been asking for a better-feeling life.

This book has evolved from the transcription of five of our original recordings from over 20 years ago. This is the first time these transcriptions have been available in print. However, they're not word for word because Abraham has now gone through every page of the original transcriptions and modified every part that might be made easier for the reader to understand and to put into immediate practical use.

There's a saying in the teaching world: "Tell them what you're going to tell them. Then tell them. And then tell them what you told them." And so, should you decide to immerse yourself in these teachings, you'll probably notice much repetition as you move forward, because we usually learn best through repetition. You can't continue the same old habitual, limiting thought patterns and get new, unlimited results. But through simple, practiced repetition, you can, over time, comfortably develop new life-enhancing habits.

In the media world there's a saying: "People would rather be entertained than informed." Well, unless you're entertained by learning new ways of looking at life, you'll probably find this book more informative than entertaining. Rather than being like a novel that's read, enjoyed, and then set aside, this—more like a textbook on the principles of achieving and maintaining wealth, health, and happiness—is a book to be read and studied and put into practiced use.

I was led to this information by my desire to help others feel better, especially in the area of financial fulfillment, so I feel especially gratified that this *Money* book is now on its way to those who are asking the questions that it will answer.

This book, *Money, and the Law of Attraction,* is the second of four scheduled *Law of Attraction* books. Two years ago we published *The Law of Attraction: The Basics of the Teachings of Abraham.* Next will be *Relationships, and the Law of Attraction;* and the final book in the series will be *Spirituality, and the Law of Attraction.*

Revisiting this life-changing material in preparation for the publication of this book has been a delightful experience for Esther and me, for we've been reminded again of these basic and simple principles that Abraham discussed with us in the beginning of our interaction.

From the beginning, Esther and I have intended to apply to our lives what Abraham has been teaching. And our resulting joyous growth experience has been remarkable: After two decades of practicing these principles, Esther and I are still in love. (Even though we have just now completed building this new home in

California and are in the process of the construction of a new home on our Texas business complex, we enjoy being with each other so much that we will still spend most of next year traveling in our 45-foot-long Marathon motor coach from workshop to workshop.) We've had no medical examinations (or insurance) for 20 years. We're debt free, and will pay more income taxes this year than the sum of all the money we earned in all of our earning years before Abraham's guidance—and although neither all our money nor all of our good health can *make* us happy, Esther and I are still finding ways to be happy anyway.

And so, it is with extraordinary joy that we can tell you—from our own personal experience: *This works!*

ᥱᧁᥱᧁᥱᧁ ᥅᪶᥅᪶᥅᪶

(**Editor's Note:** Please note that since there aren't always physical English words to perfectly express the Non-Physical thoughts that Esther receives, she sometimes forms new combinations of words, as well as using standard words in new ways—for example, capitalizing them when normally they wouldn't be—in order to express new ways of looking at old ways of looking at life.)

Pivoting and the *Book* of *Positive Aspects*

Your Story, and the *Law of Attraction*

Each and every component that makes up your life experience is drawn to you by the powerful <u>Law of Attraction</u>'s response to the thoughts you think and the story you tell about your life. Your money and financial assets; your body's state of wellness, clarity, flexibility, size, and shape; your work environment, how you are treated, work satisfaction, and rewards—indeed, the very happiness of your life experience in general— is all happening because of the story that you tell. If you will let your dominant intention be to revise and improve the content of the story you tell every day of your life, it is our absolute promise to you that your life will become that ever-improving story. For by the powerful <u>Law of Attraction,</u> it must be!

Does Life Sometimes Seem to Be Unfair?

You have wanted more success and you have applied yourself well, doing everything that everyone said you should do, but the success you have been seeking has been slow to come. You tried very hard, especially at first, to learn all the right things, to be in the right places, to do the right things, to say the right things . . . but often things did not appear to be improving much at all.

Earlier in your life, when you were first dipping your toe into the idea of achieving success, you found satisfaction in satisfying the expectations of the others who were laying out the rules for success. The teachers, parents, and mentors who surrounded you seemed confident and convincing as they laid out their rules for success:

213

"Always be on time; always do your best; remember to work hard; always be honest; strive for greatness; go the extra mile; there's no gain without pain; and, most important, never give up. . . ."

But, over time, your finding satisfaction from gaining the approval of those who laid out those rules waned as their principles of success—no matter how hard you tried—did not yield you the promised results. And it was more disheartening still when you stood back to gain some perspective on the whole picture and realized that their principles were not, for the most part, bringing *them* real success either. And then, to make matters even worse, you began meeting others (who clearly were *not* following those rules) who *were* achieving success apart from the formula that you had been so diligent to learn and apply.

And so you found yourself asking: "What's going on here? How can those who are working so hard be receiving so little, while those who seem to be working so little are achieving so much? My expensive education hasn't paid off at all—and yet that multimillionaire dropped out of high school. My father worked hard every day of his life—and yet our family had to borrow the money to pay for his funeral. . . . Why doesn't my hard work pay off for me the way it was supposed to? Why do so few really get rich, while most of us struggle to barely get by? What am I missing? What do those financially successful people know that I don't know?"

Is "Doing Your Best" Still Not Enough?

When you are doing everything you can think of, truly trying your best to do what you have been told is supposed to bring you success, and success does not come, it is easy to feel defensive, and eventually even angry at those who are displaying evidence of the success you desire. You even find yourself sometimes condemning their success simply because it is too painful to watch them living the success that continues to elude you. And it is for this reason—in response to this chronic condition in the financial affairs of your culture—that we offer this book.

When you come to the place of openly condemning the financial success that you crave, not only can that financial success never come to you, but you are also forfeiting your God-given rights to your health and happiness as well.

Many actually come to the incorrect conclusion that others in their physical environment have banded together in some sort of conspiracy to keep them from succeeding. For they believe, with all of their heart, that they have done everything possible to achieve success, and the fact that it has not come must surely mean that there are some unfriendly forces at work that are depriving them of what they desire. But we want to assure you that nothing like that is at the heart of the absence of what you desire or of the presence of things you would like to remove from your experience. No one ever has or ever could have prevented your success—or provided it. Your success is all up to you. It is all in your control. And we are writing this book so that now, finally, once and for all time, your success can be in your deliberate and conscious control.

Whatever I Can Desire, I Can Achieve

It is time for you to return to the true nature of your Being and to consciously live the success that the experiencing of your own life has helped you determine that you desire. And so, as you deliberately relax right now, breathing deeply and reading steadily, you will begin to gradually but surely remember how all success comes, for you already inherently understand it, and so you will certainly feel resonance with these absolute truths as you read about them here.

The Eternal *Laws of the Universe* are consistent and reliable and steadily hold, always, the promise of expansion and joy. They are being presented to you here in a powerful rhythm of understanding that will start small within you and then expand with each page you read, until you reawaken into the knowledge of your purpose and your own personal power as you remember how to access the power of the Universe that creates worlds.

If this time-space reality has within it the ability to inspire a desire within you, it is absolute that this time-space reality has the ability to yield you a full and satisfying manifestation of that same desire. It is Law.

To Achieve Success Is My Natural Birthright

Most people naturally assume that if their life is not going the way they want it to go, something outside of themselves must be preventing the improvement, for no one would deliberately hold their own success away. But while pointing the blame at others may feel better than assuming responsibility for unwanted conditions, there is a very big negative repercussion to believing that something outside of you is the reason for your own lack of success: *When you give the credit or the blame to another for your success or lack of it—you are powerless to make any change.*

When you desire success, but—from your perspective—you are not currently experiencing it, at many deep levels of your Being you recognize that something is wrong. And as this strong feeling of personal discord magnifies your awareness that you are not getting what you want, it often sets into motion other counterproductive assumptions that evoke jealousy toward those who *are* having more success; resentment at a myriad of people you would like to blame for your lack of success; or even self-denigration, which is the most painful and counterproductive assumption of all. And we submit that this uncomfortable upheaval is not only normal, but it is the perfect response to your feeling a lack of success.

Your emotional discomfort is a powerful indicator that something is very wrong. You are meant to succeed, and failure *should* feel bad to you. You are meant to be well, and sickness *should not* be accepted. You are supposed to expand, and stagnation *is* intolerable. Life is supposed to go well for you—and when it does not, there *is* something wrong.

But what is wrong is not that an injustice has occurred, or that the gods of good fortune are not focusing on you, or that someone else has received the success that should have been yours. What is wrong is that you are out of harmony with your own Being, with *who-you-really-are*, with what life has caused you to ask for, with what you have expanded to, and with the ever-consistent *Laws of the Universe. What is wrong is not something that is outside of you over which you have no control. What is wrong is within you—and you <u>do</u> have control. And taking control is not difficult to do once you understand the basis of <u>who-you-are</u> and the basics of the <u>Law of Attraction</u> and the value of your personal <u>Emotional Guidance System</u> that you were born with, which is always active, ever present, and easy to understand.*

Money Is Not the Root of Evil or of Happiness

This important subject of *money* and *financial success* is not the "root of all evil" as many have quoted—nor is it the path to happiness. However, because the subject of money touches most of you in one way or another hundreds or even thousands of times in every day, it is a large factor in your vibrational makeup and in your personal point of attraction. So when you are able to successfully control something that affects most of you all day, every day, you will have accomplished something rather significant. In other words, because such a high percentage of your thoughts in any given day reside around the topic of money or financial success, as soon as you are able to *deliberately* guide your thoughts, not only is it certain that your financial success must improve, but the evidence of *that* success will then prepare you for deliberate improvement in *every* aspect of your life experience.

If you are a student of *Deliberate Creation,* if you want to consciously create your own reality, if you desire control of your own life experience, if you want to fulfill your reason for being, then your understanding of these prevalent topics—*money and the <u>Law of Attraction</u>*—will serve you enormously well.

I Am the Attractor of My Every Experience

You are meant to live an expansive, exhilarating, good-feeling experience. It was your plan when you made the decision to become focused in your physical body in this time-space reality. You expected this physical life to be exciting and rewarding. In other words, you knew that the variety and contrast would stimulate you to expanded desires, and you also knew that any and all of those desires could be fully and easily realized by you. You knew, also, that there would be no end to the expansion of new desires.

You came into your body full of excitement about the possibilities that this life experience would inspire, and that desire that you held in the beginning was not muted at all by trepidation or doubt, for you knew your power and you knew that this life experience and all of its contrast would be the fertile ground for wonderful expansion. *Most of all, you knew that you were coming into this life experience with a* <u>Guidance System</u> *to help you remain true to your original intent as well as to your never-ending amended intentions that would be born out of this very life experience. In short, you felt an eagerness for this time-space reality that nearly defies physical description.*

You were not a beginner—even though you were newly beginning in your wee, small physical body—but instead you were a powerful creative genius, newly focusing in a new, Leading Edge environment. You knew that there would be a time of adjustment while redefining a new platform from which you would begin your process of deliberate creating, and you were not the least bit worried about that time of adjustment. In fact, you rather enjoyed the nest into which you were born and those who were there to greet you into your new physical environment. And while you could not yet speak the language of their words—and although you were perceived by those who greeted you as new and unknowing and in need of their guidance—you possessed a stability and a knowing that most of them had long left behind.

You were born knowing that you are a powerful Being, that you are good, that you are the creator of your experience, and that the *Law of Attraction* is the basis of all creation here in your new environment. You remembered then that the *Law of Attraction* (the essence of that which is like unto itself, is drawn) is the basis of the Universe, and you knew it would serve you well. And so it has.

You were still remembering then that you are the creator of your own experience. But even more important, you remembered that you do it through your *thought, not your action.* You were not uncomfortable being a small infant who offered no action or words, for you remembered the Well-Being of the Universe; you remembered your intentions in coming forth into your physical body, and you knew that there would be plenty of time for acclimating to the language and ways of your new environment; and, most of all, you knew that even though you would not be able to translate your vast knowledge from your Non-Physical environment directly into physical words and descriptions, it would not matter, for the most important things to set you on a path of joyful creation were already emphatically in place: You knew that the *Law of Attraction* was consistently present and that your *Guidance System* was immediately active. And, most of all, you knew that by trial, and what some may call "error," you would eventually become completely and consciously reoriented in your new environment.

I Knew of the Consistency of the *Law of Attraction*

The fact that the *Law of Attraction* remains constant and stable throughout the Universe was a big factor in your confidence as you came into your new physical environment, for you knew that the feedback of life would help you to remember and gain your footing. You remembered that the basis of everything is *vibration* and that the *Law of Attraction* responds to those vibrations and, in essence, organizes them, bringing things of like vibrations together while holding those not of like vibrations apart.

And so, you were not concerned about not being able to articulate that knowledge right away or to explain it to those around you who had seemingly forgotten everything they knew about it, because you knew that the consistency of this powerful *Law* would, soon enough, show itself to you through the examples of your own life. You knew then that it would not be difficult to figure out what kinds of vibrations you were offering because the *Law of Attraction* would be bringing to you constant evidence of whatever your vibration was.

In other words, when you feel *overwhelmed,* circumstances and people who could help you get out from under your feeling of overwhelment cannot find you, nor can you find them. Even when you try hard to find them, you cannot. And those people who *do* come do not help you, but, instead, they add to your feeling of overwhelment.

When you feel *mistreated*—fairness cannot find you. Your perception of your mistreatment, and the subsequent vibration that you offer because of your perception, prevents anything that you would consider to be fair from coming to you.

When you are buried in the *disappointment* or *fear* of not having the financial resources that you believe you need, the dollars—or the opportunities that would bring the dollars—continue to elude you . . . not because you are bad or unworthy, but because the *Law of Attraction* matches things that are like, not things that are *unlike*.

When you feel *poor*—only things that feel like *poverty* can come to you. When you feel *prosperous*—only things that feel like *prosperity* can come to you. This *Law* is consistent; and if you will pay attention, it will teach you, through life experience, how it works. *When you remember that you get the essence of what you think about—and then you notice what you are getting—you have the keys for Deliberate Creation.*

What Do We Mean by *Vibration?*

When we speak of *vibration,* we are actually calling your attention to the basis of your experience, for everything is actually *vibrationally* based. We could use the word *Energy* interchangeably, and there are many other synonyms in your vocabulary that accurately apply.

Most understand the vibrational characteristics of sound. Sometimes when the deep, rich bass notes of your musical instrumentation are played loudly, you can even *feel* the vibrational nature of sound.

We want you to understand that whenever you "hear" something, you are interpreting vibration into the sound you are hearing. What you hear is *your* interpretation of vibration; what you hear is your *unique* interpretation of vibration. Each of your physical senses of seeing, hearing, tasting, smelling, and touching exist because everything in the Universe is vibrating and your physical senses are reading the vibrations and giving you sensory perception of the vibrations.

So as you come to understand that you live in a pulsating, vibrating Universe of advanced harmonics, and that at the very core of your Being you are vibrating at what could only be described as perfection in vibrational balance and harmony, then you begin to understand *vibration* in the way we are projecting it.

Everything that exists, in your air, in your dirt, in your water, and in your bodies, is vibration in motion—and all of it is managed by the powerful <u>*Law of Attraction.*</u>

You could not sort it out if you wanted to. And there is no need for you to sort it out, because the *Law of Attraction* is doing the sorting, continually bringing things of like vibrations together while things of different vibrational natures are being repelled.

Your emotions, which really are the most powerful and important of your six physical vibrational interpreters, give you constant feedback about the harmonics of your current thoughts (vibrations) as they compare with the harmonics of your core vibrational state.

The Non-Physical world is vibration.

The physical world that you know is vibration.

There is nothing that exists outside of this vibrational nature.

There is nothing that is not managed by the *Law of Attraction.*

Your understanding of vibration will help you to consciously bridge both worlds.

You do not have to understand your complex optic nerve or your primary visual cortex in order to see. You do not have to understand electricity to be able to turn on the light, and you do not have to understand vibrations in order to feel the difference between harmony or discord.

As you learn to accept your vibrational nature, and begin to consciously utilize your emotional vibrational indicators, you will gain conscious control of your personal creations and of the outcomes of your life experience.

Whenever I Feel Abundant, Abundance Finds Me

When you make the conscious correlation between what you have been feeling and what is actualizing in your life experience, now you are empowered to make changes. If you are not making that correlation, and so continue to offer thoughts of lack about things you want, the things you want will continue to elude you.

People, often, in this misunderstanding begin to assign power to things outside of themselves in order to explain why they are not thriving in the way they would like: "I'm not thriving because I was born into the wrong environment. I'm not thriving because my parents didn't thrive, so they couldn't teach me how to do it. I'm not thriving because those people over there are thriving, and they're taking the resources that should have been mine. I'm not thriving because I was cheated, because I'm not worthy, because I didn't live the right way in a past life, because my government ignores my rights, because my husband doesn't do his part . . . because, because, because."

And we want to remind you, your "not thriving" is only because you are offering a vibration that is different from the vibration of thriving. *You cannot feel poor (and vibrate poor) and thrive. Abundance cannot find you unless you offer a vibration of abundance.*

Many ask, "But if I'm not thriving, then how in the world can I offer a vibration of thriving? Don't I have to thrive before I can offer the vibration of thriving?" We agree that it is certainly easy to maintain a condition of thriving when it is already in your experience, because then all you have to do is notice the good that is coming and your observation of it will keep it coming. But if you are standing in the absence of something you want, you must find a way to feel the essence of it—even before it comes—or it cannot come.

You cannot let your vibrational offering come only in response to *what-is* and then ever change *what-is*. You must find a way of *feeling* the excitement or satisfaction of your currently unrealized dreams before those dreams can become your reality. Find a way to deliberately imagine a scenario for the purpose of offering a vibration and for the purpose of the *Law of Attraction* matching your vibration with a real-life manifestation. . . . *When you ask for the manifestation prior to the vibration, you ask the impossible. When you are willing to offer the vibration before the manifestation—all things are possible. It is Law.*

Rather Than by Default, Live Life Deliberately

We are giving this book to you to remind you of things you already know at some level, so as to reactivate that vibrational knowledge within you. It is not possible for you to read these words, which represent the knowledge that you hold from your Broader Perspective, without a recognition of this knowledge beginning to surface from within.

This really is the time of awakening—the time of remembering your personal power and your reason for being. So take a deep breath, make an effort to get comfortable, and slowly read the contents of this book to restore yourself to your original vibrational essence. . . .

So here you are, in a wonderful state of being: no longer an infant under the control of others, somewhat acclimated into your physical environment, and now—by reading this book—returning to the recognition of the full power of your Being . . . no longer buffeted around by the *Law of Attraction* like a small cork on a raging sea, but finally remembering and gaining control of your own destiny, finally and *deliberately* guiding your life within the powerful *Law of Attraction* rather than responding in an attitude of default and just taking life as it comes. *In order to do that, you have to tell a different story. You have to begin to tell the story of your life as you now want it to be and discontinue the tales of how it has been or of how it is.*

Tell the Story You Want to Experience

To live deliberately, you have to think deliberately; and in order to do that, you must have a reference point in order to determine the correct direction of your thought. Right now, just as at the time of your birth, the two necessary factors are in place. The *Law of Attraction* (the most powerful and consistent *Law* in the Universe) abounds. And your *Guidance System* is within you, all queued up and ready to give you directional feedback. *You have only one seemingly small but potentially life-changing thing to do: <u>You have to begin telling your story in a new way. You have to tell it as you want it to be.</u>*

As you tell the story of your life (and you do it nearly all day, every day with your words, your thoughts, and your actions), you have to feel good while you tell it. *In every moment, about every subject, you can focus positively or negatively, for in every particle of the Universe—in every moment in time and beyond—there is that which is wanted and the lack of what is wanted pulsing there for you to choose between.* And as these constant choices reveal themselves to you, you have the option of focusing upon what you want or the lack of it regarding every subject, because every subject is really two subjects: what you want or the absence of what you want. You can tell, by the way you feel, which choice you are currently focused upon—and you can change your choice constantly.

Every Subject Is Really Two Subjects

The following are some examples to help you see how every subject is really two subjects:

Abundance/Poverty (absence of abundance)
Health/Illness (absence of health)
Happiness/Sadness (absence of happiness)
Clarity/Confusion (absence of clarity)
Energetic/Tired (absence of Energy)
Knowledge/Doubt (absence of knowledge)
Interested/Bored (absence of interest)

I can do that/I can't do that
I want to buy that/I can't afford that
I want to feel good/I don't feel good
I want more money/I don't have enough money
I want more money/I don't know how to get more money
I want more money/That person is getting more money than
    his/her share
I want to be slender/I am fat
I want a new car/My car is old
I want a lover/I don't have a lover

As you read this list, it is undoubtedly obvious to you which we consider to be the better choice in each example, but there is a simple and important thing that you may be forgetting. There is a tendency as you read a list such as this to feel a need to state the factual truth about the subject ("tell it like it is") rather than make the statement of what you desire. That tendency alone is responsible for more miscreating and more personal disallowing of wanted things than all other things put together, and so, the examples and exercises offered in this book are given to help you orient yourself toward what is *wanted,* not to explain what already *is. You have to begin telling a different story if you want the <u>Law of Attraction</u> to bring you different things.*

What Is the Story I'm Now Telling?

A very effective way to begin to tell that new story is to listen to the things that you are now saying throughout your day, and when you catch yourself in the middle of a statement that is contrary to what you want, stop and say, "Well, I clearly know what it is that I *don't* want. What is it that I *do* want?" Then deliberately and emphatically make your statement of desire.

I hate this ugly, old, unreliable car.
I want a pretty, new, reliable car.

I'm fat.
I want to be slender.

My employer doesn't appreciate me.
I want to be appreciated by my employer.

Many would protest, claiming that a simple rewording of a sentence will not make a shiny new car appear in your driveway, or change your fat body to one that is slender, or cause your employer to suddenly change her personality and begin to treat you differently—but they would be wrong. When you deliberately focus upon any desired subject, often proclaiming it to be as you *want* it to be, in time you experience an actual shift in the way you feel about the subject, which indicates a vibrational shift.

When your vibration shifts, your point of attraction shifts, and, by the powerful Law of Attraction, your manifestational evidence or indicator must shift, also. You cannot talk consistently of the things you do want to experience in your life without the Universe delivering the essence of them to you.

The *Pivoting Process* Can Reorient My Life

The *Process of Pivoting* is a conscious recognition that every subject is really two subjects, and then a deliberate speaking or thinking about the *desired* aspect of the subject. *Pivoting* will help you activate within yourself the aspects that you desire regarding all subjects; and once you accomplish that, the essence of the things that you desire, on all subjects, must come into your experience.

There is an important clarification that we must make here: If you are using words that speak of something that you desire while at the same time you are feeling *doubt* about your own words, your *words* are not bringing you what you want, because the way you are *feeling* is the true indication of the creative direction of your thought-vibration. *The Law of Attraction is not responding to your words but to the vibration that is emanating from you.*

However, since you cannot speak of what you *do* want and what you *do not* want at the same time, the more you speak of what you *do* want, the less frequently you will be speaking of what you *do not* want. And if you are serious about telling it like you want it to be rather than like it is, you will, in time (and usually a rather short time), change the balance of your vibration. If you speak it often enough, you will come to feel what you speak.

But there is something even more significantly powerful about this *Process of Pivoting: When life seems to have you negatively oriented toward the lack of something you want, and when you make the statement "I know what I do not want; what is it that I do want?" the answer to that question is summoned from within you, and in that very moment the beginning of a vibrational shift occurs. Pivoting is a powerful tool that will instantly improve your life.*

I Am the Creator of My Life Experience

You are the creator of your own life experience, and as the creator of your experience, it is important to understand that it is not by virtue of your action, not by virtue of your doing—it is not even by virtue of what you are saying—that you are creating. You are creating by virtue of the thought that you are offering.

You cannot speak or offer action without thought-vibration occurring at the same time; however, you are often offering a thought-vibration without offering words or action. Children or babies learn to mimic the vibration of the adults who surround them long before they learn to mimic their words.

Every thought that you think has its own vibrational frequency. Each thought that you offer, whether it has come to you out of your memory, whether it is an influence from another, or whether it is a thought that has become the combination of something *you* have been thinking and something that *another* has been thinking— every thought that you are pondering in your *now*—is vibrating at a very personal frequency . . . and by the powerful *Law of Attraction* (the essence of that which is like unto itself, is drawn), that thought is now attracting another thought that is its Vibrational Match. And now, those combined thoughts are vibrating at a frequency that is higher than the thought that came before; and they will now, by the *Law of Attraction,* attract another and another and another, until eventually the thoughts will be powerful enough to attract a "real life" situation or manifestation.

All people, circumstances, events, and situations are attracted to you by the power of the thoughts that you are thinking. Once you understand that you are literally thinking or vibrating things into being, you may discover a new resolve within you to more deliberately direct your own thoughts.

Aligned Thoughts Are Thoughts That Feel Good

Many people believe that there is more to their Beingness than what is represented in their physical reality as the flesh, blood, and bone person they know themselves to be. As people grapple with ways to label this larger part of themselves, they use words such as *Soul, Source,* or *God.* We refer to that larger, older, wiser part of you as your *Inner Being,* but the label that you choose to describe this Eternal part of you is not important. What is extremely significant is that you understand that the larger *You* does, and will eternally, exist and plays a very large part in the experience that you are living here on planet Earth.

Every thought, word, or deed that you offer is played against the backdrop of that Broader Perspective. Indeed, the reason that in any moment of clearly knowing what you *do not* want, you emphatically then realize what it is that you *do* want is because that larger part of you is giving its undivided attention to what you *do* want.

As you make a conscious effort to guide your thoughts, day by day, more in the direction of what you *do* want, you will begin to feel better and better because the vibration that is activated by your improved-feeling thought will be a closer match to the vibration of the larger Non-Physical part of you. Your desire to think thoughts that feel good will guide you into alignment with the Broader Perspective of your *Inner Being.* In fact, it is not possible for you to really feel good in any moment unless the thoughts you are thinking right now are a Vibrational Match to the thoughts of your *Inner Being.*

For example, your *Inner Being* focuses upon your value—when you identify some flaw in yourself, the negative emotion that you feel is about that vibrational discord or resistance. Your *Inner Being* chooses to focus only upon things about which it can feel love—when you are focusing upon some aspect of someone or something that you abhor, you have focused yourself out of vibrational alignment with your *Inner Being.* Your *Inner Being* focuses only upon your success—when you choose to see something you are doing as failure, you are out of alignment with the perspective of your *Inner Being.*

Seeing My World Through the Eyes of Source

By choosing better-feeling thoughts and by speaking more of what you *do* want and less of what you *do not* want, you will gently tune yourself to the vibrational frequency of your broader, wiser *Inner Being.* To be in vibrational alignment with that Broader Perspective while living your own physical life experience is truly the best of all worlds because as you achieve vibrational alignment with that Broader Perspective, you then see your world from that Broader Perspective. *To see your world through the eyes of Source is truly the most spectacular view of life, for from that vibrational vantage point, you are in alignment with—and therefore in the process of attracting— only what you would consider to be the very best of your world.*

Esther, the woman who translates the vibration of Abraham into the spoken or written word, does so by relaxing and deliberately allowing the vibration of her own Being to raise until it harmonizes with the Non-Physical vibration of Abraham. She has been doing this for many years now, and it has become a very natural thing for her to do. She has long understood the advantage of aligning her vibration so that she could effectively translate our knowledge for other physical friends, but she had not really understood another wonderful benefit of that alignment until one beautiful spring morning when she walked down the driveway by herself to open the gate for her mate, who would eventually follow in the automobile.

As she stood there waiting, she gazed up into the sky and found it to be more beautiful than it had ever appeared before: It was rich in color, and the contrast of the brilliant blue sky and the strikingly white clouds was amazing to her. She could hear the sweet songs of birds that were so far away she could not see them, but their beautiful sound made her shiver with excitement as she heard them. They sounded as if they were right above her head or sitting on her shoulder. And then she became aware of many different delicious fragrances flowing from plants and flowers and earth, moving in the wind and enveloping her. She felt alive and happy and in love with her beautiful world. And she said right out loud, "There can never have been, in all of the Universe, a more beautiful moment in time than this, right here, right now!"

And then she said, "Abraham, it is *you*, isn't it?" And we smiled a very broad smile through her lips, for she had caught us peeping through her eyes, hearing through her ears, smelling through her nose, feeling through her skin.

"Indeed," we said, "we are enjoying the deliciousness of your physical world through your physical body."

Those moments in your life when you feel absolute exhilaration are moments of complete alignment with the Source within you. Those moments when you feel powerful attraction to an idea, or keen interest, are also moments of complete alignment. In fact, the better you feel, the more in alignment you are with your Source—with *who-you-really-are*.

This alignment with your Broader Perspective will not only allow you faster achievement of the big things that you want in life—like wonderful relationships, satisfying careers, and the resources to do the things you really want to do—but this conscious alignment will enhance every moment of your day. *As you tune yourself to the perspective of your Inner Being, your days will be filled with wonderful moments of clarity, satisfaction, and love. And that is truly the way you intended to live while here in this wonderful place, this wonderful time, and this wonderful body.*

I Can Deliberately Choose to Feel Better

The reason that Esther was able to allow that fuller perspective of Abraham to flow through her, providing her with such a delicious experience, was because she had begun that day by looking for reasons to feel good. She looked for the first thing to feel good about while she was still lying in her bed, and that good-feeling thought attracted another and another and another and another and another, until by the time she reached the gate (which was approximately two hours later), by virtue of her *deliberate* choice of thoughts, she had brought her vibrational frequency to a level that was close enough to matching that of her *Inner Being* that her *Inner Being* was able to easily interact with her.

Not only does the thought you are choosing right now attract the next thought and the next . . . and so on—it also provides the basis of your alignment with your Inner Being. As you consistently and deliberately think and speak more of what you do want and less of what you do not want, you will find yourself more often in alignment with the pure, positive essence of your own Source; and under those conditions, your life will be extremely pleasing to you.

Could Illness Be Caused by Negative Emotion?

Esther's experience at the gate was dramatically enhanced by her vibrational alignment with her Source and therefore with absolute Well-Being. But it is also possible for you to experience the opposite of that enhanced experience if you are *out* of alignment with Source and Well-Being. In other words, sickness or illness, or lack of Well-Being, occurs when you vibrationally disallow your alignment with Well-Being.

Whenever you experienced *negative emotion (fear, doubt, frustration, loneliness,* and so on), that feeling of negative emotion was the result of your thinking a thought that did not vibrate at a frequency that was in harmony with your *Inner Being.* Through all of your life experiences—physical and Non-Physical—your *Inner Being,* or the *Total You,* has evolved to a place of *knowing.* And so, whenever you are consciously focused upon a thought that does not harmonize with that which your *Inner Being* has come to know—the resultant feeling within you will be one of negative emotion.

If you were to sit on your foot and cut off the circulation of the flow of blood, or if you were to put a tourniquet around your neck and restrict the flow of oxygen, you would feel immediate evidence of the restriction. And, in like manner, when you think thoughts that are not in harmony with the thoughts of your *Inner Being,* the flow of *Life Force,* or *Energy,* that comes into your physical body is stifled or restricted—and the result of that restriction is that you feel negative emotion. *When you allow that negative emotion to continue over a long period of time, you often experience deterioration of your physical body.*

Remember, every subject is really two subjects: *what is wanted* or *lack of what is wanted.* It is like picking up a stick with two ends: One end represents what you *do* want; the other end represents what you *do not* want. So the stick called "Physical Well-Being" has "wellness" on one end and "illness" on the other. However, people do not experience "illness" only because they are looking at the negative end of the "Physical Well-Being" stick, but because they have been looking at the "I know what I *don't* want" end of many, *many* sticks.

When *your* chronic attention is upon things that you *do not* want—while the chronic attention of your *Inner Being* is upon the things that you *do* want—over time, you cause a vibrational separation between you and your *Inner Being,* and that is what all illness is: separation (caused by your choice of thoughts) between *you* and your *Inner Being.*

Pivot from Feeling Bad to Feeling Good

Everyone wants to feel good, but most people believe that everything around them needs to be pleasing to them *before* they can feel good. In fact, most people feel the way they do in any moment in time because of something they are observing. If what they are observing pleases them, they feel good, but if what they are observing does not please them, they feel bad. Most people feel quite powerless about consistently feeling good because they believe that in order to feel good, the conditions around them must change, but they also believe that they do not have the power to change many of the conditions.

However, once you understand that every subject really is two subjects—what is wanted and lack of it—you can learn to see more of the positive aspects of whatever you are giving your attention to. *That really is all that the* Process of Pivoting *is: deliberately looking for a more positive way—a better-feeling way—to approach whatever you are giving your attention to.*

When you are facing an unwanted condition and are therefore feeling bad, if you will deliberately say, "I know what I *do not* want . . . what is it that I *do* want?" the vibration of your Being, which is affected by your point of focus, will shift slightly, causing your point of attraction to shift, also. This is the way that you begin telling a different story about your life. Rather than saying, "I never have enough money," you say instead, "I'm looking forward to having more money." That is a very different story—a very different vibration and a very different feeling, which will, in time, bring you a very different result.

As you continue to ask yourself, from your ever-changing vantage point, "What is it that I do *want?" eventually you will be standing in a very pleasing place—for you cannot continually ask yourself what it is that you* do *want without your point of attraction beginning to shift in that direction. . . . The process will be gradual, but your continued application of the process will yield wonderful results in only a few days.*

Am I in Harmony with My Desire?

So the *Pivoting Process* is simply: Whenever you recognize that you are feeling a negative emotion (it is really that you are feeling the lack of harmony with something that you want), the obvious thing for you to do is to stop and say, *I'm feeling negative emotion, which means I am not in harmony with something that I want. What do I want?*

Anytime that you are feeling negative emotion, you are in a very good position to identify what it is that you are, in that moment, wanting—because never are you clearer about what you *do want* than when you are experiencing what you *do not want.* And so, stop, in that moment, and say: *Something is important here; otherwise, I would not be feeling this negative emotion. What is it that I want?* And then simply turn your attention to what you do want. . . . *In the moment you turn your attention to what you want, the negative attraction will stop; and in the moment the negative attraction stops, the positive attraction will begin. And—in that moment—your feeling will change from not feeling good to feeling good. That is the <u>Process of Pivoting.</u>*

What Do I Want, and *Why?*

Perhaps the strongest resistance that people have to beginning to tell a different story about their own life is their belief that they should always speak "the truth" about where they are or that they should "tell it like it is." But when you understand that the *Law of Attraction* is responding to you while you are telling your story of "how it is"—and therefore is perpetuating more of whatever story you are telling—you may decide that it really is in your best interest to tell a different story, a story that more closely matches what you would *now* like to live. When you acknowledge what you *do not* want, and then ask yourself, "What is it that I *do* want?" you begin a gradual shift into the telling of your new story and into a much-improved point of attraction.

It is always helpful to remember that you get the essence of what you think about—whether you want it or not—because the <u>Law of Attraction</u> is unerringly consistent. Therefore, you are never only telling the story of "how it is now." You are also telling the story of the future experience that you are creating right now.

Sometimes people misunderstand what the *Process of Pivoting* is, as they incorrectly assume that *to pivot* means to look at something *unwanted* and try to convince themselves that it *is* wanted. They think that we are asking them to look at something that they clearly believe is *wrong* and to pronounce it *right*, or that it is a way of kidding themselves into accepting some unwanted thing. But you are never in a position where you can *kid* yourself into feeling better about something, because the way you feel is the way you feel, and the way you feel is always a result of the thought that you have chosen.

It is really a wonderful thing that, through the process of living life and noticing the things around you that you *do not want*, you are then able to come to clear conclusions about what you *do* want. And when you care about how you feel, you can easily apply the *Process of Pivoting* to direct your attention toward more of the *wanted* aspects, and less of the *unwanted* aspects, of life. And then, as the *Law of Attraction* responds to your increasingly improved, better-feeling thoughts, you will notice your own life experience transforming to match more of those *wanted* aspects, while the *unwanted* aspects gradually fade out of your experience.

When you deliberately apply the Process of Pivoting, which means you are deliberately choosing your own thoughts, which means you are deliberately choosing your vibrational point of attraction, you are also deliberately choosing how your life unfolds. Pivoting is the process of deliberately focusing your attention with the intent of directing your own life experience.

I Can Feel Better Right Now

People often complain that it would be much easier for them to focus on something positive if it were already happening in their life experience. They accurately acknowledge that it is much easier to feel good about something when something good is already happening. We certainly do not disagree that it is easier to feel good while noticing things you believe are good. But if you believe that you only have the ability to focus upon what *is* happening, and if what *is* happening is not pleasing, then you could wait an entire lifetime because your attention to *unwanted* things is preventing *wanted* things from coming to you.

You do not have to wait for a good thing to happen in order to feel good, for you have the ability to direct your thoughts toward improved things no matter what is currently present in your experience. And when you care about how you feel and you are willing to pivot and turn your attention toward better-feeling thoughts, you will quickly begin the positive, deliberate transformation of your life.

Things that are coming into your experience are coming in response to your vibration. Your vibration is offered because of the thoughts you are thinking, and you can tell by the way you feel what kinds of thoughts you are thinking. Find good-feeling thoughts and good-feeling manifestations must follow.

Many people say, "It would be so much easier for me to be happy if I were in a different place: if my relationship were better, if my mate were easier to live with, if my physical body didn't hurt or if my body looked different, if my work was more fulfilling, if I only had more money. . . . If the conditions of my life were better, I would feel better, and then it would be easier for me to be thinking more positive thoughts."

Seeing pleasing things does feel good, and it is easier to feel good when a pleasing thing is there, obvious for you to see—but you cannot ask others around you to orchestrate only pleasing things for you to see. Expecting others to provide the perfect environment for you is not a good idea, for many reasons: (1) It is not their responsibility to feather your nest; (2) it is not possible for them to control conditions you have created around you; and (3) most important of all, you would be giving up your power to create your own experience.

Make a decision to look for the best-feeling aspects of whatever you must give your attention to, and otherwise look only for good-feeling things to give your attention to—and your life will become one of increasingly good-feeling aspects.

Attention to Unwanted Attracts More Unwanted

For every pleasing thing, there is an unpleasing counterpart, for within every particle of the Universe is that which is wanted as well as the lack of that which is wanted. When you focus upon an unwanted aspect of something in an effort to push it away from you, instead it only comes closer, because you get what you give your attention to whether it is something that you want or not.

You live in a Universe that is based on "inclusion." In other words, there is no such thing as "exclusion" in this "inclusion-based" Universe. When you see something that you desire and you say yes to it, that is the equivalent of saying, "Yes, this thing that I desire, please *come to me.*" When you see something that you do not want and you shout no at it, that is the equivalent of saying, "*Come to me,* this thing that I do not want!"

Within everything that surrounds you is *that which is wanted* and *that which is unwanted.* It is up to you to focus upon what is wanted. See your environment as a buffet of many choices, and make more deliberate choices about what you think about. If you will try to make choices that feel good to you, as you make an effort to tell a different story about your life and the people and experiences that are in it, you will see your life begin to transform to match the essence of the details of the new-and-improved story you are now telling.

Am I Focused upon the Wanted or the Unwanted?

Sometimes you believe that you are focused upon what you want when actually the opposite is true. Just because your words sound positive, or your lips are smiling while you say them, does not mean that you are vibrating on the positive end of the stick. It is only by being aware of the way you are *feeling* while offering your words that you can be sure that you are, in fact, offering a vibration about what you *do* want, rather than what you *do not* want.

Focus on the Solution, Not the Problem

In the midst of what the television weatherman was calling "a serious drought," our friend Esther walked down one of the paths

237

on their Texas Hill Country property, noticing the dryness of the grass and feeling real concern for the well-being of the beautiful trees and bushes that were all beginning to show signs of stress from the shortage of rain. She noticed that the birdbath was empty even though she had filled it with water just a few hours earlier, and then she thought about the thirsty deer who had probably jumped the fence to drink the small amount of water that it held. And so, as she was pondering the direness of the situation, she stopped, looked upward, and—in a very positive voice, with very positive-sounding words—said, "Abraham, I want some rain."

And we said immediately back to her, "Indeed, from this position of lack, you think you will get rain?"

"What am I doing wrong?" she asked.

And we asked, *"Why* do you want the rain?"

And Esther answered, "I want it because it refreshes the earth. I want it because it gives all of the creatures in the bushes water so that they have enough to drink. I want it because it makes the grass green, and it feels good upon my skin, and it makes us all feel better."

And we said, "Now, you are attracting rain."

Our question *"Why* do you want the rain?" helped Esther withdraw her attention from the *problem* and turn her attention toward the *solution.* When you consider *why* you want something, your vibration usually shifts or *pivots* in the direction of your desire. Whenever you consider *how* it will happen, or *when,* or *who* will bring it, your vibration usually then shifts back toward the problem.

You see, in the process of taking her attention from what was wrong—by our asking her *why* she wanted the rain—she accomplished a *pivot.* She began thinking not only of *what* she wanted, but *why* she wanted it; and in the process, she began to feel better. That afternoon it rained, and that night the local weatherman reported "an unusual isolated thunderstorm in the Hill Country."

Your thoughts are powerful, and you have much more control over your own experience than most of you realize.

What I *Do* Want Is to Feel Good

A young father found himself at his wit's end because his young son was wetting the bed every night. Not only was this father frustrated about the physical disruption of finding wet bedding and clothing every morning, but he was concerned about the emotional ramifications of this continuing for such a long time. And, frankly, he was embarrassed by his son's behavior. "He's too big for this," he complained to us.

We asked, "When you come into the bedroom in the morning, what happens?"

"Well, as soon as I walk into his room, I can tell by the odor that he has wet the bed again," he answered.

"And how do you feel at that point?" we asked.

"Helpless, angry, frustrated. This has been going on for a long time, and I don't know what to do about it."

"What do you say to your son?"

"I tell him to get out of those wet clothes and get into the bathtub. I tell him he's too big for this and that we've talked about it before."

We told this father that he was actually perpetuating bed-wetting. We explained: *When the way you feel is controlled by a condition, you can never influence a change in the condition; but when you are able to control the way you feel within a condition, then you have the power to influence change in the condition.* For example, when you enter your son's bedroom and become aware that something that you do not want to happen has happened, if you would stop for a moment to acknowledge the thing that has happened that you *do not want*—asking yourself what it is that you *do* want and then further enforcing that side of the pivotal equation by asking yourself *why* you want it—not only would *you* immediately feel better, but you would soon begin to see the results of your positive influence.

"What *do* you want?" we asked.

He said, "I want my little one to wake up happy and dry and proud of himself and not to be embarrassed."

This father felt relief as he focused upon what he wanted because in making that effort, he found harmony with his desire. We told him, "As you are thinking those sorts of thoughts, then what will be oozing out of you will be in harmony with what you *do* want rather than in harmony with what you *do not* want, and you will be more positively influencing your son. Then words will come out of you such as: 'Oh, this is part of growing up. All of us have been through this, and you are growing up very fast. Now get out of those wet clothes and get into the bathtub.'" This young father called very soon after that and happily reported that the bed-wetting had stopped. . . .

Whenever I'm Feeling Bad, I'm Attracting Unwanted

While almost everyone is aware of how they feel in varying degrees, there are few who understand the important guidance that their feelings or emotions provide. In the most simple of terms: *Whenever you feel bad, you are in the process of attracting something that will not please you. Without exception, the reason for negative emotion is because you are focused upon something you do not want or upon the lack or absence of something that you do want.*

Many regard negative emotion as something unwanted, but we prefer to see it as important guidance to help you to understand the direction of your focus . . . therefore, the direction of your vibration . . . therefore, the direction of what you are attracting. You could call it a "warning bell," because it certainly does give you a signal to let you know that it is time to pivot, but we prefer to call it a "*guiding* bell."

Your emotions are your *Guidance System* to assist you in understanding what you are in the process of creating with every thought you think. Often people who are beginning to understand the power of thought and the importance of focusing upon good-feeling subjects are embarrassed or even angry at themselves when they find themselves in the midst of negative emotion, but there is no reason to be angry at yourself for having a perfectly functioning *Guidance System.*

Whenever you become aware that you are feeling negative emotion, begin by complimenting yourself for being aware of your Guidance, and then gently try to improve the feeling by choosing thoughts that feel better. We would call this a very subtle <u>Process of Pivoting</u> whereby you gently choose better-feeling thoughts.

Whenever you feel negative emotion, you could say to yourself, *I'm feeling some negative emotion, which means I'm in the process of attracting something that I do not want. What is it that I <u>do</u> want?*

Often just acknowledging that you "want to feel good" will help turn your thoughts in a better-feeling direction. But it is important to understand the distinction between *"wanting* to feel good" and "not *wanting* to feel bad." Some people think that it is just two different ways of saying the same thing, when actually those statements are exact opposites, with huge vibrational differences. *If you can begin to orient your thoughts by steadily looking for things that cause you to feel good, you will begin to develop patterns of thoughts, or beliefs, that will help you create magnificent, good-feeling lives.*

My Thoughts Dovetail into Stronger Matching Thoughts

Whatever thought you are focused upon—whether it is a memory from your past, something you are observing in your present, or something you are anticipating in your future—that thought is active within you right now, and it is attracting other thoughts and ideas that are similar. Not only do your thoughts attract other thoughts that are of a similar nature, but the longer you focus, the stronger the thoughts become and the more attraction power they amass.

Our friend Jerry likened this to the ropes he once observed while watching a large ship being docked. It was to be tied with a rope that was very large—too big and bulky to be thrown across the expanse of water. And so, instead, a small ball of twine was tossed across the water to the dock. The twine had been spliced into a little bigger rope, which had been spliced into a little bigger rope, which had been spliced into a little bigger rope . . . until eventually, the very large rope could be easily pulled across the expanse of water, and the ship was then secured to the dock. This is similar to the way your thoughts dovetail into one another, with one connecting to another, connecting to another, and so on.

Upon some subjects, because you have been pulling on the negative rope longer, it is very easy for you to get off on a negative tangent. In other words, it just takes a little negative utterance from someone, a memory of something, or some suggestion that takes you into a negative tailspin right away.

Your point of attraction predominantly occurs from the day-to-day things that you are thinking as you are moving through your day, and you have the power to direct your thoughts positively or negatively. For example: You are in the grocery store, and you notice that something that you regularly purchase has increased substantially in price, and you feel strong discomfort wash over you. You may very well think that you are just feeling shock over the sudden spike in the price of this item, and that since you have no say in what the grocer charges for any of the items in this store, you have no option other than to feel discomfort about it. However, we want to point out that your feeling of discomfort is not because of the grocer's action of raising the price of the goods for sale, but instead it is because of the direction of your own thoughts.

Just like the analogy of the rope tied to the rope tied to the rope tied to the rope, your thoughts are tied to one another and travel quickly to heightened vibrational places. For example, *Wow, the price of this is much greater than it was just last week . . . this price jump seems unreasonable . . . there's nothing reasonable about the greed in the marketplace . . . things are getting way out of hand . . . I don't know where it's all headed . . . it doesn't seem like we can go on like this . . . our economy is in trouble . . . I can't afford these inflated prices . . . I'm having a hard time making ends meet . . . I can't seem to earn it fast enough to keep up with the increase in the cost of living. . . .*

And, of course, this negative train of thought could move in many directions—toward blame of the grocer, to the economy, to your government—but it usually always turns back to the way you feel that the situation will negatively impact you, because everything that you observe feels personal to you. And everything, in truth, *is* personal to you because you are offering a vibration about it that is affecting what now is being attracted to you by your choice of thoughts.

If you are aware of how you are feeling and you understand that your emotions are indicating the direction of your thoughts, then you can more deliberately guide your thoughts. For example: *Wow, the price of this is much greater than it was just last week . . . however, I'm not aware of the other items in my basket . . . they could be the same . . . or maybe even a bit lower . . . I wasn't really paying attention . . . this one just got my attention because it was so much greater . . . prices do fluctuate . . . I always manage . . . things are going up a bit, but it's working out all right . . . it is quite an impressive system of distribution that makes this variety of goods so accessible to us. . . .*

Once you decide that you care about feeling good, you will find it easier to more consistently choose a better-feeling direction in your thoughts.

When the desire to feel good is effectively active within you, a consistent inspiration toward good-feeling thoughts will be present, and you will find it easier and easier to direct your thoughts in productive directions. Your thoughts contain enormous creative, attractive power that you harness effectively only by consistently offering good-feeling thoughts. When your thoughts constantly move back and forth between wanted and unwanted, pros and cons, pluses and minuses—you lose the benefit of the momentum of your pure, positive thought.

Creating a *Book of Positive Aspects*

In the first year of Jerry and Esther's work with us, they were using small hotel meeting rooms in different cities within 300 miles of their home in Texas to provide a comfortable place where people could gather to address their personal questions with us. There was a hotel in the city of Austin that always seemed to forget they were coming even though Esther had made arrangements with the hotel, signed contracts, and even called in the days just prior to the event to confirm. The hotel was always able to accommodate them (even though when they arrived, no one seemed to be expecting them), but it was very uncomfortable for Jerry and Esther to be in the position of urging the hotel staff to hurry to get the room ready before their guests arrived.

Finally, Esther said, "I think we should find a new hotel."

And we said, "That might be a good idea, but remember, *you will take yourselves with you.*"

"What do you mean?" Esther asked, a bit defensively.

We explained, *"If you take action from your perspective of lack— the action is always counterproductive.* In fact, it is likely that the new hotel will treat you just like the last one did." Jerry and Esther laughed at our explanation because they had already moved from one hotel to another for the very same reason.

"What should we do?" they asked. We encouraged them to purchase a new notebook and write boldly across the front cover of it: My Book of Positive Aspects. And on the first page of the book, write: "Positive Aspects of the _____ Hotel in Austin."

And so, Esther began to write: "It is a beautiful facility. It is immaculate. It is well situated. Very close to the interstate, with easy-to-find directions. There are many different-sized rooms to accommodate our increasing numbers. The hotel staff is always very friendly. . . ."

As Esther was making those entries, her *feeling* about the hotel changed from one of negative to one of positive, and in the moment that she began to *feel* better, her *attraction* from the hotel changed.

She did not write: "They are always ready and waiting for us," because that had not been her experience, and writing that would have evoked a feeling of contradiction or a feeling of defense or justification from her. By wanting to feel good, and by deliberately focusing her attention more upon the things about the hotel that did feel good, Esther's point of attraction regarding this hotel shifted, and then something Esther found very interesting happened: The hotel never forgot they were coming again. Esther was amused to realize that the hotel had not been forgetting about their agreement because they were uncaring or disorganized. The hotel staff was simply being influenced by Esther's dominant thought about them. In short, they could not buck the current of Esther's negative thought.

Esther enjoyed her *Book of Positive Aspects* so much that she began writing pages on many subjects of her life. We encouraged her to not only write about the things in which she was seeking improved feelings, but to write about things she already felt mostly positive about, just to get in the habit of good-feeling thoughts and for the pleasure of good-feeling thoughts. It is a nice way to live.

The *Law of Attraction* Adds Power to Thoughts

Often, when experiencing an unwanted situation, you feel a need to explain why it has happened, in an attempt, perhaps, to justify why you are in the situation. *Whenever you are defending or justifying or rationalizing or blaming anything or anyone, you remain in a place of negative attraction.* Every word you speak as you explain why something is not the way you want it to be continues the negative attraction, for you cannot be focused upon what you *do* want while you are explaining *why* you are experiencing something that you *do not* want. *You cannot be focused upon negative aspects and positive aspects at the same time.*

Often, in an effort to determine where your trouble started, you only hold yourself in that negative attraction longer: *What is the source of my trouble? What is the reason that I'm not where I want to be?* It is natural that you want improvement in your experience, and therefore it is logical that you are solution oriented . . . but there is a big difference between seriously looking for a solution and justifying the need for a solution by emphasizing the problem.

The realization that something is not as you want it to be is an important first step, but once you have identified that, the faster you are able to turn your attention in the direction of a solution, the better, because a continuing exploration of the problem will prevent you from finding the solution. The problem is a different vibrational frequency than the solution.

As you become aware of the value of the *Process of Pivoting*, and you become adept at identifying what is not wanted and then immediately turning your attention toward what is wanted, you will realize that you are surrounded primarily by wonderful things, for there is so much more that is going right in your world than wrong. Also, a daily utilization of the *Book of Positive Aspects* will help you to become more positively oriented. It will assist you in gradually tipping the balance of your thoughts more in the direction of what you *do* want.

The more that you focus your attention with the intention of finding increasingly *better-feeling* thoughts, the more you will realize that there is a very big difference between thinking about what you want and thinking about the absence of it. Whenever you are feeling uncomfortable as you are speaking or thinking about improving something you want—such as a better financial condition or an improved relationship or physical condition—you are in that moment preventing yourself from finding the improvement.

The *Process of Pivoting* and the *Process of the Book of Positive Aspects* are both being offered to assist you in recognizing—in the early, subtle stages of your creation—that you are pulling on the very tips of that negative ball of twine, so that you may, right away, release it and reach for the positive thread of thought.

It is much easier to go from a thought of something that makes you feel a little better, to an even better-feeling thought, to an even better-feeling thought . . . than to go directly to a wonderful-feeling thought, because all thoughts (or vibrations) are affected by (or managed by) the <u>Law of Attraction.</u>

I'll Begin My Day with Good-Feeling Thoughts

When you are focused upon something that you really do not want, it is actually easier for you to remain focused upon that unwanted topic (even finding other evidence to support that thought) than it is to move to a more positive perspective, because *thoughts that are like unto themselves, are drawn.* So if you attempt to make a big jump from a truly negative, unwanted topic immediately to a positive, delightful topic of something very much wanted, you will not be able to make the jump—for there is too much vibrational disparity between the two thoughts. A determination to gently, generally, and steadily lean more and more in the direction of wanted things is really the best way to approach your personal vibrational improvement.

When you first awaken in the morning, after a few hours of sleep (and therefore a vibrational detachment from unwanted things), you are in your most positive vibrational state. If you would begin your day, even before you get out of bed, by looking for a handful of positive aspects in your life, you will begin your day in a more positive vein, and the thoughts that the *Law of Attraction* will now provide as your springboard into each day will be much better feeling and beneficial.

In other words, every morning you have an opportunity to establish another vibrational basis (a sort of set-point) that sets the general tone of your thoughts for the rest of the day. And while it is possible that some events of your day may deviate from that starting place, in time you will see that you have established complete control of your thoughts, your vibration, your point of attraction—your life!

Sleep Time Is Realignment-of-Energies Time

While you are sleeping—or during the time that you are not consciously focused through your physical body—the attraction to this physical body stops. Sleep is a time when your *Inner Being* can realign your Energies, and it is a time for refreshment and replenishment of your physical body. If, when you put yourself in your bed, you will say, *Tonight I will rest well—I know that all attraction to this body will stop and when I awaken in the morning, I will literally reemerge back into my physical experience,* you will receive the greatest benefit from your time of sleep.

Awaking in the morning is not so different from being born. It is not so different from the day you first emerged into your physical body. So, as you awaken, open your eyes and say, *Today, I will look for reasons to feel good. Nothing is more important than that I feel good. Nothing is more important than that I choose thoughts that attract other thoughts that attract other thoughts that raise my vibrational frequency to the place where I can resonate with the positive aspects of the Universe.*

Your vibration is right where you last left it. So if you lie in your bed worrying about a situation before you go to sleep, when you awaken, you will pick up right where your thoughts or vibration left off the night before, and then your thoughts for the day will get off on that negative footing. And then the *Law of Attraction* will continue to serve up for you other thoughts that are like those thoughts. But if you will make an effort as you go to sleep to identify some of the positive aspects of your life, and then deliberately release your thoughts as you remember that during your slumber you are going to detach and refresh, and then if, when you awaken, you will open your eyes and say, *Today, I will look for reasons to feel good . . .* you will begin to gain control of your thoughts and life.

Rather than worrying about the problems of the world, or thinking about the things that you have to do today, just lie in your bed and look for the positive aspects of the moment: *How wonderful this bed feels. How comforting the fabric feels. How good my body feels. How comfortable this pillow is. How refreshing the air is that I'm breathing. How good it is to be alive! . . .* You will have begun to pull on that positive, good-feeling rope.

The *Law of Attraction* is like a giant magnifying glass amplifying whatever is. And so, as you awaken and look for some reason (something very immediate to you) to feel good about, the *Law of Attraction* will then offer you another thought that feels like it, and then another, and then another—and that is really what we call getting out of bed on the right foot.

With a little bit of effort, and a desire to feel good, you can direct your thoughts to more and more pleasing scenarios until you will change your habits of thoughts as well as your point of attraction—and the evidence of your improvement in thoughts will begin to show up right away.

An Example of a *Positive Aspects Bedtime Process*

Your action orientation in life causes you to believe that it takes hard work to make things happen, but as you learn to deliberately direct your thoughts, you will discover that there is tremendous leverage and power in thought. As you focus more consistently only in the direction of what you desire rather than diluting the power of your thought by thinking of the *wanted,* and then the *unwanted,* you will understand, from your personal experience, what we mean. Because of your *action* orientation, you often try too hard and work too hard. And as a result of that, most of you bring yourselves more to the attention of what is wrong (or more to the attention of what needs to be fixed) than you do to the attention of what you desire.

Here is a good way to apply the *Process of Positive Aspects* at bedtime: Once you are in your bed, try to recall some of the most pleasant things that happened during the day. Since many things have undoubtedly happened during this day, you may have to ponder for a little while, and you may remember some less-than-pleasant things that happened—but stick to your intention of finding something pleasing, and when you find it, ponder it.

Prime your positive pump by saying things such as: *The thing I liked about that was. . . . My favorite part of that was. . . .* Follow any positive thread that you find, thinking about the best parts of your day; and then, once you are feeling the effect of your positive thoughts, focus on your dominant intention right now: *getting a good night's sleep and awakening refreshed in the morning.*

Say to yourself, *I'm going to sleep now; and while I am sleeping, because my thoughts will be inactive, attraction will stop and my physical body will be completely refreshed at every level.* Turn your attention to the immediate things around you, like the comfort of your bed, the softness of your pillow, the Well-Being of your moment. And then softly set forth the intention: *I will sleep well, and I will awaken refreshed with another new, good-feeling, positive point of attraction.* And then, off to sleep.

An Example of a *Positive Aspects Morning Process*

As you awaken the next morning, you will be in that positive, good-feeling place, and your first thoughts will be something like: *Ah, I am awake. I have reemerged back into the physical. . . .* Lie there for a little while and bask in the comfort of your bed, and then offer a thought such as: *Today, no matter where I am going, no matter what I am doing, no matter who I'm doing it with, it is my dominant intent to look for things that feel good. When I feel good, I am vibrating with my higher power. When I feel good, I am in harmony with that which I consider to be good. When I feel good, I am in the mode of attracting that which will please me once it gets here. And when I feel good—I feel good!* (It is good just to feel good if the only thing it ever brought to you is the way you feel in the moment—but it brings ever so much more beyond that.)

We would lie in the bed for two or three minutes (that is enough), and we would look for the positive aspects of our surroundings. And then, as we move into the day, we would begin to acknowledge more positive aspects, looking for reasons to feel good no matter what the object of our attention is.

In the first moment of any negative emotion—which very likely will occur even though you have begun your day looking for reasons to feel good because there is, upon some subjects, some negative momentum already in motion—upon the first inclination of any negative emotion, we would stop and say, *I want to feel good. I'm feeling some negative emotion, which means that I'm focused upon something that I do not want. What is it that I want?* And we would turn our attention immediately to that which we want, staying focused upon the new thought, or the positive thought, long enough that we would feel the positive Energy again beginning to flow through our apparatus.

As you move through your day, look for more reasons to laugh and more reasons to have fun. When you want to feel good, you do not take things so seriously; and when you are not taking things so seriously, you are not as likely to notice the lack of things wanted; and when you are not focusing upon the lack of what you desire, you feel better—and when you feel better, you attract more of what you do want . . . and your life just gets better and better.

And then, that night, as you lie in your bed, you will have many wonderful things to ponder as you drift off into your restful, refreshing sleep; and then you will awaken into an even better-feeling new day tomorrow.

I Know How I Want to Feel

Sometimes when you are in the midst of an uncomfortable situation, you struggle to find *any* positive aspects within it. Some things are intolerable; some things are so big and so bad that it does not seem possible for you to find anything positive about them, but that is because you are attempting to take too large of a jump from the awfulness of what you are focused upon to the solution that you desire. In other words, if you want to find an action solution right now that will fix this but you find yourself in a situation where no action that you can take seems appropriate, always remember that while there may not be a positive aspect to your action in this moment—while you may not be able to figure out what to *do* that would make you feel better—*you always know how you want to feel.*

It is a bit like someone saying, "I've just jumped out of an airplane, and I have no parachute. What should I do now?" There are situations where, given the current circumstances, there is no action or thought that, at this point, will make a significant enough difference to change the outcome that is barreling in upon you. And, in the same way that sometimes you cannot find any *action* that will fix things, there is no *thought* that will immediately change it either.

But if you understand the power of your thought and the incredible leverage that consistently good-feeling thoughts provide, and you begin deliberately choosing your thoughts by utilizing the guidance that your feelings or emotions indicate, you can easily transform your life into predominantly good-feeling experiences by focusing upon the improved feeling. *If you are able to find even the smallest feeling of relief in a deliberately chosen thought—your gentle path toward your solution will begin.*

What to <u>do</u> in certain situations may not be clear to you, and you may at times not even be able to identify what it is that you want to <u>have,</u> but there is never a time that you are unable to identify, to some extent, how you want to <u>feel.</u> In other words, you know that you would rather feel happy than sad, refreshed than tired, invigorated rather than enervated. You know that you would rather feel productive than unproductive, free than confined, growing than stagnant. . . .

There is not enough action available to compensate for mis-aligned thought, but when you begin to gain control of the way you feel—by more deliberately choosing the direction of your thought—you will discover the powerful leverage in thought. *If you will bring yourself to a more deliberate control of your own thought, you will bring yourself to a more deliberate control of your own life experience.*

Nothing Is More Important Than Feeling Good

Becoming more deliberate about the things you think about is not a difficult thing. You are often particular about what you eat, the vehicle you drive, and the clothes you wear; and being a delib-erate thinker does not require much more deliberate discrimination than that. But learning to deliberately direct your thoughts toward the aspect of the subject that feels best to you will have a much greater impact on the improvement in your life than the choosing of a meal, vehicle, or wardrobe.

Once you read these words and feel your own personal resonance with their meaning and power, you will never again feel negative emotion without realizing that you are receiving important guidance to assist you in guiding your thoughts in a more productive and beneficial direction. In other words, you will never again feel negative emotion and not understand that it means you are in the process of attracting something *unwanted.* A significant thing is happening with you as you are coming into conscious awareness of your emotions and the guidance that they provide, because even in your ignorance of what negative emotion meant, you were still negatively attracting. And so, understanding your emotions now gives you control of your life experience.

Whenever you are feeling less than good, if you will stop and say, *Nothing is more important than that I feel good—I want to find a reason now to feel good,* you will find an improved thought, which will lead to another and another. As you develop the habit of look-ing for good-feeling thoughts, the circumstances that surround you must improve. The *Law of Attraction* demands it. When you feel good, you experience the sensation of doors opening as the Universe is cooperating with you; and when you feel bad, it feels as if the doors are closing and the cooperation stops.

Anytime you feel negative emotion, you are in the mode of resisting something that you want, and that resistance takes its toll on you. It takes its toll on your physical body, and it takes its toll on the amount of wonderful things that you are allowing to come into your experience.

Through your process of living life and noticing things wanted and unwanted, you have created a sort of *Vibrational Escrow*, which, in a sense, holds for you those wanted things you have identified until you become a close enough Vibrational Match to them that you allow yourself a fully manifested receiving of them. But until you find a way to feel good about them even though they have not yet manifested in your experience, it may seem to you that they are on the outside of a door that you cannot open. However, as you begin to look for more positive aspects regarding the things that occupy your thoughts—and as you deliberately choose the more positive end of the stick of possibilities regarding the subjects that dominate your thought processes—that door will open and everything that you desire will flow easily into your experience.

It Gets Better the Better It Gets

When you deliberately seek positive aspects of whatever you are giving your attention to, you, in a sense, tune your vibrational tuner to more positive aspects of everything. And, of course, you could tune yourself negatively as well. Many people struggle in an attitude of self-criticism as a result of negative comparison that has been directed to them from parents or teachers or peers, and there is nothing more detrimental to your ability to positively attract than a negative attitude toward yourself.

So, sometimes by choosing a subject about which you have practiced fewer negative thoughts, you can tune yourself to a better-feeling frequency; and then from that better-feeling place, as you redirect your thoughts toward yourself, you will find more positive aspects about yourself than usual. *Once you find more positive aspects of the world that surrounds you, you will begin to find more positive aspects about yourself. And once that happens, finding more positive aspects about your world will be easier still.*

When you find things about yourself that you do not like, you will find more of those things in others. You say, "The worse it gets, the worse it gets." But as you are deliberately looking for positive aspects in yourself or in others, you will find more of those things: "The better it gets, the better it gets."

We cannot overemphasize the value in looking for positive aspects and focusing upon more of things wanted, because everything that comes to you is dependent upon that very simple premise: *You get more and more of what you are thinking about—whether you want it or not.*

My Universe Is Positively and Negatively Balanced

So, you are the creator of your experience. Or you could say that *you are the attractor of your experience.* Creating is not about identifying something wanted and then going after it and capturing it. Creating is about focusing upon the subject of desire—tuning your thoughts more precisely to the aspects of the subject that you would like to experience and therefore allowing the *Law of Attraction* to bring it to you.

Whether you are *remembering* something from the past, *imagining* something about the future, or *observing* something from your now, you are offering thought-vibrations that the *Law of Attraction* is responding to. You may refer to your thoughts as *desires* or *beliefs* (a belief is only a thought you continue to think), but whatever you are giving your attention to is establishing your point of attraction.

Because every subject is actually two subjects—*what is wanted* and *the lack of what is wanted*—it is possible to believe that you are positively focused when in fact you are negatively focused. People may say, "I want more money," but what they are actually focused upon is the fact that they do not have as much money as they need. Most people talk most often about their desire to be healthy when they are feeling sick. In other words, their attention to what they *do not* want is what is prompting their remarks about what they *do* want, but in the majority of cases, even though they may be speaking words that seem to indicate that they are focused upon their desire, they are not.

It is only by consciously recognizing how you are feeling while you are speaking that you really know if you are positively or negatively attracting. And while you may not see immediate evidence of what you are in the process of attracting, whatever you are thinking about is amassing matching thoughts, vibrations, and Energies; and eventually the evidence of your attraction will be obvious.

My Universe Responds to My Attention to . . .

Most people believe, or want to believe, that everything in the Universe responds to their words in the same way that other people around them can sometimes be trained to behave. When you tell someone, "Yes, come to me," you expect them to come. When you say, "No, go away from me," you expect them to go. But you live in an attraction-based Universe (an inclusion-based Universe), which simply means there is no such thing as *no*.

When you give your attention to something wanted and you say, "Yes, come to me," you include it in your vibration, and the *Law of Attraction* begins the process of bringing it. But when you look at something unwanted and you say "No, I do not want you—go away!" the Universe brings that, also. *Your attention to it, and therefore your vibrational alignment with it, is what is causing the response—not your words.*

And so, as you say, "Perfect health, I seek you . . . I want you— I bask in the idea of perfect health," you are attracting health. But as you say, "Sickness, I do not want you," you are attracting sickness. As you say, *"No, no, no,"* it is coming closer, closer, closer, because the more you struggle against something that you do not want, the more engulfed in it you become.

People often believe that once they find their perfect mate, or achieve their perfect body weight, or accumulate enough money, *then, once and for all,* they will also find the happiness that they seek . . . but nowhere is there a little corner of something where only positive aspects exist. The perfect balance of the Universe says that positive and negative (wanted and unwanted) exists in all particles of the Universe. When you, as the creator, the chooser, the definer, the decider, look for the positive aspect, that becomes what you live—in *all* aspects of your life. You do not have to wait around for that perfect thing to show itself to you so that you can then have a positive response to it. Instead, you positively train your thoughts and vibrations, and then you become the *attractor* of it, or the *creator* of it.

We would encourage you to begin each day with the statement: *Today—no matter where I go, no matter what I am doing, and no matter who I am doing it with—it is my dominant intent to look for what I am wanting to see.*

Remember, when you awaken in the morning, you are reborn. While you have slumbered, all attraction has stopped. That sequestering away for a few hours of sleep—where your Consciousness is no longer attracting—gives you a refreshing new beginning. And so, unless you wake up in the morning and begin regurgitating what troubled you the day before, it will not trouble you in your new day, in your new birth, in your new beginning.

Decisions to Feel Good Attract Good Feelings

A woman said to us: "I recently found out that I'm going to be attending three or four holiday parties, and as soon as I heard that, I started thinking, *Oh, Mary's going to be there, and she's going to be gorgeous.* I started immediately comparing myself to other people. I'd like to stop doing that and feel good about *me* and just enjoy the parties, no matter who's there. Could you help me apply the processes of *Pivoting* and *Positive Aspects* regarding my self-consciousness. I really don't even want to attend these parties."

We explained: While your feeling of self-consciousness is amplified as you consider your attendance of these parties, neither the party nor Mary is the reason for your discomfort. It often seems complicated to sort out your relationships with other people, even tracing the beginning of these feelings back into your childhood, but there is no value in doing that. You have the ability, from right where you stand, to find positive aspects or negative aspects—to think of the wanted or unwanted—and whether you begin the process right now or several days before you attend your first party, or whether you wait until you are at the party, the work is the same: *Look for things that feel good when you focus upon them.*

Because you have more control over what is activated in your own mind, it is usually much easier to find the positive aspect of a situation before you are standing right in the middle of it. If you do imagine the situation as you want it to be, and you do practice your positive response to the upcoming situation, then when you are at the party you will witness the control that you set into motion days before.

You cannot feel good and bad at the same time. You cannot focus upon wanted and unwanted at the same time. If you have trained your thoughts to what you consider to be good, or wanted before you arrive at a party, the <u>Law of Attraction</u> will deliver to you things that feel good and are wanted. It really is as simple as that.

If you want to feel different at these upcoming parties than you have felt at parties in previous years, you must begin telling a different story. The story you have been telling goes something like this: "I'm only invited to these parties because of my relationship with my mate. It really isn't important to anyone that I be there. I'm not really a part of his work environment, and I don't really understand most of the things that they're interested in. I'm an outsider. Mary doesn't feel like an outsider like I do. Her confidence is obvious in the way she dresses and carries herself. I always feel less attractive, less smart, less everything when I am near Mary. I hate feeling like this. I wish I didn't have to go."

Here is an example of an attempt at a better-feeling story: "My mate is well respected at his firm. It's nice that his company occasionally provides an opportunity for people who work there to include their spouses and to get to know one another. No one there expects me to be up to speed with the inner workings of that environment. In fact, this will be a party where they will probably enjoy thinking about other things than their work.

"Life is much larger than what happens at my husband's office. And since I'm never there, I may very well appear to be a breath of fresh air to many of them because I'm not bogged down in the things they're troubled about. Mary seems light and friendly. She's clearly not bogged down in office politics or problems. It's fun to watch her. She's interesting. I wonder where she buys her clothing—they are very pretty things she wears."

You see, it is not necessary that you sort out every insecurity that you have ever felt and use this office party as a means to solve it. Just find something positive to focus upon and feel the benefit of having done so, and in time, Mary will be a nonissue, or maybe a friend. But in any case, it is your decision to make, and your vibrational practice to make it so.

How Can I Not Feel Their Pain?

Our friend Jerry asked of us: "It seems to me that the majority of my discomfort is felt because I'm observing others who are in pain. How could I use the *Pivoting Process* to not feel pain about *their* pain?"

We explained: Whatever the subject of your attention, it contains things you want to see as well as things you do not want to see. The pain you are feeling is not because the person you are observing is in pain. Your pain is because you have chosen to look at an aspect of them that causes you to feel pain. There is a big difference.

Of course, if this person were not feeling pain but were instead joyful, it would be easier for you to feel joyful, but you must not rely on conditions changing in order to control the way you feel. You must improve your ability to focus positively regardless of the condition—and to do that, it helps to remember that every subject has *wanted* and *unwanted* within it, and that, if you are deliberate, you *can* find something that feels better.

Of course, it is easier just to observe something that is right before your eyes than it is to deliberately sift for things that you would prefer to see. However, when it really matters to you that you feel good, you will be less willing to merely lazily or sloppily observe, for your desire to feel good will inspire a greater willingness to look for positive aspects. Also, the more often you do look for good-feeling things to focus upon, the more of those kinds of good-feeling things the *Law of Attraction* will bring to you, until in time you will be so positively oriented that you simply will not notice the things that don't match your positive orientation.

A mother once said to us, in response to our advising her to ignore her son's problems, "But won't he feel like I've abandoned him? Shouldn't I be there for him?"

We explained to her that there is no "abandonment" in focusing upon the positive aspects of her son's life, and there is powerful value in abandoning *any* thoughts that do not feel good when you think them. We said, "You never help anyone by being their sounding board for problems or complaints. By holding an image of improvement in your son's life, you help him move toward that. Be *there* for him. And call him *there* to a better-feeling place."

When it is your deliberate intention to feel good and you really care about how you feel, you will find more and more thoughts about more and more subjects that do feel good. And then you will be better prepared to interface with others who could be feeling good or bad. Because of your desire to feel good, you will have prepaved your experience with others with whom you will be interacting, and then it will be much easier for you to focus positively about their situation no matter what sort of mess they are in. But if you have not been tending to your own vibration and you have not been consistently holding yourself in good-feeling thoughts and vibrations, then you may be swept into their situation, and then you may very well feel discomfort.

We just want to emphasize that you are not feeling *their pain,* caused by their situation, but instead *you are feeling your own pain brought about by your own thinking.* There is great control in that knowledge, and, in fact, true freedom. *When you discover that you can control the way you feel because you can control the thoughts you think, then you are free to joyously move about your planet, but when you believe that the way you feel is dependent upon the behavior or situations of others—and you also understand that you have no control over those behaviors or situations—you do not feel free.* That, in fact, was the "pain" you were describing.

My Sympathy Is of No Value to Anyone?

Jerry said to us: "So, when I take my attention off of those who are in trouble, *I'll* feel good. But still, that doesn't help *them* feel better. In other words, I haven't solved the problem. I'm just avoiding the problem."

We replied: If you do not focus upon their problem, you can continue to feel good, but they will still have the problem. That is true, at first. But if you *do* focus upon their problem, you feel bad, they continue to feel bad—and they still have the problem. And if you continue to focus on their problem, you will have the problem, too, in time. However, if you do not focus upon their problem, but instead try to imagine their solution or a positive outcome, you feel good—and there is then the possibility of your influencing them to more positive thoughts and outcomes.

In simple terms: You are never of value to another (and you never offer a solution) when you are feeling negative emotion, because the presence of negative emotion within you means you are focused upon the lack of what is wanted, rather than what is wanted.

So if someone is having a bad experience and they come into your awareness with a powerful wind of negativity wrapped around them, if you have not already deliberately achieved your alignment with feeling good, you may be swept into their negativity; you may become part of their chain of pain, and you may very well pass your discomfort onto another, who will then pass it on to another, and so on.

But if you have been deliberately setting the tone of your day by putting your head on your pillow each night and saying, *Tonight, as I sleep, all attraction will stop, which means tomorrow I will have a new beginning; and tomorrow I will look for what I am wanting to see because I want to feel good—because feeling good is the most important thing!* as you awaken in the morning, you will be upon a fresh path bringing no negativity from the day before. And then, as you walk into a room and you see someone with pain coming toward you, as this person comes with his or her pain, you do not become part of it, but instead you provide a better example of happiness, for that which you *feel* is that which you radiate.

Now, it is not likely that just because you remain happy, others will immediately join you in your happiness. In fact, when there is a great disparity between the way you are feeling and the way others are feeling, you will have a difficult time relating to one another; but in time, if you maintain your positive vibrational stance, they will either join you in your positive place or they will vibrate right out of your experience. The only way unhappy people can stay in your experience is by your continuing attention to them.

If you and two other people were walking along a mountain ledge, and you were not watching where you were going and stumbled and fell over the edge and were hanging by a very flimsy vine, and one of your friends was very strong and sure-footed and the other was very clumsy and not focused, which one would you be glad was there? Looking for the positive aspects is the way you find your sure footing. It is *who-you-are* from an Inner Perspective. And as you consistently align with increasingly better-feeling thoughts, the powerful resources of the Universe become available to you.

To sympathize with others means to focus upon their situation until you feel as they feel, and since everyone has the potential of feeling wonderful or feeling awful—of succeeding at their desires or of failing at their desires—you have options about which aspects of them you sympathize with. We encourage you to sympathize with the best-feeling aspects of others that you can find; and, in doing so, you may influence them to an improved condition, also.

To Not Hurt When They Feel Hurt?

A man once asked, "How do you end a relationship without being hurt by the other person being hurt? If you decide that it's time to move on and the other person is not ready to move on, so he or she is very distraught, how can you keep your balance in a situation like that?"

We replied: When you attempt to guide your behavior by paying attention to how someone else feels about your behavior, you are powerless because you cannot control his or her perspective, and therefore you cannot achieve any consistent improvement in your own vibration or point of attraction or how you feel.

If you have decided to take the action of leaving a relationship before you have done the vibrational work of focusing upon *what* you want and *why* you want it, any action that you take can only bring you more of the same discomfort that you have been experiencing. And even once the relationship has ended and you are alone or beginning another relationship with another person, those old lingering negative vibrations will not allow a pleasant unfolding. Simply put, it is so much better to find your vibrational balance *before* you take the action of separation, or you may experience a rather long time of discomfort.

Let us examine the components of this situation and bring some clarity to your options: You have come to the conclusion as a result of being unhappy in this relationship for a while that it would be better to end it. In other words, you do believe that your chance of happiness is greater outside of the relationship than inside it. But when you announce that to your partner, your partner becomes even more unhappy. And now because your partner is more unhappy—you are more unhappy.

One option is to stay—to say, "Never mind. Don't be unhappy. I've changed my mind. I'll stay." But all that has happened is that you were both feeling unhappy; you made a decision to leave, which made your partner even more unhappy; and now you have pulled back from that decision, so your partner is now not quite as unhappy as before—but still neither of you are happy. So, nothing has changed except that things got a bit more intense for a while, but basically you are still unsatisfied and unhappy in this relationship.

Another option is to just leave. You could focus upon all of the things that have caused you to feel uncomfortable in the relationship and use those things as your justification for leaving. And while that negative focus upon negative things will give you the conviction to take the action of leaving, you will not really feel that much better. While you may feel some relief from the intensity of your unhappiness once you are on the outside of the relationship, you will continue to feel a need to justify your action of leaving, which will continue to hold you in an unpleasant state. So even though you have walked away from the things that were really bothering you, you will still feel bothered.

Really, there is nothing that you can *do* to prevent others from feeling bad, because they do not feel bad because of *your* behavior. There is no greater entrapment in relationships or in life than to attempt to keep others happy by observing *their* emotions and then trying to compensate with *your* actions.

The only way you can be happy is to decide to be happy. When you take upon yourself the responsibility of another's happiness, you are attempting the impossible and you are setting yourself up for a great deal of personal discord.

So now let us consider the options of *Pivoting* and *Positive Aspects:* Stay where you are for now, making no big change in your action or behavior. In other words, if you are living together, continue to do so. If you are spending time together, continue to do so. This option is a change in your *thought* process, not your *action* process. These processes are designed to help you to focus differently and to begin telling the story of your relationship, or of your life, in a better-feeling, more self-empowering way.

For example: *I've been thinking about leaving this relationship because I find that I'm not happy within it. But as I think about leaving, I realize that when I go, I'll take myself with me—and if I leave because I'm unhappy, I'll be taking that unhappy person with me. The reason that I want to leave is because I want to feel good. I wonder if it's possible to feel good without leaving. I wonder if there is anything about our relationship that I could focus upon that does feel good.*

I remember meeting this person and how that felt. I remember feeling drawn by this person and eager to move forward to see what more we might discover together. I liked the feeling of discovery. I liked our relationship as it began. I think that the more time we spent together, the more we both realized that we were not really a perfect match. I don't believe that there is any failure on either of our parts in that. Not being a perfect match doesn't mean that either of us is wrong. It only means that there are potentially better partners out there for each of us.

There are so many things about this person that I like and that anyone would easily appreciate: so smart, and interested in so many things; laughs easily and loves to have fun. . . . I'm glad that we've come together, and I believe our time together will prove to be of value to both of us.

So, our answer to your important question is this: You cannot control the pain that any other feels by modifying *your* behavior. You can, however, control your own pain by directing your thoughts until your pain subsides and is replaced by improved feelings. *As you give your attention to what you are wanting—you will always begin to feel good. As you give your attention to the lack of what you are wanting—you will always feel bad. And if you give your attention to the lack of what someone else is wanting—you will feel bad, also.*

You are so action oriented as physical Beings that you really think that you have to fix everything right now. Your partner did not get to this place all of a sudden. Your partner did not even get there only during your relationship. This has been a long path. Momentum has been gathering along the way. And so, do not expect that a conversation that you two are having in this moment is going to make all of the difference. See yourself as one who is planting a seed—a very strong, sure, powerful seed. You have planted it perfectly, and you have nurtured it for a time with your words so that long after you are gone, that seed will continue to blossom into that which it is to be.

There are many relationships that are not appropriate for you to continue, but we would never walk out of a relationship feeling angry, guilty, or defensive. Do the vibrational work, get to feeling good, and then leave. And then what comes next will not be a replay of what you just left.

I Am Not Responsible for Others' Creations

You must not accept the responsibility for what others are doing in their own life experience. See them as emerging from the lack, and know that it is going to be better for them later—and then *you* will begin to feel better. You may even inspire them, in their sleep state, to an improved direction. When you think about them, see them as happy. Do not regurgitate, in your mind, the sad conversations you have had or the parting. Envision them as getting on with their life just as you are getting on with yours. *Trust that they have the Guidance within them to find their own way.*

What trips most of you up so often in your wanting to help others is that you believe, *They need my help because they cannot help themselves,* but that belief is detrimental to them because deep down inside, they know that they *can* do it, and that they are *wanting* to do it.

Begin to say things to your partner such as: "You are such a fantastic person. And while we haven't connected on as many levels as I would like, I know that there is a perfect partner waiting for you, and I'm releasing you to that wonderful opportunity. Look for it! I don't want to keep you caged here, captive to something that neither one of us wants. I want to free us both to that which we both are wanting. I'm not telling you good-bye forever; I'm saying, 'Let this relationship have a new understanding between us, one that is inspired from passionate, positive desire, not one that is whipped into place because we are afraid of the possible consequences.'"

And then say to the person, "When I think of you, I will always know that while you are sad now, you are going to be happy later. I'm going to choose to see you as happy, because that's the way I like you best, and that's what you prefer, too."

This may sound tough or cold. But nothing else makes sense.

Listen for Guidance, or Reach for Good Feelings?

You have the ability to pivot under any and all conditions. It does not matter how negative something seems—you have the ability to give your attention to the positive aspects of it. The only things that get in your way are some old habits, or maybe some strong influences from others.

Most people are habitual in nature, and your patterns are so well entrenched that at times the fastest path to the joy you seek is for you to take your pivot as you sleep—and then awaken in the new day already in the direction of that which you are wanting. By reaching for good-feeling thoughts before you go to sleep and then experiencing the benefit of the quiet mind that occurs while you sleep—and then upon awakening, immediately turning to good-feeling thoughts—you can accomplish the ultimate *Pivoting* experience. A few days of following that pattern will provide a big change in your habit of thought and your point of attraction, and you will discover improvement in virtually every aspect of your life.

What If I Played the *What-If?* Game?

As we encourage that you do your best to find positive aspects upon whatever subject is before you, there are often those who would ask: "But what about the man who's just lost his job and has a wife and five children, his rent is due in two days, and he doesn't have the money to pay it? Or, what about the woman who has the gestapo army at her door, about to take her to be killed in a gas chamber? How could those people pivot?"

And to those extreme questions, we often reply: It is as if you have just jumped out of an airplane at an altitude of 20,000 feet and you have no parachute, and you ask, "So *now* what do I do?" You are usually not faced with such extreme circumstances from which it seems there is no possible, comfortable escape. However, these extreme situations, with all of the drama and trauma that they bring, also bring a power that, with the right focus, can provide resolutions that someone watching from the outside would find astonishing or even miraculous.

In other words, there is no situation from which you cannot find a positive resolution, but you have to be able to focus powerfully in order to accomplish such a solution. And most people who are in those kinds of situations are not adept at that kind of focus—which is why they are experiencing the negative situation to begin with.

When you are involved in extreme situations, a power comes forth from within, and so the intensity of your desire will put you upon a plateau where, if you can just get focused, you can have your greater elevation. In other words, those who are very sick are in a better position to be even more *well* than most others, because their *desire* for wellness is amplified. But unless they are able to pivot (to turn their attention to their desire for wellness and away from their concern about illness), they cannot become well.

We would encourage you to play the *What-If?* game, looking for positive aspects. In other words, rather than looking into your society for examples of disempowered people having no control over the circumstances of their lives, tell a story that gives you a feeling of empowerment. Instead of telling the story of powerless victims and thereby amplifying your own feeling of also being a victim, tell a different story.

For example: *What if* this woman, before the gestapo army came pounding on her door, had recognized the rumblings of the looming Holocaust that were in the community weeks before? *What if* she had left the community when many of the others had left? *What if* she had not been afraid of the unknown? *What if* she had not held to the familiar? *What if* she had made the decision to start a new life in a new country with her sister and her aunt and uncle two weeks ago so that she was not at home when the gestapo came calling?

When you play the *What-If?* game, look for things you *do want* to see. Look for things that make you feel better.

There is never a situation in which there is not a way out. In fact, there are hundreds and thousands of practical choices along the way— but, out of habit, most people continue to choose the "lack" perspective in situations until they eventually find themselves in an unwanted place where it seems that there are no more choices.

As you hold to your intention to look for evidence of Well-Being and thriving and success and happiness, you will tune yourself to the vibrations of *those* things—and so those kinds of good-feeling experiences will dominate your life. *Today, no matter where I am going, no matter what I am doing, it is my dominant intent to look for what I am wanting to see.*

As you make the decision that you are not a mere observer of your world, but a deliberate and positive contributor *to* your world, you will find great pleasure in your involvement with what is going on upon your planet. When you witness things that you do not want to happen in your world, in your nation, in your neighborhood, in your family, or in your personal body, and you remember that you have the power to tell a different story—and you also know that there is enormous power in telling a different story—you will then step back into the exuberant knowledge that you held when you made the decision to come forth to participate on this planet to begin with.

You cannot be in a place other than where you are right now, but you do have the power to begin to express your perspective about where you are in increasingly better ways. And as you do that consciously and deliberately, you will see the evidence of the power of your focus on every subject to which you turn your attention.

As you make the decision that you want to feel good and you consciously look for positive aspects within the subjects that you are involved in every day, and as you deliberately identify and focus upon what you *do* want regarding these subjects, you will set yourself upon a path of Eternal unfolding satisfaction and joy.

These processes are simple to understand and to apply, but do not let their simplicity cause you to underestimate their power. Consistently apply them and show yourself the leverage of the power of aligned thought. Discover the power of the Energy that creates worlds—the power that you have always had ready access to but which you now understand how to apply—and focus it toward your own personal creations.

PART II

Attracting Money and Manifesting Abundance

(**Editor's Note:** In the sections where there is a back-and-forth dialogue between Jerry and Abraham, the speaker's name is repeated at the beginning of each section for clarity.)

Attracting Money and Manifesting Abundance

While money is not absolutely essential to your experience, to most people *money* and *freedom* are synonymous. And since an intense awareness of your right to be free is at the very core of that which you are, it follows, therefore, that your relationship with money is one of the most important subjects of your life experience. And so, it is no wonder you have such strong feelings about the subject of money.

Although some people have discovered the freedom of allowing large amounts of money to flow through their experiences, it is more often the case that because you are experiencing far less money than you need or desire, most of you are not feeling free. It is our intention, here, to clearly explain why this financial disparity exists so that you can begin to allow the abundance that you want and deserve into your experience. For, as you read these words and as you begin to resonate with these *Law*-based truths, you will align your desire with the abundance of your world, and the evidence of your newfound alignment will soon become apparent to you and to others who observe you.

Whether you are one who has been working to achieve financial abundance for many years or you are a youngster just starting down that path, the journey to financial Well-Being does not have to be a long one from where you are. And it does not require large amounts of time or physical effort, for we are going to explain to you in simple and easy-to-understand terms how to utilize the leverage of Energy that is available to you. We want to show you the absolute correlation between the thoughts you have been thinking

271

about money, the way you feel when you think those thoughts—and the money that flows into your experience. When you are able to consciously make that correlation, and you decide to deliberately direct your thoughts accordingly, you will access the power of the Universe and you will then see how time and physical effort are rather irrelevant to your financial success.

So we begin with the simple premise of your Universe and of your world: *You get what you think about.* Often people say to us, "That can't be true, because I have wanted and thought about more money for as long as I can remember, but I continue to struggle with not enough money." And what we then tell them is the most important thing for you to understand if you want to improve your financial situation: *The subject of money is really two subjects: (1) money, plenty of money, the feeling of freedom and ease that plenty of money can provide; and (2) absence of money, not nearly enough money, the feeling of fear and disappointment that the thought of absence of money induces.*

Often people assume that because they are speaking the words "I want more money," they are speaking positively about money. But when you are speaking of money (or anything) and you are feeling fear or discomfort as you speak, you are not speaking of the subject of money, but instead you are speaking of the subject of not enough money. And the difference is very important, because the first statement brings money and the second holds it away.

It is of value for you to become aware of how you are really *thinking* and, more important, *feeling* about money. If you are thinking or saying things like: "Oh, that is a very beautiful thing—but I cannot afford it," you are not in a vibrational position to allow in the abundance you desire. The feeling of disappointment that is present as you acknowledge that you cannot afford it is your indicator that the balance of your thought is pointed more toward the lack of your desire than toward the desire itself. *The negative emotion that you feel as you acknowledge that you cannot afford something that you want is one way of understanding the balance of your thoughts, and the amount of abundance that you are actually experiencing is another way of knowing.*

Many people continue to perpetuate the experience of "not enough" in their lives simply because they do not think beyond the reality of what they are actually experiencing. In other words, if they are experiencing the shortage of money and are aware of it and speak of it often, they hold themselves in that chronic position. And so, many people protest when we explain to them the power of telling the story of their finances as they want it to be rather than as it is, because they believe that they should be factual about what is happening.

But we want you to understand that if you continue to look at *what-is* and speak of *what-is,* you will not find the improvement that you desire. You may see a parade of changing faces and places, but your life experience will essentially show no improvement. If you want to effect substantial change in your life experience, you have to offer substantially different vibrations, which means you must think thoughts that *feel* different as you think them.

Lackful Action Doesn't Pay Off

Jerry: Many years ago I owned a motel near El Paso, Texas, and H. L. Hunt, who at that time was one of the wealthiest men in the United States (one of the multibillionaires), called me. He had purchased Ojo Caliente, a small resort on the Rio Grande that was financially failing, and he had heard that I might have some useful information to help him turn it around. As we were visiting in my little coffee shop, I had a difficult time focusing on our conversation because I just couldn't understand why a man that wealthy would still be discontent and looking for a way of making more money. I wondered why he didn't just sell the place—at whatever price—and go on about his life enjoying the money he had already accumulated.

I have another friend who's in the multibillionaire class. We were in Rio de Janeiro, Brazil, walking on the beach, and he was talking about some business problems he was having, and it really struck me that that man—so wealthy—would have *any* kind of troubles. But what I've learned from you, Abraham (and I've learned a lot from you), is that our true success in life is not about how much money we have or about the having of things. Right?

First, I'll Find My Vibrational Balance

Abraham: The things that you *have* and the things that you *do* are all meant to enhance your state of *being.* In other words, it's all about how you feel, and how you feel is all about coming into alignment with *who-you-really-are.* When you tend to your alignment first, then the things you gather and the actions you perform only enhance your good-feeling state of being . . . but if you do not find that vibrational balance first and attempt to make yourself feel better by bringing more things into your experience or participating in more activities in order to try to make yourself feel better, you just get further out of balance.

We are not guiding you away from accumulating things or from taking action, because all of that is an essential part of your physical experience. In other words, you intended the wonderful experience of exploring the details of your physical world in order to help you to personally determine your own joyous growth and expansion, but when you try to move forward from an imbalanced footing, it is always uncomfortable. *If you will begin by identifying how you want to _feel,_ or _be,_ and let your inspiration to _accumulate_ or to _do_ come from that centered place, then not only will you maintain your balance, but you will now enjoy the things you gather and the things that you do.*

Most people do most of their wanting from a place of lack. They want things, in many cases, simply because they do not have them, so the having of them does not really satisfy anything deep within them because there is always something else that they do not have. And so, it becomes a never-ending struggle to try to bring one more thing (one more thing that still will not be satisfying) into their experience: *Because I don't have this, I want it.* And they really think that getting it will fill the void. But that defies *Law.*

Any action that is taken from a place of lack is always counterproductive, and it always leads to more of a feeling of lack. The void that these people are feeling cannot be filled with things or satisfied with action because the feeling of void is about the vibrational discord between their desires and their chronic habits of thought.

Offering better-feeling thoughts, telling a different story, looking for positive aspects, *Pivoting* to the subject of what you really *do* want, looking for positive *what-ifs*—that is how you fill that void. And when you do, a most interesting thing will occur in your experience: The things you have wanted will begin to flood into your experience. But these things you have been wanting will flood in not to fill your void, because that void no longer exists—they flow in *because* your void no longer exists.

Certainly, you will gather many magnificent things into your experience. *Our message is not for you to stop <u>wanting, having,</u> or <u>doing.</u> Our message is for you to <u>want</u> and <u>accumulate</u> and <u>do</u> from your place of feeling good.*

Neither Money Nor Poverty Makes Joy

Jerry: Abraham, there's a saying that money doesn't make for happiness. On the other hand, I've noticed that poverty doesn't make for happiness either, but still it's obvious that money isn't the *path* to happiness. So, if the *idea* of achieving something does bring us happiness, does that mean the *achievement* is an appropriate goal for us to set? And how does a person maintain his or her feeling of happiness when reaching one's goal is taking a lot of time and energy? It often seems that there is a sort of uphill climb to reach the goal and then a short plateau of rest, but then an almost immediate tedious climb to achieve the next goal.

How does a person keep all of the climbing toward their goals joyous so there's not that struggle, struggle, struggle, and then: "Wow, I've made it!" but then struggle, struggle, struggle—"Oh, here I've made it again"?

Abraham: You are right! Money is not the path to happiness, and as you have observed, poverty certainly is not the path to happiness either.

It is so important to remember that when you offer any action for the purpose of achieving happiness, you are truly going about it in a backward way. Instead, use your ability to focus your thoughts and words toward things that cause you to feel better and better; and once you have deliberately achieved a state of happiness, not only will wonderful actions be *inspired,* but wonderful results must follow.

Most people give the majority of their attention to whatever is happening in their experience right now—which means if the results please them, they feel good, but if the results do not please them, they feel bad. But that is really going about life the hard way. If you only have the ability to see *what-is,* then things cannot improve. You must find a way to look optimistically forward in order to achieve any improvement in your experience.

When you learn how to deliberately focus your thoughts toward good-feeling things, it is not difficult to find happiness and maintain it even before your goal has been accomplished. The feeling of struggle you were describing happens because of the continual comparison of where you are right now in relationship to the goal you are reaching for. When you constantly take score, noticing the distance that still needs to be traveled, you amplify the distance, the task, and the effort; and that is why it feels like such an uphill struggle.

When you care about how you feel, and so choose thoughts on the basis of how they feel, you then develop patterns of thought that are more forward looking. And as the *Law of Attraction* then responds to those better-feeling thoughts, you get more pleasing results. *Struggle, struggle, struggle never leads to a happy ending. It defies Law. "When I get there, then I'll be happy" is not a productive mind-set because unless you are happy, you cannot get there. When you decide to first be happy—then you will get there.*

I Am Here as a Joyful Creator

Abraham: You are here not as accumulators or regurgitators. You are here as *creators.* When you are looking toward an ending place, you exaggerate the feeling of lack between where you are now and that ending place—and that habit of thought can not only slow the progress of your creation, but can hold it apart from you indefinitely. *You are the attractor of your experience. As you look for positive aspects and make an effort to find good-feeling thoughts, you will hold yourself in a place of positive attraction and what you want will come faster.*

The sculptor of a work of art does not derive his greatest satisfaction from the finished piece. It is the process of creation (the sculpting of the piece) that gives him pleasure. That is the way we would like you to view your physical experience of creating: *continual, joyful becoming.* As you focus your attention upon things that feel good and achieve a consistently joyful state of being, you will then be in the position of attracting more of whatever you want.

Sometimes people complain that it seems unfair that they have to become happy before things that bring more happiness can then come to them. They believe that when they are unhappy, they "need" the happy events to come, but when they are already happy, then the happy events are unnecessary—but that would defy the *Law of Attraction. You have to find a way of feeling the <u>essence</u> of what you desire before the <u>details</u> of that desire can come to you. In other words, you have to begin to feel more prosperous before more prosperity can come.*

Often people tell us that they want more money, and when we ask them what their balance of thought is about money, they proclaim that they have a very positive attitude about money. But as we probe a bit deeper, asking them how they feel when they sit to pay their bills, they often then realize that while they may have been attempting to sound positive about the subject, they have actually been feeling a great deal of worry or even fear around the subject of money. In other words, often without realizing it, the majority of their thoughts about money have been on the *not-enough* side of the subject rather than on the *abundant* side of the subject.

The Power of Vibrationally Spending Vibrational Money

Abraham: Here is a process that can quickly help you shift the balance of your thoughts regarding money to a place where you can begin to let more money flow easily into your experience: Put $100 in your pocket and keep it with you at all times. As you move through your day, deliberately notice how many things you could exchange this money for: "I could purchase that. I could do that."

Someone replied to us that $100 really does not buy that much in today's economy, but we explained that if you mentally spend that $100 one thousand times today, you have vibrationally spent $100,000. That sort of positive focus will dramatically change your vibrational balance about money. This vibrational spending process will cause you to feel differently about money; and when that happens, your point of attraction will shift—and more money must flow into your experience. *It is Law.*

Someone said to us, "Abraham, I didn't have the $100, but I put an IOU in my pocket." And we said, that is defeating the process, because you are walking around with a *feeling* of debt in your pocket, which is exactly the opposite of what you want to do. You want to *feel* your prosperity. And so, even if it is only $20 or $50, or if it is $1,000 or $10,000, that you have in your pocket, *utilize it effectively to help you notice how good things are—now.* Because in your acknowledgment of your prosperous *now*—your prosperity must become more.

Needing Money Won't Attract It

Jerry: Abraham, one of my greatest disappointments as I have worked to help people find greater financial success is that those who *needed* the money the *most* had the *least* success with what I was teaching them, while those who *needed* it the *least* had the *most* success with it. That always seemed backward to me: It seemed like those who needed it more would try harder, and eventually they should succeed.

Abraham: Anyone who is in a place of lack—no matter how much action they offer—attracts more lack. In other words, the powerful *feeling* outweighs any *action* that they offer. *Any action that is offered from a place of lack is always counterproductive.* Those who were not feeling need were not in a place of lack, and so their action was productive. Your experience was in absolute harmony with the *Law of Attraction*—as is every experience. There is not a shred of evidence anywhere in the Universe that is to the contrary of this that we are speaking of.

Jerry: Also, what I noticed was that by and large, those who didn't achieve much success, or weren't very interested in even hearing about achieving success, were people who had been taught that to want money was evil or immoral, and that the best thing for them to do was to remain as they were even though they were unfulfilled.

Abraham: The reason that many reach a place where they say that they do not have desire is because they have wanted and wanted and wanted, but because they have not understood that every subject is two subjects, they have given more of their attention to the lack of what they have wanted than to what they wanted. And so, they continued to attract the lack of what they want. And then, eventually, they were just worn down by it. As a person begins to associate wanting with not having, so much so that to want is an unpleasant experience, then he or she says, "I no longer want, because every time I want something, I get myself in this place of discomfort, and so it is easier for me not to want in the first place."

What If a "Poor" One Doesn't Feel Poor?

Jerry: If others who are noticing you and comparing you to themselves come to the conclusion that you are poor but *you* don't *feel* poor, then you wouldn't be in a state of lack—and so you would be able to move quickly toward more abundance in that case, right?

Abraham: That is correct. Others' assessment of you has no bearing on your point of attraction unless you are bothered by their assessment. Comparing your experience to the experiences of others can amplify a feeling of lack within you if you come to the conclusion that they have succeeded more greatly than you have, and you then activate within yourself a feeling of being "less than." Also, noticing a lack of prosperity in the experiences of others does not put you in a place of attracting greater prosperity for yourself, because you will be getting what you think about.

What you draw to you—or keep from you—has nothing to do with what anyone else is doing. *An improved feeling of prosperity, even if your current reality does not justify the feeling, will always bring more prosperity to you. Paying attention to the way you feel about money is a much more productive activity than noticing how others are doing.*

Allowing more money to flow into your experience requires far less than most people understand. All that is required is that you achieve a vibrational balance in your own thoughts. If you want more money but doubt you can achieve it—you are not in balance. If you want more money but you believe there is something wrong in having money—you are not in balance. If you want more money and you are angry at those who have more money—you are not in balance. When you are feeling those emotions of inadequacy, insecurity, jealousy, injustice, anger, and so on, your *Emotional Guidance System* is letting you know that you are out of alignment with your own desire.

Most people make no effort in coming into personal alignment with the subject of money. Instead, they spend years, even lifetimes, pointing out perceived injustices, attempting to define the rightness or wrongness of the subject, and even trying to put laws in place to orchestrate the flow of money in the civilization, when a rather small effort—in comparison with the impossible attempt at controlling those outside circumstances—would yield them an enormous return.

Nothing is more important than that you feel good, for when you feel good, you are in harmony with your greater intent. Many believe that hard work and struggle are not only a requirement to achieve success, but that working hard and struggling long is a more honorable way of living life. Those hard times of struggle certainly do help you in the defining of what you desire, but until you release the feeling of struggle, what you desire cannot come into your experience.

Often people feel as if they need to prove their worthiness, and that once that is accomplished, then and only then will rewards be given—but we want you to know that you are already worthy, and that proving yourselves worthy is not only not possible, but unnecessary. What *is* necessary for you to receive the rewards or benefits that you seek is alignment with the essence of those benefits. You have to first bring yourself into vibrational alignment with the experiences you wish to live.

We recognize that words do not teach and that our knowledge regarding the *Laws of the Universe* and of your value do not necessarily mean that now that you have read our words, you now know your value. However, as you consider the premises that we are laying out for you here, and as you begin the application of the processes that we are suggesting here, it is our knowing that the Universe's response to your improved vibration will give you the evidence of the existence of these *Laws*.

It will not be long and it will not require much deliberate application of what you are reading here before you will be convinced of your own value and of your ability to create whatever you desire. The primary reason that people do not believe in their own value is because they often have not found a way to get what they want, and so they incorrectly assume that someone outside of them does not approve and is somehow withholding the reward. That is never true. You are the creator of your experience.

Make statements such as: *I want to be the best that I can be. I want to do and have and live in a way that is in harmony with my idea of the greatest goodness. I want to harmonize physically here in this body with that which I believe to be the best, or the good way, of life.* If you will make those statements, and then do not take action unless you feel good, you will always be moving upon the path in harmony with your idea of that which is good.

What Is My "Financial Abundance" Story?

Abraham: A belief in lack is the reason that more people are not allowing themselves the financial abundance they desire. When you believe that there is a finite pile of abundance and that there is not enough to go around—and so you feel injustice when someone has more than others, believing that because they have it, others are deprived of having it—you are holding yourself apart from abundance. It is not another's achievement of success that is responsible for your lack of achievement, but rather it is your negative comparison and your attention to the lack of your own desire. When you feel the negative emotion that you feel as you accuse others of injustice or of squandering wealth or hoarding—or when you simply believe that there is not enough to go around—you hold yourself in the position of denying your own improved condition.

What anyone else has or does not have has nothing to do with you. The only thing that affects your experience is the way you utilize the Non-Physical Energy with your thought. Your abundance or lack of it in your experience has nothing to do with what anybody else is doing or having. It has only to do with your perspective. It has only to do with your offering of thought. If you want your fortunes to shift, you have to begin telling a different story.

Many people criticize those who are living well, who accumulate land and money and things; and that criticism is symptomatic of their own lackful habit of thought. They want to feel better and often believe that if they can make that which they are unable to achieve "wrong," then they will feel better—but they never do feel better, because their attention to lack perpetuates lack everywhere they look. They would not feel uncomfortable in seeing someone else's achievement if that desire for achievement were not present within themselves as well. And that criticism that they often keep alive within themselves only serves to hold them in vibrational discord with what they want.

In other words, if someone called you on the telephone and said to you, "Hello, you don't know me, but I'm calling to tell you that I will never call you again," you would not feel negative emotion about the caller's absence from your life, because his or her presence was not something that you desired to begin with. But if someone you care about were to make that announcement to you, you would feel strong negative emotion, because your desire and your belief would then be at odds.

When you feel negative emotion about anything, it always means that you have a desire that has been born from your personal life experience that you are, right now, opposing with other thoughts. *Vibrational discord is always the reason for negative emotion. And negative emotion is always guidance to help you redirect your thoughts to find vibrational alignment with <u>who-you-really-are</u> and with your current desires.*

What If the Poor Criticize the Rich?

Jerry: When I was a kid, I associated with poor people primarily, and we used to make fun of those who were wealthy—we criticized those who drove luxury cars, for instance. And so, as an adult, when it came time that I would like to have owned a Cadillac, I couldn't bring myself to drive one because I felt that people would make fun of me as I had made fun of the others. So I drove a Mercedes because years ago people kind of thought that they were "economy" cars.

The only way I could bring myself to drive a Cadillac, which I finally did, was to bridge my thoughts by saying, *Well, by buying this car, I put all those people to work who put this car together. I created jobs for all the people who supplied the parts and the materials—the leather, the metal, the glass—and the craftsmen, and so on. . . .* And in that justification, then I was able to buy the car. So somehow I discovered a process of bridging my thoughts that helped me allow that symbol of success into my experience.

Abraham: Your process of bridging thoughts is an effective one. When you want to feel good and you gradually find increasingly better-feeling thoughts, you are bringing yourself into alignment with your desire and you are releasing the resistance that is preventing your improved conditions. *Focusing on opposing opinions of others is never productive because it always causes discord within you, which also prevents your improved condition. There will always be others who disagree with you, and your attention to them will always cause you to <u>vibrationally</u> disagree with your own desires. Listen to your own <u>Guidance System</u>—by paying attention to how you are feeling—in order to determine the appropriateness of your desires and behaviors.*

There will always be someone, no matter which side of any subject you choose, who does not harmonize with you. And that is why we speak so firmly, and want so much for you to understand, that your greatest endeavor is to find harmony with *who-you-really-are*. If you would trust in yourself—if you could believe that through all that you have lived you have come to a place of very strong knowing, and that you can trust the way you feel as your personal form of Guidance about the appropriateness or inappropriateness of what you are contemplating doing—then you would utilize your *Guidance System* in the way that it was really intended.

What If Our Money Loses Value?

Jerry: Abraham, in the past our money was primarily coins—metal that had a value in and of itself: Like the $20 gold piece, the gold itself was worth $20; and the silver in the silver dollar had value. And so, it seemed simple to understand the value of the coin. But now our money in and of itself has no actual value; the paper and coins are essentially valueless.

I've always appreciated the convenience of money as a way of exchanging goods and talents rather than trading a chicken for a container of milk or for a basket of potatoes. But now our money is being artificially devalued, and it's becoming increasingly difficult to really understand the value of a dollar. In other words, it reminds me of my own searching for my own value: "How much is my talent worth? How much should I ask for in exchange for the time and energy that I put forth?" But now I'm learning from you that we don't have to consider our value in that way. We have only to consider what it is that we want and then allow it in.

I'm aware that many people are feeling insecure about their financial future because they feel they don't have control over what may happen to the value of the dollar—because it's typically a handful of people who seem to control or manipulate that. Many worry that there's going to be more inflation, or even another depression. I'd like people to understand what you've been teaching us about the *Law of Attraction* so that they won't be concerned with things that are outside of their control, like the value of the dollar.

Abraham: You have hit upon something very essential here regarding the subject of money because, you are right, many of you are recognizing that the dollars today just are not worth what they were at one time. But that is another position of lack you very often stand firmly upon that keeps you from attracting the abundance that is yours.

We would like you to understand that the dollar and its assigned value is really not as important to your experience as you are believing, and that if you could put your attention upon what you are wanting, in terms of *being* and then *having* and then *doing,* that all of the money—or other means for bringing about what you want—could then flow easily, and much more effortlessly, into your experience.

We keep coming back to the same terminology: *From your place of lack, you cannot attract its opposite. And so, it really is a matter of adjusting your thinking so that your thinking harmonizes with that which feels good within you.*

Every thought that you think vibrates, and it is by virtue of having that vibrating thought that you attract. When you think a thought of lack, that thought is vibrating at a place that is so alien to that which your *Inner Being* knows to be that your *Inner Being* cannot resonate with you at all—and the resultant feeling within you is one of negative emotion. When you think a thought of upliftment or abundance or Well-Being, those thoughts do harmonize with that which your *Inner Being* knows to be. And under those conditions, you are filled with a feeling of positive emotion.

You may trust the way that you feel as the indicator as to which side of this subject (that is really two subjects) you are on. *Whether it is the subject of money or lack of it, or health or lack of it, or a rela-tionship or the lack of one—always, when you feel good, you are in the place of attracting that which you are wanting.*

To Reverse a Downward Spiral?

Jerry: When I would see people having financial problems, I used to worry about them. I would watch as they spiraled down, down, down, until they would finally come crashing down in bank-ruptcy. But then in a very short time, they would have another new boat, a new luxury car, and another beautiful home. In other words, no one I watched seemed to stay down. But why couldn't they stop the downward spiral somewhere earlier along the way and start back upward sooner? Why did so many of them have to go all the way to the bottom before they could start back up again?

Abraham: The reason for any downward spiral is attention to lack. In their fear that they might lose something, or in their attention to things that they were losing, they were focused upon the lack of what they wanted; and as long as that was their point of attention, only more loss was possible. As they felt guarded or defensive, or as they began to justify or rationalize or blame, they were on the lack side of the equation and only more lack could be their experience.

But once they hit bottom and were no longer in a place of guardedness because there was nothing else to lose, their attention shifted, and so their vibration shifted—and so their point of attrac-tion shifted. Hitting what they believed to be the bottom caused them to begin to look up. You could say that it forced them to begin telling a different story.

Your life experience has caused you to ask for many wonderful things that are making their way into your experience, but your worry or doubt or fear or resentment or blame or jealousy (or any number of negative emotions) would indicate that the predomi-nant thoughts you were thinking were holding those things away. It would be as if you had drawn them right outside your door, but your door was closed. As you begin to tell a different story of the things you could buy with a $100 bill, as you relax and focus more upon the positive aspects of your life, as you more deliberately choose the better-feeling end of the vibrational stick—that door will open and you will be flooded with manifestations of those wanted things and experiences and relationships.

A War Against War Is War

Abraham: Recognizing that you are the creator of your own life experience and learning to deliberately do so by directing your thoughts is an adjustment for most people, because most have long believed that you *make* things happen through *action*. Not only have you erroneously believed that action is what makes things happen, but you have also believed that if you apply pressure to unwanted things, they will go away. That is why you have a "war against poverty" and a "war against drugs" and a "war against AIDS" and a "war against terrorism."

And although you may believe that pushing against these unwanted things will cause them to leave your experience, that is not how the *Laws of the Universe* work, and that is not the proof of your experience, for all of those wars are getting bigger. *Attention to the lack of what is wanted causes it to increase and come closer to you, just as focusing upon what is wanted causes it to increase and come closer to you.*

When you relax into your natural Well-Being, when you make statements such as: "I seek abundance, and I trust the *Laws of the Universe*—I have identified the things that I want, and now I am going to relax and allow them into my experience," more of what you desire will come. If your financial situation feels like a struggle, you are pushing your financial Well-Being farther away, but when you begin to feel ease regarding your financial situation, you are then allowing more abundance to flow into your experience. It really is as simple as that.

And so, when you see others excelling in their attraction of money and you feel negative emotion about it, that is your signal that your current thought is not allowing the abundance that you desire into your experience. *When you find yourself critical of the way anyone has attracted or is using money, you are pushing money away from yourself. But when you realize that what others do with money has nothing to do with you, and that your primary work is to think and speak and do what feels good to you, then you will be in alignment not only about the subject of money, but about every important subject in your physical experience.*

Can We Succeed Without Talent?

Jerry: What bearing does talent or skill or ability have on bringing abundance or money into our lives?

Abraham: Very little. Those are all *action* aspects for the most part, and your *action* is responsible for but a minuscule part of what comes to you. Your *thoughts* and *words* (words are *thoughts* articulated) are the reason your life unfolds as it does.

Jerry: So then would you say that people with no salable skill or talent could still receive all the financial abundance they want in their lives?

Abraham: Absolutely, unless in comparing themselves to others (and concluding that they have no salable skill or talent), they feel diminished and therefore defeat their own experience with their own negative expectation.

The most valuable skill that you could ever develop is the skill of directing your thoughts toward what you want—to be adept at quickly evaluating all situations and then quickly coming to the conclusion of what you most want—and then giving your undivided attention to that. There is a tremendous skill in directing your own thoughts that will yield results that cannot be compared with results that mere action can provide.

Can We Get Something Without Giving?

Jerry: So, how can people get past the belief that they must *give* a dollar's worth of something in order to *get* a dollar's worth of something?

Abraham: Your knowledge in all things comes only through life experience, but your life experience comes as a result of the thoughts that you are thinking. So even though you may have wanted something for a very long time, if your thoughts have been upon the absence of it, then it could not come to you. And so, from your personal experience, you come to the conclusion that it *is not* possible, or that it *is* a struggle. In other words, you come to many valid conclusions about things being hard when you have led a difficult life.

It is our desire to help you understand what is really at the heart of that self-created struggle. We want to help you begin from a different premise and understand the *Laws* at the basis of all things. A new understanding of the *Laws of the Universe* and a willingness to begin telling a different story will give you different results, and those different results will then give you different beliefs or knowledge.

You are the one, and the only one, who can evaluate your effectiveness. No one else has the ability to discern where you stand relative to where you are wanting to be, and nobody else can decide where you should be—only you.

They Want to Win the Lottery Fortune

Jerry: Many people are hoping for some major financial windfall to come to them to free them from debt or to release them from working at something they don't want to work at in order to receive money. The thing I hear them say most often is that they want to win the lottery, where they'll get their abundance in exchange for someone else losing theirs.

Abraham: If their *expectation* were in a place that would allow it, then that could be a way for money to come to them. But most know the odds against that, and so their *expectation* for winning the lottery is not in a powerful place either.

Jerry: So, how does *hoping to win* relate to *expecting to win?*

Abraham: Just as *hoping* is more productive than *doubting—expecting* is much more productive than *hoping.*

Jerry: Then how could people begin to expect something that their life experience hasn't yet shown them? How can you expect something that you haven't experienced?

Abraham: You do not have to *have* money to *attract* money, but you cannot *feel poor* and attract money. The key is, you have to find ways of improving the way you feel from right where you stand before things can begin to change: *By softening your attention to the things that are going wrong, and by beginning to tell stories that lean more in the direction of what you want instead of in the direction of what you have got, your vibration will shift, your point of attraction will shift, and you will get different results. And in a short time, because of the different results you are then getting, you will then have beliefs or knowledge of abundance that will easily perpetuate more of the same. People often say, "The rich get richer, and the poor get poorer," and that is why.*

Look for reasons to feel good. Identify what you want—and hold your thoughts in a place that feels good.

Living Abundantly Is Not "Magic"

Abraham: As we explain, from our perspective, the abundant nature of your Universe and the potential for abundance that is always available to you, we understand that our knowledge does not become your knowledge only because you have read our words. If we were to ask you to trust what we say or to "just try" to understand, you cannot just adopt our understanding as your own—for it is only your own life experience that brings knowledge to you.

The beliefs that you hold as a result of your own experience are very strong, and we understand that you cannot release them immediately and replace them with others, even though we know there are many more productive beliefs that you could foster. But there is something that you can begin today that will make a profound difference in the way your life unfolds that does not require an immediate releasing of the beliefs that you currently hold: *Start telling a more positive, better-feeling story about your life and the things that are important to you.*

Do not write your story like a factual documentary, weighing all the pros and cons of your experience, but instead tell the uplifting, fanciful, magical story of the wonder of your own life and watch what happens. It will feel like magic as your life begins to transform right before yours eyes, but it is not by magic. It is by the power of the *Laws of the Universe* and your deliberate alignment with those *Laws.*

Trading Freedom for Money?

Jerry: Well, I know we titled this book *Money, and the Law of Attraction,* but it's really more about attracting *abundance* in all areas of our lives. Since my childhood, we (in the U.S.) have been fighting strongly against crime. And there's much more crime now than when I was a kid. I read recently that our nation has a higher percentage of its population in prisons than any other country in the "free" world.

We've been fighting against illness, and yet there are more hospitals and more sick people than ever before—there's so much more physical suffering in this nation percentage-wise now than I've ever seen.

We've been pushing against warfare in our search for world peace, and yet it seems like such a short time ago that everyone was raving, "Isn't it wonderful [as the Berlin wall came down] that we're finally in peace?" But we hardly took four breaths until we were back in another series of wars, and now *we're* even putting more walls up around *this* nation.

Also, I hear of so much concern about child abuse and the mistreating of other people, and yet the more I hear of our pushing against child abuse, the more child abuse I hear of.

It seems like everything we're trying to do to stop what we don't want isn't working for us. But the area where this nation seems to continue to go in a more positive direction is that of *abundance.* We have so much food and money that we're able to give the world over from our excess abundance, and I see many more material things in the hands of more people in this country than during my early years, so there have been some major positive changes there.

But so many people, in their quest for more financial abundance, seem to be losing quite a bit of their personal freedom as a trade-off for the money. It seems like there are those who seem to have a lot of free time, but they have so little money that they don't enjoy their time. And then there are those with more money, but little time to enjoy the money. But it's rare that I meet someone who has both an abundant flow of money combined with the time to really enjoy it. Abraham, would you please comment on your perspective of my perceptions?

Abraham: Whether you are focused upon the lack of money or the lack of time, you are still focused upon the lack of something you want and therefore holding yourself in resistance to the things you really want. Whether your negative emotion is because of your feeling of shortage of time or whether it is because of your feeling of shortage of money, you are still feeling negative emotion and you are still in a state of resistance, and therefore you are holding away what you really want.

As you feel that you do not have enough time to do all of the things you need or want to do, your attention to lack negatively impacts you much more than you realize. *A feeling of being overwhelmed is your indicator that you are denying yourself access to ideas, rendezvous, conditions, and all manner of cooperation that could assist you if you were not disallowing them. It is an uncomfortable cycle where you feel a shortage of time, you focus upon your overloaded schedule, and you feel overwhelmed—and in all of that, you offer a vibration that makes improvement impossible.*

You have to begin telling a different story, for you cannot continue to comment on how much you have to do without holding assistance away. There is a cooperative Universe at your fingertips, ready and able to help you in more ways than you can begin to imagine, but you deny yourself that benefit as you continue to complain about too much to do.

As you feel that you do not have enough money, your attention to the lack of money disallows the avenues that could bring you more—you just cannot look at the opposite of what you want and get what you want. You have to begin telling a different story. You have to find a way to create a feeling of abundance before abundance can come.

As you begin to feel freer regarding the expenditure of time and money, doors will open, people will come to assist you, refreshing and productive ideas will occur to you, and circumstances and events will unfold. As you change the way you feel, you access the Energy that creates worlds. It is there for your ready access at all times.

Feeling Negative with Respect to Money or Cancer?

Jerry: So what's the difference between having a negative feeling about money and therefore you *don't* get money and saying, "I don't want cancer," but you *do* get cancer?

Abraham: Here is the way it works: You get the essence of what you think about, and so as you are thinking about the *lack* of health, you are getting the lack of health. As you are thinking about the lack of money, you are getting the lack of money. You can tell by the way you *feel* as you are offering your thought whether you are attracting the positive or the negative aspects of the subject.

The Universe does not hear *no.* When you are saying, *No, I do not want illness,* your attention to the subject of illness is saying, *Yes, come unto me, this thing I do not want.*

Anything you are giving your attention to is an invitation to the essence of it. When you are saying, *I want money, but it will not come,* your attention to its absence is the same as saying, *Come to me, absence of money, which I do not want.*

When you are thinking of money in the way that will make it come to you, you always feel good. When you are thinking of money in the way that keeps it from coming to you, you always feel bad. That is how you know the difference.

So, you are asking, "If I can get cancer by focusing upon the lack of health, then why couldn't I get money by focusing on the lack of it?" The receiving of money, *which you do want,* is the same as the receiving of health, *which you do want.* The receiving of cancer, *which you do not want,* is the same as the receiving of no money, *which you do not want.*

Just make sure that whatever thoughts you are thinking, or whatever words you are speaking, evoke from you positive emotion, and then you will be in the mode of attracting what you *do* want. When negative emotion is present, you are in the mode of attracting something that you *do not* want.

He Didn't Struggle for Money?

[The following is an example of an audience member's question at an Abraham-Hicks workshop.]

Question: I have a friend who had basically financially supported her former husband for about ten years. She worked hard and took care of him for all of that time, often struggling to earn enough money to support them. Eventually she grew tired of his unwillingness to contribute financially, and they separated. Her husband never showed any evidence that money was important to him, but he has now just inherited over a million dollars—and now he will not share his money with his ex-wife (my friend), who supported him for all of those years.

It doesn't seem fair that she cared about money and worked hard for it and received so little, while he barely worked, didn't seem to care about money, and has now inherited over a million dollars. How can this be?

Abraham [the rest of the chapter is Abraham speaking]: Understanding the *Law of Attraction* as we do, this story makes perfect sense. This woman worked hard, felt resentment, focused upon lack—and the Universe matched those *feelings* precisely. Her husband felt ease, refused to feel guilty, expected things to come to him easily—and the Universe matched those *feelings* precisely.

Many believe that they must work hard, struggle, pay a price, and feel pain, and that they will then be rewarded for their struggle—but that is not consistent with the *Laws of the Universe: You cannot find a happy ending to an unhappy journey. That defies <u>Law.</u>*

There is not a shred of evidence to the contrary of the *Law of Attraction;* and you had the benefit of knowing these two people, seeing their attitudes, and watching their results: one struggling, working very hard, doing what society has taught her—and not getting what she wants . . . the other refusing to struggle, insisting on a feeling of ease—and being the recipient of the resources that support more ease.

Many would say, "Well, it might be consistent with the *Laws of the Universe,* but it's still not right," but we want you to know that when you get in sync with this powerful *Law,* you will then understand the absolute justice of it.

Since you have control over what you offer, what could be more just than the Universe giving you exactly what you offer vibrationally? What could be more just than the powerful *Law of Attraction* responding equally to everyone who offers a vibration? Once you gain control over the thoughts you think, your sense of injustice will subside and will be replaced with the exuberance for life and the zest to create that you were born with. *Let everything in the Universe be an example to you of the way the <u>Laws of the Universe</u> work.*

If you believe that you must work hard in order to deserve the money that comes to you, then money cannot come to you unless you do work hard. But the money that comes in response to physical action is very small in comparison with what comes through alignment of thought. Surely you have noticed the enormous disparity between some people who apply tremendous action for little return while you see others seemingly offering very little action for an enormous return. We want you to understand that the disparity exists only in the comparison of the *action* they are offering—but there is no disparity or injustice relative to the *alignment* of Energies within them.

Financial success, or any other kind of success, does not require hard work or action, but it does require alignment of thought. You simply cannot offer negative thought about things that you desire and then make up for it with action or hard work. When you learn to direct your own thoughts, you will discover the true leverage of Energy alignment.

Most of you are much closer to a financial fortune than you are even allowing yourself to purely desire, because, in the thought that it might come, you right away begin thinking of how disappointed you will be if it does *not* come in. And so, in your lackful thought, you do not allow yourself to desire or to expect anything magnificent in terms of money; and that is the reason why, for the most part, you are living rather mediocre financial experiences.

You are right when you think, *Money isn't everything.* You certainly do not need money to have joy in your experience. But in your society—where so much of what you live is tied to money in some way—most of you associate money with freedom. And since freedom is a basic tenet of your Being, then coming into alignment with money will help you establish a balanced footing that will be of value to you in all other aspects of your experience.

Is Spending Money Comfortable?

A very prevalent way of looking at money was expressed to us by a woman who explained that she always feels uncomfortable when she spends her money. She had, over time, managed to save quite a bit of money, but whenever she would think about spending some of it, she would "freeze up" and "feel afraid to go another step further."

We explained: It is certainly understandable that when you believe that your money is coming to you because of the action that you are offering and you also believe that you will not always be able to offer that action, you would want to hold on to your money and spend it sparingly to make it last. However, that feeling of shortage slows the process of more money flowing into your experience.

If you feel uncomfortable with the idea of spending money, then we absolutely do not encourage you to spend the money while you are feeling uncomfortable, because any action taken amidst negative emotion is never a good idea. But the reason for your discomfort is not about the action of spending the money, but instead it is an indication that your thoughts about money in that moment are not a Vibrational Match to your own desire. *A belief in shortage will never resonate with your broader knowing, because there is no shortage. Any attention to lack of something wanted will always produce negative emotion within you because your Guidance is letting you know that you have strayed from your broader basic understanding of abundance and Well-Being.*

Find a way to ease your *discomfort* and eventually transform it into a feeling of hope, and then positive *expectation;* and then from that stable place of feeling better, that feeling of "freezing up" will be replaced with *confidence* and *enthusiasm.* Whether you are focused upon the shortage of *money*—or seeing yourself as having only so many *years* to live (and so each day that is expended is one day closer to the end of your years)—that feeling of decline is contrary to your broader understanding of the Eternal nature of your Being.

In the same way that you understand that you do not have to attempt the impossible task of drawing enough air into your lungs to last all day or all week or all year—but instead you easily breathe in and out, always receiving what you want or need whenever you want or need it—money can flow in and out of your experience with the same ease once you achieve that expectation of Eternal abundance.

All of the money that you want is available for you to receive. All you have to do is *allow* it into your experience. And as the money flows in, you can gently allow it to flow out, for like the air you breathe, there will always be more to flow. You do not have to guard your money (like holding your breath and not letting it out) because there will not be any more coming. More *is* coming.

People sometimes protest as they tell their tales of shortage or scarcity, pointing out the "reality" of the shortage that they have experienced, witnessed, or heard about. And we understand that there are plenty of examples to point to of people who are experiencing shortages of many things that they desire. But we want you to understand that those experiences of shortage are not because abundance is not available, but because it is being *disallowed.*

Continuing to tell stories of shortage only continues to contradict your desire for abundance, and you cannot have it both ways: You cannot focus upon *unwanted* and receive *wanted.* You cannot focus upon stories about money that make you feel uncomfortable and allow into your experience what makes you feel comfortable. You have to begin telling a different story if you want different results.

We would begin by saying, *I want to feel good. I want to feel productive and expansive. My thoughts are the basis for the attraction of all things that I consider to be good, which includes enough money for my comfort and joy, which includes health and wonderful people around me who are stimulating and uplifting and exciting. . . .*

Begin telling the story of your desire, and then add to it the details of the positive aspects that you can find that match those desires. And then embellish your positive expectation by speculating with your good-feeling *Wouldn't it be nice if . . . ?* examples.

Say things like: *Only good things come to me. While I don't have all of the answers, and while I don't know all of the steps, and I can't identify all of the doors that will open for me, I know that as I move through time and space, the path will be obvious to me. I know I will be able to figure it out as I go along.* Every time you tell your better-feeling story, you will feel better and the details of your life will improve. The better it gets, the better it gets.

How to Change My Point of Attraction?

Sometimes people worry that they have been telling the story of what they do not want for such a long time that they now do not have the time left in their lives to make up for all of those years of focusing upon the shortage of money—but they have no cause for worry.

Although it is true that you cannot go backward and undo all of that negative thinking, there is no reason to do that even if you could, because all of your power is in your *now*. As you find a better-feeling thought right now, your point of attraction shifts—now! *The only reason it may seem like some negative thinking that you picked up many years ago is having an impact on your life now is because you have been continuing the negative train of thoughts or beliefs through all of those years. A belief is only a thought you continue to think. A belief is nothing more than a chronic pattern of thought, and you have the ability—if you try even a little bit—to begin a new pattern, to tell a new story, to achieve a different vibration, to change your point of attraction.*

Just the simple act of noticing how many things you could purchase in this one day with the $100 you are carrying with you would dramatically alter your financial point of attraction. That one simple process is enough to tip the balance of your Vibrational Scale enough to show you actual tangible results in your attraction of money. Mentally spend your money and imagine an improved lifestyle. Deliberately conjure a feeling of freedom by imagining what it would feel like to have a large amount of money at your disposal.

You see, the *Law of Attraction* is responding to your vibration, not to the reality you are currently living—but if your vibration continues to be only about the reality you are living, nothing can change. *You can easily change your vibrational point of attraction by visualizing the lifestyle you desire and holding your attention upon those images until you begin to feel relief, which will indicate that a true vibrational shift has occurred.*

My Standards Are Mine to Set

Sometimes from an awareness of a shortage of money, you think that you want everything that you see. A sort of uncontrollable craving rises within you, which tortures you when you do not have the money to spend or causes even more distress when you give in to the craving and spend money you do not have, going deeper into debt. But that craving to spend money under those conditions is really a false signal, for it is not coming from a real desire to have those things. *Buying one more thing and bringing it home will not satisfy that craving, for what you are really feeling is a void that can only be filled by coming into vibrational alignment with who-you-really-are.*

You are currently feeling insecure, when *who-you-really-are* is someone who is absolutely secure. You are currently feeling inadequate, when *who-you-really-are* is someone who is adequate. You are feeling lack, when *who-you-really-are* is someone who is abundant. It is a vibrational shift that you are craving, not the ability to purchase something. Once you are able to achieve and consistently maintain your personal alignment, a great deal of money will flow into your experience (if that is your desire), and you will very likely spend large amounts of money on things that you desire, but your purchases will feel very different to you then. You will not feel need or a void that you are attempting to fill with a purchase, but instead you will feel a satisfying interest in something, which will easily make its way into your experience, and every part of the process—from the inception of the idea to the full-blown manifestation of it into your experience—will bring to you a feeling of satisfaction and joy.

Do not let others set the standards about how much money you should have—or about what you should do with it—for you are the only one who could ever accurately define that. Come into alignment with who-you-really-are, and allow the things that life has helped you to know that you want to flow into your experience.

Does "Saving for Security" Work?

A man related to us that he once had a teacher who told him that to set money aside for security was the same as "planning for a disaster," and in fact the very act of trying to feel more secure would actually lead to more insecurity because it would attract the unwanted disaster. He wanted to know if that philosophy fit in with our teachings about the *Law of Attraction*.

We told him: This teacher was right in pointing out that attention to anything brings more of the essence of it to you, and so if you were to focus upon the idea of possible bad things looming out there in your future, the discomfort that you would feel as you pondered those unwanted things would be your indication that you are, indeed, in the process of attracting them. But it is absolutely possible to briefly consider something unwanted occurring in the future, such as a financial situation that makes you feel insecure as you consider it, which could cause you to then consider the financial *stability* that you *desire*. And as you focus upon the security that you *desire*, you may very well be inspired to an action that enhances that state of security.

The action of saving money, or investing in assets, in and of itself is neither positive or negative, but that teacher would be correct to say that you cannot get to a place of security from an insecure footing. *Our encouragement is to use the power of your mind to focus upon the good-feeling security you seek and then take whatever positive action that is inspired from that place of feeling good. Anything that feels good to you is in harmony with what you want. Anything that feels bad to you is not in harmony with what you want. It is truly as simple as that.*

Some say that you should not want money at all because the desire for money is materialistic and not Spiritual. But we want you to remember that you are here in this very physical world where Spirit has materialized. You are here in your very physical bodies on this very physical planet where that which is Spirit and that which is physical or material blend. *You cannot separate yourself from the aspect of yourself that is Spiritual, and while you are here in these bodies, you cannot separate yourselves from that which is physical or material.*

All of the magnificent things of a physical nature that are surrounding you are Spiritual in nature.

Telling a New Story about Abundance, Money, and Financial Well-Being

The *Law of Attraction* is not responding to the reality that you are currently living and perpetuating, but instead it is responding to the vibrational patterns of thoughts that are emanating from you. So as you begin to tell the story of who you are—in relationship to money—from the perspective of what you *desire* rather than from the perspective of what you are actually currently living, your patterns of thoughts will shift, and so will your point of attraction.

What-is has no bearing on what is coming unless you are continually regurgitating the story of what-is. By thinking and speaking more of how you really want your life to be, you allow what you are currently living to be the jumping-off place for so much more. But if you speak predominantly of what-is, then you still jump off—but you jump off into more of the same.

So consider the following questions, letting your natural answers flow in response to them, and then read some examples of what your new story regarding money might sound like. And then, begin to tell your own new-and-improved story of your financial picture, and watch how quickly and surely circumstances and events will begin to move around you to make your new story a reality:

- Do you have as much money in your life experience as you want right now?

- Is the Universe abundant?

- Do you have the option of having plenty of money?

- Was the amount of money that you would receive in this lifetime already decided before you were born?

- Are you now setting into motion, through the power of your current thought, the amount of money that will flow?

- Do you have the ability to change your financial situation?

- Are you in control of your financial condition?

- Do you want more money?

- Knowing what you now know, is financial abundance guaranteed?

An Example of My "Old" Story about Money

There are so many things that I want that I just can't afford. I'm making more money today than ever before, but money feels as tight as ever. It just seems like I can't get ahead.

It seems like I've worried about money my whole life. I remember how hard my parents worked and my mother's constant worry about money, and I guess I've inherited all of that. But that isn't the kind of inheritance I had hoped for. I know there are really wealthy people in the world who don't have to worry about money, but they aren't anywhere near me. Everyone I know right now is struggling and worried about what's going to happen next.

Notice how this story began by noticing a current unwanted condition; then moved to justification of the situation; then looked into the past for more emphasis of the current problem, which amplified the resentment more; then moved to a broader view of perceived shortage. *When you begin to tell a negative story, the Law of Attraction will help you reach from your present perspective, into your past, even into your future—but the same vibrational pattern of lack will persist. When you focus upon lack in an attitude of complaining, you establish a vibrational point of attraction that then gives you access only to more thoughts of complaint whether you are focused in your present, your past, or your future.*

Your deliberate effort to tell a new story will change that. Your new story will establish a new pattern of thought, providing you with a new point of attraction from your present, about your past, and into your future. The simple effort of looking for positive aspects from right where you stand will set a new vibrational tone that will not only affect the way you feel right now, but will begin the immediate attraction of thoughts, people, circumstances, and things that are pleasing to you.

An Example of My "New" Story about Money

I like the idea that money is as available as the air I breathe. I like the idea of breathing in and breathing out more money. It is fun to imagine a lot of money flowing to me. I can see how my feeling about money affects the money that comes to me. I am happy to understand that with practice I can control my attitude about money, or about anything. I notice that the more I tell my story of abundance, the better I feel.

I like knowing that I am the creator of my own reality and that the money that flows into my experience is directly related to my thoughts. I like knowing that I can adjust the amount of money that I receive by adjusting my thoughts.

Now that I understand the formula for creating; now that I understand that I do get the essence of what I think about; and, most important, now that I understand that I can tell by the way I am feeling whether I am focused upon money or lack of money, I feel confident that in time, I will align my thoughts with abundance—and money will flow powerfully into my experience.

I understand that the people around me hold many different perspectives about money, wealth, spending, saving, philanthropy, giving money, receiving money, earning money, and so forth, and that it is not necessary for me to understand their opinions or experiences. I am relieved to know that I do not have to sort all of that out. It is very nice to know that my only work is to align my own thoughts about money with my own desires about money, and that whenever I am feeling good, I have found that alignment.

I like knowing that it is all right for me to occasionally feel negative emotion regarding money. But it is my intention to quickly direct my thoughts in better-feeling directions, for it is logical to me that thoughts that feel good when I think them will bring positive results.

I understand that money will not necessarily manifest instantly in my experience with the changing of my thinking, but I do expect to see steady improvement as a result of my deliberate effort to think better-feeling thoughts. The first evidence of my alignment with money will be my improved feeling, my improved mood, and my improved attitude—and then real changes in my financial situation will be soon to follow. I am certain about that.

I am aware of the absolute correlation between what I have been thinking and feeling about money and what is actually happening in my life experience. I can see the evidence of the Law of Attraction's absolute and unerring response to my thought, and I look forward to more evidence in response to my improved thoughts.

I can feel a powerful leveraging of Energy in being more deliberate about my thoughts. I believe, at many levels, that I have always known this, and it feels good to return to my core beliefs about my power and value and worthiness.

I am living a very abundant life, and it feels so good to realize that whatever this life experience causes me to desire—I can achieve that. I love knowing that I am unlimited.

I feel tremendous relief in recognizing that I do not have to wait for the money or the things to materialize before I can feel better. And I now understand that when I do feel better, the things and experiences and money that I want must come.

As easily as air flows in and out of my being—so it is with money. My desires draw it in, and my ease of thought lets it flow out. In and out. In and out. Ever flowing. Always easy. Whatever I desire, whenever I desire, as much as I desire—in and out.

There is no right or wrong way to tell your improved story. It can be about your past, present, or future experiences. The only criterion that is important is that you be conscious of your intent to tell a better-feeling, improved version of your story. Telling many good-feeling short stories throughout your day will change your point of attraction. Just remember that the story *you* tell is the basis of *your* life. So tell it the way you want it to be.

ఇ§ ఇ§ ఇ§ ఠ౾ ఠ౾ ఠ౾

PART III

Maintaining My Physical Well-Being

My Thoughts Create My Physical Experience

The idea of "success," for most people, revolves around money or the acquisition of property or other possessions—but we consider a state of joy as the greatest achievement of success. And while the attainment of money and wonderful possessions certainly can enhance your state of joy, the achievement of a good-feeling physical body is by far the greatest factor for maintaining a continuing state of joy and Well-Being.

Every part of your life is experienced through the perspective of your physical body, and when you feel good, everything you see looks better. Certainly it is possible to maintain a good attitude even when your physical body is diminished in some way, but a good-feeling body is a powerful basis for an ongoing good attitude. And so, it is not surprising that since the way you feel affects your thoughts and attitudes about things, and since your thoughts and attitudes equal your point of attraction, and since your point of attraction equals the way your life continues to play out—*there are few things of greater value than the achievement of a good-feeling body.*

It is quite interesting to note that not only does a good-feeling body promote positive thoughts, but that, also, positive thoughts promote a good-feeling body. That means you do not have to be in a perfect state of health in order to find feelings of relief that eventually can lead to a wonderful mood or attitude, for if you are able to somehow find that relief even when your body is hurting or sick, you will find physical improvement, because your thoughts create your reality.

Complaining about Complaining Is Also Complaining

Many complain that it is easy to be optimistic when you are young and in good health, but that it is very difficult when you are older or sicker . . . but we never encourage using your age or a current state of failing health as a limiting thought that disallows improvement or recovery.

Most people have no idea of the power of their own thoughts. They do not realize that as they continue to find things to complain about, they disallow their own physical well-being. Many do not realize that before they were complaining about an aching body or a chronic disease, they were complaining about many other things first. It does not matter if the object of your complaint is about someone you are angry with, someone who has betrayed you, behavior in others that you believe is wrong, or something wrong with your own physical body—complaining is complaining, and it disallows recovery.

So whether you are feeling good and are looking for a way to maintain that good-feeling state of being or if your physical body is diminished in some way and you are looking for recovery, the process is the same: *Learn to guide your thoughts in the direction of things that feel good, and discover the power that only comes from vibrational alignment with Source.*

As you continue to read this book, things that you have known long before you were born will be remembered, and you will feel a resonance with these *Laws* and processes that will give you a feeling of empowerment. And then all that is required for the achievement and maintenance of a healthy, good-feeling body is some deliberate attention to thoughts and feelings and a sincere desire to feel good.

I Can Feel Good in My Body

If you are not feeling good or looking the way you want to look, it has a way of reflecting out into all other aspects of your life experience, and it is for that reason that we want to emphasize the value in bringing your physical body into balance and comfort and well-being. There is nothing in the Universe that responds faster to your thoughts than your own physical body, and so aligned thoughts bring a quick response and obvious results.

Your physical well-being is really the easiest of subjects over which you have absolute control—for it is what *you* are doing about *you*. However, because you are translating everything in this world through the lens of how your physical body feels, if you do get out of balance, it can negatively affect a much larger part of your life than only your physical body.

You are never more clear about wanting to be healthy and to feel good than when you are sick and feeling bad, and so the experience of being sick is a powerful launching pad for the asking for wellness. So, if, in the moment that your sickness has caused you to ask for wellness, you could turn your undivided attention to the idea of being well, it would occur immediately—but for most, now that you are feeling bad, *that* is what has your attention. *Once you are sick, it is logical that you would now notice how you feel, and in doing so, you would prolong the sickness . . . but it was not your attention to the lack of wellness that made you sick. Instead, it was your attention to the lack of many things that you desire.*

Chronic attention to unwanted things holds you in a place of disallowing your physical well-being, as well as disallowing the solutions to other subjects you are focused upon. *If you could focus your attention upon the idea of experiencing physical well-being with as much passion as you focus upon the absence of it, not only would your recovery come quickly, but maintaining your physical well-being and balance would also be easy.*

Words Do Not Teach, but Life Experience Does

Simply hearing words, even when they are perfect words that accurately explain truths, does not bring understanding, but the combination of careful words of explanation, coupled with life experience that is always consistent with the <u>Laws of the Universe,</u> does bring understanding. It is our expectation that as you read this book and live your life, you will achieve a complete understanding of how all things occur in your experience and you will accomplish complete control of all aspects of your own life, especially things that have to do with your own body.

Perhaps your physical condition is exactly as you want it to be. If that is the case, then continue to focus upon your body as it is, feeling appreciation for the aspects that are pleasing you—and you will maintain that condition. But if there are changes that you would like to make, whether it is in appearance or stamina or well-ness, then it will be of great value for you to begin telling a different story—not only about your body, but about all subjects that have been troubling to you. As you begin to positively focus, getting to feel *so* good about so many subjects that you often feel passion rise within you, you will begin to feel the power of the Universe—the power that creates worlds—flowing through you.

You are the only one who creates in your experience—no one else. Everything that comes to you comes by the power of your thought.

When you focus long enough that you feel passion, you harness more power and you achieve greater results. The other thoughts, while they are important and have creative potential, usually are only maintaining what you have already created. And so, many people continue to maintain unwanted physical experiences simply by offering consistent—not powerful, and not accompanied by strong emotion—thoughts. In other words, they merely continue telling the same stories about things that seem unfair, or unwanted things that they disagree with, and in doing so, they maintain unwanted conditions. *The simple intention of telling better-feeling stories about all subjects that you focus upon will have a great effect on your physical body. But since words do not teach, it is our suggestion that you try telling a different story for a while and observe for yourself what happens.*

The *Law of Attraction* Expands My Every Thought

The *Law of Attraction* says that *that which is like unto itself, is drawn.* In other words, that which you think, in any moment, attracts unto itself other thoughts that are like it. That is why whenever you are thinking about a subject that is not pleasant, more unpleasant thoughts regarding that subject are quickly drawn. You find yourself, in very short order, not only experiencing what you are experiencing in *this* moment, but reaching into your past for more data that matches that vibration—and now, by the *Law of Attraction,* as your negative thought expands proportionately, so does your negative emotion.

Soon you find yourself discussing the unpleasant subject with others, and now *they* add to it, often reaching into *their* past . . . until, *in a very short period of time, most of you, upon any subject that you ponder very long, attract enough supporting data that it does bring forth the essence of the subject of the thought into your experience.*

It is natural that by knowing what you *do not want,* you are able to clarify what you *do want;* and there is nothing wrong with identifying a problem before beginning to look for a solution. But many people, over time, become problem oriented rather than solution oriented, and in their examination and explanation of the problem, they continue the perpetuation of the problem.

Again, a telling of a different story is of great value: Tell a solution-oriented story instead of a problem-oriented story. *If you wait until you are sick before you begin to try to focus more positively, it is much harder than if you begin to tell the story of Well-Being from your place of feeling good . . . but, in any case, your new story will, in time, bring you different results. That which is like unto itself, is drawn—so tell the story you want to live and you will eventually live it.*

Some people worry that since they are already sick, they cannot now be well because their sickness now has their attention, and therefore their attention to sickness is perpetuating more sickness. We agree. That would be correct if they only have the ability to focus upon *what-is* at this time. But since it is possible to think about things other than what is happening right now, it is possible for things to change. However, you cannot focus only upon current problems and get change. You have to focus upon the positive results you are seeking in order to get something different.

The Law of Attraction is responding to your thought, not to your current reality. When you change the thought, your reality must follow suit. If things are going very well for you right now, then focusing upon what is happening now will cause the well-being to continue, but if there are things that are happening now that are not pleasing, you must find a way of taking your attention away from those unwanted things.

You have the ability to focus your thoughts—about yourself, about your body, and about the things that matter to you—in a different direction from only what is happening right now. You have the ability to imagine things that are coming or to remember things that have happened before, and when you do so with the deliberate intent of finding good-feeling things to think and speak about, you can quickly change your patterns of thought, and therefore your vibration, and eventually . . . your life experience.

15 Minutes to My Intentional Well-Being

It is not easy to imagine a healthy foot when your toe is painfully throbbing, but it is of great value for you to do everything you can do to distract yourself from your throbbing toe. However, a time of acute physical discomfort is not an effective time to try to visualize well-being. The best time to do that is when you are feeling the best you usually feel. In other words, if you usually feel physically better during the first part of the day, choose that time for the visualization of your new story. If you usually feel best after taking a long, warm bath, choose *that* time for visualization.

Set aside approximately 15 minutes where you can close your eyes and withdraw as much as possible from your awareness of *what-is*. Try to find a quiet place where you will not be distracted, and imagine yourself in a state of physical thriving. Imagine walking briskly and breathing deeply and enjoying the flavor of the air you are breathing. Imagine walking briskly up a gentle incline, and smile in appreciation of the stamina of your body. See yourself bending and stretching and enjoying the flexibility of your body.

Take your time exploring pleasant scenarios with the sole intent of enjoying your body and appreciating its strength and stamina and flexibility and beauty. *When you visualize for the joy of visualizing rather than with the intention of correcting some deficiency, your thoughts are more pure and therefore, more powerful. When you visualize to overcome something that is wrong, your thoughts are diluted with the lackful side of the equation.*

Sometimes people explain that they have long-held desires that have not manifested, and they argue that the *Law of Attraction* is not working for them—but that is because they have been asking for improvement from a place of keen awareness of the lack of what they desire. It takes time to reorient your thoughts so that they are predominantly focused toward what you want, but in time it will feel perfectly natural to you to do so. In time, your new story will be the one that you tell most easily.

If you do take the time to positively imagine your body, those good-feeling thoughts will become dominant, and then your physical condition must acquiesce to those thoughts. If you only focus upon the conditions as they exist, nothing will change.

As you imagine and visualize and verbalize your new story, in time you will *believe* the new story, and when that happens, the evidence will flow swiftly into your experience. A belief is only a thought you continue to think, and when your beliefs match your desires, then your desires must become your reality.

Nothing stands between you and anything that you desire other than your own patterns of thought. There is no physical body, no matter what the state of decline, no matter what the conditions, that cannot achieve an improved condition. Nothing else in your experience responds as quickly as your own physical body to your patterns of thought.

I Am Not Bound by Others' Beliefs

With a little bit of effort focused in the right direction, you will achieve remarkable results, and in time, you will remember that you can be or do or have anything that you focus upon and achieve vibrational alignment with.

You came into your physical body and into this physical world from your Non-Physical perspective, and you were very clear about your intention to be here. You did not define all of the details of your physical life experience before you got here, but you did set forth clear intentions about the vitality of your physical body from which you would create your life experience. You felt enormous eagerness to be here.

When you first arrived in your small infant body, you were closer to the Inner World than to the physical world and your sense of Well-Being and strength was very strong, but as time passed and you became focused more into your physical world, you began to observe others who had lost their strong Connection to Well-Being, and—bit by bit—your sense of Well-Being began to fade as well.

It is possible to be born into this physical world and continue to maintain your Connection to *who-you-really-are* and to your absolute Well-Being; however, most people, once they are focused into this time-space reality, do not. The primary reason for the fading of your awareness of personal Well-Being is the clamoring of those around you for you to find ways to please them. *While your parents and teachers are, for the most part, well-meaning people, they are nevertheless more interested in your finding ways to please <u>them</u> than in your finding ways to please yourself. And so, in the process of socialization, almost all people in almost all societies lose their way because they are coaxed or coerced away from their own <u>Guidance System.</u>*

Most societies demand that you make your action your top priority. You are rarely encouraged to consider your vibrational alignment or your Connection to your Inner World. Most people eventually become motivated by the approval or disapproval that is directed at them by others—and so, with their misplaced attention upon accomplishing the action that is most respected by the onlookers of their lives, they lose their alignment, and then everything in their experience is diminished.

But you were eager about being born into this physical world of such amazing variety because you understood the value of that contrast from which you would build your own experience. You knew that you would come to understand, from your own experience, what you preferred from the variety of options that would be available to you.

Whenever you know what you *do not want,* you understand more clearly what it is that you *do want.* But so many people take that first step of identifying what is *not* wanted, and instead of then turning toward what *is* wanted and achieving vibrational alignment with that, they instead continue to talk about what they do *not* want—and, in time, the vitality that they were born with wanes.

There Is Time Enough to Accomplish It

When you do not understand the power of thought and you do not take the time to align your thought to allow this power, you are then resigned to create through the power of your action—which, comparatively, is not much. And so, if you have been working hard with your action to accomplish something and have not managed to achieve it, often you feel overwhelmed or incapable of now making it happen. Some people simply feel they do not have enough time left in their lives to be and do and have the things that they have dreamed of. But we want you to understand that if you will take the time to deliberately align with the Energy that creates worlds, through the power of focusing your thoughts you will discover a leverage that will help you quickly accomplish things that have formerly seemed not possible.

There is nothing that you cannot be or do or have once you accomplish the necessary alignment, and when you do, your own life experience will give you the evidence of your alignment. Before things actually manifest, your proof of alignment comes in the form of positive, good-feeling emotion; and if you understand that, then you will be able to hold steady to your course while the manifestations of the things you desire are making their way to you. The *Law of Attraction* says: *That which is like unto itself, is drawn. Whatever your state of being—whatever the way you feel—you are attracting more of the essence of that.*

To want or desire something always feels good when you believe you can achieve it, but desire in the face of doubt feels very uncomfortable. We want you to understand that wanting something and believing you can accomplish it is a state of alignment, while wanting something and doubting it is misalignment.

317

Wanting and believing is alignment.
Wanting and expecting is alignment.
Expecting something unwanted is not alignment.
You can *feel* your alignment or misalignment.

Why Do I Want Perfect Bodily Conditions?

Although it may seem strange to you, we cannot begin to address your physical body without addressing your Non-Physical roots and your Eternal Connection to those roots, because you, in your physical body, are an extension of that *Inner Being*. In very simple terms, in order to be at your maximum state of health and Well-Being, you must be in vibrational alignment with your *Inner Being*—and in order to do that, you must be aware of your emotions or feelings.

Your physical state of well-being is directly related to your vibrational alignment with your *Inner Being* or Source, which means every thought that you think on every subject can positively or negatively affect that Connection. In other words, it is not possible to maintain a healthy physical body without a keen awareness of your emotions and a determination to direct your thoughts toward good-feeling subjects.

When you remember that feeling good is natural and you make an effort to find the positive aspects of the subjects that you are considering, you will train your thoughts to match the thoughts of your <u>Inner Being,</u> and that is of tremendous advantage to your physical body. When your thoughts are chronically good-feeling—your physical body will thrive.

Of course, there is a broad range of emotions—from those that feel very bad to those that feel very good—but in any moment in time, because of whatever you are focused upon, *you actually only have two choices in emotion: a <u>better-feeling one</u> or a <u>worse-feeling one.</u>* So you could accurately say there are really only two emotions, and you effectively utilize your *Guidance System* when you deliberately choose the better-feeling of those two options. And, in doing so, in time you can tune yourself to the precise frequency of your *Inner Being*—and when you do that, your physical body will thrive.

I Can Trust My Eternal *Inner Being*

Your *Inner Being* is the *Source* part of you that continues to evolve through the thousands of life experiences that you live. And with each sifting and sorting experience, the Source within you always chooses the best feeling of the available choices, which means your *Inner Being* is eternally tuning itself to *love* and *joy* and all that is good. That is the reason that when you choose to love another or yourself rather than find fault, you feel good. Good feeling is confirmation of your alignment with your Source. When you choose thoughts that are out of alignment with Source, which produces an emotional response like *fear* or *anger* or *jealousy,* those feelings indicate your vibrational variance from Source.

Source never turns away from you but offers a steady vibration of Well-Being, and so when you feel negative emotion, it means that you are preventing your vibrational access to Source and to the Stream of Well-Being. As you begin telling stories about your body and your life and your work and the people in your life that feel good as you tell them, you will achieve a steady Connection with that Stream of Well-Being that is ever flowing to you. And as you focus upon the things that you desire, feeling positive emotion as you focus, you access the power that creates worlds and you flow it toward your object of attention.

What Is the Role of Thought in Traumatic Injuries?

Jerry: Are traumatic injuries created in the same way that diseases are created, and can they be resolved through thought? Are they like a breakage of something that happened in a momentary incident as opposed to a long series of thoughts leading up to it?

Abraham: *Whether the trauma to your body seemed to come suddenly as a result of an accident or whether it came from a disease such as cancer, you have created the situation through your thought—and the healing will come through your thought as well.*

319

Chronic thoughts of *ease* promote wellness, while chronic *stressful* or *resentful* or *hateful* or *fearful* thoughts promote disease, but whether the result shows up suddenly (as in falling and breaking your bones) or more slowly (as in cancer), *whatever you are living always matches the balance of your thoughts.*

Once you have experienced the diminishment of Well-Being, whether it has come as broken bones or internal diseases, it is not likely that you will suddenly find good-feeling thoughts that match those of your *Inner Being.* In other words, if before your accident or disease you were not choosing thoughts that aligned with Well-Being, it is not likely that now that you are faced with discomfort or pain or a frightening diagnosis, you will now suddenly find that alignment.

It is much easier to achieve great health from moderate health than to achieve great health from poor health. However, you can get to wherever you want to be from wherever you are if you are able to distract your attention from the unwanted aspects of your life and focus upon aspects that are more pleasing. It really is only a matter of focus.

Sometimes a frightening diagnosis or traumatic injury is a powerful catalyst in getting you to focus your attention more deliberately on things that do feel good. In fact, some of our best students of Deliberate Creation are those who have been given a frightening diagnosis where doctors have told them that there is nothing more that can be done for them, who now (since they have no other options) deliberately begin to focus their thoughts.

It is interesting that so many people will not do what really works until all other options have been exhausted, but we do understand that you have acclimated to your action-oriented world, and so action does seem to most of you to be the best first option. *We are not guiding you away from action, but instead encouraging that you find better-feeling thoughts first, and then follow with the action that you feel inspired to.*

Could a Congenital Illness Be Vibrationally Resolved?

Jerry: Can a *congenital illness*—something a person came into physical form with at birth—be resolved by thought?

Abraham: Yes. From wherever you stand, you can get to wherever you want to be. If you could understand that your *now* is only the jumping-off place for that which is to come, you could move quickly (even from dramatic unwanted things) to things that please you.

If this life experience contains the data that causes you to give birth to a desire, then the wherewithal to accomplish it is available to you. But you must focus upon where you want to be—not where you are—or you cannot move toward your desire. However, you cannot create outside your own beliefs.

Major Diseases Come and Go, but Why?

Jerry: In my earlier years, there were major diseases (tuberculosis and polio) that we hear very little of anymore. But we're not short of diseases, because now we have heart disease and cancer, which we almost never heard of back then. In those days syphilis and gonorrhea were constantly in the news. We don't hear much of those, but now AIDS and herpes stay foremost in the news. Why do there always seem to be more diseases cropping up? As cures are being discovered, why don't we finally run out of diseases *to* cure?

Abraham: Because of your attention to lack. Feelings of powerlessness and vulnerability all produce more to feel powerless and vulnerable about. You cannot focus upon the conquering of disease without giving your attention to disease. But it is also very important to understand that looking for cures for diseases, even when you find them, is a shortsighted and, in the long run, ineffective process because, as you have pointed out, new diseases are continually being created. *When you begin to look for and understand* *the <u>vibrational causes</u> for diseases rather than looking for <u>cures,</u> then you will come to the end of the pile of diseases. When you are able to deliberately accomplish the emotion of ease and its accompanying vibrational alignment, it is possible to live disease free.*

Most people spend very little time basking in appreciation for the wellness they are currently experiencing, but instead they wait until they are sick and then they turn their attention to recovery. Good-feeling thoughts produce and sustain physical well-being. You live in very busy times, and you find many things to fuss and worry about; and in doing so, you hold yourself out of alignment— and disease is the result. And then you focus upon the disease and perpetuate more disease. But you can break the cycle at any time. You do not have to wait for your society to understand in order to achieve wonderful physical wellness yourself. *Your natural state is one of wellness.*

I've Witnessed My Body Heal Itself Naturally

Jerry: I became aware early in life that my body heals quickly. If I cut or scratched my body, I could almost watch it heal right before my eyes. Within five minutes, I could see that healing had begun, and then in a very short time, the wound would be completely healed.

Abraham: Your body is made up of intelligent cells that are always bringing themselves into balance, and the better you feel, the less you are vibrationally interfering with the cellular rebalancing. If you are focused upon things that are bothering you, the cells of your body are hindered in their natural balancing process—and once an illness has been diagnosed and you then turn your attention to that illness, the hindering is greater still.

Since the cells of your body know what to do to come into balance, if you can find a way of focusing your attention upon good-feeling thoughts, you will stop your negative interference and your recovery will come. Every dis-ease is caused by vibrational discord or resistance, without exception, and since most people were unaware of their discordant thoughts prior to the illness (usually making little effort to practice good-feeling thoughts), once the illness occurs it is very difficult to then find pure, positive thoughts.

But if you could understand that your thoughts and your thoughts alone are causing the resistance that is preventing the wellness—and you could turn your thoughts in a more positive direction—your recovery could be very fast. No matter what the disease is, and no matter how much it has progressed, the question is: *Can you direct your thoughts positively regardless of the condition?*

Usually at this point someone asks, "But what about the sick child who has just been born?" Do not assume because a child is not yet speaking that the child is not thinking or offering vibration. There are tremendous influences to wellness and sickness that occur even when the child is still in the womb or is newly born.

By Attention to Wellness, I'll Maintain Wellness?

Jerry: Because I've seen my body heal, and because that healing has been visible to me, I expect that. But how can we get to the point that we *know* that *all* parts of the body will heal? People seem to be most frightened of the parts they can't see—those hidden inside of the body, so to speak.

Abraham: It is a wonderful thing to see the results of your thoughts out in the open in an obvious fashion, and just as your wound or sickness is evidence of misalignment, your healing or wellness is evidence of alignment. *Your tendency toward wellness is much stronger than your tendency for illness, and that is the reason that even with some negative thinking, most of you do remain mostly well.*

You have come to *expect* your wounds to heal, which helps tremendously in the healing process, but when the evidence of your illness is something that you cannot see—where you must rely on the investigation of your doctor who uses his medical tests or equipment to probe for information—you often feel powerless and fearful, which not only slows the healing process, but also is a strong reason for the creation of illness. Many people have come to feel vulnerable about the unseen parts of their bodies, and that feeling of vulnerability is a very strong catalyst in the perpetuation of illness.

Most people go to the doctor when they are sick, asking for information about what is wrong, and when you look for something wrong, you usually find it. *The Law of Attraction insists on it, actually. A continual searching for things wrong with your body will, in time, produce evidence of something wrong, not because it was lurking there all along and you finally probed long enough to find it, but because repeated thought eventually creates its equivalent.*

When Inspired to Visit a Medical Doctor?

Abraham: There are many who would protest our perspective, claiming that we are irresponsible when we do not encourage regular checkups on the quest for things that have gone wrong, or are getting ready to go wrong, or could potentially go wrong, with your physical body. And if we did not understand the power of your thoughts, we might even say that if it makes you feel more secure to go to the doctor, then by all means go.

In fact, sometimes when you go looking for trouble and do not find it, you do feel better. But more often than not, the repeated looking for something wrong over time creates it. It is really that simple. We are not saying that medicine is bad or that there is no value to be received by a visit to your doctor. Medicine, doctors, and all healing professions in general are neither good nor bad at their own face value, but instead they are as valuable as your vibrational stance can allow them to be.

Our encouragement is that you pay attention to your emotional balance, work deliberately to find the best-feeling thoughts you can find, and practice them until they are habitual . . . and, in doing so, you will tend to your vibrational alignment first—and then follow through with whatever action you feel inspired to. In other words, a trip to your doctor—or action toward anything—when accompanied by joy or love or good-feeling emotion, is always valuable; while action that is motivated by your *fear* or *vulnerability,* or any bad-feeling emotion, is never valuable.

Your physical well-being, like everything else, is profoundly affected by the *beliefs* that you hold. Usually when you are younger, your expectation of wellness is stronger, but as you get older most of you degenerate on a sort of sliding scale that reflects what you are seeing in others around you. And, your observation is not inaccurate. *Older people often do experience more illness and less vitality. But the reason for the decline of people as they get older is not because their physical bodies are programmed to break down over time, but because the longer they live, the more they find to fuss and worry about, causing resistance to their natural Stream of Well-Being. <u>Illness is about resistance, not about age.</u>*

Euphoria in the Jaws of a Lion?

Jerry: I heard that a famous man, Dr. Livingstone, while in Africa, was dragged off by a lion that grabbed him with its jaws. He said that he went into a sort of euphoric state and felt no pain. I've seen prey go limp like that when they're about to be eaten by a larger animal. It's kind of like there is a giving up and the struggle is over. But my question is about his statement about feeling no pain: Was what he was calling *euphoria* a mental condition or a physical condition? And is it something that only happens in extreme conditions like when you're about to be eaten or killed, or could it be utilized by anyone when there is something that's painful in order not to feel the pain?

Abraham: First, we will say that you cannot accurately separate that which is physical from that which is mental from that which is coming from your Higher or *Inner* Being. In other words, you are a physically focused Being, *yes;* and you are a thinking, mental Being, *yes;* but the Life Force or Energy that comes forth from within you is offered from a Broader Perspective. In such a situation where it is likely that you would not recover—in other words, once a lion has you in his jaws (usually, *he* is going to be the victor)—*your <u>Inner</u>*

Being intervenes and offers a flow of Energy that would be received by you as that sort of euphoric state.

You do not have to wait until you are in such an intense situation before you have access to the Stream of Well-Being from Source, but most people do not allow it until they have no other choice. You were right in your choice of words that there was a _giving up_ that allowed that Stream of Well-Being to flow powerfully. But we want you to understand that what was actually "given up" was the _struggle,_ the resistance—not the _desire_ to continue to live in this physical body. You have to take all of that into consideration as you are examining specific situations. Someone with less enthusiasm for life, with less determination to live and continue to accomplish, may very well have experienced a different outcome and have been killed and devoured by the lion. _Everything that you experience is about the balance of thought between your desires and your expectations._

A state of _allowing_ is something that must be practiced in normal day-to-day circumstances, not in the midst of attacks by lions. But even in the middle of such an intense situation, the power of your intentions always causes the outcome. Practiced alignment—brought about by consistently good-feeling thoughts—is the path to being pain free. Pain is only a more emphatic indicator of resistance. First there is negative emotion, then more negative emotion, then more negative emotion (you have tremendous leeway here), then sensation, then pain.

We tell our physical friends: If you have negative emotion and you do not realize that it is an indicator letting you know about resistant thought and you do not do something to correct your resistant thought, by the _Law of Attraction_ your resistant thought will grow stronger. If you still do not do anything to bring yourself into alignment and better-feeling thoughts, it will grow stronger still, until eventually you will experience pain and illness or other indicators of your resistance.

How Could Someone Feeling Pain Focus Elsewhere?

Jerry: Okay, so I've heard you say that in order to heal ourselves, we want to get our thoughts off of the problem and onto what we're wanting. But if we're in pain, how can we not feel it? How can we get our attention off the pain long enough to concentrate on something we do want?

Abraham: You are right. It is very difficult not to think about the "throbbing toe." Most of you do not think clearly about what you *do* want until you are living what you *do not* want. Most of you sort of drift into your day, blundering here and there, not offering any real conscious thought. Because you do not understand the power of your thought, you usually do not offer any really deliberate thought until you are faced with something that you do not want. And then, once you are faced with something that you do not want, then you attack it fully. Then, you give it your attention, which—knowing the *Law of Attraction,* as we do—only makes things worse. . . . And so, our encouragement would be: *Look for times (or segments) when you are not feeling such intensity of throbbing pain—and then focus upon the Well-Being.*

You have to find a way of separating what is happening in your experience from your emotional response to what is happening. In other words, you could have pain in your body and during the pain you could be feeling *fear,* or you could have pain in your body while feeling *hopeful.* The pain does not have to dictate your attitude or the thoughts that you are thinking. It is possible to think about something other than the pain. And if you can achieve that, then in time the pain will subside. However, if once the pain occurs, you give the pain your undivided attention, then you will only perpetuate more of what you do not want.

Someone who has been focusing negatively upon any variety of subjects and *now* is experiencing pain, now has to overcome the pain *and* focus positively. You see, your negative habit of thought brought about the illness, and to suddenly switch to the positive thought required to allow wellness is not likely to be a fast process, because now you have the hindering pain or illness, or both, to contend with. _Preventive wellness is far easier to accomplish than cor-rective wellness, but, in either case, improved-feeling thoughts—thoughts of greater and greater relief—are the key._

Even in situations where a lot of pain is being experienced, there are times of greater and lesser discomfort. Choose the best-feeling times from the range you are experiencing to find positive aspects and to choose better-feeling thoughts. And as you continue to reach for thoughts that bring greater emotional relief, that positive leaning will eventually bring you back to Well-Being—every time, no exceptions.

My Natural State Is One of Well-Being

Abraham: At the core of that which you are is wellness and Well-Being, and if you are experiencing anything less than that, there is resistance present within your vibration. _Resistance_ is caused by focusing upon the lack of what is wanted. . . . _Allowing_ is caused by focusing upon what is wanted. . . . _Resistance_ is caused by thought that does not match the perspective of your Source. . . . _Allowing_ is experienced when your current thoughts _do_ match the perspective of your Source.

Your natural state is one of wellness, one of absolute health, one of perfect bodily conditions—and if you are experiencing anything other than that, it is only because the balance of thought within you is toward the lack of what you want instead of what you do want.

It is your resistance that causes an illness in the first place, and it is your resistance to illness that holds it to you once it is there. It is your attention to what you do _not_ want that creates unwanted things in your experience, and so it is logical that your attention to what you _do_ want would be appropriate.

Sometimes you think you are thinking about being well, when you are really worried about being sick. And the only way to be sure of the vibrational difference is by paying attention to the emotion that always accompanies your thought. _Feeling your way to the thoughts that promote wellness is much easier than trying to think yourself there._

Make a commitment to yourself to feel good and then guide your thoughts accordingly, and you will discover that without even realizing it you have been harboring resentments, feeling unworthy, and feeling powerless. But now that you have decided to pay attention to your emotions, these resistant, illness-producing thoughts will no longer go unnoticed. It is not natural for you to be sick, and it is not natural for you to harbor negative emotion—for, at your core, you are like your *Inner Being: You are well; and you feel very, very good.*

But Could a Baby's Thoughts Attract Disease?

Jerry: How could a new baby attract a disease that it doesn't have a conscious awareness of yet?

Abraham: First, we want to state unequivocally that no one is creating your reality other than you, but it is important to realize that the "you" that you know as you did not begin as that small infant born to your mother. You are an Eternal Being, having lived many experiences, who came forth into this physical body from a long background of creating.

People often think that it would be a much better world if all newborn babies could be born meeting all of the standards of a "perfect" physical body, but that is not necessarily the intention of every Being who comes forth into a physical body. There are many Beings who, because the contrast creates an interesting effect that proves valuable in many other ways, deliberately intend to vary from what is "normal." In other words, you just cannot assume that something has gone wrong when babies are born with differences.

Imagine an athlete who has become very good at playing tennis. People sitting courtside watching the match may assume that this player would be happiest always playing against an opponent with less skill whom she can easily beat, but the athlete may very well prefer exactly the opposite: She may prefer people who are at the top of their game, who draw forth from her focus and precision that has not been drawn before. And, in like manner, *many who are at the top of their game in physical creating want opportunities to view life differently so that new options can be evoked and new experiences can be lived. And these Beings also understand that there can be tremendous benefit to those others who are close by when something different from what is "normal" is being experienced.*

People often incorrectly assume that since the baby cannot speak, it could not be creating its own reality, but that is not the case. Even those who do have language are not creating through words, but through thoughts. Your babies are thinking when they are born, and before they are born they are vibrationally aware. Their vibrational frequencies are immediately affected by the vibrations that surround them in their birth environment, but there is no need to worry about them, for they, like you, were born with a *Guidance System* to help them to discern the difference between the offering of beneficial thoughts and the disallowing of Well-Being thoughts.

Why Have Some Been Born with Illnesses?

Jerry: You speak of the "balance of thought," but are you saying balance of thought even from before we're born? Is that why someone can be born with a physical problem?

Abraham: It is. Just as the balance of your thought now is equaling what you are living, the balance of thought that you held prior to your birth is also what has equaled what you are living. But you must understand that there are those who have come forth deliberately wanting physical "disability" because they wanted the benefit that they knew would come from it. They were wanting to add some balance to their perspective.

Before you came into this physical body, you understood that from wherever you stand, you can make a new decision about what you want. And so, there was no concern about your starting place in your physical body because you knew that if that condition inspired a desire for something different, the new desire was attainable. There are many people who have achieved tremendous success in many areas of life who were born into what would be considered conditions that are the extreme opposite of success. And those raw-and-ragged beginnings served them extremely well, because born out of that poverty or dysfunction was strong desire, which was the beginning of the *asking* that was necessary before success could begin to flow to them.

All Beings who come forth into a physical body have full understanding of the body they are coming into, and you may trust that if they come forth, and remain, it was their intention from the Non-Physical to do so. And, without exception, when where you are currently standing causes you to make another decision about what you *now* desire—you have the ability, if you focus your thought, to accomplish the essence of that creation.

Most who are attracting less than wellness are doing so by default. They may very well desire wellness, while the majority of their thoughts are upon subjects that do not support wellness. *It is not a good idea to stand in your perspective and try to evaluate the appropriateness of what anyone else is living because you will never be able to figure it out. But you always know where you stand relative to what you are wanting. And if you will pay attention to what you are thinking and let your thoughts be guided by the feeling that comes forth within you, you will find yourself guiding your thoughts more of the time in the direction of that which will ultimately please you.*

Let's Discuss the Concept of "Incurable" Diseases

Jerry: The most recent of what we call our "incurable" diseases is AIDS, and yet we're now beginning to see AIDS survivors—people who have lived way beyond the time they were told they were going to be able to live. What would you suggest to someone who is already afflicted with AIDS and now wants help?

Abraham: *There is not a physical apparatus, no matter what the state of deterioration, that cannot achieve perfect health. . . .* But that which you *believe* has everything to do with what you *allow* in your experience. If you have been convinced that something is not cur-able—that it is "fatal"—and then you are told that you have it, usually your *belief* will be that you will not survive . . . and you will not.

But your survival has nothing to do with the disease and everything to do with your thoughts. And so, if you say to yourself: *That may be true for others, but it is not so for me, for I am the creator of my experience, and I choose recovery, not death, at this time* . . . you *can* recover.

These words are easily said by us and not so easily heard by those who do not believe in their power to create, but your experi-ence always reflects the balance of your thoughts. *Your experience is a clear indication of the thoughts that you think. When you change the thoughts you are thinking, your experience, or indicator, must change, also. It is <u>Law.</u>*

Focus on Fun to Regain One's Health?

Jerry: Norman Cousins was an author who contracted a disease that was considered to be incurable. (I don't think anyone had ever recovered from it.) But he survived it, and he said he was able to do so by watching a series of humorous television programs. I under-stand that he just watched these programs—and laughed—and the disease went away. What would you say was behind his recovery?

Abraham: His recovery was accomplished because he achieved vibrational alignment with Well-Being. There are two primary fac-tors involved in his finding vibrational alignment: First, *his desire for wellness was dramatically enhanced by his illness;* and second, *the programs he watched distracted him from the illness—the pleasure that he felt as he laughed at the humor of the programs was his indication that his disallowance of Well-Being had ceased.* Those are the two fac-tors required in the creation of anything: <u>*Want*</u> *it and <u>allow</u> it.*

Usually, once people have focused upon problems and such enough that they have disallowed their Well-Being and they are seriously ill, they then turn their undivided attention to the illness—thus perpetuating it more. Sometimes a doctor can enhance your belief in wellness if he has a process or a remedy that he believes will help you. In that case, the *desire* is amplified because of the illness, and the *belief* is enhanced because of the proposed remedy—but in the case of the supposedly incurable disease, or in the case of the supposedly *curable* disease, the two factors that brought about the healing were the same: <u>*desire and belief.*</u>

Anyone who can come to expect Well-Being can achieve it under any conditions. The trick is to *expect* Well-Being or, as the man in your example did, simply distract yourself from the *lack* of Well-Being.

Did Ignoring the Illness Resolve the Illness?

Jerry: Throughout my adult life, I've never been so sick that I wasn't able to do the work I intended to do that day. In other words, I always felt my work was so important that I didn't consider *not* doing it. I noticed, however, that if I was beginning to feel less than good—like if I was in the beginning stages of a cold or flu—once I got focused on what I needed to do in terms of my work, the symptoms went away. Is that because I was focused upon something that I *wanted?*

Abraham: Because you had a strong *intention* to do your work—and because you enjoyed it when you did it—you had the advantage of a strong momentum toward your Well-Being. So when it seemed that something was detracting from that Well-Being because of some attention to something unwanted, you had only to focus upon your usual intention and your alignment returned quickly—and the symptoms of misalignment faded quickly.

Often you try to accomplish too much through action, and, in doing so, you feel tired or overwhelmed, and those feelings are your indicator that it is time to stop and refresh. But often you push forward in action rather than taking the time to refresh and realign, and that is a very common reason for uncomfortable symptoms to begin to surface.

Most people, when they feel a symptom of sickness, begin to give their attention to the symptom and usually slide rapidly into more discomfort and misalignment. The key is to catch your misalignment early. In other words, whenever you feel negative emotion, that is your signal to reach for a different thought to improve your vibrational balance—but if you do not, your signal will get stronger, until eventually you may feel physical discomfort. But even then, as in the example you just stated, you can still refocus upon something that you desire (taking your attention from whatever has you out of balance) and come into alignment, and the symptoms of sickness must then leave. *There is no condition from which you cannot recover, but it is much easier if you catch it in the early, subtle states.*

Sometimes being sick provides you an escape from something else that you do not want to do, and so, in your environment, there is much *allowing* of sickness for the sake of not having to do something else. But when you begin playing that sort of game with self, you are opening the door to greater and greater and greater sickness.

What's the Effect of Vaccines on Diseases?

Jerry: Since we create our illnesses through thought, then why do *vaccines*—like the one we have for polio—seem to almost put an end to the spread of those particular types of diseases?

Abraham: The illness amplifies your *desire,* and the vaccine amplifies your *belief.* Therefore, you have accomplished the delicate balance of creation: *You want it and you allow it, or <u>believe</u> it—and so it is.*

What about Medical Doctors,
Faith Healers, and Witch Doctors?

Jerry: Well, that would lead me to my next question. People like *witch doctors, faith healers,* and *medical doctors* . . . all of them have the reputation for *healing* some people and for *losing* some of their patients, too. Where do you see the place for such people in thought, or in life?

Abraham: The important thing that they have in common is that they stimulate *belief* in their patients. The first part of the balance of creation has been accomplished because the illness has enhanced the *desire* for wellness, and anything that brings about *belief* or *expectation* will give positive results. When medicine and science stop looking for *cures* and begin to look for *vibrational causes,* or imbalances, they will see a much higher rate of recovery.

If a doctor does not *believe* that you can recover from your illness, your association with that doctor is extremely detrimental. And often, well-meaning doctors will defend their doubt for your recovery by pointing out the odds against it, telling you that it is not likely that you will be an exception. The trouble with that logic—even though it is based on the facts or evidence that medicine and science have come to expect—is that it has nothing to do with you. There are only two factors that have anything to do with your recovery: your *desire* and your *belief.* And this negative diagnosis is hindering your *belief.*

If you have a *strong* desire for recovery, and doctors are giving you no *hope,* it is logical that you would turn to alternative approaches where hope is not only allowed but encouraged, for there is much evidence to show that people can recover from supposedly "incurable" diseases.

Your Physician as a Means to Well-Being

Abraham: Do not condemn your modern medicine, for it has been created because of the thoughts, desires, and beliefs of the members of your society. But we want you to know that you have the power to accomplish anything that you desire, but you cannot look outside of yourself for the validation to do so; your validation will come from within you in the form of emotion.

Seek your vibrational alignment first, and then follow through with inspired action. Let your medical community assist you in your recovery, but do not ask them to do the impossible—do not ask them to give you a cure to compensate for your misalignment of Energy.

Without *asking* there can be no *answering,* and attention to a problem is really an *asking* for a solution, so it is not unusual that doctors would be examining the physical body looking for problems for which they might have a solution. But *looking for problems* is a powerful catalyst for *attracting* them, and so, often well-meaning doctors are instrumental in perpetuating more illness than they are able to find cures for. *We are not suggesting they are not wanting to help you; we are saying their dominant intent, when they examine you, is to find some evidence of something wrong. And since that is their dominant intent—that is more of what they attract than anything else.*

In time, after they have been involved in it for a long period of time, they begin to believe in the fallibility of man. They begin to notice more often what is wrong than what is right, and that is the reason so many of them begin to attract illness into their own experience.

Jerry: So, is that the reason why often doctors can't heal themselves?

Abraham: That is the reason. It is not easy to be focused upon others' negatives without experiencing the negative emotion within your own being—and illness exists because of the allowance of negativity. *One who never experiences negativity will not be sick.*

What Can I Do to Help Them?

Jerry: What's the best thing that I, as an individual, can do for other people who are having physical problems?

Abraham: *You never help others when you allow yourself to be a sounding board for their complaints. Seeing them as you know they want to be is the most valuable thing you can do for them.* Sometimes that means removing yourself from their vicinity because when you are near them, it is difficult not to notice their complaints. You might say to them, "I've learned the power of my attention and thought, and so as I hear you speaking of what I know you don't want, I must tell you that I must remove myself, for I don't want to contribute to your miscreating." Try to distract them from their complaints; try to help them focus upon some positive aspects . . . do your best to imagine their recovery.

You will know when you are of value to anyone when you are able to think about the person and feel good at the same time. When you love others without worry, you are an advantage to them. When you enjoy them, you help them. When you expect them to succeed, you help them. In other words, when you see them as your own Inner Being sees them, then and only then is your association with them to their advantage.

But What If They're in a Coma?

Jerry: From time to time, someone will say, "I have a friend or family member who's in a coma." Is there anything we can do for a loved one who's in an unconscious state?

Abraham: You are communicating with those around you vibrationally even more than with your words, so even though your loved one may show no signs of recognition, it does not mean that your communication is not being received on some level. *You can even communicate with those who have made their physical transition in what you call "death," so do not assume that a seeming unconscious state has barred your communication.*

The primary reason why people remain in a coma or unconscious state is that they are seeking refreshment from the lackful thoughts that have been hindering them. In other words, while they have withdrawn their conscious attention from the details of their normal life, they are in a state of vibrational communication with their own *Inner Being*. It is an opportunity for refreshment and is often a time of decision making where they are actually determining whether they will find their alignment by returning to the Non-Physical or whether they will awaken again back into their physical body. In many regards, it is not very different from being born into their physical body in the first place.

Here is the best attitude for you to hold regarding such people: *I want you to do what is important to you. I approve of whatever you decide. I love you unconditionally. If you stay, I will be ecstatic . . . and if you go, I will be ecstatic. Do what is best for you.* That is the best you can do for them.

Jerry: And so, those people who are in a state like that for many years . . . they're doing what they *want* to do?

Abraham: *Most of them, if it is that length of time, made the decision not to return long ago, and someone in the physical overrode their decision and kept them plugged into a machine, but their Consciousness has long gone and will not return to this body.*

Could I Inherit My Grandmother's Illness?

Jerry: I've heard people say, "I have migraine headaches because my mother had migraine headaches," or "My mother is overweight, my grandmother was overweight, and my children are also overweight." Do some people inherit physical problems?

Abraham: What appears to be an inherited tendency is usually the *Law of Attraction*'s response to the *thoughts* that you learned from your parents. However, the cells of your body are thinking mechanisms, also, and your cells—like you—can learn vibration from those around them. However, when you identify a desire and you find thoughts that feel good—which indicate that you are in vibrational alignment with your *Inner Being* or Source—the cells of your body will quickly align to the vibration of Well-Being that your positive thought has established. The cells of your body cannot develop negative tendencies that lead to disease when you are in alignment with your Source. Your cells can only get out of alignment when *you* are.

Your body is an extension of your thought. Your contagious or "inherited" negative symptoms are supported by your negative thought and could not occur in the presence of chronically positive thoughts no matter what diseases had been experienced by your parents.

Jerry: If I hear my mother speak of her headaches and I accept that, then I can start having headaches myself?

Abraham: *Whether you heard it from your mother or from any other, your attention to something you do not want will, in time, bring the essence of it to you.* The headache is a symptom of resistance to Well-Being, which occurs when you hold yourself in vibrational contradiction to the Well-Being of your *Inner Being.* For example, worrying about work or feeling anger at your government can cause physical symptoms— *you do not have to focus upon a headache to have one.*

Jerry: If I hear my mother complain of headaches and I consciously reject that and say, "That may be for you, but that's not for me," does that protect me to some degree?

Abraham: It is always to your advantage to speak of what you want, but you cannot stay in alignment with *who-you-really-are* and focus upon your mother's headache at the same time. *Speaking of what you do want while looking at what you do not want does not put you into alignment with what you do want. Take your attention from the things you do not want to attract and put it upon the things you do want to attract.* Focus upon some aspect of your mother that causes you to feel good, or focus upon something other than your mother that causes you to feel good.

What Is the Media's Role in Epidemics?

Jerry: I've been hearing in the media recently that there are free flu shots in town for those who want to go and get them. Will that news affect the spread of the flu virus?

Abraham: Yes, it will be of great value to the spread of the flu virus. There is no greater source of negative influence in your environment today than your television. Of course, as in every part of your environment, there is wanted and unwanted, and you do have the ability to focus and therefore to receive value from your television and media—but those sources do bring you a tremendously distorted, imbalanced point of view. They look all around your world for pockets of trouble, shining spotlights upon them and magnifying them and enhancing the trouble with dramatic music and then funneling it into your living rooms, giving you a tremendously distorted picture of the trouble, versus the Well-Being, of your planet.

The constant barrage of medical commercials is a powerful source of negative influence as they explain to you that "one out of every five people has this disease lurking, and you are probably the one." They influence you to give thought, and then they say, "See your physician." And when you go to your physician (remember, the *intent* of the physician is to find something *wrong*), now your negative expectation is born or enhanced. And, with enough of that influence, your body begins to manifest the evidence of those pervasive thoughts. Your medicine is more advanced today than ever before, and yet more of you are sick than ever before.

Remember, to create anything, you have only to give *thought* to it—and then expect it—and it is. They show you the statistics; they tell you the horror stories; they stimulate your thought, and as you are being stimulated by the thought in great detail, you have the emotion: the *dread,* the *fear . . . I do not want that!* And one half of the equation is complete. Then they encourage you to go in for a checkup or to come and get the free flu shots: "Obviously, we know it's an epidemic or we wouldn't be offering the free flu shots," and that completes the *expectation* or the *allowing* part—and now you are in the perfect position for the receiving of the flu or the essence of whatever else it is they are talking about.

You get what you think about whether you want it or not. And so, it is of great value for you to begin practicing your own story about your Well-Being so that when the television presents that frightening story (one that you do not want to live), you can hear their version and feel humor about it rather than fear.

Catch Uncomfortable Sensations While They're Small?

Abraham: The first indication that you are disallowing your physical well-being comes to you in the form of negative emotion. You will not see a breakdown of your physical body at the first sign of negative emotion, but focusing upon subjects that cause a prolonged feeling of negative emotion will eventually cause dis-ease.

If you are unaware that negative emotion indicates the vibrational disharmony that is hindering the level of Well-Being that you are asking for, you may be, like most people, accepting a certain level of negative emotion and feeling no need to do something about it. Most people, even when they feel alarm at the level of negative emotion or stress they are feeling, do not know what to do about it because they believe they are reacting to conditions or circumstances that are outside of their control. And so, since they cannot control those unpleasant conditions, they feel powerless to change the way they feel.

We want you to understand that your emotions come in response to your focus, and under all conditions you have the power to find thoughts that feel slightly better or slightly worse— and when you consistently choose slightly better, the *Law of Attraction* will bring steady improvement to your experience. *The key to achieving and maintaining a physical state of well-being is to notice the indicators of discord in the early stages. It is much easier to refocus your thoughts in the early, subtle stages than after the* <u>Law of Attraction</u> *has responded to chronic negative thoughts, bringing bigger negative results.*

If you could make a decision to never allow negative emotion to linger within you—and at the same time acknowledge that it is your work alone to refocus your attention in order to feel better rather than asking someone else to do something different or for some circumstance to change to make you feel better—you will not only be a very healthy person, but you will be a joyful person. *Joy, appreciation, love, and health are all synonymous. Resentment, jealousy, depression, anger, and sickness are all synonymous.*

Are Arthritis and Alzheimer's
Disease Somehow Resolvable?

Jerry: Can the gnarled joints caused by arthritis or the memory loss caused by Alzheimer's be resolved? Is it possible to recover from those types of illnesses at whatever age?

Abraham: The conditions of your physical body truly are vibrational indicators of the balance of your thoughts—and so when you change your thoughts, the indicators must change, also. The only reason that some diseases seem stubborn and unchangeable is because your thoughts are often stubborn and unchanging.

Most people learn their patterns of counterproductive thought often based on "truths" they have witnessed or learned from others, and as they hold stubbornly to those patterns of thought (which do not serve them), they then experience the results of those thoughts. And then an uncomfortable cycle occurs where they think about *unwanted* things (valid, true unwanted things) and, in doing so, by the *Law of Attraction,* they prevent *wanted* things from coming into their experience and allow *unwanted* things to come instead—then they focus even more upon those unwanted things, causing more unwanted things to come.

You can accomplish change in every experience, but you have to begin to see your world differently. You have to tell the story the way you want it to be rather than like it is. When you choose the direction of your thoughts and conversations by the way they feel as you think them or speak them, then you begin to *deliberately* offer vibrations. You are Vibrational Beings, whether you know it or not, and the *Law of Attraction* is eternally responding to the vibrations you are offering.

Jerry: Can chemicals, such as alcohol, nicotine, or cocaine, negatively affect the body?

Abraham: *Your physical wellness is affected much more by your vibrational balance than it is by the things that you put into your body. And, even more significant to your question is the fact that from your* *place of vibrational alignment, you would not feel inclined toward any* *substance that would detract from that balance.* Almost without exception, the seeking of those substances comes from a place of less alignment. *In fact, the impulse to participate in those substances comes* *from a desire to fill the void that is present because of the vibrational* *imbalance.*

Are Exercise and Nutrition a Health Factor?

Jerry: Does better nutrition or more exercise add to our health?

Abraham: You may have noticed that there are those who are very deliberate about food and exercise whose physical well-being is obvious. And there are those who seem to be offering tremendous effort regarding food and exercise who struggle for years to gain benefit and still have no success in maintaining their physical well-being. What you do in terms of action is far less important than the thoughts you think, the way you feel, your vibrational balance, or the story you tell.

When you take the time to find vibrational balance, the physical *effort you apply will yield you wonderful results, but if you do not tend* *to your vibrational balance first, there is not enough action in the world* *to compensate for that misaligned Energy. From your place of alignment,* *you will feel inspired to the beneficial behavior, just as from your place* *of misalignment, you are inspired to detrimental behavior.*

Jerry: I remember hearing a line from Sir Winston Churchill. (He was the British leader during World War II.) He said, "I never run if I can walk, and I never walk if I can stand, or stand if I can sit, or sit if I can lie down," and he always smoked a big cigar. He lived to be 90 years of age and, as far as I know, was in good health. But his lifestyle was clearly not what we consider today to be healthy, so was it just a *belief* factor then?

Abraham: Leaving at such an early age? (Fun) The reason that so many are confused about the correct behavior for healthy living is because they are only factoring in behavior and they are leaving out the part of the equation that is most responsible for every outcome: the way you think, the emotions you feel, and the story you tell.

What If a Healthy Person Feels Mostly Tired?

Jerry: If a person seems to be in good health but feels tired or listless most of the time, what would you suggest as a solution?

Abraham: People often refer to that state of being tired or listless as a state of low energy, and that is really a good way of saying it. While you cannot cut yourself off from your Energy source, when you offer thoughts that contradict that source, your resulting feeling is one of resistance or low energy. *The way you feel is always about the degree to which you are in alignment or out of alignment with your Source. No exceptions.*

As you tell the story of what you want (which is the story the Source within you is always telling), you feel happy and energized. The feeling of low energy is always a result of telling a different story than the expanded, Source Energy part of you is telling. When you tell a story that focuses upon the positive aspects of your life—you feel energized. When you tell a story that focuses upon the negative aspects—you feel enervated. When you focus upon the absence of something that you desire in your present experience—you feel negative emotion. When you imagine an improved condition—you feel positive emotion. *The way you feel is always about the relationship between the object of your attention and your true desire. Giving thought to what is wanted will give you the invigoration that you seek.*

What Is the Chief Cause of Illness?

Jerry: So in simple terms, what do you see as the chief cause of illness?

Abraham: Illness is caused by giving thought to unwanted topics, feeling negative emotion but ignoring it, and continuing to focus upon *unwanted* such that negative emotion is getting greater—but still ignoring it and maintaining attention upon *unwanted* . . . until, by the *Law of Attraction,* still more negative thoughts and experiences are attracted. *Illness exists when you disregard the early, subtle signs of misalignment that come in the form of emotion.*

If you feel negative emotion and you do not change the thought to relieve the discomfort of the negative emotion, it always gets bigger, until eventually the negative emotion becomes physical sensation—then physical deterioration. *However, the illness is only an indication of your vibration, and whenever you change your vibration, the indicator will change to match the new vibration. Illness is nothing more than a physical indicator of Energy out of balance.*

Many people who are experiencing illness disagree with our explanation of the cause of their illness being that the *Law of Attraction* is responding to their thoughts, as they protest that they have never thought about *that* particular illness. But illness does not occur because you are thinking about *that* illness or about *any* illness. *Illness is an exaggerated indicator of negative thoughts that began as a subtle indicator of negative emotion and grew larger as the negative thoughts persisted. Negative thought is resistance, no matter the subject of the negative thought. That is the reason that new diseases continue to come about, and until the actual cause of the disease is addressed, there will never be a final cure.*

You have potential for every illness in your body right now, and you have potential for a perfect state of health in your body right now—and you will solicit one or the other, or a mixture, depending upon your balance of thought.

Jerry: So, in other words, from your perspective there is no *physical* cause for illness or disease? It's all *thought?*

Abraham: We understand your urge to give credence to action or behavior in attempting to explain causes. As you explain where your water comes from, you would be accurate to point to the faucet as the source of the water coming into your kitchen sink. But there is much more to the story of "where the water comes from" than only the faucet. And in like manner, there is much more to the story about the source of wellness or of illness. *Your ease or dis-ease are symptoms of the balance of your thought, and that balance will manifest through the path of least resistance as surely as water flows downhill.*

An Example of My "Old" Story about My Physical Well-Being

I'm noticing symptoms in my body that worry me. As I get older, I feel less strong, less stable, less healthy, less secure. I worry about where I'm headed healthwise. I've tried to take care of myself, but I don't see that it has helped that much. I guess it's just normal to feel worse as time goes on. I saw that with my parents, so I'm really worried about my health.

An Example of My "New" Story about My Physical Well-Being

My body responds to my thoughts about it and to my thoughts about everything I think about. The better my thoughts feel when I think them, the more I allow my own personal Well-Being.
I like knowing that there is an absolute correlation between how I feel and what my chronic thoughts have been and how those thoughts felt as I thought them. I like knowing that those feelings are meant to help me choose better-feeling thoughts,

which produce better-feeling vibrations, which will produce a better-feeling body. My body is so responsive to my thoughts, and that is such a good thing to know.

I am getting rather good at choosing my thoughts. No matter what condition I find myself in, I have the power to change it. My state of physical health is simply an indication of the state of my chronic thoughts—I have control of both.

A physical body is an amazing thing in the way it began as a glob of fetal cells to become this full-blown human body. I am impressed with the stability of the human body and the intelligence of the cells that make up the human body as I notice how my body accomplishes so many important functions without my conscious involvement.

I like that it is not my conscious responsibility to move the blood through my veins or the air through my lungs. I like that my body knows how to do that and does that so well. The human body in general is quite an amazing thing: an intelligent, flexible, durable, resilient, seeing, hearing, smelling, tasting, touching thing.

My own body serves me very well. I love my exploration of life through my physical body. I enjoy my stamina and flexibility. I like living life in my body.

I am so pleased with my eyes that look out into this world, seeing near and far from where I stand, distinguishing shapes and colors with such vivid perception of depths and distances. I so enjoy my body's ability to hear and smell and taste and feel. I love the tactile, sensual content of this planet and my life in my wonderful body.

I feel appreciation and fascination for my body's self-patching ability as I watch wounds cover over with new skin and as I discover renewed resiliency when traumas to my body occur.

I am so aware of my body's flexibility, my fingers' dexterity, and the immediate response that my muscles show to any task I attempt.

I like understanding that my body knows how to be well and is always moving toward wellness, and that as I do not get in the way of that with negative thought, wellness must prevail.

I like understanding the value of my emotions, and I under-stand that I have the ability to achieve and maintain physical well-being because I have the ability to find and maintain happy thoughts.

On any day in this world, even when some things in my body may not be at their best, I am ever aware that far, far, far, far more things are functioning as they should, and that the aspects of Well-Being of my body are dominant.

And most of all, I love my body's quick response to my attention and intentions. I love understanding my mind-body-spirit connections and the powerful productive qualities of my deliberate alignment.

I love living life in my body.

I feel such appreciation for this experience.

I feel good.

There is no right or wrong way to tell your improved story. It can be about your past, present, or future experiences. The only criterion that is important is that you be conscious of your intent to tell a better-feeling, improved version of your story. Telling many good-feeling short stories throughout your day will change your point of attraction. Just remember that the story *you* tell is the basis of *your* life. So tell it the way you want it to be.

PART IV

Perspectives
of Health,
Weight, and Mind

I Want to Enjoy a Healthy Body

Bringing your physical body into alignment is a tremendously valuable thing to do for two reasons:

- First, there is no subject that people think more about than their own body. (And that is logical since you take it with you everywhere you go.)

- Second, since every perspective or thought that you have flows through the lens of your physical body, your attitude on virtually every subject is influenced by the way you feel about your physical body.

Because science and medicine have been slow to acknowledge the connection between mind and body, between thoughts and outcomes, and between attitudes and results, most people are reeling in a plethora of contradictory guidance relative to their bodies. *Whenever the basis of an understanding is flawed, no amount of patching it with methods, potions, or remedies can bring consistently provable results. And because the alignment of Energies for each individual varies because of such a variety of factors in beliefs, desires, expectations, and early and current influences, it is little wonder that remedies that "work every time" are nonexistent, and it is no wonder that most are truly confused about their physical bodies.*

When you attempt to gather and process information about what is happening with other people's bodies instead of utilizing your own *Emotional Guidance System* to understand *your* current alignment or misalignment of Energy, it is tantamount to using a road map from a different country to plan your route in your own country: That information simply has no bearing on you and where you are right now.

You have been given so much information that is contradictory to that which we know to be (and to the *Laws of the Universe*) that we are extremely happy to talk to you about you and your body relative to the greater picture. We want to assist you in finding a clear understanding of how to be a healthy Being who is physically fit, who looks as you want to look (whole in terms of mind and spirit and body); and when you use your mind to deliberately focus your thoughts to align with the thoughts of your *Inner Being* (or spirit), your physical body will be the manifestational evidence of that alignment.

I Want to Balance My Desires and Experiences

It is not possible to bring your physical body to a state of perfect health by only thinking about the physical aspects of your being and then offering action regarding your physical body. Without an understanding of the Connection between the physical you and the Non-Physical Vibrational Inner You, there can be no consistent understanding or control. In other words, while it may feel to you that the path to a good-feeling, good-looking body will be a result of your behavior in terms of food intake and activity, it is really much more about your vibrational alignment between the physical and Non-Physical aspects of your being.

Once you accept the totality of your Being and you make that vibrational alignment your top priority, you are well on your way to achieving and maintaining your desired physical body. But if you use conditions of others, experiences of others, and opinions of others as your gauge for wellness, you will not be able to control the condition of your own physical body. In other words, as you strive for a physical standard based on comparison with the experiences of others rather than striving for your personal alignment between you and *You,* you will never discover the key to control over your own body.

I Needn't Compare My Body to Others

We would like to assist you in understanding that there is not one state of being that is the correct one, or even the most wanted one, for there are a great many varieties of states of physical bodies that have been intended by you as you emerged into this physical body. If it had been your intent to all be the same, more of you would be the same—but you are not. You come forth with all sorts of varieties of size and shape and flexibility and dexterity. Some are stronger, and others are more agile. . . . You came with great variety, adding all sorts of differences that are of tremendous advantage to the whole. You came forth in your great variety to add balance to this time and place.

And so, we would like to encourage you: Rather than looking at yourselves and acknowledging that you are lacking in this or in that characteristic, as most of you do, we would like to assist you in looking toward the advantages of that which *you are.* In other words, as you are assessing or analyzing your physical body, spend a greater part of your time looking for the advantages that it offers not just to you, but to the balance of *All-That-Is.*

Jerry: I recall that when I used to work out on a trapeze (with the circus), I was too heavy to be what they called a "flyer," and I was too light to be what they called a "catcher." So the trapeze wasn't my place to be comfortable unless we got a heavier catcher or a lighter flyer, so to speak. So, I was still an *aerialist,* but I performed what was called an aerial bar act, where nobody had to catch me and I didn't have to catch anyone. But I didn't see myself lacking because I didn't think that I should have been bigger or smaller. I just found something I liked to do that still gave me the same general feeling of performing as an aerialist. [**Abraham:** Good. That is excellent.]

What If I Saw Myself as Perfect?

Jerry: So couldn't we look at our weight, then, and our state of mental ability or talent in the same way? Could each of us see ourselves as perfect?

Abraham: We are not necessarily encouraging you to look at whatever your current state is and proclaim it as "perfect," because you will always be striving for something that is just beyond *what-is*. But finding aspects of your current experience that feel good when you focus upon them will cause you to align with the perspective of your *Inner Being,* who is always focused upon your Well-Being. *We encourage you to feel for the agreement between your thoughts about your body and your Inner Being's thoughts about your body rather than trying to get the conditions of your body to agree with conditions of other bodies that you see around you.*

Pushing Against Unwanted Attracts More Unwanted

Abraham: As you are understanding that you are creating through your thoughts rather than through your action, you will accomplish many more of your desires with far less effort—and in the absence of struggle, you will have much more fun. You are offering thought in every waking moment, and so achieving a propensity to positive, good-feeling thoughts will serve you extremely well.

You were born into a society that began warning you against unwanted things as soon as you arrived, and over time, most of you have taken on a guarded stance. You have a "war against drugs" and a "war against AIDS" and a "war against cancer." Most of you really believe that the way to get what you *do* want is to defeat what you *do not* want, and so you give so much of your attention toward pushing away from you what you do not want, where, if you could see the *Law of Attraction* as we see it—if you could accept yourselves as the attractors by virtue of the thought that you are holding—you would understand what a backward approach most of you are taking.

As you say, "I'm sick and I want not to be sick, so I'll beat this illness—I'll take this action and I'll defeat this illness," you are, from your position of guardedness and defensiveness and negative emotion, holding on to that illness.

My Attention to Lack Attracts More Lack

Abraham: Every subject is really two subjects: There is the subject of what you are wanting, and there is the subject of its lack. Regarding your body, since every thought that you think is filtered through your perspective of this body, if this body does not feel the way you want it to feel or look the way you want it to look, it is very natural that a large number of your thoughts (a very imbalanced proportion of your thoughts) would be slanted toward the lack side of the equation rather than toward the truly desired side of the equation.

From your place of lack, you will attract only more of that, and that is the reason most diets do not work: You are aware of your fat—you are aware of your body looking the way you do not want it to look—and so when it gets bad enough that you cannot stand it anymore (either from your own perspective or because others are scowling at you), then you say, "I can't bear this negative place anymore. I'm going to go on a diet, and I'm going to get rid of all of this stuff that I do *not* want." And yet, your attention is given to the stuff that you do not want, and so you hold it to you. *The way to get to where you want to be is to give your full attention to what you do want, not to give your attention to what you do not want.*

Planting Fear Seeds Does Grow More Fear

Jerry: A dear friend, my mentor in business, volunteered to be a part of a medical study. He said that even though he was in brilliant health, he was willing to participate if it could be of value to others, because so many men his age in that area were dying from a certain disease. Well, it seemed like only a matter of weeks before we received a message from him that he had been diagnosed with the illness. And now he's no longer in physical form, but he didn't seem to have a fear of the disease. Did he create it in his body by merely focusing on it?

Abraham: It was his attention to it—in other words, it was his intent to be of value for others. And so, he allowed them to probe and poke and look. And in the probing and poking and looking, he received enough stimulation of thought from the others to make him aware of the possibility—not only the possibility, the *probability. They planted within him the seed of probability, and then, with the probing and the poking and the looking, his body responded to what then became the balance of his thought.*

It is a wonderful example that you have offered because that disease was not within him until the *attention* to the disease was within him, but once the attention to the disease was within him, then his body responded in kind.

The potential for wellness or illness is always within you. The thoughts you choose determine which you experience and to what degree you experience it.

Must Attention to Illness Attract Illness?

Jerry: How much can we toy with these thoughts of illness? For instance, a person can watch on television an offer to come down for a free examination of some part of his or her body, and if the person says, "Oh well, I think I'll just go do that—I feel fine, but why not, since it's free?" what are the chances of that leading to what you're talking about: a stimulation of thought and, eventually, an unwanted result?

Abraham: Nearly 100 percent. Because of the attention to illness in your society, your diseases are running rampant. With all of your medical technology—all of the tools, all of the discoveries—there are more people who are critically ill today than ever before.

The prevalence of so much severe illness is predominantly because of your attention to illness.

You said: "How much can we toy" with it? And we say: You are very particular about what you eat and what you wear and what you drive, and yet you are not particular about what you think. *We would encourage you to be particular about what you think. Keep your thoughts on the side of the subject that is in harmony with your wanting. Think about wellness—not about lack of it. Think about being as you want to be rather than the lack of it.*

Your illnesses are not born and perpetuated only because of your negative attention to illness. Remember that illness stems from your feelings of vulnerability and guardedness. Train your thoughts on all subjects (not only the subject of physical health) in the direction of what you desire, and through the improved emotional state that you accomplish, your physical well-being will then be assured.

Is My Attention Predominantly Focused on Well-Being?

Jerry: Another dear friend of ours recently built a room onto her house so that her mother-in-law, whose health had really worsened, could come to live with her. Her mother-in-law spoke almost constantly about how bad she felt, how bad her health was, how unhappy she was with life, and about this surgery and that surgery.

Then our friend's mother, who was 85 years old, came out to visit for the holidays. She had never been in a hospital in her life before, but within a week of staying in that house with this other lady—who was continually speaking of illness—her own health plummeted dramatically. She was hospitalized and then was placed in a nursing home. Could someone's health fail so dramatically as a result of only a few days of negative influence?

Abraham: *The potential for illness or wellness lies within all of you at all times. And whatever you give your attention to begins to foster within you the manifestation of the essence of that thought. Thought is very powerful.*

While it is not necessary, most people who have lived to be 85 years of age have already been receiving substantial negative influence about their physical body. You are constantly bombarded with thoughts of failing health: a need to buy medical insurance, a need to buy burial insurance, a need to get your will in order to prepare for your death, and so on. So this woman did not receive her first negative influence about her physical well-being from the other woman in that house.

However, since she was already teetering there, somewhat unstable about her own longevity, the intensity of the other woman's conversation—and the responses she noticed that it extracted from the people who surrounded her—did tip the balance of her thoughts enough that negative symptoms became immediately apparent. And then, as she turned her attention toward her own negative symptoms, in that intense environment those symptoms increased even more rapidly.

When someone comes into your experience who stimulates your thought so that your thought is predominantly upon illness rather than wellness, upon lack of Well-Being rather than upon Well-Being, where you are in a place where you are feeling vulnerable or defensive or even angry—then the cells of your body begin to respond to the balance of that thought. And yes, it is possible that in a matter of weeks, or even days—or even hours—this negative process could begin. *Everything that you are living is as a result of the thoughts that you are thinking, and there is not an exception to that.*

Others' Physical Evidence Needn't Be My Experience

Abraham: As you see physical evidence around you, very often that *physical evidence* seems more real to you than a *thought*. You say things to us such as: "Abraham, this is really real—this isn't just a thought," as if what is *really real* and a *thought* are two separate things. But we want you to remember that the Universe does not distinguish between your thoughts of current reality and thoughts of imagined reality. The Universe and the *Law of Attraction* are simply responding to your thought—real or imagined, current or remembered. *Whatever evidence you see around you is nothing more than the manifestational indicator of someone's thought, and there is no reason for what others are creating with their thoughts to cause you to feel frightened or vulnerable.*

There is no such thing as an unchangeable condition. There is not a physical situation, no matter what the state of negative degeneration, that cannot receive wellness. But it requires an understanding of the Law of Attraction, *the guidance represented by emotion, and a willingness to deliberately focus upon things that make you feel good. If you could understand that your body is responding to what you are thinking, and if you could hold your thoughts where you want them to be—all of you would be well.*

How Can I Influence All Toward Maintaining Health?

Jerry: So, what would be the best thing we could do to either maintain or regain perfect health or to influence others around us toward *their* perfect health?

Abraham: Actually, the process for regaining health and maintaining health are one and the same: *Focus upon more things that feel good.* The biggest difference between regaining and maintaining is that it is easier to think good-feeling thoughts when you feel good than when you feel bad, so *maintaining* health is much easier to do than *regaining* health. *The best way to influence others to good health is to live it. The best way to influence others to sickness is to get sick.*

We understand that for those who are now in a place where they do not want to be, it sounds very simplistic to just find a better-feeling thought. But it is our absolute promise to you that if you were to be determined to improve the way you feel by deliberately choosing thoughts that feel better, you would begin to see immediate improvement in anything that is troubling you.

I'll Relax and Sleep Myself into Well-Being

Abraham: Your natural state is one of absolute Well-Being. You do not have to fight anymore against illness. Just relax into your wellness. Put yourself in your bed tonight, and as you are going to sleep, feel the wonderful comfort of the bed beneath you. Notice how big it is. Notice the pillow beneath your neck. Notice the fabric upon your skin. Give your attention to things that feel good, for every moment that you can think about something that feels good, you are cutting the fuel to that illness. *In every moment that you think about something that feels good, you are stopping the illness from going forward; and in every moment that you are thinking about the illness, you are adding a little more fuel to the fire, so to speak.*

As you are able to accomplish holding your thoughts on something that feels good for five seconds, then for that five seconds you will stop fueling your illness. As you accomplish it for ten seconds, then for ten seconds you have stopped fueling the illness. As you think about how good you feel right now, and as you think about your natural state as being a state of wellness—*you begin fueling your wellness.*

Do Negative Emotions Indicate Unhealthy Thoughts?

Abraham: As you think thoughts of illness, the reason you feel such negative emotion about it is because that thought is so out of harmony with your greater knowing that you are not resonating with *who-you-really-are.* The negative emotion that you feel, in the form of *concern* or *anger* or *fear* about your illness, is your real indicator that you have put a very strong restriction on the flow of Energy between you and *who-you-really-are.*

Your wellness comes forth as you allow the full flow of Non-Physical Energy from your *Inner Being.* And so, as you think, *I am well* or *I am becoming well* or *I am whole; it is my natural state to be well,* those thoughts vibrate in a place that is in harmony with that which your *Inner Being* knows to be, and you receive the full benefit of the thought Energy that comes forth from your *Inner Being.*

Every thought vibrates. And so, focus upon thoughts that make you feel good, which will attract others and others and others and others and others . . . until your vibrational frequency will raise to the place that your <u>Inner Being</u> can fully envelop you. And then you will be in the place of Well-Being, and your physical apparatus will catch up very quickly— it is our absolute promise to you. You may begin to watch for dramatic physical evidence of your recovery—for it is <u>Law.</u>

To What Degree Can I Control My Body?

Jerry: Well, this subject is "Perspectives of Health, Weight, and Mind": *How can I get there and stay there?* I see an absolutely overwhelming number of people who are concerned about the state of their weight and their physical and mental health. And because of the amount of attention to physical health failures, I understand why people are concerned.

As a kid, I had the good fortune, somehow, of realizing that I was in control of my own body. I recall when I was about nine years old going to the county-fair carnival, where two professional fighters would take on all comers. In other words, any of the farmers around there could pay to get in the boxing ring and fight them, and if the farmers could beat those professional fighters, they'd win money. But the farmers always got beaten to a pulp. . . .

I remember standing in this little canvas tent lit by kerosene or gas lamps, and I can recall watching the lights flickering on the sweating back of the professional fighter. And I was just absolutely entranced with the fact that his backbone was hidden between two beautiful muscles running down his back, whereas mine was more like our Arkansas state mascot: the razorback hog. In other words, my backbone stuck way out and had no muscles around it, while his was beautifully embedded where I couldn't even see it. I so enjoyed observing these beautiful back muscles. I really appreciated what I saw that day, and within about eight years the muscles on my back did look like that, and so from that experience, I realized that I could create my physical body.

As a result of the extreme ill health that I experienced as a child, I learned somehow to be able to *control* my own health. I experimented with doctors a few times, but their diagnoses and treatments were mostly always wrong. And so, it didn't take me long to realize that I'd be better off staying away from doctors because I couldn't find one I could count on to be right. They were nearly always wrong when it came to helping me, so I decided I'd be better off just handling my own body.

But I still find myself thinking a little bit about how my body is going to hold up and what my future condition is going to be. Will I be able to, as I say, maintain this perfect state of weight, health, and mind? I feel I'm there now, but I'm at the point of sometimes wondering, *Will I be able to always stay there?* And so, I'd like you to address that general subject.

Abraham: We are appreciating the combination of words that you have put there, for your body and your mind are forever connected. *Your body is responding to your thoughts continually—in fact, to nothing else. Your body is absolutely a pure reflection of the way you think. There is nothing else that is affecting your body other than your thoughts.* And it is a good thing that at that early age you proved to yourself that you did have some control over your own body.

When you consciously acknowledge the absolute correlation between what you are thinking and what you are getting, you can then eventually, under all conditions, control your own experience. All that is required for you to get only what you want, versus getting some of what you do *not* want, is to recognize that the control that you seek you already have, and then to deliberately think about things that you want to experience.

Thoughts of decline always feel bad because you do not want decline. So utilize your Guidance and choose good-feeling thoughts and you will have no reason to worry about moving through time. Really, it is simply a matter of making the decision: *I want to acknowledge that I have the only—and the absolute—control of my own physical apparatus. I acknowledge that <u>I am as a result of the thoughts I think.</u>*

The day you were born, you possessed knowledge (not *hope* or *desire,* but deep *understanding*) that your basis is absolute freedom, that your quest is joy, and that the result of your life experience would be growth; and you knew that you are perfect and still reaching out for even more perfection.

Can We Consciously Grow New Muscle and Bone?

Jerry: I consciously, deliberately, added muscle to my body in my early years because I wanted to, but can we consciously affect our bones as well?

Abraham: You can—in the same way. The difference is that the current *belief* about the muscle is there. The current belief about the bone is not.

Jerry: That's true. I saw a man who had developed tremendous muscles, and I wanted that. And because many others were doing it, I believed I could, too. But I haven't seen bone changed.

Abraham: The reason that more things do not change more quickly in your societies today is because most people are giving their attention predominantly to *what-is.* In order to effect change, you must look beyond *what-is.*

It slows you down tremendously if you need to see evidence of something before you believe it, because that means you have to wait for someone else to create it before you can believe it. But when you understand that the <u>Universe,</u> and the <u>Law of Attraction,</u> will respond to your imagined idea as quickly as it responds to an observed idea, then you can move quickly into new creations without having to wait for someone to accomplish it first.

Jerry: So, the challenge is being that "pioneer"—the first one out.

Abraham: The Leading Edge requires vision and positive expectation, but it is really where the most powerful exhilaration is. To be in a state of desire and to have no doubt is the most satisfying experience possible, but to want something and not believe in your ability to achieve it does not feel good. When you think only of what you desire, without constant contradictions that are filled with doubt or disbelief, the Universal response to your desire comes quickly, and in time you begin to feel the power of your deliberate thought. But that kind of "pure" thought takes practice, and it requires that you spend less time observing *what-is,* and more time visualizing what you would like to experience. In order to tell the new-and-improved story about your physical experience, you must spend time thinking and speaking about the experience you would like to live.

The most powerful thing you can do—the thing that will give you much greater leverage than any action—is to spend time every day visualizing your life as you want it to be. We encourage that you go to a quiet and private environment for 15 minutes every day where you can close your eyes and imagine your body, your environment, your relationships, and your life in ways that please you.

What has been has nothing to do with what will be, and what others experience has nothing to do with your experience . . . but you must find a way to separate yourself from all of that—from the past and from the others—in order to be what you want to be.

What about When One's Desire Overrules One's Belief?

Jerry: People have been running for thousands of years, and no one had been able to cover a mile in four minutes. And then a man named Roger Bannister did it, and once *he* did it, now many others have run the "four-minute mile" as well.

Abraham: When people do not allow the fact that no one else has ever done something to prevent *them* from doing it, they are of great advantage to others, because once they break through and create it, then others can observe and, in time, can come to *believe*

or *expect* it—and for that reason, everything that you accomplish is of value to your society.

Your platform for progressive living continues to expand, and life does get better and better for everyone. However, we are wanting to take you beyond the need to see it before you can believe it. We want you to understand that if you believe it, *then* you will see it. Anything that you practice in your mind until the idea begins to feel natural to you must come to physical fruition. The *Law of Attraction* guarantees it.

You will feel enormous liberation when you realize that you do not have to wait for someone else to do something in order to prove that it can be done or before you allow yourself to do it. As you practice new thoughts, reaching for improved emotions, and then see the evidence that the Universe will provide, you will come to know your own true power. *If someone were to tell you that you are experiencing an incurable disease, you could then say with confidence, "I will decide what I will live, for I am the creator of my experience." If your desire is strong enough, it can outweigh your negative beliefs and your recovery will begin.*

It is not so different from the story of the mother whose child is pinned beneath the object that weighs many, many times more than anything she has ever lifted, but in her powerful desire to save her child, she does lift it. Under normal conditions, she could not begin to lift this object, but with such powerful desire, her normal beliefs become temporarily irrelevant. If you said to her, "Do you *believe* you can lift that object?" she would say, "Of course not. I can't even pick up my suitcase when it's full." But *belief* had nothing to do with *this:* Her child was dying, and her *wanting* was to free her child—and so she did.

But What If I Believe in Dangerous Germs?

Jerry: I really do want to be healthy, but I also believe that I might catch some things. And so, whenever I visit people who are in the hospital, I hold my breath as I walk down the corridor to avoid germs.

Abraham: You must have very short visits. (Fun)

Jerry: I do have short visits, and I keep going to a window and trying to get some air. . . . So if I believe that I can avoid the germs by holding my breath, then will that belief keep me from getting sick?

Abraham: In your strange way you are maintaining a vibrational balance. You *want* health, you *believe* that germs could make you sick, you *believe* that your behavior of avoiding the germs is preventing sickness—and so you achieve a balance that works for you. You are, however, going about it the hard way.

If you were really listening to your *Guidance System*, you would not enter an environment where you believe there are germs that could compromise your Well-Being. The dread you feel about going into the hospital is your indicator that you are about to take action before you have achieved vibrational alignment. You could just not go to the hospital, but then you would feel uncomfortable because you know that your sick friend would enjoy a visit from you. So you find a way to visit your friend without feeling dread. And that is what we mean by finding vibrational alignment *before* you take the action of entering the hospital. In time, you can come to *believe* so much in your Well-Being, or your *desire* for Well-Being can become so vivid, that you could be in any environment and not feel a threat to your Well-Being.

When you are in alignment with *who-you-really-are* and you are listening to your powerful *Guidance System*, you would never enter an environment where your Well-Being could be threatened. Unfortunately, many people override their own *Guidance System* for the sake of pleasing others. Two people could enter the hospital as you have described it, one feeling no threat to Well-Being and the other feeling great threat. The first would not get sick; the second one would—not because of the germs that are present in the hospital, but because of the person's vibrational relationship to his or her own sense of Well-Being.

We are not attempting to alter your beliefs, for we do not see your beliefs as inappropriate. It is our desire to make you aware of your own

Emotional Guidance System so that you can achieve the balance of vibration between your *desires* and your *beliefs*. Doing the "right" thing means to do that which is in harmony with your intent *and* with your current beliefs.

Jerry: So there's nothing wrong with taking "the coward's way out"?

Abraham: There are many people who override their own *Guidance System* by trying to please others, and there are many people who will call you "selfish" or "cowardly" when you have the audacity to please yourself rather than them. Often others will call you "selfish" (because you are unwilling to yield to *their* own selfishness) without realizing the hypocrisy of their demand.

Sometimes we are accused of teaching *selfishness,* and we admit that it is true, because if you are not selfish enough to tend to your own vibration and therefore hold yourself in alignment with your Source (with *who you-really-are*), then you have nothing to give to another anyway. When others call you "selfish" or "cowardly," their own vibrations are clearly out of balance, and a modification of *your* behavior will not bring them into balance.

The more you think and speak of your own physical well-being, the more entrenched your own vibrational patterns of wellness will be, and the more the *Law of Attraction* will then surround you with things that enhance and support those beliefs. *The more you tell your own story of Well-Being, the less vulnerable you will feel, and then not only will your point of attraction shift so that different situations will surround you, but you will also feel different about the situations as they come.*

I Am Guided *Toward* What I *Do* Like

Abraham: The only path to the life you desire is through the path of less resistance, or the path of most allowance: allowance of your Connection to your Source, to your *Inner Being,* to *who-you-really-are,* and to all that you desire. And that allowance is indicated

to you in the form of good-feeling emotions. If you will let feeling good be your most important priority, then whenever you are having a conversation that is not in harmony with the health you desire, you will feel bad, and so you will be alerted to your resistance . . . and then you can choose a better-feeling thought and you will be right back on track.

Whenever you feel negative emotion, it is your *Guidance System* helping you realize that you are, in this moment, offering resistant thought that is hindering the Stream of Well-Being that would otherwise be reaching you fully. It is as if your *Guidance System* is saying: *Here, you're doing it again; here, you're doing it again; here, you're doing it again. This negative emotion means you are in the process of attracting what you do not want.*

Many people ignore their *Guidance System* by tolerating negative emotion and, in doing so, deny themselves the benefit of Guidance from Broader Perspective. But once life has caused you to identify that you desire something, you will never again be able to look at its opposite or at the lack of it without feeling negative emotion. Once a desire has been born within you, you must look at the desire if you are to feel good. And the reason for that is, *you cannot revert back to less than life has caused you to become.* Once you identify a desire for wellness, or for a specific bodily condition, you will never be able to focus upon the lack of it again without feeling negative emotion.

Whenever you feel negative emotion, just stop whatever it is you are doing or thinking and say, "What is it that I do want?" And then, because you have turned your attention to what you do want, the negative feeling will be replaced by a positive feeling, and the negative attraction will be replaced by positive attraction—and you will be right back on track.

First, I Must Be Willing to Please Myself

Abraham: When you have been on a particular train of thought for a while, it is not easy to abruptly change the direction of your thought, because the *Law of Attraction* is supplying you with

thoughts that match your current train of thought. Sometimes while you are in that negative-feeling mode, another who is not in that negative place will not agree with your negative view of your current subject, which only serves to make you want to defend your position all the more. *Trying to defend or justify your opinion only causes you to stay in your resistant state longer. And the reason so many people hold themselves in resistance unnecessarily is because it is more important to them to be "right" rather than to feel good.*

When you meet those who are determined to convince you that they are right, and they try to hold you in a negative conversation in an attempt to convince you, sometimes you are considered "uncaring" or "coldhearted" if you do not hear them and eventually agree with their point of view. But when you forfeit your good feeling (that comes when you choose thoughts that harmonize with your Broader Perspective) to try to please a negative friend who wants to use you as a sounding board, you are paying a very big price for something that will not help him or her either. That uncomfortable knot in your stomach is your *Inner Being* saying, *This behavior, this conversation, isn't in harmony with what you want.* You must be willing to please yourself first or you will often be swept up by the negativity that surrounds you.

Is There an Appropriate Time to Die?

Jerry: Are there any limits of control for our bodily conditions as we approach 100 years of age?

Abraham: Only the limitations caused by your own limited thinking—and all are self-imposed.

Jerry: Is there a time to die, and if so, when is it?

Abraham: There is never an ending to the Consciousness of You, so really there is no "death." But there will come an end to the time that your Consciousness will flow through this particular physical body that you identify as *you.*

369

It is up to you when you withdraw your focus from this body. If you have learned to focus upon good-feeling subjects, and you continue to find things in this environment that excite you and interest you—there is no limit to the amount of time that you can remain focused in your physical body. But when you focus negatively and chronically diminish your Connection to the Stream of Source Energy, your physical experience is then shortened, for your physical apparatus cannot sustain long-term without Source Energy replenishment. *Your negative emotion is a signal that you are cutting off the Source Energy replenishment. Get happy and live long.*

Are All Deaths a Form of Suicide?

Jerry: So, all deaths are a form of "suicide"?

Abraham: That would be one way of stating it. Since everything that you experience comes about because of the balance of your thought, and no one else can think your thoughts or offer your vibration, then everything that happens in your life experience—including that which you term your physical death— is self-inflicted. *Most do not decide to die—they just do not decide to continue to <u>live.</u>*

Jerry: How do you feel about those who *do* decide to die and commit what we call *suicide?*

Abraham: It makes no difference whether the thought you are thinking is one you have deliberately chosen to focus upon or whether you are merely lazily observing something and therefore thinking the thought—you are still thinking the thought, offering the vibration, and reaping the manifestational result of that thought. So you are always creating your own reality whether you are doing it purposefully or not.

There are those who seek to control your behavior for many different reasons, who even wish to control your behavior regarding

your own personal experience, but their frustration level is great because they have no way of controlling others, and every attempt at that control is futile, wasted effort. So, many are uncomfortable with the idea of people deliberately removing themselves from this physical experience by way of "suicide," but we want you to understand that even if you do that, you do not cease to exist, and whether you depart this physical experience by way of deliberate "suicide" or by way of not-deliberate release, the Eternal Being that you are continues to be and looks back on the physical experience you have just left behind only with love and appreciation for the experience.

There are those who are filled with so much hatred as they live in their physical experience that the chronic pinching off from Source and Well-Being is the reason for their death. There are those who simply are no longer finding interesting reasons to focus and remain, who turn their attention to the Non-Physical, and that is the reason for their death. And there are those who have not come to understand Energy or thought or alignment, who desperately want to feel good and can find no way of stopping the chronic pain they have lived for so long that they deliberately choose to reemerge back into the Non-Physical. But in any case, you are Eternal Beings, who, once refocused in the Non-Physical, become whole and renewed and completely aligned with *who-you-really-are*.

Jerry: So, do we each then choose, to some degree, how long we're going to live in each life experience?

Abraham: You come forth intending to live and joyfully expand. When you disregard your *Guidance System*, continuing to find thoughts that disallow your Connection to your Source, you diminish your Connection to your replenishing Source Energy Stream, and without that support, you wither.

A Process to Manage One's Body Weight?

Jerry: What process would you recommend to those wanting to control their body weight?

Abraham: There are so many beliefs upon this subject. So many different methods have been tried, and most Beings who are struggling with the control of body weight have tried many of those methods with little lasting success. And so, their *belief* is that they cannot control their body weight—and so they do not.

We would encourage a visualization of self as you are wanting to be, seeing yourself in that way, thereby attracting it. The ideas and the confirmation from others and all of the circumstances and events that will bring it about easily and quickly for you will come into your experience once you begin to see yourself that way.

When you feel fat, you cannot attract slender. When you feel poor, you cannot attract prosperity. That which you are—the state of being that you *feel*—is the basis from which you attract. That is why "the better it gets, the better it gets; and the worse it gets, the worse it gets."

When you feel very negative about something, do not try to hammer it out and solve it immediately, because your negative attention to it just makes it worse. Distract yourself from the thought until you feel better; and then take another run at it from your positive, fresh perspective.

Jerry: So, is that why people will often go on a "crash diet" and lose massive pounds, and then they'll find themselves gaining it back? Is it because the *desire* was strong, but they didn't have the *belief* and the picture of themselves as this thin person, so they filled the fat picture back in again?

Abraham: They *want* the food; they *believe* that the food will make them fat. And so, as they are giving thought to that which they do *not* want—in *belief,* they create that which they do not want. But that, again, is going about it in the hard way. For the most part, the reason why they lose the weight and then gain it back quickly is that they never gain an image of self as they want

it to be. They keep feeling fat. They keep thinking of themselves as that, and that is the image that they hold. . . . Your body will respond to the image of self—always. That is why if you see yourself as healthy—you will be. If you see yourself as slender, or whatever it is you are wanting in terms of muscle or shape or weight—that is what you will be.

Regarding Food, Can I Follow My Bliss?

Abraham: Some have argued that if they do take our advice and follow their bliss—always looking for things that feel good—they would happily eat things that are detrimental to their health or their body weight. People do often choose food to try to fill the void when they are not feeling good. However, if you have been tending to your vibrational balance for a while and you have learned the power of positively directing your thoughts toward an image of your body as you want it to be, then if you believe that eating a particular food is contrary to accomplishing that desire, negative emotion would come forth as guidance. *It is never a good idea to pursue any action that brings forth negative emotion, because the negative emotion means there is an Energy imbalance, and any action that you participate in during negative emotion will always produce negative results.*

Negative emotion does not occur within a person because a particular food is contrary to Well-Being, but because of current contradictory thoughts. Two people could eat identical diets and follow similar exercise programs and get opposite results, which means there is much more to the equation than the consumption of the food and the burning of calories. *Your results are always and only about your alignment of Energy caused by the thoughts you think.*

A good rule of thumb is: "Get happy, then eat. But do not try to eat your way to happiness." As you have come to make your emotional balance your top priority, your relationship with food will change and your impulse toward food will change, but even more important, your response to food will change. Altering <u>behavior</u> about food without tending to your vibration nets minimal results,

while altering *thought* will yield great returns without the necessity of altering the *behavior.*

And so, let us say that you have decided that you want to be very slender, but you currently do not see yourself as you want to be. And your belief is: *If I eat this food, I will be fat.* As you have a *desire* to be slender, but a *belief* that eating this food will make you fat, you would feel negative emotion if you begin to eat the food. You might call it *guilt, disappointment,* or *anger*—but whatever it is, *eating the food feels bad because, given the set of beliefs that you hold, and given the desire that you hold, this action is not in harmony. And so, if you are following your bliss, you would find yourself feeling good about eating the things that do harmonize with your beliefs and bad about eating the things that do not. Once a desire has been established within you, it is not possible to offer behavior that you believe contradicts it without feeling negative emotion.*

What Are My Beliefs about Food?

Abraham: The beliefs that you hold regarding food are boldly reflected in the experiences you are living:

- If you *believe* that you can eat most anything and not gain weight, that is your experience.

- If you *believe* that you gain weight easily, then you do.

- If you *believe* that certain foods give you an energy boost, they do.

- If you *believe* that certain foods deflate your energy, they do.

- If you want to be slender, but you *believe* that a particular diet is not conducive to being slender, and you take the action of eating that diet, you will gain weight.

374

People often initially balk at our seemingly simplistic analysis of your beliefs about food and how they affect your physical reality, because they believe that their beliefs have come about by observing experience, and it is hard for them to argue with the "factual" evidence that the living of their own life and the observation of others' lives has provided them.

However, observation of results gives you scanty and inadequate information, for unless you are factoring in *desire* and *expectation*, then calculating the action of what has or has not been eaten is irrelevant. You simply cannot leave out the most important ingredient in the recipe of creation and understand the outcome.

People respond differently to the food because the food is not the constant—the thought is. It is the way you are thinking about the food that is making the difference.

Opinions of Others about My Body Are Insignificant

Question: A significant other pointed out to me that I have a little roll along my belt line and it would be good if I worked hard to get rid of it—I could exercise more or eat less or order salads. And because she's a significant other, I took it to heart—and my roll got bigger.

Abraham: The most important thing that we want you to understand is that when you are using the word *other,* always use the word *insignificant* regarding him or her. (Fun)

Of course we understand that people in your life are significant, but you must not let their opinions of you be more important than your own, and anytime anyone influences you to focus upon something that makes you feel bad, you have received negative influence.

We want you to practice your own thoughts so steadily that opinions of others become irrelevant to you. The only freedom you will ever experience comes when you achieve an absence of resistance, which means you will have figured out how to align your chronic thoughts with the thoughts of your own *Inner Being.*

We have never seen anyone achieve that alignment or the feeling of freedom when they are factoring the desires and beliefs of others into the equation. There are just too many moving parts, and it cannot be sorted out.

And so, if someone says to you, "I see something about you that I don't like," we would say, "Look someplace else. What do you think of my nose? Cute little thing, is it not? (Fun) What about this ear over here?" In other words, we would encourage the other to look for positive aspects, and we would be playful and not allow our feelings to be hurt. In fact, we would practice positive thought about our life until we render our feelings unhurtable.

An Example of My "Old" Story about My Body

I'm not happy about the way my body looks. I've been trim and fit at times in my life, but it has never been easy, and those periods never lasted very long. It seems to me that I always had to work irrationally hard to even get close to the way I wanted to look, and then I just couldn't manage to stay there. I'm tired of depriving myself of good things to eat only to end up not looking good anyway. This is hard. I just don't have the kind of metabolism that allows me to eat much of anything that tastes good. It's really not fair. But I don't like being fat either. . . .

An Example of My "New" Story about My Body

My body is a reflection mostly of the thoughts I think. I am happy to understand the power of directing my thoughts, and I am looking forward to seeing physical changes in my body, which reflect my changes in my thinking. I feel good as I anticipate my improved size and shape—and I am confident that those changes are in progress. And, in the meantime, I am generally feeling so good that I am not unhappy with where I currently am. It is fun to think on purpose, and even more fun to see the results of those deliberately chosen thoughts. My body is very responsive to my thoughts. I like knowing that.

There is no right or wrong way to tell your improved story. It can be about your past, present, or future experiences. The only criterion that is important is that you be conscious of your intent to tell a better-feeling, improved version of your story. Telling many good-feeling short stories throughout your day will change your point of attraction. Just remember that the story *you* tell is the basis of *your* life. So tell it the way you want it to be.

PART V

Careers, as Profitable Sources of Pleasure

My First Steps in Career Choice?

Jerry: How would you suggest we know if we've chosen the right career? And how can we be successful at the career we've chosen?

Abraham: What is your definition of *career?*

Jerry: A *career* is like a life's work. An occupation that people could throw themselves into and put the best and the most of themselves into. And, of course, in most cases, people would also want to get a financial return on that.

Abraham: What are you meaning by *life's work?*

Jerry: Some work that people would plan to spend the rest of their lives doing, like a job, profession or business, or a trade. . . .

Abraham: Are you telling us that it is a widespread belief, or accepted desire, of your culture to choose a career and expect to live happily ever after within one topic, forevermore?

Jerry: Well, as long as I can remember, it has been traditionally so. From the time I was very young, people began asking me what I was going to be when I grew up. It is interesting to me now to realize that even when I was a very young child, the adults around me had instilled a sense of urgency in me to choose a career; and I remember watching the milkman delivering the beautiful, delicious

381

milk in glass bottles and thinking as I watched him drive away that that would be my choice for a career. And then I witnessed a policeman actually *making* my mother stop her car by running her off the road, and I was in such admiration of anyone who was able to get my mother to do anything that for a while I decided that I'd be a policeman. Not long after that, a doctor set my broken arm, and I thought I'd like to be a doctor; and then our house caught fire, and the idea of being a fireman seemed like the best idea.

And even after becoming what many would consider to be an adult, I was still observing and considering the multitude of options from my ever-changing perspective. And so, those around me were a bit disappointed that I kept moving from thing to thing rather than settling on one thing for my "life work" or "career."

Abraham: Many people, as they read your childhood story of the events of your life influencing your ideas of what you wanted to be when you grew up, might call your ever-changing ideas childish or unrealistic. But we want to acknowledge: You are always inspired from the events of your life, and when you allow yourself to follow the flow of those inspired ideas, your potential for a joyous experience is much greater than if you were to select your career based on other reasons that people use to justify their choices, such as family tradition or income potential.

It is not surprising that so many have a difficult time deciding what they will do for the rest of their lives, because you are multifaceted Beings and your dominant intent is to enjoy your absolute basis of freedom and, in your quest for joyful experiences, to experience expansion and growth. In other words, without a real perception of *freedom,* you will never be *joyful;* and without *joy,* you cannot experience true *expansion.* So, childish as it may seem to many, it is natural that your life inspires your next adventure and your next and your next.

We encourage you to decide, as early in life as possible, that your dominant intent and reason for existence is to live happily ever after. That would be a very good career choice: to gravitate toward those activities and to embrace those desires that harmonize with your core intentions, which are freedom and growth—and joy. *Make a "career" of living a happy life rather than trying to find work that will produce enough income that you can do things with your money that will then make you happy. When feeling happy is of paramount importance to you—and what you do "for a living" makes you happy—you have found the best of all combinations.*

You can become very good at feeling good under all conditions, but when you become good at reaching for your vibrational balance first—and then attract circumstances and events to yourself from that happy place—your potential for sustained happiness is much greater.

"What Do You Do for a Living?"

Jerry: There are cultures still today (usually we call them primitive or savage) who seem to live in the moment, without jobs. In other words, when they're hungry, they catch a fish or find fruit in a tree.

Abraham: Will they be reading this? (Fun) [No, they won't.] What is the basic category of people you believe will be reading this?

Jerry: People who believe it is essential to have some sort of an income-producing job.

Abraham: What do you believe is the predominant reason that people believe they should find a career early in life and then pursue it the rest of their lives?

Jerry: Of course, I can't speak for everyone, but it seems to almost be a moral or ethical position that we *should,* or *ought,* to find work that produces money. In other words, it's considered to be inappropriate to receive money without giving something back for it or without being productive in some way.

Abraham: You are right. Most people do feel a need to justify their existence through effort or work, and that is perhaps the reason why the first question that you ask one another upon meeting for the first time is: *What do you do for a living?*

Jerry: For about 40 years, I earned my living by working about an hour and a half a day. And often people would voice a sort of resentment that I could have such an income without putting out more time, which would usually evoke a justification from me as I would then explain how much energy I expended during that 90 minutes, how many years it took me to become good at what I did, or how much driving I had to do to even begin my work. In other words, I always felt a need to justify that I *was* actually paying a fair price for what I was receiving.

Abraham: When you are in vibrational alignment (which means that you are in alignment with the Source within you and that your own desires and beliefs are in balance), you never feel a need to justify to another. Many people attempt to justify their behavior or ideas to others, but it is never a good idea to use opinions of others as the guide that you are seeking alignment with rather than your own *Guidance System.*

Many people early on in your experience attempt to demand your compliance with their rules and opinions, but if you allow what they want to be central to the decisions that you make, you only get further and further out of alignment with *who-you-really-are* and with the intentions that you were born with as well as those that have evolved from the life experience you are living. *You will never experience the deliciousness of feeling free until you release your desire to please others and replace it with your powerful intention to align to <u>who-you-really-are</u> (to your Source) by caring how you feel and choosing good-feeling thoughts that let you know you have found your alignment.*

When you sense that someone is disapproving of you or attacking you, it is a natural response to defend yourself, but that need to defend will quickly subside when you have trained yourself into alignment with your *Inner Being,* because all feelings of vulnerability will have been replaced with a sure-footed sense of *who-you-really-are.*

No matter what choices you make, there will always be someone who does not agree with those choices, but as you find your balance and maintain your alignment, most who are observing you will be more inclined to ask you what your secret to success is rather than criticizing you for being successful. And those who continue to criticize you would find no satisfaction in your justification, no matter how compelling your argument is.

It is not your role to fix the feeling of lack within others; it is your role to keep *yourself* in balance. When you allow your society, or even one other person, to dictate to you what you should want or how you should behave, you will lose your balance, because your sense of freedom—which is core to your very Beingness—is challenged. *When you pay attention to the way you feel and you practice the self-empowering thoughts that align with <u>who-you-really-are,</u> you will offer an example of thriving that will be of tremendous value to those who have the benefit of observing you.*

<u>*You cannot get poor enough to help poor people thrive or sick enough to help sick people get well. You only ever uplift from your position of strength and clarity and alignment.*</u>

The *Law of Attraction,* and Career?

Abraham: What is the primary reason for the desire for a career?

Jerry: I read a study done recently that concluded that what most people are looking for is *prestige.* In other words, if offered the choice of having a higher title or more money, most chose the title.

Abraham: Those who are seeking prestige have replaced their own *Guidance System* with seeking approval from others, and that is a rather unfulfilling way to live because the onlookers you are seeking to please do not sustain long-lasting attention upon you.

That study is very likely accurate because most people do care more about what others think about them than they do about how they personally feel, but there can be no consistency in that form of guidance.

Sometimes people worry that if they selfishly consider what makes them happy above all other things, they will be uncaring and unfair to those around them, but we know that the opposite is true. *When you care about your alignment with Source, which is represented by the way you feel, and you work to maintain your Connection, anyone who is then your object of attention receives benefit from your gaze. You cannot uplift another unless you are connected to the Stream of Well-Being yourself.*

We understand that it can feel very good when others hold you as their object of attention as they are feeling appreciation for you, because they are then doing exactly what we were just explaining to you: In their appreciation of you, they are connected to Source and showering it all over you. But to ask others to always be in alignment with Source and to always hold *you* as their object of attention so that you can be showered with the Well-Being they are providing is not practical, because you cannot control their connection and you will not always be their only object of attention. You do, however, have absolute control over your own Connection to Source, and when your dominant intent is to maintain your Connection while leaving others out of that equation, then you will be free of trying to please others (which you cannot consistently do), and you will be able to maintain a consistent Connection and feeling of Well-Being.

An interesting thing to note is, those who care about how they feel—who consistently hold themselves in an attitude of good-feeling emotions; who are connected to Source and flowing positive thoughts outward toward whatever they are focused upon—are usually seen by others to be *attractive,* and they are often the recipients of much appreciation and approval.

You just cannot get the approval you seek from the place of *needing* it or from the place of the *lack* of it. An office with a wonderful window view or a parking place with your name on it or an impressive title accompanying your name cannot fill the void caused by not being in alignment with *who-you-really-are*. When you achieve that alignment, those things feel less important—but then, interestingly enough, they come anyway.

Filling My Void Through Service?

Jerry: So during my 20 years in a wide variety of positions in the entertainment industry, I really had a lot of fun; it required only a few hours of my time, and I had a lot of adventurous challenges because I had so many new experiences . . . and yet I often told people that I felt like I was walking across the sands of life, but when I looked back, there were no tracks. In other words, I felt that I was bringing my audiences some temporary pleasure, but I wasn't leaving them with anything of permanent value.

Do we all inherently have those drives to uplift others? Do they come from another level of ourselves, or do we pick those intentions up from others around us once we're born into this physical environment?

Abraham: *You are born wanting to be of value, wanting to uplift. And you are born understanding that you have value.* Most of that feeling of lack that you were describing was not about your not being able to provide lasting value to others, but because your thoughts were keeping you away from your own personal alignment. It works like this: When you are in alignment with *who-you-really-are* (with your *Inner Being* or Source), you cannot help but uplift those with whom you come into contact, *and* in that alignment, you do not notice so many others who are not in alignment. *The Law of Attraction does not surround you with dissatisfied people when you are satisfied. And the Law of Attraction does not surround you with satisfied people when you are dissatisfied.*

You simply cannot compensate for your own misalignment by offering more time or energy or action. You cannot find ideas that are effective enough to make up the difference. Your value to those around you hinges upon only one thing: your personal alignment with Source. And the only thing you have to give to another is an example of that alignment—which they may observe, then desire, and then work to achieve. But *you* cannot give it to them.

The entertainment that you provided to your audiences was actually a much bigger gift than you were able to acknowledge at the time, for you were providing distraction from troubling things; and in the absence of your audience members' attention to their problems, they did achieve, in many cases, temporary alignment with Source. But you cannot go with each of them, holding yourself as their only object of attention in order to maintain their good feeling. *Everyone is responsible for the thoughts they think and the things that they choose as their objects of attention.*

All of you have, deep within you, an understanding that you are here as joyous creators, and you are always being called toward that fulfillment, but there is not a long list of requirements that you are expected to accomplish. Your intention was to let your physical environment inspire your never-ending ideas of expansion or desire, and then you intended to align with the Source Energy within you for the achievement of those ideas. In other words, you knew your desires would be born from your participation here, and then, once the desire was alive within you, you could focus your thoughts until you accomplished a feeling of expectation—and then your desire would come to fruition.

The primary role that others around you play in that equation for creation is they provide variety from which your desires are born. *It was not your intention to measure your value against the value of others, but to be inspired to new ideas by the combination of things going on around you. Any comparison to others is only meant to inspire expanded desire. It was never intended as a means to diminish you or to discount your value.*

Your life is not about what you will do after work, on the weekend, or after you retire. Your life is happening now and is really represented by how you are feeling now. If your work feels unpleasant or unfulfilling or hard, it is not because you are standing in the wrong place, but because your perspective is clouded by contradicted thought.

You cannot have a happy ending to a journey that has not been pleasant along the way. The end absolutely does not justify the means.

The means, or the path along the way, always brings about the essence of an identical ending.

Will My Success Uplift Others?

Jerry: My freedom has always been what was most important to me, so I've never been willing to give up much of it for money. I always said that I had very little interest in money because I wasn't willing to give up my freedom for it, but then over time that "leaving no footprints in the sand" feeling made me question if there wasn't really something more to life than just having fun.

Shortly after that awareness, I found the book *Think and Grow Rich,* and even though the idea of *thinking* or of *growing rich* was something that I would have denied having any interest in, the book got my attention and I felt a strong draw toward it. I picked it up and the hair stood up on my body as if I had found something that would have major meaning in my life. The book said: *Make a decision about what you want!* It was a seemingly simple statement, but I felt the power of it in a strange and new way, so for the first time in my life, I consciously started making decisions about what I wanted and writing them down: "I want to be self-employed; I want a business of my own; I want no place of business; I don't want my foot nailed to the floor; I want no employees—I don't want that kind of responsibility. What I want is *freedom.*"

I wanted to be able to control my income. I wanted to be mobile so I could travel or be anywhere that I wanted to be. *I wanted my work to be something where every life I touched I elevated in some way (or just let people be where they were) but that no one would ever be diminished as a result of knowing me.*

People used to laugh when I'd tell them that. They'd say, "Oh, Jerry, you're such a dreamer. There's no such thing as that." And I said, "Well, there has to be. Emerson said, 'You wouldn't have the desire if you didn't have the ability to achieve it.'" And I believed that. And so, I really expected, somewhere along the line, opportunities to show up. . . .

Within about 30 days of my clarifying what I *wanted*, I met a man who showed me a business that I could take to California and start—and it answered everything I was asking for. And so, for the next years of my life, that business really took hold. And again, it fulfilled the essence of everything that I'd written down that I wanted.

I Want Freedom, Growth, and Joy

Jerry: I didn't say it had to be something I was capable of doing or that I had the talent or the ability or the intelligence for; I just said: *This is what I want.*

Can any of us have that? Can any of us have whatever we want once we clarify what it is that we want?

Abraham: Yes. *If this life experience has inspired the desire within you, this life experience has the wherewithal to fulfill it down to the very last detail.*

You had been coming to those decisions about what you wanted over a long period of time because of the life experiences that you had been living. Your decision point of focusing upon those decisions and writing them down in a comprehensive manner caused an emphasizing of your *belief* regarding them. And when your *desires* and *beliefs* come together, *expectation* occurs. And once *expectation* for anything is within you, it then comes quickly into your experience.

Being free was the most important element in the desires that you had held for some time, and when you saw something that you believed would not threaten your desire for freedom but had the potential of bringing income, you then allowed your desire for more income to expand, where previously anything that you perceived as having the potential to dampen your freedom you repelled immediately.

You were all born with a triad of intentions pulsing within you: *freedom, growth,* and *joy. Freedom* is the basis of that which you are because everything that comes to you comes in response to the thoughts you think—and no one has control over the thoughts that you think other than you. When *joy* is your dominant quest so that you gently train your thoughts into alignment with *who-you-really-are*, all resistance subsides, and you then allow the *expansion* or *growth* that your life experience has inspired within you.

I Want My Life to Feel Good

Abraham: *When choosing a career, or when doing the things that your work currently requires, if your dominant intent is to feel joy while you are doing the work, your triad of intentions will come quickly and easily into alignment, because in your accomplishment of feeling good, you come into complete alignment with the broader, Non-Physical aspects of your Being. That alignment then allows the expansion toward all of the things that your life has helped you identify that you want, so your growth becomes swift and satisfying.*

Freedom is the basis of your life experience; it is not something that you have to earn. *Joy* is your objective. *Growth* is the result of all of that. But if you believe that you are unworthy and you set out to prove worthiness through action, you cannot find your balance. Often we explain this perfect triad of intentions of *freedom and growth and joy,* but most physical Beings then turn their attention immediately to the idea of *growth* in their misguided attempt of proving worthiness—worthiness that has never been in question. You have nothing to prove to anyone and nothing to justify. *Your reason for existence needs no justification, for your very existence is justification enough.*

I Create My Own Joyous Career

Abraham: *We would like you to see your "career" as one of creating a joyful life experience. You are not a creator of things or a regurgitator of what someone else has created or a gatherer of stuff. <u>You are a creator, and the subject of your creation is your joyful life experience. That is your mission. That is your quest. That is why you are here.</u>*

Is It Immoral to Get Without Giving?

Jerry: Abraham, would you say that it would be morally or ethically correct for people to never give back? In other words, if they just lived on inherited money or won money, like the lottery, or lived off of welfare or donated money, would you say that would be appropriate for *all* of us?

Abraham: Your question still implies that there is a price to pay for the Well-Being that flows to you, and that some sort of action is required to justify the flowing of the Well-Being. That is not the case. *It is neither necessary nor possible to justify the Well-Being that flows to you, but it is necessary to <u>align</u> with the Well-Being. You cannot focus upon lack of Well-Being and allow Well-Being into your experience.*

Many people focus upon *unwanted* things, with no deliberate attention to the emotional Guidance within them, and then they try to compensate for their lackful thinking with physical action. And because of the misalignment of Energy, they do not get results from their action, so then they try harder by offering more action, but still things do not improve.

Like the air you breathe, abundance in all things is available to you. Your life will simply be as good as you allow it to be.

If you believe that you must work hard for the abundance that comes to you, then it cannot come without hard work. But in so many cases, the harder you work, the worse you feel, and the worse you feel, the more you disallow the results that you wanted to receive from your hard work. It is no wonder so many people are discouraged and do not know which way to turn, for it seems that no matter what they do, they do not thrive.

Appreciation and *love,* and *alignment* to that which is Source, is the ultimate "giving back," so to speak. In your *pain* or *struggle,* you have nothing to give back. Many complain of unfairness or injustice when they see some people receiving greatly but offering seemingly little effort, while others who work very hard often show very little success—but the *Law of Attraction* is always consistently just. <u>*What you are living is always an exact replication of your vibrational*</u>

patterns of thought. Nothing could be more fair than life as you are living it, for as you are thinking, you are vibrating, and as you are vibrating, you are attracting—and so you are always getting back the essence of what you are giving.

Jerry: If we take money out of the equation, so to speak, then if we're not *doing* for the sake of money, what *should* we be doing with our life?

Abraham: What most people *are* doing with most of their lives is offering action to try to compensate for vibrational imbalance. In other words, they think so much of things they *do not want,* and in doing so, they prevent what they *do want* from easily flowing into their experience, and then they try to compensate for the misalignment through action. If you would tend to your vibrational alignment first—by recognizing the value of your emotions and trying to focus upon things that feel good—you would benefit tremendously by that alignment, and wonderful things would flow to you with far less action.

The majority of action that is offered today is offered amidst tremendous vibrational resistance, and that is the reason why so many people have come to believe that life is a struggle. It is also the reason why many, like you, believe that success and freedom are at odds with one another, when, in reality, they are actually synonymous. *It is not necessary to take money out of the equation, but it is necessary that you make your quest for joy be the most dominant part of your equation. When you do that, abundance in all manner will flow to you.*

Welcome to Planet Earth

Abraham: If we were talking to you on your first day of physical experience, we could be of great advantage to you because we would say, "Welcome to planet Earth. There is nothing that you cannot be or do or have. And your work here—your lifetime career—is to seek joy.

"You live in a Universe of absolute freedom. You are so free that every thought you think will attract unto you.

"As you think thoughts that feel good to you, you will be in harmony with *who-you-really-are*. And so, utilize your profound freedom. *Seek joy first, and all of the growth that you could ever imagine will come joyously and abundantly unto you.*"

But this is not the first day of your life experience. In most cases, you are reading this long after you have been convinced that you are not free and that you are unworthy and that you must prove, through your action, that you are worthy of receiving. Many of you are currently involved in careers or work that you do not find pleasing, but you feel that you cannot just walk away because the financial repercussions would cause even greater discomfort than what you are already experiencing. Many others who do not currently have work that is producing income feel the discomfort of having no means of support or promise of future security. But, no matter where you are currently standing, if you will make a decision to look at the positive aspects of where you are right now, you will stop the offering of resistance, which is the only thing holding you apart from what you desire.

You do not have to go back and undo anything or beat up on yourself for what you have not yet accomplished. If you could, in essence, regard this moment as the beginning of your life experience —doing your best to resist the bad-feeling, resistant thoughts of unworthiness or resentment that often surround the subject of money—your financial picture would begin to change right now. You only have to say, *Here I am, on the first day of the rest of my physical life experience. And it is my dominant intent, from this moment forward, to look for reasons to feel good. **I want to feel good. Nothing is more important to me than that I feel good.***

Most Important Is Feeling Good

Abraham: Often there are things in your work environment that are not conducive to feeling good, and often you believe that your only chance of ever really feeling good is to get away from those negative influences. But the idea of quitting and leaving does not feel good either because that could cause a lapse in your income when things are already financially tight, so you continue on, unhappy and feeling trapped.

If you could stand back a little bit and see your career not as work that you are doing in exchange for money but as the expenditure of your life experience in return for your joyful experience, then you would realize that many of the thoughts you think and the words you speak are not in alignment with that quest for joy. If you will say, "Nothing is more important than that I feel good," you will find yourself guiding yourself to different thoughts, words, and behaviors.

The simple exercise of deliberately looking for positive aspects of your current work and the people who work there with you will give you an immediate feeling of relief. And that relief will indicate a shift in your vibration, which means your point of attraction has shifted. Once that occurs, the *Law of Attraction* will cause you to rendezvous with different people and will even cause you to have different experiences with the same people. It is a sort of creating from the inside out, rather than the outside-in, action version that never works. *From your simple but powerful premise of deciding that you want to feel good, things will begin to improve in dramatic ways.*

What Is Holding Back My Career?

Jerry: What would you say to those who are moving toward their first field of employment or are making a career change and are considering things like income or growth potential, product or service demand, and so forth in trying to decide what direction to take?

Abraham: The life you have already lived has caused you to determine the details of the experience you are looking for, and the perfect situation is already lined up for you. Your work right now is not to get out there and find the perfect set of circumstances, but instead to *allow* the unfolding of the circumstances that will lead you right to a position that satisfies the myriad of intentions that you have come to through your life experience. In other words, you never know more clearly what it is that you *do want* than when you are living what you *do not want.*

So, not having enough money causes you to *ask* for more money. An unappreciative employer makes you *ask* for someone who appreciates your talent and willingness. A job that asks very little from you causes you to *desire* something that inspires more clarity and expansion through you. A job that requires a long commute in traffic gives birth to a *desire* for work that is closer to where you live . . . and so on. *We would like to convey to anyone looking for a change in their work environment: It is already queued up for you in a sort of Vibrational Escrow. Your work is to align with what your past and current experiences have helped you identify that you want.*

It may sound strange, but the fastest way to an improved work environment is to look for things in your current environment that make you feel good. Most people do exactly the opposite by pointing out the flaws in where they stand in an effort to justify an improved environment. But since the *Law of Attraction* always gives you more of whatever you are giving your attention to, if your attention is upon unwanted things, then more unwanted things are on the way as well. *When you leave one situation because of the unwanted things that are present, you find the essence of the same unwanted things in your next environment as well.*

Think and speak of what you *do* want.

Make lists of things that are pleasant about where you are.

Think excitedly about the improvements that are on the way to you.

De-emphasize what you do not like.

Emphasize what you do like.

Observe the Universe's response to your improved vibration.

I'll Seek Reasons to Feel Good

Jerry: So, in other words, unless people now focus on what they *do* want and get their focus off of what they *don't* want in their current or previous position, they'll just continue to—in some form—re-create a negative situation?

Abraham: That is absolutely correct. *No matter how justified you are in your negative emotion, you are still messing up your future.*

Most of you have given enough thought to what you want to keep you happily busy for 10 or 20 lifetimes, but your manifestations cannot get to you because your door is closed. And the reason that your door is closed is because you are so busy complaining about *what-is* or busy defending where you now stand. . . . *Look for reasons to feel good. And in your joy, you open the door. And as you open your door, all of these things that you have said "I want" can then flow in. And it is our expectation that, under those conditions, you would live happily ever after—which, after all, is that which you have truly intended as you have come forth into this career of physical life experience.*

Do I *Want* to, or Do I *Have* to?

Jerry: Through my early years while we lived on a series of 40-acre farms in Oklahoma, Missouri, and Arkansas, I did many different things to earn money, all of them very hard work and none of them fun. From picking berries; to raising and selling chickens; to planting, harvesting, and selling tomatoes; to chopping and selling firewood, I earned quite a bit of money (for those times), but I didn't enjoy my work at all. Then, during my high school years in New Orleans, I worked at another series of non-fun jobs as a roofer, a sheet-metal mechanic, and an elevator operator. The first job I had that was any fun at all was being a lifeguard at Pontchartrain Beach.

I guess I was like most others around me, and it didn't occur to me that fun and earning money could coincide. During the time I was doing all of that not-fun, very hard work, I was doing fun things *after* work. I got together with other kids in the park at night and played my guitar, and I sang at church and in the choir with the New Orleans Opera. I led a Cub Scout group, performed acrobatics, and volunteered as a teacher of gymnastics and dance. I did many wonderful, fun things, but I didn't earn money from any of them.

However, once I became an adult, I never again worked very long at anything I didn't enjoy. Instead, I became self-employed, and those things I'd been doing free for fun, I just kept doing—but then I started receiving money in return for performing them.

I hadn't been training for, or planning for, a career in music or singing or dancing or acrobatics—but then the sheet-metal workers' union called a strike, and while I was out of work, a man at the YMCA gym asked me to join "El Gran Circo de Santos y Artigas" in Cuba as an aerial bar performer (*artista*). And so I didn't go in the "secure" direction in roofing and sheet metal that my father wanted me to plan for. (It paid a steady wage, and I was trained for it and was very good at it even though I disliked so much about it.) But as a result of the *unwanted* union strike, I turned easily in the direction of what then became a truly joyous life of adventure and earnings. I began as an acrobat with that Cuban circus and then stayed in show business, in one aspect or another, for over 20 years.

Abraham: Hear how the details of your life clearly demonstrate the things we have been offering here. Do you see how those early years of working so hard at things you did not enjoy helped you to not only identify what you did not want, but also helped you to determine what you did prefer? And even though you were working as a teenager still at things you did not enjoy doing, you were spending a great deal of your time—every spare minute, really—doing things that you really *did* like very much to do. So the two parts of your equation for joyful creation were in place: The hard work caused you to *ask;* your time playing music and doing the gymnastics and such that you loved put you in a chronic place of *allowing;* and then, through the path of least resistance, the Universe delivered to you a viable path to get the freedom, growth, and joy that you wanted.

Because of the intense unpleasantness of those early years of very hard work, you were one of the few who was strange enough or weird enough or different enough to allow yourself to seek your bliss. And that led to many things that you had come to desire.

Most people feel a stark difference between the things that they *want* to do and the things that they believe they *have* to do. And most have put anything that earns money in the category of *the things that I have to do.* That is why the money often comes so hard, and that is why there is usually not enough.

If you are wise enough to follow the trail of good-feeling thoughts, you will discover that that blissful path will lead you to all things you desire. By deliberately looking for positive aspects along your way, you will come into vibrational alignment with who-you-really-are and with the things you really want, and once you do that, the Universe must deliver to you a viable means to achieve your desires.

What If My Pleasure Attracts Money?

Jerry: For example, Esther and I had no intention of receiving income from our work with you, Abraham. We were really enjoying learning from you, and we were thrilled by the positive results we were personally receiving as we applied what we were learning, but it was never our intention for our work with you to become a business. It was an enlightening experience of just plain fun (and it still is fun), but now it has expanded dramatically into a worldwide enterprise.

Abraham: So, are you saying that as your life experience expanded, your ideas and desires expanded, also? And even though in the beginning you were not able to see or describe the details of *how* things would unfold . . . because it was fun and because you felt good, this became a powerful avenue to fulfill desires and goals that had been in place long before you met us or began this work?

Jerry: Yes. My original intention in visiting with you was to learn a more effective way to help others become more financially successful. And, also, I wanted to learn how to live our lives more in harmony with the natural *Laws of the Universe.*

I Want My Work to Feel Free

Jerry: So, most of what you might call my *careers* through the years almost never began as a means to earn money. They've mostly been things that I just enjoyed doing, which ended up earning money.

Abraham: Well, that truly is the secret to the success that you have enjoyed for so many years. Because you determined early on that feeling good was what mattered most to you, you managed to find a variety of interesting ways to maintain that intention, not realizing at the time that *the secret to all success is keeping yourself happy.*

Many of you have been taught that your own happiness is a selfish and inappropriate quest, and that your real objectives should revolve around commitment and responsibility and struggle and sacrifice . . . but we want you to understand that you can be committed and responsible and an uplifter—*and* happy. In fact, unless you do find a way of connecting to your true happiness, all of those other quests are usually just empty, hollow words not backed up by any true value. *You only ever uplift from your position of connection and strength.*

People often say, "I don't want to work," meaning: "I don't want to go someplace where I have to do unwanted things to earn money." And when we ask why, they say, "Because I want to be free." But it is not freedom from action that you are seeking, because action can be fun. And it is not freedom from money that you want, because money and freedom are synonymous. *You are seeking freedom from negativity, from resistance, from the disallowance of who-you-really-are, and from the disallowance of the abundance that is your birthright. You are seeking freedom from lack.*

What Are Its Positive Aspects?

Abraham: *Whenever you feel negative emotion, that is your Emotional Guidance System giving you an indication that you are, in that* *moment, looking at negative aspects of something, and in doing so, you are depriving yourself of something wanted.*

If you will set an intention to look for positive aspects in whatever you are giving your attention to, you will begin to immediately see the evidence of the lifting of patterns of resistance as the Universe is then allowed, by your shift in vibration, to deliver your long-wanted desires to you.

People often move from job to job, profession to profession, employer to employer, only to find the next place no better than the last—and the reason for that is, they take themselves everywhere they go. When you go to a new place and you continue to complain about what was wrong with your last position in order to explain why you came to the new position, the same vibrational mix of resistance goes with you and continues to prevent the things you want from coming to you.

The best way to accomplish an improved work environment is to focus upon the best things about where you currently are until you flood your own vibrational patterns of thought with *appreciation,* and in that changed vibration, you can then allow the new-and-improved conditions and circumstances to come into your experience.

Some worry that if they follow our encouragement to look for good things about where they are, it will only hold them longer in an unwanted place, but the opposite is really true: *In your state of appreciation, you lift all self-imposed limitations (and all limitations are self-imposed) and you free yourself for the receiving of wonderful things.*

Jerry: Abraham, what is the role of *appreciation* in the creation equation? And how does a condition of appreciation equate to what's called the attitude of gratitude? From Napoleon Hill's book *Think and Grow Rich,* I learned to decide what I wanted and then to focus on it (or think about it) until it came into being. In other words, I set goals and timetables for their achievement. But then after meeting you, I became aware that most of what I would describe as the most wonderful things that came into my life weren't so much things that I had specified that I *wanted* (although much of that came to pass, also). What actually manifested was the essence of something that I had greatly *appreciated.*

In other words, I knew Esther for years before we came together. And I never *wanted* her through those years, but I did greatly *appreciate* so many aspects of who she was . . . and then she (and all of her delightful aspects) came completely into my life. And look at what a magnificent difference she has made in the joyous aspects of my life.

Also, I read the *Seth* books over and over and never *desired* to have a "Seth" in my life. But I greatly *appreciated* the teaching of that "Non-Physical Entity" named Seth, as well as Jane Roberts and Robert Butts, who facilitated that experience. And now, here you are, not "Seth" per se, but you bring with you the essence of everything that I *appreciated* so much about Jane and Rob and Seth's phenomenal metaphysical experiences.

Over 40 years ago, I was visiting a family near San Francisco who earned their money from a very basic, almost primitive, mail-order lapidary business that they conducted from their home. I never, ever said that I *wanted* that business, but in my *appreciation,* I told thousands of people the story of that experience. And then one day (about 20 years ago) as I was at the post office picking up orders for some *Teachings of Abraham* recordings, I realized that I was now experiencing the essence of that mail-order business that I had so much *appreciated*—and now look at how many millions of people have been positively touched as a result of the business aspects of disseminating this philosophy!

I could list many more, but I'll add one more scenario: Esther and I, when we first moved to San Antonio, Texas, found a small temporary rental house where we could enjoy a vegetable garden, laying hens, a milk goat, and our own water well. . . . We used to take our walks by crossing the road in front of the house and then walking across a small airplane landing strip into a grove of large cedar and live-oak trees. Even in the heat of the summer, we were able to enjoy our walks by following the deer trails that tunneled through the dense growth of trees.

One day we discovered that one of the deer trails opened into a tiny "meadow" hidden among the oaks. It was so beautiful! The grass and flowers and general atmosphere would be best described as "enchanting." Esther and I loved that good-feeling spot in the woods, and we returned there many times. We conjured scenarios of how this seemingly ancient, seemingly natural clearing could have come about and who might have discovered and enjoyed it before us. We questioned why it was so inexplicably pleasing to us—and we *appreciated* it greatly! We *never* said that we *wanted* that piece of land—we purely *appreciated* it.

And then about five or six years later, a stranger called us and said he had heard that we were looking for land to build our office complex on . . . and the seven acres that he offered us contained that small hidden meadow. And now our office sits exactly on that beautiful, enchanting spot. That 7 acres became part of 20 . . . and then one day I was *appreciating* the beautiful oak trees on our neighbor's prime 20 acres, and to make a long, delightful story relatively short—that little meadow has now evolved to 40 prime acres with Interstate 10 frontage . . . with a plane hangar, a helicopter pad, and a stable (we don't have a plane or horses). *And it all evolved from our appreciation of that small meadow in the woods.*

Abraham, would you please respond to my perspective regarding the emotion of *appreciation?*

Abraham: The vibration of true love, that feeling of being in love, that feeling that you have sometimes when you see someone and you feel like you are moving through one another. The feeling that you have when you are looking at the innocence of a child and feeling the beauty and power of that child. *Love* and *appreciation* are identical vibrations.

Appreciation is the vibration of alignment with <u>who-you-are.</u> It is the absence of resistance. It is the absence of doubt and fear. It is the absence of self-denial or hatred toward others. Appreciation is the absence of everything that feels bad and the presence of everything that feels good. When you focus upon what you want—when you tell the story of how you want your life to be—you will come closer and closer to the vicinity of appreciation, and when you reach it, it will pull you toward all things that you consider to be good in a very powerful way.

Conversely, let us talk about the difference between, let us say, *gratitude* and *appreciation.* Many people use the words interchangeably, but we do not feel the same vibrational essence in them at all, because when you feel gratitude, often you are looking at a struggle that you have overcome. In other words, you are happy that you are still not in the struggle, but there is still some of that "struggle" vibration present. In other words, the difference between *inspiration,* which is being called to *who-you-are,* and *motivation,* which is trying to make yourself go somewhere, is a similar difference.

Appreciation is that tuned-in, tapped-in, turned-on feeling. Appreciation is vibrational alignment with "who I have become." The state of appreciation is "me being in sync with the whole of that which I am."

Being in the state of appreciation is seeing whatever you are looking at through the eyes of Source. And when you are in that state of appreciation, you could walk down a crowded street with all kinds of things that a lot of other people would find reason to criticize or worry about, and you would not have access to them because your vibration of appreciation is picking out for you things of a different vibrational nature.

A state of appreciation is a state of Godliness. A state of appreciation is being *who-you-really-are.* A state of appreciation is who you were the day you were born and who you will be the moment you die, and it would be (if we were standing in your physical shoes) our quest in every moment.

Joseph Campbell used the word *bliss,* and we think it is equal: "Follow your bliss." But sometimes, you cannot get a whiff of bliss from where you are. So we say, if you are in despair, follow your revenge; it is *downstream.* If you are in revenge, follow your hatred; it is *downstream.* If you are in hatred, follow your anger; it is *downstream.* If you are in anger, follow your frustration; it is *downstream.* If you are in frustration, follow your hope; it is *downstream.* If you are in hope, now you are in the vicinity of appreciation.

Once you get into the vibration of hope, now begin making lists of things that you feel good about, and fill your notebooks full of them. Make lists of positive aspects. Make lists of things you love. Go to the restaurant and look for your favorite things, and never complain about anything. Look for the thing that you like the best . . . even if there was only one thing in all of it that you like, give it your undivided attention—and use it as your excuse to be *who-you-are.*

And as you use those things that shine bright and make you feel good as your excuse to give your attention and be *who-you-are,* you will tune to *who-you-are,* and the whole world will begin to transform before your eyes. *It is not your job to transform the world for others—but it is your job to transform it for you.* A state of *appreciation* is pure Connection to Source where there is no perception of lack.

My Time at Work Is Perceptual

Abraham: In the same way that many people are focused upon a shortage of *money,* there are also many who are focused upon a shortage of *time,* and often these two lackful subjects are intertwined to negatively impact one another. Usually the reason for this detrimental coupling of lackful subjects is the feeling that there just is not enough time to do what is necessary to achieve success.

The primary reason that people feel a shortage of time is because they are trying to get too much leverage out of their action. If you are unaware of the power of alignment and are making little or no effort at finding your personal alignment—if you are overwhelmed or angry or resentful or ornery, and from those emotional perspectives, you are then offering your action to try to accomplish things—you are very likely experiencing a severe shortage of time.

There simply is not enough action in the world to compensate for the misalignment of Energy, but when you care about how you feel and you tend to your vibrational balance first, then you experience what feels like a cooperative Universe that seems to open doors for you everywhere. The physical *effort* required of someone who is in alignment is a fraction of that required to someone who is not. The *results* experienced by someone who is in alignment are tremendous in comparison with the results experienced by someone who is not.

If you are feeling a shortage of time or money, your best effort would be to focus upon better-feeling thoughts, to make long lists of positive aspects, to look for reasons to feel good, and to do more things that make you feel good when you do them. Taking the time to feel better, to find positive aspects, to align with who-you-really-are, will net you tremendous results and help you balance your time much more effectively.

Shortage of time is not your problem. Shortage of money is not your problem. Shortage of Connection to the Energy that creates worlds is what is at the heart of all sensations of shortage that you are experiencing. Those voids or shortages can be filled with only one thing: Connection to Source and alignment with *who-you-really-are.*

Your time is a perceptual thing, and even though the clock is ticking the same for everyone, your alignment affects your perception, as well as the results that you allow. When you set time aside to envision your life as you want it to be, you access a power that is unavailable to you when you focus upon the problems of your life.

As you observe the enormous differences in the effort that people apply and the results they achieve, you have to conclude that there is more to the equation of achieving than action alone. The difference is that some receive the benefit of the leverage of alignment because of the thoughts they think—while others disallow that leverage because of the thoughts they think.

Imagine yourself running one mile, and in this mile there are 2,000 doors to move through. Imagine coming to each door and then having to personally open it before you can run through it. Now imagine running the mile, and as you approach each door, the door is opened for you, so you are able to continue the pace, slowing not at all upon approaching each door. *When you are in alignment with the Energy that creates worlds, you no longer have to stop and open the doors. Your Energy alignment allows things to line up for you, and the action that you offer is the way you enjoy the benefit of the alignment you have accomplished.*

Should I Try to Work Harder?

Abraham: You are a powerful creator who came into this Leading Edge environment understanding that you would create through the power of your thought by deliberately directing your focus toward things that you want. You did not intend to rely on your action for that creation.

It may take some time to adjust to the understanding that you are creating through your thoughts, not through your action—but we cannot overstate the value of thinking and speaking of things as you would like them to be rather than as they are. *Once you not only understand the power of your thought, but you deliberately direct this powerful tool in the direction of things that you desire, then you will discover that the action part of your life is the way you enjoy what you have created through your thought.*

When you achieve vibrational alignment (which means your thoughts are pleasing as you think them) and you feel an inspiration to act, you have accomplished the best of both worlds. Your action feels effortless when you are tuned in to the vibrational frequency of Source, and then you feel an inspiration to offer action. Those outcomes are always pleasing. But action taken without tending to vibrational alignment first is hardworking, inefficient action that, over time, wears you down.

Most are so busy dealing with that which is immediate that they do not have time to tend to that which is important. Many tell us that they are so busy making their money that they do not have time to enjoy it . . . for when you rely on your action to create, often you are too tired to enjoy your creation.

Question: My work is an adventure, and I really do enjoy it. But when I tie money and earnings to my work, I can feel a tension that then takes the joy out of it. Do they not go well together?

Abraham: This is a common story that we hear from creative people who are involved in music or art that they love, but when they decide to make this thing they love the primary source of their income, not only do they often struggle in making enough money, but their previous joy is diminished as well.

Most people have a rather negative attitude about money, simply because most people speak more often of what they cannot afford or the lack of the money they desire than they speak of the *benefit* of money. Also, most people spend much more time thinking about what is currently happening in their experience rather than what they would prefer to happen, and so without meaning to, most people are thinking rather lackfully about money.

So then, when you couple an idea of something that you enjoy—your adventure, your music, your art—with something that you have felt strong lack about for a long time (money), the balance of your thought tips toward the dominant feeling.

As you begin spending more time visualizing what you desire and less time observing *what-is,* and as you then practice your more positive, better-feeling story, in time your *adventure* will become the dominant vibration within you, and then as you couple your adventure with your means of earning, the two will blend perfectly and enhance each other.

There is no better way to earn money than to do the things that you love to do. Money can flow into your experience through endless avenues. It is not the choice of the craft that limits the money that flows—but only your attitude toward money.

That is why so many niche markets are continually opening, with people becoming very wealthy from ideas that only recently were not viable markets at all. You are the creator of your own reality, and you are the creator of your own markets of enterprise and your own flow of money.

You cannot accurately define some activities as <u>hard</u> and others as <u>easy</u>, because all things that are in harmony with what you are wanting are easy and flowing, while all things that are not in harmony with what you are wanting are harder and are more resistant.

Anytime what you are doing feels like a struggle, you must understand that your contradictory thought is introducing resistance into the equation. Resistance is caused by thinking about what you do not want, and that is what makes you tired.

An Example of My "Old" Story about My Career

I've always worked hard in every job I've had, but I've never really been appreciated. It seems to me that employers always take advantage of me, getting everything from me that they can and giving as little in return as they can get away with. I'm tired of working so hard for so little. I'm going to start holding back, too—no point in my knocking myself out when no one else notices. Many of the people around me at work know less than I know, work less than I work, and make more money than I make. That's just not right.

An Example of My "New" Story about My Career

I know that I will not always be right here in this place doing this same work. I like understanding that things are always evolving, and it is fun to anticipate where I am headed.

While there are many things that could be better where I am, it is not really a problem because "where I am" is constantly changing to something better. I like knowing that as I look for the best things around me where I am, those things become more prevalent in my experience.

It is fun to know that things are always working out for me, and I watch for the evidence of that . . . and I see more evidence of that every day.

There is no right or wrong way to tell your improved story. It can be about your past, present, or future experiences. The only criterion that is important is that you be conscious of your intent to tell a better-feeling, improved version of your story. By telling many good-feeling short stories throughout your day, you will change your point of attraction.

Time to Tell a New Story

My old story is about . . .

. . . things that have gone wrong.
. . . things that aren't the way I want them to be or think
    they should be.
. . . others who have let me down.
. . . others who have not been truthful with me.
. . . not enough money.
. . . not enough time.
. . . how things usually are.
. . . how things have been all my life.
. . . how things have been lately.
. . . injustices that I see in the world.
. . . others who just don't understand.
. . . others who don't make an effort.
. . . others who are capable but who don't apply themselves.
. . . dissatisfaction with my appearance.
. . . worry about my body's health.
. . . people who take advantage of others.
. . . people who want to control me.

My new story is about . . .

. . . the positive aspects of my current subject of attention.
. . . the way I really want things to be.
. . . how well things are going.
. . . how the *Law of Attraction* is the true manager of all
    things.
. . . abundance that flows abundantly.
. . . how time is perceptual and endless.
. . . the best things I see.
. . . my favorite memories.
. . . the obvious expansion of my life.
. . . the amazing or interesting or wonderful aspects of my
    world.

. . . the incredible variety that surrounds me.

. . . the willingness and effectiveness of so many.

. . . the power of my own thoughts.

. . . the positive aspects of my own body.

. . . the stable basis of my physical body.

. . . how we all create our own reality.

. . . my absolute freedom and my joyous awareness of it.

Each and every component that makes up your life experience is drawn to you by the powerful *Law of Attraction*'s response to the thoughts you think and the story you tell about your life. Your money and financial assets; your body's state of wellness, clarity, flexibility, size, and shape; your work environment, how you are treated, work satisfaction, and rewards—indeed, the very happiness of your life experience in general—is all happening because of the story that you tell. *If you will let your dominant intention be to revise and improve the content of the story you tell every day of your life, it is our absolute promise to you that your life will become that ever-improving story. For by the powerful <u>Law of Attraction,</u> it must be!*

BOOK 3

The Vortex

Where the *Law of Attraction*
Assembles All Cooperative Relationships

❦ ❦ ❦

This book is dedicated to all of you who, in your desire for enlightenment and Well-Being, have asked the questions that this book has answered; and to four delightful children of our children, who are examples of what the book teaches: Laurel (almost 11), Kevin (8), Kate (7), and Luke (almost 4), who are not yet asking because they have not yet forgotten.

This book is also dedicated to our friends Louise Hay (founder), Reid Tracy (president), Jill Kramer (editorial director), and the entire staff at Hay House. We are most appreciative of what they have done, and continue to do, to bring to the entire world the Teachings of Abraham.

❦ ❦ ❦

Preface

by Jerry Hicks

You are about to delve into the subject of *relationships* from a different perspective, perhaps, than you have previously considered. The teachings contained in this book have to do with aspects of our relationships that are far broader and deeper than "security-loving girl meets freedom-loving boy; they fall in love; they move in together; they work to earn money to acquire stuff; they (in most cases) have children; they continue to work 'full-time' and play 'part-time'; they usually attempt to train their children to match (fit in with) the prevailing cultural, social patterns of 'politically correct' words, behaviors, and beliefs . . . if they live long enough, they retire from working full-time—hopefully to play full-time—and then they move on to . . . ?"

Although the questions and subsequent answers in the book will certainly guide you to a deeper and more practical understanding of those typical family relationships, our intention here is to give you a more conscious awareness of the potential depth and breadth of the vast network of relationships that, on a practical, day-to-day basis, affect your swirling Vortex of natural Well-Being.

At the hub of these teachings of Abraham (not the biblical or presidential *Abraham*) is a profound concept: *the basis of life is freedom; the result of life is expansion—and the purpose of life is joy.*

And so, as you play the words from this book across the life that you have already knowledgeably experienced, the thrust of these teachings will be felt by you as an empowering sense of clarity as you discover concepts whereby you can, more deliberately, create the relationships that feel best to you. *Simply put: regarding every relationship in which you are now, or would like to be, engaged—the Teachings of Abraham are being offered here to guide you to allowing yourself more of what you do want, and less of what you don't want.*

This is the third of four scheduled books in the *Law of Attraction* Series. Our first, *The Law of Attraction: The Basics of the Teachings of Abraham®*, was originally published in book form in 2006; and it quickly became our second book to make the *New York Times* bestseller list.* *Money, and the Law of Attraction,* released in 2008, was the second; and *Spirituality, and the Law of Attraction,* due to be released in 2011, will be the final book in this series.

The material that was to later form our first *Law of Attraction* Series book was first published in 1988 (over 20 years ago) as part of two Special Subjects cassette albums. These original 20 tapes outlined for the listeners practical perceptions of the relationships between the *Universal Law of Attraction* and their finances, careers, bodily conditions, relationships. . . . Our hundreds of questions, and Abraham's forthcoming answers, were focused on 20 practical topics about which people could learn to improve their allowance of their natural state of Well-Being. (If you would like to hear [free] one of those original recordings detailing our introduction to Abraham, you can find our *Introduction to Abraham* recording as a 70-minute free-to-listen-to download at our Website: **www .abraham-hicks.com**; or you can order the CD version from our San Antonio, Texas, business center.)

It was in 2005, while conducting one of our *Law of Attraction* Cruise Seminars, that we were approached by Rhonda Byrne, an Australian television producer. She wanted us to allow her to create an Australian TV series based on the Teachings of Abraham®. And, as a result of our ensuing contractual agreement, Rhonda

---

Ask and It Is Given, our first **Amazon.com** bestseller, was published in 2004; and it was followed by four Abraham-Hicks books (all published by Hay House, Inc.) that rapidly reached the *New York Times* bestseller list: *The Amazing Power of Deliberate Intent,* 2005; *The Law of Attraction,* 2006; *The Astonishing Power of Emotions,* 2007; and then, in August of 2008, *Money, and the Law of Attraction: Learning to Attract Wealth, Health, and Happiness* became the first of the Abraham-Hicks books to reach the #1 position on the *New York Times* bestseller list.

brought her Australian film crew on board our 2005 Alaskan *Law of Attraction* cruise and filmed about 14 hours of seminar material. And, as a result, in 2006, the basic tenet of our 1988 album—*The Law of Attraction*—was used as the foundation for the original version of the phenomenally successful DVD movie and subsequent book *The Secret.*

Esther and I don't appear in the revised edition of *The Secret.* We can only be seen in the original version, but between the viral distribution of the original edition and the standard distribution of the revised, "expanded" edition, *The Secret* has added a powerful impetus to the worldwide dissemination of Abraham's teachings regarding the *Universal Law of Attraction.* And we are most appreciative that Rhonda fulfilled her dream of bringing an awareness of Abraham's basic *Law of Attraction* concepts to the world—for, in doing so, she has instilled a *belief,* and evoked an *asking,* in the minds of millions of viewers who have now come to *believe* that they *do* have the ability to achieve better-feeling lives. . . . And so, they are now *asking.* (And Abraham teaches us that "asking" is the first step in the creation process.) And as they have asked, what they have asked for has been given. . . . Their next step now will be to learn to *allow* themselves to receive that which they have been given.

If you were already feeling good when you found this book, then by utilizing these materials, your life can now, by your deliberate intention, spiral toward that which allows you to feel even better. However, if, in this moment, you are feeling less than good—or even if you think your life is as bad as it can possibly get—you can still learn perspectives here that can enable you to allow your life to begin to incrementally improve . . . or, you may be one of those rare ones who, from something you read here, receive a paradigm shift in your Beingness that somehow propels you from a long-term feeling of powerlessness, up into a fresh, long-term joyous alignment with your natural state of Well-Being. And once you reach that state, you will feel like a magnet, attracting to yourself everything—and every relationship—to which you are a Vibrational Match.

I've said that if I receive one practical idea that I can put into practice from a book, a lecture, or a visit with someone, it is well worth spending my time and/or money, because a single new perspective can redirect my thoughts and thereby redirect my life. For instance, a minister friend, Chet Castellaw, said to me back in 1970, "Jerry, you'll never receive the kind of success you're saying you want."

I asked him, "Why not?"

And Chet responded, "Because you are critical of successful people."

"Well," I said, "that's because they lie, cheat, and steal."

And Chet said to me, *"You can be critical of their lying, cheating, and stealing, but you are critical of their success at lying, cheating, and stealing. You can't be critical of huge success and achieve huge success!"*

There it was! Just one idea, a different perspective, that, 38 years ago, I immediately began to act on, which preceded a giant wave of what most would call "coincidental" events that carried me on—joyously—to receiving the essence of everything that I have ever wanted to be, do, or have. . . . And our intention for you is that you will receive ideas from this book that will inspire within you new patterns of thought that will attract to you whatever brings *you* the most of whatever *you* want to be, do, or have.

In this *relationships* book, Abraham* focuses the light of their Broader Perspective to reveal a wide array of *flawed premises* (which most of us are living by) relative to our varied relationships. And as you come upon those false-premise segments ("false," relative to the natural *Laws of the Universe*), if you will superimpose Abraham's perspective over your personal life experience (known only by you), and if you see room for improvement in your life, you will have the opportunity to shift your life—from as good as it is, right now, to whatever you perceive as a better-feeling experience.

Here are a couple of examples of flawed premises under which I operated for many years. Note how those "false" beliefs caused me so much discontent, but even more important, take notice of how a simple change in my perspective led to an immediate major positive change in my life experience:

My mother was born a dyed-in-the-wool nonconformist. I, too, was born as an adamant nonconformist. For over 30 years, Mother

---

*Abraham is considered a group consciousness, so is referred to in the plural.

tried, even quite violently, to get me to conform with what she wanted me to be. Every time I came in contact with her, I tried to vehemently and defensively get her to conform to how *I* wanted her to treat me. Also, I was always a bit embarrassed in public (but somehow proud) of her obvious lack of conformity.

And so, for more than 30 years, every time we came together, we fought! But then, soon after my father died, I adopted a new premise—it just came to me as a complete idea: The "flawed" premise each of us had been operating under for all of those terrible years, was: "If I try hard enough, I can get a 'natural-born nonconformist' to conform." (And how was that working out? It wasn't!) And so, I adopted a new premise: "Since I cannot control Mother—and Mother can't control me—I'll just continue to be the delightful, uncontrollable me that I am; and I will *allow* Mother to be my uncontrollable Mother . . . and, since strangers find Mother's idiosyncrasies entertaining (rather than repulsive), I'll look for and find entertainment in her differences . . ." and we lived happily ever after!

After over 30 years of beatings, restraints, fights . . . I decided to change to a new premise (I didn't ask *her* to change); and, for the next 40 years, we never had another cross word! If it hadn't happened to me, I probably wouldn't have believed it possible—but it did happen.

I'll close this Preface with one more personal "premise" experience: The "abundance" premise of those I associated with in my early days was that those of us who managed to remain poor would always be able to get through a needle's eye, but if we slipped up and were no longer poor, we would get so fat that we wouldn't be able to get through the eye of a needle. (Or something like that—it was a story we were taught in our church.) Another premise that my associates lived by was: "The rich get rich by taking (or somehow keeping) money away from us poor people." For instance, under that premise, if a rich person acquired a luxury automobile, then he or she was leaving less money, or luxury, for us poor, used-economy-car people. And so, operating under that flawed premise, I was unable to comfortably bring myself to potentially impoverish others by buying a luxury vehicle for myself.

And then the idea of *a Universe of never-ending abundance* somehow came to me—another simple thought that I adopted, and adapted, that changed my life, and the lives of those who may have been influenced by my example, in a very dramatic way. My new premise was: "When I buy a series of luxury vehicles, I am creating jobs and redistributing money in a luxurious way. In other words, when I purchase an expensive vehicle, I create work for—and redistribute dollars to—thousands of persons who made the vehicle possible. Some of them are rich, some are on their way to rich, some have no intention of ever being rich, and some believe that being rich will restrict them from entering the eye of a needle. But every one of them has the option of improving their level of joy in some way. And each one of them—whether rich or poor—gained, to some degree, by my purchase of that vehicle: there was the luxury-vehicle salesperson; the dealer; the prep team; the distributor; the wholesaler; the manufacturer; the shareholder; (maybe) the assembly worker; the inventors of the thousands of parts; the designers of the steering wheel, wheel covers, sound systems . . . ; the diggers of the iron ore; the makers of the glass and plastics . . . ; the manufacturers of the paint and tires; the drivers of the many delivery trucks; the manufacturers of the delivery trucks." (Oops! I'd better stop before I get too carried away.)

But I'm sure you get the point I'm making. Once I accepted the premise that *everything is working out for everyone,* then I was able to allow myself to let the floodgates to my financial well-being swing (almost) wide open. And from that decision, I went on to purchase a string of luxury vehicles, always knowing I was passing potential well-being on to anyone who was open to receive it.

And so, as I write this Preface, I am seated at my front desk and Esther is working at her rear office desk in our $2 million tour bus—and I remind myself, often, that this vehicle has brought some degree of pleasure to not only us, but to the thousands of others who had a hand in, and earned money from, its creation.

At any rate, I give you these personal examples to let you feel the long-term power of the adoption of just one good idea; as well as the dynamic value in the recognition, and resolution, of one flawed premise.

This *Vortex* book has been planted with good ideas that are available for you to transplant into your own life experience. And it also recognizes a string of flawed premises, any one of which—if it has been ruling your life—you can now decide to resolve, and replace with a premise that best serves you.

Esther and I are so pleased to participate in this co-creative adventure with you and with Abraham, and we look forward to the joy that you are about to receive as you play with the processes and perspectives embedded in these teachings.

Love ya,
Jerry

(**Editor's Note:** Please note that since there aren't always physical English words to perfectly express the Non-Physical thoughts that Esther receives, she sometimes forms new combinations of words, as well as using standard words in new ways—for example, capitalizing them when normally they wouldn't be—in order to express new ways of looking at old ways of looking at life.)

PART I

Your Vortex, and the *Law of Attraction:* Learning to Attract Joyous Co-creators

Learning to Attract Joyous Co-creators

Your life is supposed to feel good to you.

Before your birth, you knew that the primary component of your physical experience that would offer the greatest value for your personal and collective expansion and joy would be the component of the relationships that you would experience with each other. It was your plan to relish the diversity of your relationships and to choose from them the details that would make up your creations—and here you are.

Before your birth, as you were making the decision to focus yourself into this Leading Edge time-space reality, it was your powerful intention to enjoy every moment of the process. You understood then, from your Non-Physical perspective, that you are a creator and that you were coming into an environment with enormous potential for joyful, satisfying experiences in creation. You understood that you are a creator, and that the Earth experience would be the perfect platform from which you would launch numerous satisfying creations—and here you are.

Before your birth into your physical body, you knew that once you were here, you would be surrounded by others and that your relationships with those others would be the primary source of the contrast you would live. You understood, also, that these contrasting relationships would provide the very basis of your personal expansion, as well as the very basis of your enormous contribution to Eternal expansion, and you eagerly welcomed your interaction with all of them—and here you are.

There was nothing in your plan about being here that included struggle or hardship. You did not believe that you were coming into physical form to right past wrongs, or to fix a broken world, or even to evolve (in the sense that you were currently *lacking* in something). Instead, you knew this physical experience would be an environment that would provide a balance of contrast from which you would personally make increasingly improved choices that would add to your own expansion as well as to the collective expansion of *All-That-Is.* You knew that this world of contrast would induce in you the expansion that literally puts the Eternalness into Eternity; and your appreciation for the contrasting environment on planet Earth was enormous, for you understood that contrast is the basis of expansion, and that the expansion would be joyous—and here you are.

Before your birth into your physical body, you knew the value of variety and of diversity, for you understood that every new preference, desire, or idea would be born from that contrast. And you knew that this contrast not only provided the literal basis for expansion, but also the basis for your joyful experience. And, most of all, you knew that your joyful experience would be the ultimate reason for every part of every part of every part of all of this Being-ness. You knew that it all exists for the joyful moments that would constantly explode into your awareness along the way—and here you are.

Before your birth, you understood *contrast* to be the variety from which you would make your choices. You knew that your surrounding environment would be like a dining buffet spread out before you, from which you would choose, and that nothing about that environment was permanent because your constant new choices would cause it to continually change—and here you are.

Before your birth, you understood that all choices are made by giving attention to something. You knew that you were about to focus your Consciousness into a physical body and into a physical time-space reality; and that you would make your selections from the contrasting buffet of choices that would surround you by your attention, focus, or thought—and here you are.

Before your birth, you understood that the Earth environ-ment, like all environments—physical and Non-Physical—is a Vibrationally based environment, which is managed by the *Law of*

Attraction (that which is like unto itself, is drawn); and you knew that your attention to any subject was your invitation for your personal participation with it—and here you are.

Before your birth, in considering your physical experience on planet Earth, you did not request to be born into an environment of sameness or agreement, where all of the variety had already been considered and all of the decisions about how life should be lived had been made, for you were a powerful creator who was coming forth for the purpose of making your own decisions and of creating your own joyful experience. You knew that *diversity* would be your best friend, and that *conformity*, on every level, would be the opposite. You literally dived in, in eagerness to find your bearings and to then begin to explore, from your own personal, important, and powerful viewpoint, your contrasting surroundings, from which you would carve out your creations—and here you are.

Many people express concern and frustration—and, at times, anger and resentment—that they did not retain conscious awareness of these prebirth decisions, but we submit that you arrived in your physical body with something even more important intact: *you were born with a personal <u>Guidance System</u> to help you to know— every step (or thought) along the way—when you are diverging from your prebirth understanding of life, and when you are on track.*

It is our desire that you become consciously aware of your own *Guidance System* so that you can explore this new frontier of creation in alignment with the stability of your Non-Physical knowledge.

It is our desire to help you consciously reconnect with *who-you-really-are* and to help you replace myriad false premises—which you have erroneously picked up along your physical trail—with Universal, *Law*-based premises of life.

It is our desire to help you to solve the mystery of seemingly impossible relationships; to sort out the details of sharing your planet with billions of others; to rediscover the beauty of differences; and, most of all, to re-establish the most important relationship of all: your relationship with the Eternal, Non-Physical Source that is really you—and here we are.

427

Life Is about Our Relationships

You will never find yourself in a point in time when the subject of relationships is not an active part of your <u>now</u> experience, for everything you perceive or notice or know is because of your relationship with something else. Without a comparative experience, you would be unable to perceive or focus any kind of understanding within yourself. Therefore, it is accurate to say that without relationships you could not exist at all.

It is our desire that an even greater awareness of *who-you-are* will awaken within you by reading this book, as you begin to explore the variety of relationships that you are already living.

It is our desire that you experience an enhanced appreciation of your planet; your body; your family; your friends; your enemies; your government; your systems; your food; your finances; your animals; your work; your play; your purpose; your Source; your Soul; your past, your future, and your present. . . .

It is our desire that you come to remember that every relationship is Eternal and that once it has been established, it is a part of your Vibrational makeup forevermore, and that, in your powerful now—where all that you have become converges with all that you are now becoming—you hold the power to create.

Often, when you observe an unwanted or unpleasant experience, you believe that you are not personally a part of it, but instead a distant, dissociated, unattached observer of it; but that is never the case. *Your observation of a situation—no matter how remote you believe yourself to be—makes you a co-creative partner of the experience.*

Over time, as you have interacted with one another, many of you have arrived at collective preferences about how life should be lived; and while you have come nowhere close to an agreement about what the appropriate way to live is, still, on the myriad subjects that *you* are experiencing, you continue to try to convince others to accept the preferences that *you* most prefer.

Find Alignment First and Then Take Action

In every society of the vast number of societies on your planet today, you have instituted rules, requirements, taboos, laws—along with a great variety of rewards and punishments for conforming or not conforming—as each society seems determined to sort into separate piles the *wanted* from the *unwanted.* And although you work very hard at the sorting process, the piles continue to shift around; and you never come even close to a consensus of *wanted* and *unwanted, right* and *wrong, good* and *bad.*

It is our desire that, as a result of just reading this one book, you will never again require global, community, or even a partner's agreement in order to find your confidence, direction, and power. *We want you to remember that the need for agreement from others comes from a basis of misunderstanding of the* <u>Laws of the Universe</u> *and runs counter to* <u>who-you-really-are.</u>

It is our desire that, by understanding your own personal *Guidance System,* you will return to alignment with the power that flows to you and through you. For by your finding agreement with the power that flows forth from within you, the harmony that you seek on all other levels and all other subjects—and with all others—will then (and only then) be possible.

Most people would deem it unwise to load a big clumsy truck, which has a very bad suspension system and a steering mechanism so worn-out that it is almost impossible to keep the truck on the road, with their most precious cargo. Or, most people would deem it unwise to gather a load of precious glass antiques and put them in the carrying basket of the bicycle that their five-year-old son is taking on his first bicycle ride today. Or, most people would deem it unwise to carry a sack containing their life's savings and all of their favorite jewelry and then walk out onto the iced-over lake before they were sure that the ice was actually strong enough to hold their weight.

In other words, it always makes sense to first find fundamental stability before embarking on any journey, especially those journeys that matter most to you. And yet, as people interact with one another on important subjects, they commonly plunge headlong into conversations and decisions and behaviors before they have achieved any sense of true stability, and then the return to stability is often very long in coming. And often, once out of balance, they stumble into the next and then the next and then the next out-of-control experience. *Through the examples in this book, it is our desire to help you remember the art of alignment first—then action. Alignment first—then conversation. Alignment first—then interaction. Alignment first—then anything else.*

People sometimes say, "Think before you speak." A wise intention, but we would take it further. We would suggest, *"Think—and then evaluate the value of that thought by noticing how it feels; and do that often enough that you know, without question, that you are in alignment—then speak, then act, then interact."*

Someone who takes the time to understand their relationship with Source, who actively seeks alignment with their Broader Perspective, who deliberately seeks and finds alignment with *who-they-really-are,* is more charismatic, more attractive, more effective, and more powerful than a group of millions who have not achieved that alignment.

The historical masters and healers whom you revere understood the value of this personal alignment. And in this book about *relationships,* we submit to you: *There is no relationship of greater importance to achieve than the relationship between you, in your physical body, right here and now, and the Soul/Source/God from which you have come. If you tend to that relationship first and foremost, you will then, and only then, have the stable footing to proceed into other relationships. Your relationship with your own body; your relationship with money; your relationship with your parents, children, grandchildren, the people you work with, your government, your world . . . will all fall swiftly and easily into alignment once you tend to this fundamental, primary relationship first.*

Are We Living Under Flawed Premises?

You may have chosen to read this book because of a particular issue that you are having with someone in your life, and we want you to know that the answers you are looking for *are* contained within the covers of this book. If you were to read the Contents pages at the beginning of this book, you might even be able to pin-point the specific relationship that you most want to address. And we understand how tempting it is to simply turn to those pages to find your answer—and if you were to do that, you *would* find your answer, and it would be the *right* answer—but if, instead of doing that, you will systematically read through the pages of this book in the order that they are written, then when you come to the sec-tion of the book that pertains to the relationship issue you are most interested in soothing, it is our promise to you: the soothing will be greater, the solution easier to understand, and your relationship issue will be more quickly reconciled.

Whether you read this book in one sitting or over a period of several days, an important transformation will take place within you: *Flawed premises that you have picked up along your physical trail will fall by the wayside, one by one, and you will return to the understanding that is at the core of that which you are. And when that happens, not only will you begin to understand every current and past relationship, but the benefit that every relationship has given you will become immediately apparent to you.*

Without exception, the flawed premise or unstable footing that most people stand on is because they care more about what someone else is thinking about them than how they themselves are feeling. So, over time, by interacting with many others (who also want to feel better and have trained those around them to offer behavior that does make them temporarily feel better—that is, "Don't please you, but instead please me"—that is, "Don't you dare be selfish and satisfy yourself, but instead please me"), they have lost sight of their own Guidance and have become further and further separated from *who-they-are*. And so, they feel worse and worse as time goes on, and so they come to incorrect conclusion after incorrect conclusion until they are completely lost.

It seems logical that an exposing of those flawed premises would clear things up and put them back on their path of Well-Being. However, when you are standing in the middle of a flawed premise, focusing upon the results of it, you are usually so engulfed in the

Vibration of it—and therefore so actively attracting because of it—that you cannot see its inherent flaw. It does not feel false when your life continues to unfold in the way you "believed" it would.

In order to discover or understand a false or flawed premise, you have to stand back far enough and reconnect with *who-you-really-are* before you can see it. In other words, if you were to interact with an unkind (disconnected) person who told you continually that you are not smart, at first you would take issue with the idea. The negative emotion you would feel is because the words *You are not smart* are so contradictory to the true knowledge of your Source. *But if you were to hear this again and again, until you yourself began to believe and repeat the false premise, now your own activation of the contradictory Vibration would interfere with your own sense of intelligence, and you would begin to attract evidence of your lack of intelligence, in effect proving the false premise to be true. It becomes increasingly hard for you to call this a "false" premise when the evidence seems to be telling you that it is true. Over time you come to believe it is true.*

The good news in all of this is that whenever you know what you *do not* want, an equal and proportionate desire for what you *do* want erupts from you, and a rocket of desire shoots forward into your Vibrational Reality. In other words, the potential for a greatly improved experience is always born from an unwanted experience; and, in time (whenever the resistance ceases), the improvement will come.

We write this book so that you can allow your improvement sooner rather than later, or sooner rather than not in this lifetime—but in any event, future generations will benefit dramatically from the contrast your current generation is living. It is our desire to assist you in unraveling and releasing these erroneous, incorrect, unhelpful beliefs, to help you free yourself from the bondage of these false premises. We want you to remember *who-you-really-are* and to stand in that fresh light, in that fresh place of attracting on all subjects.

Most people who are in the midst of observing something unwanted in another person believe that if the unwanted condition were not there to be observed, they would not be observing it.

Most people who are in the midst of observing something unwanted in another person believe that the discomfort they are feeling is because of the unpleasant condition that is being offered by the other person, and that if the other person would no longer offer the unpleasant condition, then they (the ones observing) would feel better.

Most people who are in the midst of observing something unwanted in another person believe that if they could control the behavior of the other—through influence, persuasion, coercion, rules, laws, or threat of punishment—in the gaining control of unwanted situations, they would feel better.

Most people believe that control of conditions and of others is the key to feeling better, but that belief is the greatest flawed premise of all. The belief that if you could get all circumstances to change so that your observation of them would then feel good to you defies the *Laws of the Universe,* as well as your reason for being here. *It was never your intention to control everything around you. It was your intention to control the direction of your thought.*

Throughout this book, we will identify a series of flawed premises that are at the heart of the confusion and distortion of your physical reality. It is our desire that, as you make your way through the pages of this book, you will be able to release the flawed premises that contradict your Broader knowing so that you can return to the natural state of allowing the Well-Being of your life to flow to you.

Gaining a Clear View by Stepping Back

While we are eager to rendezvous with you, right where you are, in order to help you improve every relationship that is currently active in your experience, it will be of value for you to first relax and walk with us down the path of the usual human interactions experienced from the time of physical birth until the time of physical death. Of course, you are different in many ways from one another—but, for the most part, no matter when you were born or what part of the world you live in, there are typical, predominant relationship patterns that are really worth considering. This overview of the evolution of the relationships that you experience as physically focused humans has the potential of helping you to realize—no matter what phase of human evolution you are currently focused within—a myriad of flawed beliefs that humans have been passing on to one another for a very long time. By stepping back from the immediacy of your current experience and seeing the full spectrum of your physical human life experience in the way we present it here, you will gain a clear view of your life's purpose, and you will discover an immediate stable footing that will set you on your course for joy for the rest of this life experience.

Before Your Birth into This Physical Body

Before you focused a part of your Consciousness into the physical body that you now recognize as *you,* you were an intelligent, clear, happy, nonresistant Consciousness eager for this new experience into which you were emerging. Before your birth, the only relationship you experienced was your relationship with your Source; but since you were, at that time, Non-Physical, and therefore nonresistant, you experienced no discernible separation, and therefore no discernible "relationship," between you and Source. *You were Source.*

In other words, while you have fingers and toes and arms and legs, you do not see them as separate Beings. You see them as a part of you. So you usually do not try to describe your *relationship* with your leg, because you understand that your leg is you. And so, before your physical birth, you were Vibrationally intertwined with *Source,* or with what humans often call *God,* but the full integration of you with *God* was such that there was no relationship between the two—because you were all One.

The Moment of Your Birth

In the moment of your birth, a part of the Consciousness that is you focused itself into your physical body, and your first relationship began: the relationship between the physical you and the Non-Physical You.

Here we come upon a significant flawed premise, or misunderstanding, of many—in fact, most—of our physical human friends:

Flawed Premise #1: *I am either physical or*
Non-Physical, either dead or alive.

Many people do not understand that they existed before their physical birth. Many others believe that if they existed in the Non-Physical before their birth, the Non-Physical part of them ceased to be once they were born into this body. In other words, "I am either Non-Physical or physical, either dead or alive."

We want you to remember that while you are focused here in this Leading Edge body in this Leading Edge time, the Eternal, Non-Physical, older, wiser, larger part of you remains Non-Physically focused. And because that Non-Physical part of you exists, and because *You* exist, there is an Eternal, undeniable relationship between those two important aspects of you.

This relationship (this Vibrational relationship) that exists between the physical you and the Non-Physical You is significant for many reasons:

1. The emotions that you feel (your *Emotional Guidance System*) are because of the relationship between these two Vibrational parts of you.

2. As you reach for new thoughts and expansion, out here on the Leading Edge of life, you have the benefit of the stable knowledge of your Non-Physical counterpart.

3. As you reach for new thoughts and expansion, out here on the Leading Edge of life, the Non-Physical part of you has the benefit of the expansion that you carve out of your physical experience.

4. Every other relationship you have (that is, with other people, with animals, with your own body, with money, with concepts and ideas, with life itself) is profoundly affected by this all-important relationship between *you* and *You.*

Your Relationship with Your Parents

Of course, your physical parents are of great significance to you, for if it were not for their relationship with each other, you would not exist in your current physical form. But there are many misunderstandings, or what we are calling *flawed premises,* around your relationships with your parents.

From your Non-Physical vantage point, you understood that your physical parents would be your important avenue into physical experience, and that you would be born into a stable enough environment to be able to get your physical footing. You knew that your parents, or others like them, would receive you and introduce you to your new environment. You knew that there would be a time of acclimation, and you felt enormous appreciation for those who would welcome you.

You understood that your parents, who were already acclimated to their physical environment, would help you in finding food, shelter, and physical stability. But you did not intend to look to them to determine your life's purpose for you, or for guidance about the correctness or effectiveness of your physical journey. In fact, from your Non-Physical perspective before your birth, you knew that *your personal guidance* would be more intact (and therefore more effective) on the day that you were born than would be the guidance of the adults who would greet you. In other words, when you were first born into your physical body, the relationship between you and You (your Non-Physical *Inner Being*) was such that you were nearly still that *One* Pure, Positive Energy.

But in those very first new days in your physical body, you began to experience a gradual shift in your own Consciousness (just as you knew you would) as you began to garner your personal perspective (from your *physical* vantage point) of your new Earth environment. And in that process, your Energy, or Consciousness, became two instead of one. In other words, as the new infant in your mother's arms, you had two Vibrational vantage points active within you—*and so, you then began to feel emotions.*

Since you just came from an environment where you had absolute knowledge of the Well-Being of the Universe and of planet Earth and of *All-That-Is,* when your mother held you and worried about you—you felt uncomfortable. When your parents felt overwhelmed with their lives—you felt uncomfortable. When they gazed at you in pure love and appreciation—you felt the alignment of their Beings, and you felt comfort. But, even in your infancy, you remembered that it was not their job to shine their alignment on you. You remembered, even then—even before you could talk or walk—that it was not their job to provide a haven of comfort and aligned Energy for you. You knew it was *your* job, and you knew you would figure it out. And, meanwhile, you were able to easily withdraw back into the alignment of your Oneness—and so you slept. Often.

You came into this physical environment knowing that you would be surrounded by *contrast* right from the beginning, and that this contrast would provide the nucleus of the creation of your own life experience. You understood that just by being present in this Earth environment, you would automatically find your own preferences, and that both *wanted* and *unwanted* aspects would be of benefit to you. And, most of all, you knew that you would be the one (the only one) who would (or could) choose for you. However, by the time you came into the life experience of your parents, they had (in most cases) all but forgotten that about you. Which brings us to another flawed premise:

> **Flawed Premise #2:** *My parents, because they were here long before I was born, and because they are my parents, know better than I do what is right or wrong for me.*

437

You did not intend to use the opinions of your parents to measure against your beliefs, desires, or actions in order to determine the appropriateness of them. Instead, you knew (and still remembered, long after you were born) that it was the relationship between the opinion (or knowledge) of the Source within you and your current thoughts, in any moment, that would offer you perfect guidance in the form of emotions. You did not intend to replace your <u>Emotional Guidance System</u> with the opinions of your parents even if they were in harmony with their <u>Emotional Guidance System</u> in the moment of their trying to guide you. It was much more important to you to recognize the existence of your own <u>Guidance System,</u> and to utilize it, than to be deemed correct by, or to find approval from, others.

Much of the imbalance that people feel long after they leave the immediate environment of their childhood home stems from the impossible effort of replacing their own <u>Guidance System</u> by seeking approval from their parents. Your feeling of freedom is trampled whenever you try to align with the opinion of someone outside of you (that is, your parents) rather than aligning with the Vibration that comes forth from within you (that is, your *Inner Being*). Of course, it is possible to have a wonderful, effective relationship with your parents if you first find the alignment between *you* and *You.* But, unless you have achieved alignment between *you* and *You,* no other relationship can be a good one.

Your Relationship with Your Siblings

Whether you were the first child your parents welcomed into your childhood home or if you came after another who was already there, multiple children certainly can change the dynamics of your parental relationships. In most relationship settings, the more people involved, the more the possibility that personal misalignment will occur; but that does not have to be the case.

Often the family dynamics are as follows: Your mother and father have not been consciously aware of their own *Guidance*

Systems, and so they do not offer to themselves—or to each other—consistent patterns of alignment. They often believe that it is up to you to alter your behavior in order to positively affect their experience. So, not long after you have settled into their life experience, they attempt to train you into patterns of behavior that *they* have deemed favorable. But, they are attempting the impossible. Instead of achieving their alignment with *who-they-really-are,* they are asking *you* to behave in a way that makes *them* feel better. That is what *conditional love* is: "If you will change your behavior or condition, then as I observe it, I will feel better. So I am giving you the responsibility for the way I feel."

When the second child enters the mix, not only is there now more behavior for your parents to attempt to control, but an even more confusing thing occurs for you: now, not only are you considering your own behavior in relationship to your parents' response to what you are doing, but you are observing the way your parents are responding to the behavior of the other child. *The potential for distortion and confusion exponentially expands with each new person who enters the mix.*

Trying to achieve your proper personal behavior is not possible through trying to adjust to the desires and demands of the people you live with. There is simply too much variety in personality, interest, intention, and life purpose coming in for you to sort it out on a behavior level. But there is something you can do that will bring each of these relationships into perspective and satisfaction for you: <u>Seek alignment between you and You, first, before you engage with any other. And never ask for a behavioral change from any other to use as your basis of improved emotion or perspective. There are simply too many moving parts, and you will not succeed.</u>

Our Vortex, and the *Law of Attraction*

It is our desire that, through reading this book, you will discover a new sense of clarity about how your physical life experience fits into the greater scheme of things. We want you to remember *who-you-really-are* and why you are here in this physical body. Most of all, it is our desire that you regain your sense of worthiness and absolute Well-Being; and, it is our desire that you understand the important role that you fulfill by being here in the Leading Edge, contrast-filled time-space reality.

Before you came into this body, you were Non-Physical Energy; and from that Non-Physical perspective of Source, you extended or focused a part of your Consciousness forward into your physical time, physical Earth, and physical body. And when you were born into this body, achieving awareness through your physical senses of your new surroundings—the Consciousness known as *you* became two specific aspects: the Non-Physical part of you and the physical part of you.

Some refer to their Non-Physical aspect as their *Soul* or *Source;* and while we prefer labels like *Inner Being, Broader Non-Physical Perspective,* or *who-you-really-are,* there is an even more important distinction that we would like you to understand: *both the Non-Physical and physical aspects of you exist at the same time.* Most people acknowledge that some aspect of them existed prior to their physical birth, and most believe that after their physical death, they will again be Non-Physical, but something quite different from that is occurring: *You are extensions of Source Energy, and when you became physically focused, your Non-Physical aspect did not cease to be. In fact, your Non-Physical aspect began to expand because of the existence and experience of your physical aspect.*

It was your clear intention to come forth into your magnificent physical body and to interact with the variety of intentions and beliefs and desires of others upon your planet for the purpose of expansion. You understood that by your exposure to the variety that surrounds you, on all subjects, you would naturally come to specific conclusions of improvement. You knew that by living an unpleasant experience, a request for an improved experience would be born. You knew that a request, or asking, or desire would emanate from you Vibrationally; and that your *Inner Being* would be aware of your new request and would follow it and focus upon it and become it. You knew that your *Inner Being* would immediately become the Vibrational equivalent of every request that your physical environment inspired.

And so, if you can now turn your attention to the idea of your expanded *Inner Being,* who stands as the culmination of all that you have lived, who emits a Vibration that expresses the whole of that which you have become—then you will more fully understand who your *Inner Being* is and how the physical aspect of you has added to that expansion.

We want you to realize that while you are focused in your physical body, thinking thoughts, speaking words, involved in action . . . at the same time there is a Non-Physical aspect of you who exists in the Non-Physical realm from which you have come—and the Non-Physical aspect of you has expanded because of your physical experiences.

Many people refer to their physical life experience as *reality.* You decipher your physical reality through your physical senses, and as you look around your planet at the places and people and experiences, you pronounce it *reality.* We want you to understand that even though you are seeing and hearing and tasting and smelling and touching the evidence of your physical reality, it is much more than the flesh, blood, and bone reality that you believe it is. *Everything that you perceive here in your physical environment is Vibration, and the life you are living is your Vibrational interpretation.*

The powerful *Law of Attraction* is at the root of everything that you experience; and the stable, never-changing, always-accurate premise of this *Law* is: *that which is like unto itself, is drawn.*

When you give thought to something, you begin the attraction process of the essence of that subject into your own life experience. Once you have activated a thought-Vibration within yourself by giving your attention to the subject, the progression of expansion occurs. In other words, the more attention you give to any subject, the more active the Vibration of that subject is within you. And the longer that occurs, the more powerful the attraction is, until, eventually, you will have irrefutable evidence in your own experience of that active Vibration. All things that happen in your experience come because of the requests that you are sending out with your thoughts.

The Law of Attraction is the Universal manager of all Vibration, which expands to everything that exists through the Universe. And so, at the same time that the Law of Attraction is responding to the Vibrational content of your physical thoughts, it is also responding to the Vibrational content of your Inner Being.

We want to draw your attention toward that powerful, Non-Physical aspect of you and the effect that the *Law of Attraction* has upon it: Each time your physical life experience causes you to ask for something, a Vibrational, rocketlike request shoots forward and is received by your *Inner Being* and becomes the Vibrational, expanded version of your request. In order to help you get a sense of that process of expansion, we have called it your *Vibrational Escrow* or your *Vibrational Reality.* It is the furthermost, expanded version of you.

In the same way that the Law of Attraction is responding to the thoughts, words, and actions that you are offering here in your physical reality, the Law of Attraction is always responding powerfully to your Vibrational Reality. When the Law of Attraction, the Universal manager of all Vibrations, responds to the clarity of Vibration offered by your newly expanded Inner Being, the result is a powerful swirling Vortex of attraction.

So here is this Vortex of becoming—a Vortex that contains all of the requests, all of the amended requests, each and every detail of each and every asking that has emanated from you—and the *Law of Attraction* is responding to that. Envision this swirling, swirling, swirling Vortex and the power of attraction that is amassed as the *Law of Attraction* responds to this pure, nonresisted, focused desire. *The Vortex is literally drawing in all things necessary for the completion of every request it contains. All cooperative components are being summoned and are coming for the completion of these creations, for the answering of these questions, for the solutions to these problems.*

The purpose of this book is not only to help you remember the process of creation—and remember the Pure, Positive Energy platform from which you have come—but to help you remember the power of this Vortex and to remind you of your *Emotional Guidance System* so that you can *consciously* and *deliberately* achieve the Vibrational frequency of your Vortex.

The purpose of this book is:

- To help you remember *who-you-really-are*

- To help you remember the purpose of your physical experience

- To restore your feeling of self-appreciation for what you are accomplishing here in your physical body

- To help you remember that you are, first and foremost, a Vibrational Being

- To help you remember that there is a Non-Physical aspect of you that exists now, also

- To help you be aware of the relationship between the two Vibrational aspects of you

- To help point your awareness consistently toward the swirling Vortex of Creation, which contains all that you desire and all that you have become.

In short, this book is written to help you get into your Vortex.

Everyone who turns up in your life—from the people you call friends or lovers, to the people you call enemies or strangers—comes in response to your <u>Vibrational asking.</u> You not only invite the person, but you also invite the personality traits of the person. Many people have a difficult time accepting this as they think of many of the unwanted characteristics of people in their lives. They argue that they would never have asked for something so unwanted to come into their experience, for they believe that "asking" for something means "asking for something wanted." But by "asking," we mean offering a matching Vibration. . . . *We know that many of the relationships or experiences you have attracted, you would not have <u>deliberately</u> attracted if you had been doing it on purpose, but much of your attraction is not done by deliberate intent, but rather by default. . . . It is important to understand that you get what you think about, whether you want it or not. And chronic thoughts about unwanted things invite, or ask for, matching experiences. The <u>Law of Attraction</u> makes it so.*

Relationships, or co-creating with others, is responsible for nearly all of the contrast in your life. They are responsible for the troubles of your life *and* your greatest pleasures. But, most important of all, the relationships that you experience with one another are the basis of the majority of the expansion that you achieve; and because of that, it is accurate to also say that the relationships of your life are the reason for the potential for your joy—or your pain—in any moment in time. Simply put, if someone had not prodded you into more expansion, you could not feel the pain of not keeping up with that expansion. The interaction, intertwining, and co-creation of relationships enhances your individual experience enormously. *Your greatest joys and your greatest sorrows come from the basis of your relationships, but you have more control over whether you experience joy or sorrow than you realize.*

The Powerful, Eternal, Universal *Law of Attraction*

The powerful *Law of Attraction* (that which is like unto itself, is drawn) is at the root of everything that you experience. So, when you give thought to something, you begin the attraction process of the essence of that subject into your own life experience. Once you have activated a thought-Vibration within yourself by giving your attention to the subject, the progression of expansion occurs. In other words, the more attention you give to any subject, the more active the Vibration of that subject is within you; and the longer that occurs, the more powerful the attraction is . . . until, eventually, you will have irrefutable evidence in your own experience of that active Vibration. All things that happen in your experience come because of the requests that you are sending out with your thoughts.

Remember that whether you are thinking about <u>wanted</u> things or <u>unwanted</u> things, you are still sending out a "request" to attract more things like the subject of your thought. And all things that happen to you—all people, things, experiences, situations that come to you—come in response to your Vibrational invitation.

The culmination of relationships and circumstances and events that you draw to you is utterly accurate in its response to your Vibrational requests. Noticing how things are turning out for you is one very clear way of understanding which Vibrational requests you are emanating, because you always get the essence of what you are thinking about, whether you want it or not. We call that *post-manifestational awareness:* vibrating with no deliberate direction of thought, but then noticing the results of the thoughts only after they have manifested into something real or tangible, such as a low balance in your bank account, an unwanted physical condition, or an unpleasant relationship.

It is possible to become aware of the attracting of an unwanted situation and to head it off before it comes into full realization in your experience by becoming aware of, and utilizing, the wonderful *Emotional Guidance System* you were born with. But most people indiscriminately give attention to whatever is in their view, and then accept the inevitability of their emotional responses to those thoughts. They accept that there are bad things out there in the world, and when they focus upon those bad things, they expect to feel bad—and they do. Rarely do they understand the important reason for their bad feeling, but we will state it simply for you here:

When you focus upon a subject or situation and you feel bad, it is not the subject or the situation that is the reason for your bad feeling. You feel bad because the thoughts have caused a Vibrational separation in you. In other words, you have chosen to give your attention to something that the Source within you is not giving attention to. And it is with good reason that the Source within you is not giving attention to the thing that makes you feel bad when *you* do. <u>Source understands the power of attraction and does not want to add to the creation of unwanted things; and when you do, you feel bad. Every time.</u>

And, conversely, when you think thoughts during which you feel passionate or happy or loving or eager, you are choosing thoughts in which the larger part of you is also completely immersed; but instead of causing a separation between you and your Source, you are now creating a partnership or relationship with power and clarity and Well-Being.

There is no understanding on any subject that is of greater value to you than the understanding of the existence of your personal

Emotional Guidance System. When you are aware of the existence of your two significant Vibrational perspectives and how they relate to one another, you consciously hold the key to your joyful Deliberate Creation. And without that understanding, you are a bit like a small cork bobbing atop a raging sea, blown by the current and the wind, out of your personal control.

You could say that, in any moment, you really only have access to two emotions: one that feels better and one that feels worse. If you will make a determination that, from wherever you stand and no matter what you are focusing upon, you will reach for the best-feeling thought you can find from where you are, then you will develop an ongoing relationship with your *Inner Being,* with Source, and with all that you desire—and your life will become consistently joyous. That was your plan: to sift through variety, come to personal clarity about what you prefer on topic after topic, and then to come into alignment with your eternally evolving self.

Are We Tolerating Others, or Allowing Them?

Jerry: But since we are all so different, it doesn't seem to me that there is much chance of us ever coming together on common agreements about how we should all live life.

Abraham: We agree. And it would be a very boring place if that were the case.

Jerry: Since we are all different and we want different things, how can we move forward without feeling the pain of having to put up with, or tolerate, those differences in others?

Abraham: Your pain, or negative emotion, is not because of your disagreement with another person. It is always about the disagreement between *you* and *You.* If you will withdraw your attention from the unwanted and put it upon something you *do* like, your pain will subside. As you focus longer still upon something that you *do* want, not only will you no longer feel pain, but you will feel positive emotion, such as interest or eagerness or happiness.

Jerry: But since we are all somehow connected, how can a person learn to allow the uncomfortable things that are occurring in other people's lives?

Abraham: All understanding comes through the comparative living of life. And by "comparative," we mean weighing all current observations against the true knowledge that emanates from your Source. From your Broader Perspective, you know that attention to unwanted things adds to them—and so, the Source part of you withdraws attention from all things that are unwanted. When you, in your physical body, give your attention to unwanted things, you cause a disparity in the Vibrational relationship between *you* and *You*, and your negative emotion is your indication of that discord or lack of alignment. And in that absence of alignment, you are of no value to the person you are worrying about or angry with. And when you think about it, since you cannot control the circumstances of the lives of others, you have no real choice—if it is your desire to be happy—other than to withdraw your attention from their uncomfortable situation.

Jerry: But won't others feel abandoned if we withdraw our attention from the pain they are experiencing? Don't we have some responsibility to help those in need?

Abraham: Here is an opportunity to begin to understand a basic flawed premise of your society:

> **Flawed Premise #3:** *If I push hard enough against unwanted things, they will go away.*

You live in a Universe that is based upon the *Law of Attraction*. That means that this is an inclusion-based Universe, not an exclusion-based Universe. In other words, in an inclusion-based, attraction-based Universe, there simply is no such thing as "no." When you look at something wanted and you say "yes" to it, you are including it in your Vibration; and it then becomes a part of your Vibrational offering, which means it is a part of your point of attraction, which means—it begins to come to you. But when you shout "no" at something, you are including *it* in your Vibration, also, so it then becomes a part of your Vibrational offering, which means it is a part of your point of attraction, which means—it begins to come to you.

You are of no advantage whatsoever to anyone who has your negative attention. When you observe something in another that causes you to feel bad while you are observing it, your negative emotion is your indicator that you are adding to something unwanted. In the early stages of negative emotion, you merely feel discomfort, but if you continue your focus upon unwanted things, unwanted things will begin to appear in your own experience in increasingly prominent ways.

In every conscious moment, your point of attraction is active, which means that the *Law of Attraction* is responding to your active Vibration and you are in the state of becoming more. Your emotions are your indication of whether you are becoming *more* like the positive, uplifting Being of your *Source* or whether you are becoming *more* of the opposite of that. *You cannot stand still. If you are awake, you are in the process of expansion.*

Whenever you know what you do not want, you always know more clearly what you do want, so in a poignant moment of awareness of another person's undesirable situation, you automatically launch your version of an improved situation forward into your Vibrational Reality. Now, your work, your value to that person, your value to yourself, your natural state of being . . . is to give your undivided attention to the idea of improvement that has hatched from your interaction/observation. And as you learn to do that, not only will you be of increasing value to others, but you will see how your relationships with others add immeasurably to your own becoming.

Learning the *Art of Allowing*

Jerry: You have spoken to us often of the *Art of Allowing*. Is that what you are speaking of here?

Abraham: Yes. The *Art of Allowing* is what you want most to understand, because, in deliberately applying it, you "allow" yourself to be all that you have become. And anything less than the allowing of you to be *You* feels less good. In other words, every contrasting experience causes an expansion of *who-you-are* because the larger Non-Physical part of you always moves to that point of farthest expansion. But if you continue to look back to the events or circumstances or reasons that caused the expansion, you then hold yourself in opposition to the very expansion. You disallow it—and then you feel bad.

The *Art of Allowing* is simply your allowing yourself, by virtue of your deliberately chosen thoughts, to keep up with the expansion of yourself. And since the expansion is happening—because the contrast of your time-space reality insists that it does—if you are to be happy, you have no other choice than to keep up.

The Broader Non-Physical part of you, to whom you have an Eternal relationship, is one who loves. When you are not loving, you are not practicing the *Art of Allowing*.

The Broader Non-Physical part of you is one who knows your worthiness. When you feel unworthy, you are not practicing the *Art of Allowing*.

Here is an opportunity to begin to understand another basic flawed premise of your society:

Flawed Premise #4: I have come here to live the right way of
life and to influence others to the same right way of living.
And what feels right to me must be the right way of living for all.

You did not come into this physical experience intending to take all of the ideas that exist and whittle them down to a handful of good ideas that everyone agrees on. In fact, the opposite was your intention. You said, "I will go forth, into a sea of contrast; and from it, more ideas will be born." You understood that joyous expansion would be born from diversity.

Since everyone wants to feel good, but there are so many things that others are doing that, as you observe them, you do not feel are good, it is easy to understand how you would come to the conclusion that your path to feeling good is through influencing or controlling the behavior of others. But as you attempt to control them (through influence or coercion), you discover that not only can you not contain them—but your attention to them brings more like them into your experience. Your current society is waging a war against illegal drugs, a war against poverty, a war against crime, a war against teenage pregnancy, a war against cancer, a war against AIDS, a war against terrorism . . . and all of them are getting bigger. You simply cannot get to where you want to be by controlling or eliminating the unwanted.

And who among you gets to decide which way of living is the "right" one, anyway? Is the largest group the one that holds that "knowledge," or is the group with the greatest capacity to kill the other groups the one who is "right"? Do poor people have the answer? Do rich people hold the key? Which religion is the "right" religion? Which way of life is the "right" one? Is it right to have children? How many is the correct number? And if a woman has children, is it appropriate for her to think of other things? Can she have a career, or is she now obligated to think of nothing other than her children? How should a man treat his wife? How many wives should he have?

The flawed premise "My group's/our way of life is the only correct way, therefore all other ways must be stopped, because when I look at what I do not agree with, I feel bad" is the basis of the majority of unhappiness on your planet. Not only do those being pushed against feel the pain, but those doing the pushing feel it as well. In fact, the unhappiest, least fulfilled among you are those who are pushing against others, because, in doing so, you are disallowing the most important relationship of all: the relationship between you and You.

While it was your intention for new desires to be born within you and to accomplish those desires, you had no intention of hindering, in any way, the desires of others. You knew that this world is big enough for everyone to create their own desires. And you were not worried about being hindered by your observation of their creations (even if you did not like what you saw) because you knew you had the power to focus upon what is wanted. And so, ridding your world of your personal unwanted was not necessary. *You intended to decide what you want and, by the power of your focus and the Law of Attraction, to attract it—and to allow all others to do the same. You understood that diversity not only provides the basis of your strength and of your expansion, but of your very existence—because if there is not expansion, existence cannot continue to be.*

Do We Have Power to Influence Others
Rather Than Control Them?

Jerry: I'd like to talk more about the power of *influence,* or the power of *control,* we have over one another in our relationships. How much power over others do we actually have? And how can we avoid being influenced away from something that we want by another who thinks that we should want something different?

Abraham: It is good that you see that there is a distinction between *control* and *influence,* and we would like to take your understanding further still: When someone seeks control over another person, or over a situation, they never achieve it, because in the attitude of control there is such a big component of knowing what you *do not* want that your Vibration and point of attraction are working in opposition to your actual desire. *Even though you may join forces with others to push against the unwanted, and even when it appears that your forces have overwhelmed the opposing forces, you never actually gain control—but, instead, you enhance, or add to, your attraction of more unwanted. The faces and places may change, but more unwanted keeps coming, and you find no sustainable control.*

Also, there is little distinction between *seeking control of a situation* and *wanting to influence a situation to be something different than it is* other than the extent to which you are willing to go to try to achieve it. In other words, in the seeking of *influence,* you may use words to try to persuade—or even use threats of action to coerce— where in an actual attitude of *control,* you may offer stronger words or even take specific action to affect the behavior of another.

But there is an even more important distinction that we want to make here than the one between *influence* and *control,* and that is the distinction between trying to get to where you want to be from your awareness of what you *do not* want, as compared to getting to where you want to be from your awareness of what you *do* want. The first is more about trying to *motivate* another to a different behavior; the latter is more about *inspiring* another to a different behavior.

In your effort at motivation, because you are focused upon what you do not want, you do not have the benefit or help of your true power. But when you are focused completely upon what you do want—thereby releasing all resistance or opposition to your own desire—you are engaging the Energy that creates worlds, and your power of influence is mighty. In your connection to, and allowance of, your true power, your influence to bring others into their own power is great.

How Do We Harmonize a Diverse Family?

Jerry: Regarding the family relationships between parents and children: How can an independently thinking, Leading Edge child who is learning and growing exist in harmony with parents who want to train him in their static way of thinking and behaving? In other words, what if your parents don't want to see change or new thought?

Abraham: This leads us to the explanation of yet another flawed premise:

Flawed Premise #5: Because I am older than you, I am wiser than you; and therefore you should allow me to guide you.

While your parents, and others who arrived on your planet before you, do help to provide a platform of stability for you when you are born, they do not possess the wisdom that you are seeking. Your expansion will come from your personal experiences, and your knowledge will come from your Connection to your Broader Perspective. *Most of the guidance, rules, and laws that are passed down from generation to generation are written by people who are not in the state of "allowing" their Connection with their Broader knowledge. In other words, the majority of the guidance that is thrust upon you has come from a perspective of lack, and it cannot lead you to an improved situation.*

Of course there are things of a physical nature than you can learn from each other. There are many inventions and skills that have been discovered before your birth that you do not have to start from scratch in order to realize the benefit of. But there is a pervasive belief on your planet that is absolutely contradictory to *who-you-really-are* and to your reason for being, which leads us to the next flawed premise:

Flawed Premise #6: *Who I am began the day I was born into my physical body. As an unworthy Being, I was born into a life of struggle in order to try to achieve greater worthiness.*

You did not begin on the day you were born into your physical body. You are Eternal Consciousness, with an Eternal history of becoming and of worthiness. And while a part of that worthy, Non-Physical, Eternal, *God Force,* Creative Consciousness expressed itself into the Being you know as you—the larger part of *You* remained, and remains, Non-Physically focused in Pure, Positive Energy and absolute worthiness.

You eagerly came into this physical time-space reality because it is the Leading Edge of creation and you are a creator. You adored the idea of focusing on this world of contrast because you understood the value the contrast would have

453

in helping you, a creator, to focus and create. You understood that your own life would draw from you continual new ideas, and that, by the power of your focus, those ideas could become "reality," as it is known in the physical world. And you knew the joy of *choosing, focusing,* and *allowing* the creative manifestations. You knew that, in every moment, you would be able to feel the degree of Vibrational alignment you were achieving between your current thoughts and the understanding that the *Source* within you has on the same subject at the same time, and you understood that those feelings of positive and negative emotion would be the sole source of your guidance to help you create and discover and expand along your Eternal path of becoming.

You may remember how you felt as a child when someone focused their disapproval of you at you. The negative feeling you experienced was your indication that their opinion of you was out of alignment with *who-you-really-are* and what you really know. In that moment, you felt the beginning of the tugging of that other person pulling you away from your Broader Perspective of *who-you-are* with their distorted view of you. Your Guidance (the negative feeling) was letting you know that the focus that they had caused you to achieve was out of alignment with the focus of your *Source*. *While it never feels good to you to view yourself (or anything else) differently than the <u>Source</u> within you sees it, over time you became accustomed to the discomfort of your gradual disempowerment—until, eventually, you began looking to others for guidance, leaving your own Guidance to fade into the background.*

So now, getting back to your question of how a child can exist in harmony with parents who want to train him into *their* way of thinking . . . our dominant intent would be to, first, assist the child in remembering *who-he-is.* We want to remind him of his own *Guidance System;* we want to help him reconnect with his own personal power and realize his own personal dreams. But many would argue that it is just not as simple as that: "Even if the child were to remember all of that, he is still trapped in a relationship with people who don't remember, who don't agree with that, who are bigger than he is, and who are in control of his experience. How could a child ever find harmony under those conditions?"

First we will direct our response to the child in this situation, then to the parents, and finally to you who are asking the question:

To the Child . . .

Your parents mean well. They are mostly just trying to prepare you for the struggles of life that *they* have found along *their* way. Their behavior indicates that they not only do not remember *who-you-are*, but they also do not remember *who-they-are*. That is why their behavior is guarded. They feel vulnerable, and they believe that you are vulnerable, too.

It would take quite a bit of explaining to your parents to help them remember; and if they were not asking, they would not hear anything that we have to say, anyway. . . . There is a good chance that you will be all grown up and out of their house before *they* ask, or listen, or remember.

If you are asking and listening (no matter how old you are), then we want to tell you the most important thing that anyone could ever tell you: *It does not matter what anyone else thinks about you. It only matters what you think. And if you are willing to let them think whatever they want to think—about anything, even about you—then you will be able to hold your thoughts steady with who-you-really-are; and you will, in time, feel good, no matter what.*

As you hear this and remember that it is true that *you are a powerful creator who wanted to experience contrast in order to help you decide the things that you now want,* it will help you to feel more patient about others' not remembering. When you remember that everything is responding to you and the way you feel, and you then gain control of how you are feeling, you will find tremendous cooperation from many different places helping you gain control of your own experience.

When you are alone and thinking about some of the trouble you have been in with your parents—you are inviting more incidents of being in trouble. But if, when you are alone, you are thinking about more pleasing things—you are not inviting more trouble. *You have much more control over the way others treat you than you sometimes realize. The less you think of trouble, the less of it you get. The less you think of your parents trying to control you, the less they try to control you. The more you think of things that please you, the better you will feel. The better you feel, the better things will go for you.*

It feels to you as if your parents are in charge of the way they treat you, but that is not true. *You* are in charge of the way your parents treat you; and as you hear this, and practice this, their change in behavior will be your evidence. And the best part is that you will be showing them (even if they do not realize it) how to enjoy harmony by *inspiring it* rather than *demanding it.*

To the Parents . . .

The more you see things in your child that you do not want to see— the more of that you will see. The behavior that you elicit from your child is more about you than it is about your child. This is actually true of all of your relationships, but since you think about your child more than most others, your opinion about your child plays a greater role in his behavior.

If you could de-emphasize the unwanted behavior you see in your child by ignoring it—not replaying it over again in your mind, not speaking to others about it, and not worrying about it—you would not be a continuing contributor to the unwanted behavior.

When you hold anyone or anything as your object of attention, you are leaning in one of two directions: toward what *is* wanted, or toward what is *not* wanted. If you will practice leaning toward what *is* wanted when you think about your child, you will begin to see behavior patterns shifting to more of what you are wanting to see. *Your child is a powerful creator who wants to feel good and be of value. If you do not take score in the moment and decree him otherwise, he will rise to the goodness of his natural Being.*

When you are in a state of *fear, worry, anger,* or *frustration*—you will evoke *unwanted* behavior from your child.

When you are in a state of *love, appreciation, eagerness,* or *fun*—you will evoke *wanted* behavior from your child.

You child was not born to please you.

You were not born to please your parents.

To You Who Are Asking the Question . . .

Do not worry about a child losing freedom to unknowing parents, and do not worry about unknowing parents losing freedom to their children. Understand that all of them wanted the experience of co-creating in order to come to a new awareness of desire. Just see them all as having *Step One* (asking) experiences where they are continually clarifying what they want.

Through feeling parental domination, the *child* gives birth to desires about . . .

> . . . greater freedom.
> . . . being appreciated.
> . . . appreciating others more.
> . . . independence.
> . . . opportunities to expand.
> . . . opportunities to excel.

Through offering parental control, the *parent* gives birth to desires about . . .

> . . . having more freedom.
> . . . experiencing more cooperation.
> . . . the child having a good life.
> . . . the child being ready for the world he will step
>   out into one day.
> . . . being understood.

In other words, this co-creative, contrasting experience is causing everyone involved to launch more rockets of desire and therefore to Vibrationally expand to those new places. And the only reason any of them ever feel negative emotion is because, in the moment of their negative emotion, they have not yet *allowed* the expansion. *Life caused them to become something that they are not currently allowing themselves to be; and both of them, parent and child, are using the other as their excuse for not being it. . . . Before your birth, you relished the idea of the contrasting relationships that would cause your expansion, and whenever you allow your own catching up with that expansion, you will then bless the seeming struggle that made it so.*

Will the *Law of Attraction* Do Household Chores?

Jerry: Would you elaborate a little more on ways in which family members could *harmoniously* share in the responsibilities of common home maintenance and help with the general flow of the activities of the family, and still maintain their individual feeling of freedom.

Abraham: When you speak of *responsibilities,* you are usually speaking of *action,* and we certainly understand that there are plenty of action responsibilities to be shared in the making and managing and maintaining of a home environment. And we also understand how it seems logical to most people that when there are a specific number of things that need to be done and there are a specific number of people to share those tasks, an *action* regimen seems logical. The thing that usually goes wrong in such situations is that the people who are assigning the activities of the family are often doing so from a personal place of imbalance—not out of balance because of the amount of work that they are personally doing, but because of the resentment they feel about having to do more than what they feel is their fair share, or the frustration they feel about the work not being done the way they want it to be done. . . . *Even though we are talking about taking action to organize and maintain the home, it is still necessary to find personal alignment first. Which leads us to another flawed premise:*

*Flawed Premise #7: With enough effort,
or hard work, I can accomplish anything.*

When you are Vibrationally out of balance with your desired results, there is not enough action in the world to compensate. Without working to achieve Vibrational alignment with what you really want, but instead, offering action to push against, or fix, existing problems, the *Law of Attraction* will bring you a steady stream of problems to fix—and you will never get out ahead of them. If you are focused upon problems—the *Law of Attraction* will bring problems to you faster than you can fix them. If you are focused upon a disorganized home—the *Law of Attraction* will bring more experiences of disorder, disruption, and problems than you can keep up with.

In simple terms, the power of the <u>Law of Attraction</u>'s response to your Vibration will always be stronger than your ability to keep up in terms of action. You just cannot get there from there. The only way to bring order to your life or your home—or your relationships—is to tap the powerful leverage of Energy alignment. And when you do, things that were formerly a struggle will seem to flow effortlessly.

Unless you are able to let go of your chronic awareness of unfinished tasks and uncooperative family members, you will never be able to elicit good-feeling cooperation from others. You have to let go of the struggle, and focus upon the end result that you are seeking. *You have to find the <u>feeling-place</u> of a cooperative home that is organized and good-feeling before you can inspire that behavior from others. <u>The people in your life will always give you exactly what you expect. No exceptions.</u>*

Many people tell us that they believe that their negative expectations were born from observing negative behavior, and not the other way around. "I didn't *expect* my son to refuse to take out the garbage until he consistently refused to take out the garbage."

You can find yourself in an endless loop where you explain that you feel negative because of the negative behavior of someone else. But if, instead, you take control of your own emotions and you think an improved thought because it feels better to do so, you will discover that no matter how the negative trend got started, you can turn it around. You have no real control of what anyone else is doing with their Vibration (or with their actions, for that matter), but you have complete control over your own thoughts, Vibrations, emotions, and point of attraction.

But What about When Our Interests No Longer Match?

Jerry: When people in a relationship that was once harmonious find that their interests have changed, and so now they are often in disagreement with one another, how can they find harmony when they have opposing beliefs or desires?

Abraham: This question brings us to another flawed premise:

Flawed Premise #8: To be in harmony with another,
we have to want and believe the same things.

Often people are pushing so hard against so many things they do not want that they come to believe that when they find people who believe as they believe—who are willing to also push against those same unwanted things—in the joining of forces, they have found *harmony.* But the problem with that is, as they are focused upon what they do *not* want, they are neither in harmony with their own desires nor with the larger part of themselves (who is always in harmony with their desires). So their basic state of being, as they are pushing against their foes, is one of utter disharmony. And while they may find agreement with others who are also pushing against the same concept, or enemy, they could not be further from harmony.

You must first find harmony between you and You, and then, and only then, is any other harmony possible. And when you consistently achieve harmony between you and You (which is what we refer to as the state of allowing), then it is possible to find harmony with others even though you have disagreements. In fact, that is the perfect environment for expansion and joy: diversity of beliefs and desires—but alignment with Source.

Relationships are usually better in the beginning because you are both looking for things you want to see. And so, your expectation is usually more positive in the beginning of your relationship. Also, looking for positive aspects is a powerful tool in finding your own harmony, or alignment with Self. In the beginning, you both probably think that the wonderful way you feel is because of the harmony you have discovered with the other person, when what has actually happened is that you are using one another as your positive reason to find harmony with *who-you-really-are.*

The Source within you only sees positive aspects in your partner, and whenever you are finding positive aspects, you are in alignment with <u>who-you-really-are.</u>

What If One Doesn't Want the Relationship to End?

Jerry: But what if your desires are *really* different from those of your mate? What if one of you has decided to bring your relationship to an end and the other wants it to continue?

Abraham: *We understand how that may seem like "different desires," but actually there is a powerful mutual desire at the heart of what both people want: the desire to feel better.* One believes that the action of separation is the most likely path to feeling better, while the other believes that staying together is the path.

Let us begin this discussion by pointing out another flawed premise, which is a big part of the basis of confusion on this issue:

Flawed Premise #9: The path to my joy is through my action. When I am feeling bad, I can get to a better-feeling place by taking action. I can focus upon a situation that I think is the reason I am feeling bad, and walk away from it. And once away from it, I will feel better. I can get to what I want by leaving what I don't want.

The positive moments you may have once felt within your relationship were not about the harmony you found with each other (that now seems to be gone), but instead about your own alignment with *who-you-really-are*. It is true that it is easier for you to be in alignment with yourself when you are not focused upon unwanted things. So a person near you who is pleasing to you *can* serve as a positive object of attention, causing no distraction from your alignment. But the belief that another person is "making" you happy is incorrect. *Your happiness is your natural state of being.* The correct understanding is that you are using this currently pleasant person as your reason *not* to focus yourself away from *who-you-really-are;* while, in your state of unhappiness, you may be using this currently unpleasant person as your reason *to* focus yourself away from *who-you-are.*

Your true happiness happens when you discover that no one other than yourself is responsible for the way you feel. If you believe that others are responsible for the way you feel, you are in true bondage, because you cannot control how they behave or how they feel.

It is natural that you would want to remove yourself from things that do not feel good, but in an inclusion-based Universe, that is not possible. You cannot focus upon unwanted things— and therefore activate the unwanted in your Vibration—and get away from it, because the pulling power of the *Law of Attraction* is stronger than any action that you may offer.

As you walk away from one unpleasant situation, the <u>Law of Attraction</u> will bring another that feels very much like it, and usually quickly. You just cannot get there from there. To get to where you want to be—to that place of <u>feeling</u> better—you have to reach for alignment between you and You.

A 30-Minute Energy-Alignment Process

You can get a running start on a day of aligned Energy as you put yourself to bed the night before:

Find things in your immediate vicinity—such as your bed, your bed linens, and your pillow—to direct your appreciation toward. Then set your intention to sleep well and to awaken refreshed. When you find yourself awake in the morning, lie in more appreciation for at least five minutes, and then refresh yourself by bathing and eating. Then, sit for 15 minutes and quiet your mind. Feel whatever resistance you may have fall away, and feel your Vibration rise. Then open your eyes, and sit for five or ten minutes writing a list of things you appreciate about your life.

In doing this Energy-alignment work, your point of attraction will not only yield to you activities and rendezvous with good-feeling people, places, and things—but your ability to experience the delicious depth of them will be dramatically enhanced. Rather than doing things and going places to try to *make* yourself feel good, deliberately get to *feeling good*—and let those things and people and places come to you. It is possible that once you come into alignment with *who-you-really-are,* you will gravitate to a different relationship. But it is also likely that the relationship that you are already in was attracted from your point of being in alignment to begin with, and now that you have achieved alignment again, it will renew itself for you.

If you entered your current relationship from a place of mostly alignment, its potential for returning to a wonderful *feeling-place* is great. If you entered this relationship because you were in the process of escaping from something unpleasant, then the basis of this relationship may be more about what you *do not* want than about what you *do* want.

In any case, getting yourself feeling good before you take any action is always the best process; and when you do not feel good, you cannot be inspired to any action that will solve the problem.

Is There One Perfect Person for Me?

Jerry: Is there the "one perfect person" for us to be in a relationship with? And if there is, do you have any recommendations of how to find that person? Also, what is your opinion about what we call a "Soul Mate"? In other words, is there an ideal Spiritual mate for each of us?

Abraham: Throughout your lifetime, and because of your interaction with others, you have been identifying the characteristics in others that are most appealing to you; and you have, incrementally, been sending out rockets of desires about those desirable traits. In other words, bit by bit, you have created (in your own Vibrational Reality) your version of the perfect mate for you. But before you can find your perfect mate, you must be a Vibrational Match to that desire, which means, you must consistently be a Vibrational Match to what you want.

If you are feeling lonely or frustrated about not yet meeting your mate, you are *not* a match to your Vibrational Reality, and so your rendezvous is postponed. When you are envious of others who have wonderful relationships, you are *not* a match to your Vibrational Reality, and so your rendezvous is postponed. *If you are remembering past unpleasing relationships and using those as your justification for wanting or needing a better one, you are a match to what you do not want, and what you do want is postponed. But if you can bring yourself to a place of consistently feeling good, even in the absence of the relationship that you desire, the rendezvous is certain. In fact, it is Law.*

The "perfection" of that partner means that your partner matches the things that your life has caused you to ask for, but the finding of that partner hinges upon you becoming a match to those desires first. You cannot find your perfect mate from your awareness that your mate is missing from your life. You have to find a way to no longer offer the Vibration of a "missing partner."

In the same way that from the sifting through your *now* physical experience, you are continually launching new desires—you also launched desires about your physical experience from your

Non-Physical vantage point before your birth. And sometimes those desires, or intentions, did include such specific things as creative traits or talents, specific things you wanted to do, or specific people you intended to co-create with. A "Soul Mate" would be such a person. But we usually downplay the idea of "Soul Mates" in the way that so many people want to address them because, really, *every person with whom you share your planet is a sort of soul mate.* And the feeling of Connection that people are looking for, the exhilaration of being with someone with their hearts soaring, really is not a function of the person you are with, but instead it is a function of your own Connection with You. We would prefer to think of *Soul Mate* as you mating, or consciously Connecting, with your own *Soul* or *Source* or *Inner Being* or *Self.* When you, in your physical moment and time, are offering a similar Vibration to that of your *Inner Being,* you have indeed found your *Soul Mate.* And if you *consistently* do that, the people who will gravitate to you will be enormously satisfying in nature.

Think about __what__ you want in a relationship and __why__ you want it. Look for those around you who are experiencing good relationships, and feel appreciation for them. Make lists of the positive aspects of those you have spent time with. . . . __In fact, one of the fastest ways to make your way to a wonderful relationship is to find any subject that consistently feels good, and focus on that even if it has nothing to do with relationships.__

When you remember that you have already Vibrationally created your perfect relationship, and that it is all queued up for you in your Vibrational Reality, and that your work now is to just not offer an opposing Vibration about it—and that it *has* to come to you—then it must come quickly. The number one thing that prevents people from rendezvousing immediately with their perfect mate is simply their awareness and discomfort about not yet finding one. Remind yourself, often, that you have done the work, you have clarified your desire, you have shot off the rockets of desire, Source is tending to those combined wishes, the *Law of Attraction* has organized the circumstances and events through which the rendezvous will occur, and now your work (your only work) is to stop doing that thing you do that *prevents* your meeting. When you are "doing that thing you do," you always, without exception, feel negative emotion. So when you are lonely, or ornery, or impatient, or discouraged, or jealous—you are delaying the meeting.

If we were standing in your physical shoes, we would remind ourselves that we have already done the work of specifying and asking. We would accept that the creation is already accomplished. It is done! And then we would think about it only for the sake of the pleasure of the thought. *When the moment of thought is blissful and satisfying—without the contradictory energy of trying to make something that has not yet happened, happen—your Vibration is pure and powerful, and your creation can easily flow without hindrance.*

How Does One Find the Perfect Business Partner?

Jerry: If you were looking for a business partner, would you look for someone with exceptional ability and specific skills, or would you look for someone who is more compatible with your overall intentions?

Abraham: We want to answer your question fully, but first, you have led us to another widely believed flawed premise:

> *Flawed Premise #10: I cannot have everything that I desire, so I have to give up some things that are important to me in order to get others.*

If you have experienced relationships with others where there were some pleasing characteristics and some unpleasing characteristics, it is easy to understand why you would come to believe that you just have to take the bad with the good and put up with the unwanted parts in order to have access to the favorable parts. And since most people make very little effort to guide their thoughts beyond mere observation of *what-is*, they usually continue the pattern of focusing upon *what-is*—therefore getting more of what they are focusing upon—therefore focusing upon it—therefore getting more of what they are focusing upon . . . and then concluding that they have little or no control of those with whom they interact.

By focusing upon the <u>wanted</u> *characteristics of those around you, you train your Vibrational offering to match only the best in them—and then the* <u>Law of Attraction</u> *can no longer match you up with the worst in them. When you focus upon the worst of them, and train your Vibrational offering to match only the worst in them—the* <u>Law of Attraction</u> *can no longer match you up with the best of them.*

The people you would describe as having "exceptional ability" are usually those who are in alignment with *who-they-really-are. The brilliance or clarity or intuitiveness that denotes "exceptional ability" are also characteristics of a person in alignment.*

If we were seeking a partner of any kind, business or personal, we would first seek someone in alignment with him- or herself, because when people are tuned to the fullness of *who-they-really-are,* they are feeling good; they are inspired; they are a match to Well-Being, love, and all good things. . . . *The most significant thing that we could say about you finding such a person is that unless you yourself are in alignment, you would not be a Vibrational Match to such a person. . . .*

Many people who are not in alignment then look to their partners to make things better, but the inherent flaw in that reasoning is that you do not have access to the aligned person you need to make it better for you if <u>you</u> *are not in alignment. You just cannot get there from there.*

So our answer to this important question is: There are clearly happy people who do not have the skills or interest in your specific business, and there are people who may have all of those necessary skills required for your business who are not happy. *We would look for a talented person—with abilities that matched the needs of our business—who is obviously happy. In short, seek compatibility between you and You (which means, be happy), and then everything that you are looking for will find its way to you.*

Who Is Best Qualified to Govern Us?

Jerry: In the area of government, who do you feel, among us, is the best qualified to set the standards, terms, and conditions of life for the rest of us?

Abraham: Your question leads us back to an earlier-mentioned flawed premise, that there are *right* ways to live and *wrong* ways to live, and therefore your objective as a society is to eventually find the right way to live and then to convince all others to agree or comply with this "right" way.

The diversity of your planet is of tremendous value and benefit because *from variety, springs all new ideas and expansion. Without the diversity, there would be complacency and endedness.*

Let us carry the flawed premise a bit further by pretending that your current population were to come into complete agreement with one another. Let us say that, by persuasion or coercion, you came to a worldwide consensus on the proper way to live. But new babies are being born every day from *their* powerful Non-Physical vantage points of understanding—and they are seeking diversity. It is such a perfect process where a small portion is coming into your environment (through birth) and a small portion is leaving (by death), while the largest part of your population remains, providing you with both continuity and stability.

As individuals living life, you are individually, but also collectively, making constant Vibrational requests about an improved life upon your planet; and there is no possible way that you can individually or collectively cease the offering of these Vibrational requests—and the responsive Universe steadily responds to those requests.

That stable central part of your population that we were just speaking of usually stubbornly holds to its limited beliefs (by attention to *what-is*), which prevents it from receiving the immediate benefit of the improvement it is seeking . . . but then the old, and therefore "more set in their ways," among you die; while the open and eager ones are born. *And so, life continues to improve in response to the asking that life summons from you.*

There are many who would argue that there are ideologies that are more conducive to a better life, and that even within those ideologies there are those who are better suited to lead and guide and make laws and decide what is the better approach to life, and all of that molding of the clay of your lives is pleasurable and satisfying. But there is something very much larger than that happening upon your planet: *You are billions of people, living the perfect diversity, just as you knew you would, constantly asking for improvement and thereby setting up, for the next generation, that improved life experience. If you understood that, and no longer clamored for the "one right way to live," things would go better for you sooner.*

So the answer to your question, "Who, among us, is the best qualified to set the standards, terms, and conditions of life for the rest of us?" is: *No one is more qualified than you to set the standards for you.* But there is nothing to worry about because you cannot cease making your requests, and Source never ceases answering them. And when you, right here, right now, no longer offer resistance to what you are asking for (by focusing on the opposite of it), it will reveal itself in your life experience immediately. In other words, if you focus upon something that your government, or someone in leadership, is doing that pleases you—then you are not resistant to the things you have chosen by the living of your life. But if you are bothered by something you see and are chronically pushing against it, you then use that unwanted thing as your reason to hold yourself in resistance to what you have chosen.

Appreciate your government, or any other, in every way you can; and, in doing so, you will not disallow the thriving that is already set up for you, and by you, that is on its way to you. The powerful Law of Attraction always, no exceptions, is best qualified to deliver to you the standards that your own individual lives have set.

What Is the Perfect Form of Government?

Jerry: So, how would you envision the perfect form of government for us here?

Abraham: It would be a government that allows you freedom to be or do or have as you want. And that will come only when there is an understanding of *how* you are getting what you are getting. You see, your government, for the most part, has become one of rules and regulations primarily established to protect one of you from the other of you. *When you come to understand that you invite through thought, then you will not feel so much need for all of that restriction, and then your government can be established as it was begun—more to offer services rather than restriction or control.*

What Is Our Natural Relationship with the Animals?

Jerry: How would you describe our natural relationship with the animals of our planet?

Abraham: The most important thing to remember about the animals with whom you share your planet is that they have come into this environment as extensions of Source Energy just as you have. In other words, like you, your animals also have an *Inner Being* or *Source* point of view; and, like humans, when their *physical* point of view varies from their *Source* point of view, they can also be in a state of resistance. However, the animals of your planet are less often in a state of resistance or separation. Unlike humans, they primarily remain in a state of Connection or alignment with their Broader Perspective.

When humans witness an animal who is tuned in to the Vibration of its Broader Perspective, they often comment about the "instinct" of the animal. What humans refer to as an animal's "instinct," we call an animal's "state of alignment with Broader Perspective."

Evidence of the alignment of the physical animal with its Broader Non-Physical counterpart is all around you, and so you accept it as animal behavior or "instinct," when what you are actually witnessing is a physical animal who, because it is offering no resistance, has full access to the Broader Perspective, and who understands, always, the larger picture.

The Three-Step Process of Creation

In the Process of Creation there are three steps:

- **First:** *Ask.* (And the contrast of life experience causes you to do that.)

- **Second:** *Answer.* (That is not the work of you from your physical perspective, but, instead, the work of Non-Physical Source Energy.)

- **Third:** *Allow.* (You must find a way to be a Vibrational Match to what you are asking for or you will not allow it into your experience even though the answer is available for you.)

When humans and animals come forth from Non-Physical, you come with different intentions. Humans are more naturally involved in *Step One:* focusing, and sifting through the contrast of your time and space for the express purpose of *asking,* with ever-increasing clarity, for improved life experience. Animals are more naturally involved in *Step Three:* maintaining their alignment with their Broader Perspective. *Humans are here to specifically create through more specific focus. Animals do less specific creating and are much less inclined to sift through contrast and make decisions. In simple terms, humans are more creative, and animals are more allowing. That is your natural bent.*

While animals do experience contrast, and they do Vibrationally ask for improved conditions, they remain more often in alignment with their Broader Perspective than humans do. It is possible to be actively involved in sifting through contrast, as humans are, and to deliberately guide your thoughts into resonance with your Broader Perspective and experience the benefit of being an active creator at the same time that you are in the state of allowing. And while the animals of your planet are an important source of food for each other and for humans, the greatest value they bring to life on planet Earth is the Vibrational balance they provide, as they are extensions of *Source Energy* and remain predominantly in alignment with that Energy. *Humans and animals make a very nice combination, just as you knew you would.*

Can We Influence Animals, or Only Control Them?

Jerry: Can humans *influence* the other living things on the planet, or do humans only have *control* over them? Like breaking or controlling a horse?

Abraham: <u>Control</u> *never proves to be satisfying for the one attempting the control or the one being controlled, because both—controlling others and being controlled <u>by</u> others—are unnatural to man and beast.*

With the absence of the offering of control, all would find alignment with *Source,* and all would experience harmonious co-creating with one another. Whether man or beast, you have inherent, innate selfish natures that you Eternally seek to satisfy. In other words, when you are in complete alignment with the Source within you, and therefore experiencing the benefit of that Broader Perspective, control of another is never necessary to your survival or Well-Being. In that state of alignment, you are always guided to circumstances that will accommodate the Well-Being that you seek. Only someone not in that state of alignment would ever seek control over another.

While in the state of alignment, you offer no Vibration contradictory to your intent; and when it is without contradiction, in that powerful state of alignment, the *Law of Attraction provides evidence of that nonresisted intention. That is what influence is: when you are in that state of Connection, your power of influence is very strong, because it is only your contradictory Vibration that ever causes you to be weak.*

Being in a state of powerful influence does not mean that you can get someone to stop doing what he intends to do and to begin pleasing you instead. It means that when you are not contradicting your own intentions—and are therefore offering a powerful Vibrational signal—the *Law of Attraction* will immediately bring to you people, circumstances, and events that match that signal. Everyone with whom you interact holds myriad intentions; and at the core of every one of them is a Being who is Pure, Positive Energy. And so, when you are in a state of alignment, you can then connect with the true nature of them. *Focusing upon your own alignment is the best way to maintain your power of influence.*

Animals intuitively move toward anything or anyone who offers benefit, and away from anyone or anything who does not offer benefit.

What about Our Optimal
Physical/Non-Physical Relationship?

Jerry: How would you describe the relationship between us current human Beings and *Non-Physical Intelligence?* And what would you describe as the optimal relationship between the two?

Abraham: This is a profoundly important question, and, in fact, is at the basis of this entire book on *relationships. The relationship between you and your Source is the most significant relationship of all, and unless this relationship is understood, all other relationships cannot be clearly understood.*

As you stand in your physical body, it is rather easy for you to perceive yourself as separate from others whom you can see. You make clear distinctions between "me" and "you" as you integrate your life with the lives of those who surround you. And, in a similar way, "mankind" has perceived what it calls *"God"* or *"Source"* or *"Non-Physical"* as separate, also.

While focused into your physical body, you are an extension of that which is "Source," and the most important clarification of all here is that Source sees no separation at all between you, in your physical body, and Source. Any separation, or disallowing of a complete integration or alignment between you in your physical body and the Source within you, is caused from your physical viewpoint and behavior, not the viewpoint or behavior of Source.

Source, or your *Inner Being*—or whatever you want to call that Non-Physical part of you—understands the Eternal relationship between the physical and Non-Physical aspects of you. *Source* also understands the Eternal relationship between you and every other physical Being with whom you share your planet, but we will discuss that more fully in other sections of this book.

So, here, in this book about *relationships,* we are asking you to reframe your definition of your relationship with Non-Physical Intelligence in this important way: Usually, when you think of a relationship between two people, you see them as separate individuals, or entities, who behave or interact with one another. We want you to understand that you are not separate from your Source, but an extension of your Source; and we want you to be aware of, or feel, your Vibrational alignment, or discord, with that Broader part of you at all times. We want you to be consciously aware when the thought you are thinking right now harmonizes so completely with your Broader Perspective that the full knowledge of your Broader Perspective flows through you, causing you to feel enlivened, clear-minded, and joyous. And when you feel confused or angry, or uncomfortable in any way, we want you to recognize that the thought you are thinking is discordant and out of harmony with your Broader Non-Physical viewpoint.

The relationship between "mankind" and "Non-Physical Intelligence" equals your *Guidance System.*

The relationship between "mankind" and "Non-Physical Intelligence" equals the expansion of *All-That-Is.*

The relationship between "mankind" and "Non-Physical Intelligence," from the viewpoint of *Source,* is that there is no separation, ever, between the two.

The relationship between "mankind" and "Non-Physical Intelligence," from your physical point of view, is a variable. The better you feel, the more complete the Connection or relationship. The worse you feel, the more fragmented the Connection or relationship.

Your question comes right to the heart of the intention of this book and the intention that "mankind" held when you came forth into your physical bodies: *You came as physical extensions of Source Energy, understanding that you would explore contrast, causing expansion not only for you but for All-That-Is. And you knew that, at all times, even while you were reaching into uncharted territories, the Guidance from within would not waver, but would remain a constant signal of Well-Being that you could reach toward and find at all times.*

You knew that under all conditions, you could find your way back to the resources of your Source by "feeling" your way—by understanding that the relationship between you and You is not one of separateness but one of alignment and resonance. . . . When you master the Art of Allowing your consistent alignment with the Source within you—every other relationship will be beneficial and pleasurable.

What If One's Workplace Feels Uncomfortable?

Jerry: Abraham, if a person has a job that he enjoys, but he's being harassed by an oppressive, overbearing superior, would you recommend that he change jobs, or can you offer a better solution?

Abraham: This leads us to another flawed premise:

Flawed Premise #11: If I leave an unwanted situation, I will find what I am looking for.

Whatever you are giving your attention to is offering a Vibrational frequency, and your attention to it for an extended period of time causes that same frequency to be active within you. It is important to remember that when a Vibration is active within you, taking the physical action of walking away from it will not prevent it from being present in your experience. In clearer terms, the *action* of walking away does not hold enough power to compensate for the *attraction power* of your thoughts.

By the time you come to the point of using strong labels such as *oppressive* or *overbearing* to describe someone you are working with, you have undoubtedly been observing unwanted conditions for some time, which means you have been practicing a pattern of thought and a pattern of resistant Vibration, and that means your point of attraction now is quite strong. So even if you take the physical steps to remove yourself from the situation by quitting your job and finding another—or by asking to be removed from the specific department of this supervisor and moving to another—*wherever you go, you will be taking yourself with you.*

Taking the action of walking away does not mean that your Vibrational patterns have changed; and, usually, even though someone may not now be observing the unwanted characteristics of his former superior, often he justifies the necessity of the move to the new location by continuing to remember or explain what the previous experience was like, therefore keeping that Vibration active within him.

You have received tremendous value in this *harassing, oppressive* relationship even though it is difficult to recognize it while it is happening, because during those uncomfortable moments when you knew so very clearly how you did *not* want to be treated, how you did *not* want your job to be, how you did *not* want to be devalued, how you did *not* want to be disrespected, how you did *not* want to be misunderstood—during those experiences, you were launching rockets of desire about what you *did* prefer and how you *did* want to be treated. In other words, those unpleasant experiences were the bouncing-off place for your expanded and improved life experience.

Every time something happened that caused you to launch one of those rockets of desire, the larger part of you—your *Source,* or *Inner Being*—followed the rocket, took the expansion, and held for you the position of the improved experience. The only open question, then, is: *Where are you in relationship to the expansion? Are you imagining the improvement, appreciating the contrast that caused it? Are you looking forward with optimism to the improved life experience regarding your work environment? Or are you continuing to speak of the injustices of your past experience and therefore holding yourself out of alignment with the new expansion that this relationship has spawned?*

Negative emotion means that your life has caused expansion, which, in the moment of the negative emotion, you are disallowing. Every time. No exceptions. That means that no matter what you believe is the cause of your negative emotion (and certainly we understand why you want to justify your negative feelings, because it *would* feel better if *they* would be nicer), *your negative emotion means that you are disallowing your own expansion.* Period.

If your harassing supervisor had not inspired your desire and expansion into something more, you would not suffer the discomfort of not allowing the expansion. So the better solution you are asking for is this: *Try to make peace with where you are,* perhaps by acknowledging that this unpleasant person has helped you become very clear about how you want to be treated and about how you want to treat others; look for the benefit of the relationship rather than pushing against the unwanted aspects of it; and, in the simple, and much-easier-than-you-may-at-first-believe, process of just chilling out a bit—and maybe even trying to give the benefit of the doubt to your supervisor—your resistance will subside and you will then be allowing yourself to move in the direction of your newfound expansion. . . . *If your life has caused you to ask for an improved situation—no matter what it is—and you are no longer offering chronic thought-Vibrations that are opposite of your desire, your desire must come to you. But you cannot continue to keep alive within you Vibrational patterns of what you do not want, and receive what you do want. That defies the <u>Law of Attraction.</u>*

How Can We All "Have It All"?

Jerry: You said that we can have it *all,* but how does that work when there are others who are also wanting it *all?* What keeps our desires from clashing?

Abraham: There is a very large flawed premise that must be reconciled here before you will be able to understand our answer to your very important question:

Flawed Premise #12: There is a finite container of resources that we are all dipping into with our requests. Therefore, when I satisfy my request for something, I deprive others of that resource. All of the abundance, resources, and solutions already exist, merely waiting to be discovered; and if someone else gets there first, then the rest of us will be deprived of that discovery.

What many are regarding as the "discovery" of abundance or resources or solutions, we want you to understand is actually the "creation" of abundance, resources, and solutions. *When the living of your life causes you to desire an improvement—your Vibrational request for that improvement sets forth the process of the attraction and actualization of that improvement. In living your Leading Edge lives, you are not merely discovering improved benefits. You are creating them.*

Many people deprive themselves of much that they desire because of their misunderstanding of the ever-evolving, ever-expanding, ever-created pool of resources. If you do not understand the Creative Process of your planet, and the important role that you play in the expansion, you may fall into the ranks of the many who experience the shortage Consciousness that is caused by this misunderstanding.

This misunderstanding is at the heart of the feeling of competition. You did not come here to compete for the resources of your planet. You came as creators. *If your time-space reality has the wherewithal to inspire a desire within you, it is our absolute promise to you that your time-space reality has the ability to deliver, in full-manifested form, the reality of the desire it has inspired.* You came here knowing that; and until you remember it fully, and apply it deliberately, you will pinch yourself off from your largest of resources—the clarity, knowledge, and Energy of your *Source.* That is truly the only shortage that can exist in your world; and it is wonderful when you realize that that shortage is always, without exception, self-inflicted.

And so, you are not in competition with the others who share your planet. They could never deprive you of something by taking it for themselves. In fact, their existence *enhances* your ability to receive, for in your interaction with them, your own desires are inspired. *Any and all desires can be fulfilled unless you are holding yourself out of alignment with your own desire. The feeling of competition or shortage, or limitation of resources, means you are out of alignment with your own desire.*

Are Legal Contracts Counterproductive to Creativity?

Jerry: I understand that you are encouraging us to be aware of our current emotions in order to make our best choices. So how can we live and create "in the moment" while, at the same time, entering into long-term relationships or agreements where our legal documents are often binding far into our future?

Abraham: Whether you are focused upon an immediate situation, which requires your thought and action right now, or whether you are thinking about a future or even a past event—you are doing it right now. Therefore, it is causing an activation of Vibration right now. In other words, you can tell how you are affecting a future event, right now, by the way you are feeling about it right now as you are thinking about it. Therefore, if you are aware of how you are feeling in every present moment, and it matters to you that you feel good, and so you are deliberately making an effort to align your current thought with the thought of your *Inner Being*—not only will you have many more pleasant moments, *but every subject that you have pondered will benefit by the focus of your Source-aligned thought.*

Sometimes people disagree with the premise that "if you feel really good about something, it will continue to evolve in a pleasing way," by pointing out how happy they felt at the beginning of a relationship that turned out badly. But if you remember that each time you focus upon something, your current thought is affecting it, then you may understand that between the time you felt good about your relationship and the time it turned out badly, your current thought moved often to what you did *not* want rather than to what you *did* want. Sometime, in the interim between the happy beginning and unhappy ending of your relationship, your thoughts turned consistently toward unwanted things, and you experienced the inevitable negative emotion that always accompanies such thoughts. *It requires continual deliberate focusing upon the positive aspects of any relationship to maintain the good-feeling productivity of it over time. You cannot allow your "now" thoughts to drift toward unwanted without having both current and future negative impact upon the object of your attention.*

Many long-term agreements are sought from a standpoint of wanting to protect against future unwanted situations, and that is not a good basis from which to begin any relationship. *When you come to understand the power of your focused thought, any need to protect will dissipate, and your sense of continual Well-Being will dominate.*

If your current circumstances, or the laws of your government, require that you enter into binding, long-term agreements, you can still maintain your balance and feeling of alignment, or freedom, by remembering that even those agreements can be changed. You may enter into a 20- or 30-year agreement regarding the purchase of your home, but later on, if you wish, you could sell your home and therefore end that agreement. Many people enter into "until death do us part" marriage relationship agreements, later to amend those agreements with new agreements of "divorce."

It is liberating to realize that by utilizing the power of your thoughts— by deliberately aligning them with the expanded version of your life that you have given birth to—you can get anywhere you want to be from wherever you are.

What Perpetuates Chronic Therapeutic Problems?

Jerry: It seems to me that when people enter into therapy where they are trying to work out or fix specific problems, the problems often seem to continue for years. What's the cause of that? Why does their pain continue?

Abraham: Because every moment is new; and, under all conditions, the components of the moment are changing and different from every moment that has been before. *Nothing ever remains the same. Things are constantly changing, but often, because of chronic patterns of thoughts, even though things are changing—they are changing to more of the same.*

It is not possible to create an improved future by dwelling on the problems of the past. That simply defies *Law. Focusing on problems of the past, or the present, will prevent you from moving to the solutions in your future. Focusing on the problems of the past, or the present, will guarantee a problematic future.*

Therapy can be of value in the sense that any discussion about the unwanted aspects of your life experience can help you to know more clearly what changes you prefer, but beyond that discovery, *a continued discussion of unwanted things will only hold you in those unwanted patterns of attraction. If, however, once you are keenly aware of what you do prefer, you will focus upon that, your life must improve.*

There is a tremendous difference in the Vibrational frequency of the *problem* and that of the *solution*. The *question* is one Vibration, while the *answer* is something quite different. Your unwanted experience has launched an amended desire, and your *Inner Being* is now focused entirely upon that *improvement;* and when you join your *Inner Being* in the thought and Vibration of that desire, you will feel immediate improvement in your emotion—and the manifestation of the improvement will begin to move into your experience. But as long as you continue to beat the drum of injustice, unfairness, or that which is unwanted, you will hold yourself apart from the improvement.

What Is Our Greatest Value to Those in Need?

Jerry: If we see a friend in a negative situation, living something truly unwanted or without something the person very much does want, how can we help? In other words, how can we be of an advantage to others rather than a disadvantage?

Abraham: Whether your friend is feeling negative emotion because of the situation he is in, or whether you are feeling negative emotion because of your awareness of the situation your friend is in, neither of you is aligned with your Broader Perspective. *Your awareness of your friend's problem is a true disadvantage to him, because you are amplifying the Vibration of the problem and therefore adding to it.*

Often your friend draws you into keener awareness of the problem by continually discussing specific aspects of it, but with every moment of attention that you give to your friend's problem, the further from really helping him you are.

In this contrasting world in which you are focused, any attention to your problems *does* cause you to Vibrationally ask for solutions, and those solutions *do* begin lining up for you. And so, you could actually add to the power with which your friend is asking for solutions by discussing the specifics of the problem, but he does not need help in amplifying his problems in order to intensify his asking. That is a natural process that the contrast of the Universe provides. . . . *There is no reason to deliberately stir up problems in order to stir up solutions.*

You are of no discernible assistance to your troubled friend unless you are able to focus in the direction of the solution, in the direction of what he wants, or in the direction of what you desire for him. *If you are determined to feel good and are able to focus in the direction of improvement for him despite his continual prodding at his problem, your power of influence toward improvement will be powerful.* In other words, when you focus in the direction of the solution, you join forces with your own *Inner Being,* with his *Inner Being,* and with all of the cooperative components that the *Law of Attraction* has already assembled. *If you allow yourself to be the sounding board for your friend's problems, your power of influence will be paltry, and you will be of no value to your friend.*

But something even more troubling is now occurring: Your friend's problem not only launched rockets of desire into *his* Vibrational Reality, but your association with him and your focus has caused you to launch rockets of desire about your friend into *your* Vibrational Reality. In other words, this experience has caused an expansion in you, and if you do not focus in the direction of your expansion—if you do not focus on the possible improvement for your friend—you will pull against your own expansion.

It is important to realize that the negative emotion that you often feel when you are worried about a troubled friend is actually present because your focus is pulling you apart from yourself. Your friend may be the reason for your focus, but your friend is not the reason you are pulling against yourself. Your focus is the reason for that.

Looking for positive aspects and expecting good outcomes for your friends is the only way you can be of value to them, for there is no action that you can offer that is strong enough to buck your current of negative attention.

Jerry: So we're not doing ourselves or the other person any favor when we discuss our problems or concerns with them?

Abraham: Indeed not. *Nothing good ever comes from focusing in opposition to what you desire. It is detrimental to you and to whomever you draw into your negative conversation.*

Why Do Some People Repeatedly Attract Painful Relationships?

Jerry: What is it that causes some people to repeatedly attract relationships that bring them pain and anger—to the degree that they finally end the relationship—but then they soon find themselves engaged in another relationship with essentially the same sort of negative conditions? And what would you recommend to change that pattern?

Abraham: It is possible to walk away from an unwanted situation without repeating it again, but that would require not talking about it, not thinking about it, and not pushing against it. It would require a complete deactivation of the Vibration of the troubling experience. And the only way to deactivate a thought, or Vibration, is to activate another. *The way to avoid repeating <u>unwanted</u> situations is to talk about <u>wanted</u> situations. Talk about what you do want; and discontinue dialogue about any unwanted experiences, situations, or results.*

Monitoring thoughts can be tedious and tiring, so the best approach to deliberately change the direction of your thought is to reinforce your desire to feel good. *Once you are determined to improve the way you feel, you will begin to catch yourself in the more early, subtle stages of negative attraction. It is easier to release a negative thought in the beginning stages of it than after it has gained more momentum.*

Are Some Doomed by Their Childhood Influence?

Jerry: Don't many of our disempowering thoughts begin in childhood? In other words, how much influence do adults have on the way children begin to think? And are children doomed to continue the patterns of resistant thoughts that they learn from their parents?

Abraham: *Doomed* is a stronger word than we would use, but there is no question that children are influenced by the thoughts of their parents, because anyone who is giving their attention to anything begins to offer a similar Vibration. But it is of value to remember that no matter what your age, there is always a Vibrational Relationship occurring between the Vibrational content of whatever you are focused upon in the moment and the point of view about the same subject from the Source within you.

For example, when an adult disapproves of the behavior of a child and speaks his condemnation of the child, as the child observes the adult's disapproval, a Vibration occurs within the child that corresponds with that disapproval. But, at the same time, the *Source* within is offering appreciation and approval of the child, because, no matter the situation, Source never withdraws love or offers condemnation. Ever! So the discord between the active Vibration, influenced by the physical adult's disapproval, and the active Vibration of the love of Source causes discord in the child, which feels like negative emotion. *When negative emotion is present, it always indicates discord between the perspective of Source and the perspective of you in your physical body.*

It is of value to note here that no negative emotion is present until opposing Vibrations have actually occurred. In other words, no matter how much disapproval another feels for you, unless you focus upon their disapproval long enough to activate it in your own Vibration—you will not feel the discord. But most parents are so certain they are right that they work quite hard at staying focused upon what they believe is wrong behavior until they do manage to influence enough attention to their object of disapproval that the discord begins within the child.

It is interesting to note the striking difference between the behavior or approach of your Source and most of your parents: Your Source, no matter how extreme the situation, will never withdraw its love and appreciation from you. There is no behavior that you could offer that would result in the withdrawal of the Love of Source—while, quite often, your physical parent, who has lost conscious Connection with Source, seemingly demands your attention to what he deems your failure or misconduct.

Notice how reluctant your children are, especially in the beginning, to admit their wrongdoing to you. It is their natural instinct to continue to feel good about themselves even when you are finding flaws or misbehavior.

From the moment that you are influenced to deviate from your awareness of your own value, the most powerful desire that flows forth from you is to reconnect with that awareness of your value. There is no greater driving force in the Universe than the force of Well-Being and self-value. So even if you are like most children who have been born into an environment where most adults have lost their conscious awareness of that Connection, whenever you catch a glimpse of it, it calls you. And you feel it. *There is no greater purpose of this book than to activate within you a conscious decision to seek alignment with the Source within you.*

Whenever others attempt to guide or influence your behavior by the offering of approval or disapproval . . . as you try to please them, you are diminishing your awareness of your own *Guidance System. If we were parents standing in your physical shoes, our dominant intent regarding our children would be to make them aware of their own Guidance System and to encourage them to utilize it always. For we understand that there is no amount of physical knowledge that we could convey that could begin to approach the magnitude of the value of their continual alignment with their Broader Perspective. In other words, the coaxing of anyone into pleasing you, from your physical perspective, and thereby ignoring their Broader Perspective of Source, is a sacrifice that we would never ask of anyone.*

Are You Blessed with a Difficult Child?

Many children are able to hold to their Broader Perspective even amidst strong human influence. They are often labeled by their parents and teachers as "problematic" or "troubled" children. They are often deemed "stubborn" and "incapable of learning," but we want you to know that a determination to guide oneself, and follow one's personal guidance, is an inherent intention that all are born with. Many are coming into physical form with an even more powerful intention of remaining connected to their own Broader Perspective, and the physical people who surround them are finding them less easy to dissuade from their own determinations. That is a good thing.

Many people have been socialized, in the sense that they commonly seek the approval of others, and they often live very difficult lives because it is no simple task to determine which, of the influential people who surround them, they should bend to.

And many people who have spent many years making an effort to fit in, to not make trouble, and to find approval from others finally reach the point of recognizing the futility of it, because no matter how hard they try to please others, the list of those who are *not* pleased with them always remains longer than the list of those who *are* pleased. And who gets to decide what the right way of living is, anyway?

You are living in the wonderful time of Awakening. This is the time when more people will come into conscious realization of their own value. It is the time when fewer people will attempt the impossible task of pushing the unwanted far enough away that they will be left with only that which is wanted. It is the time when more people will come to the realization that what they have been long seeking is not a change in the behavior of others, or in the world outside of them—over which they have no control—but, instead, an understanding of their own Vibrational relationship with *Source*, over which they have complete control.

How Can One Move from Disharmony to Harmony?

Jerry: If you were a child born into a disharmonious environment—or even an employee finding yourself in an unpleasant work environment—how could you remain in such a situation and still maintain a positive personal life experience?

Abraham: The first thing we would encourage you to do is to lay low, so to speak. Try to be as inconspicuous as possible in your awareness of the disharmony. In fact, do your best to be unaware of the disharmony, because in actually being unaware of the disharmony, there will be no active Vibration of it present within you, and the *Law of Attraction* will then leave you out of any discordant rendezvous.

But if, instead, you *are* aware of the unpleasant occurrences—if you seek to quell the injustices by drawing attention to them—then you activate a Vibration within you that draws you closer into the unpleasant mix. If, from your point of view, you identify wrongdoing and you point it out, those participating in the behavior you believe is wrong will rise up larger and push back at you in an attempt to convince you that it is really your point of view that is wrong. Then you push back, and they push back, and the discord looms larger while both sides are deprived of any lasting solution.

All *contrast* causes an asking for improvement by all parties involved, but usually those involved are pushing so hard against someone else that they render themselves incapable of seeing the solution, even though it may be quite near.

Seeing what you do not want until you can no longer stand it, and then leaving the situation and going somewhere else, does not bring a lasting solution, because the reason you left is the dominant Vibration within you, which means more scenarios like the one you just walked away from are making their way into your experience again. In other words, you did not change your point of attraction by moving to a new location, to a new job, or to a new relationship.

It may sound odd, but the fastest way to get to a new-and-improved situation is to make peace with your current situation. By making lists of the most positive aspects you can find about your current situation, you then release your resistance to the improvements that are waiting for you. But if you rail against the injustices of your current situation, you hold yourself in Vibrational alignment with what you do not want, and you cannot then move in the direction of improvement. It defies <u>Law.</u>

Since a powerful desire for improvement is always born out of unpleasant situations, the larger part of you is already experiencing the benefit of the contrast you have lived, and you can—much more easily than many of you believe—begin, right now, to receive the benefit of that contrast. It may not be easy at first, but it really is as simple as making the best of where you are.

In every particle of the Universe, there is that which is wanted—and the lack of it. By making a decision to orient yourself to look for what is wanted, you will change your Vibrational patterns of resistance, and it will not be possible to remain in unwanted situations for long periods of time.

Must a Negative Childhood Lead to a Negative Adulthood?

Jerry: So, a child could be negatively influenced by a parent, but that doesn't have to be a continuing influence through the adult life of the child, does it? In other words, that's an individual decision that can be made, at any time, by that child who is now an adult?

Abraham: It is clear, by the way you have worded your questions here, that you believe that the small child has little or no control in relationship to the older, bigger adult. And so, you are delaying your expectation of things getting better for this child until he becomes an adult and can gain control of his own life and make his own decisions.

As an adult reading this book, you are in a position where you can consciously make your Vibrational relationship with your *Inner Being* your highest priority by getting into the Vortex of Well-Being and positively controlling everything about your life experience. But there is another way of looking at this: As a child, even a child in a negative situation who seems to have little control of your own experience, you have a better relationship between the physical you and the Non-Physical You than most adults. In other words, for most, the Vibrational variance between your two Vibrational aspects is much less in the early days of your life than in the later years because you pick up and continue more and more resistant thoughts as you move through time. That is why most children are much happier than most adults even though they seemingly have far less control. And this book is written to help you reverse that process.

We want you to understand that at any point when you make the decision to be consciously aware of the relationship between your Vibrational vantage points (which means, anytime you decide that how you feel is of utmost importance to you), you can come into alignment, you can access the Energy that creates worlds, you can fulfill your reason for being—and you can live happily ever after.

But until you decide to focus your thoughts into alignment with the Source within you, you will not feel good. *A joyful life is not about gaining control of the factors that surround you. A joyful life is about coming into alignment with who-you-are. Joy is not about controlling other people or circumstances. Joy is about controlling your own Vibrational relationship between the physical you and the Non-Physical You. It is alignment with Source that is joy or love or success or satisfaction.*

Blaming Past Suffering Magnifies Current Suffering

Jerry: There are a large number of adults who are experiencing trauma in their lives who believe that their parents are the root of their current problems. As long as they continue to blame their parents, won't they continue to experience problems?

Abraham: For adults to be able to use something from their distant past (such as from their childhood) as their reason for not feeling good in their present, it is necessary to keep that unpleasant thought alive and active in their Vibration. *Whether their unpleasant memory is about a parent, a sibling, a bully at school, or an angry teacher, it is only their continued thought about that relationship that would cause it to still be an issue years later.*

We would define a *belief* as a thought you continue to think. In other words, whatever you are focused upon, thinking about, speaking about, observing, remembering, or contemplating—whether it is about your past, present, or future—that thought-Vibration is active right now. And your emotions are giving you, in the moment, feedback of how that current active thought is blending with the perspective of your *Inner Being.* When your current thought is not resonating with what your *Inner Being* knows about the subject, your negative emotion indicates the disharmony. And often, because you are not aware of the existence of this *Emotional Guidance System,* and you do not realize that you could shift your focus and improve the way you feel, you continue your discordant thought, and you feel bad and blame the object of your attention.

You innately understand that you are supposed to feel good, and when you do not, you know something is wrong. And it is easy to understand how, under those conditions, you would blame whatever or whomever has your attention while the negative emotion is present.

So, over a longer period, each time that unpleasant memory surfaces and you feel the negative emotion but you make no effort to control your thought and focus into alignment with the perspective of your *Inner Being*—your Vibrational discord gets stronger. In other words, your negative beliefs about your earlier life not only get larger and gain momentum, but you continue to bring them forward and to use them as reasons for your current disconnection from Source.

Many feel the futility of trying to resolve those past conflicts because often the main characters in their past dramas are deceased, and even if they are still living somewhere on the planet, most feel that the likelihood of their recognizing their wrongdoing is small; and, anyway, they believe the damage is done. . . . During those traumatic or dramatic childhood moments of real or perceived mistreatment, they were influenced by the situation to focus themselves out of alignment with their *Source Energy,* and they did it often enough that they established a belief (a chronic pattern of thought) that held them out of alignment whenever they focused upon that misaligned thought.

What this blaming adult does not realize is that the relationship that is disharmonious here is the one between him, in his physical form right now, and his Broader, Pure, Positive Energy *Inner Being.* . . . *His suffering is not because of childhood mistreatment, over which he had no control. His suffering is about his current, in-this-moment misalignment between physical self and Non-Physical Source—over which he has complete control.*

It can be so liberating to focus your thoughts and therefore train your beliefs into alignment with your own Source and power. And it is so debilitating to continue the flawed premise that "others need to be different before I can feel good."

When Does "Fixing Problems" Simply Increase Problems?

Jerry: I guess my tendency, in years gone by, was to try to fix the problems. I believed that if I could think about them enough, I could get them fixed. But then most of the problems just increased.

Abraham: *The only way to solve a problem is to look toward the solution. And, when you are looking in the direction of the solution, you always feel an improvement in your emotions. Looking back at the problem always feels worse.*

It is that old *flawed premise* again: "If I push hard enough against what I do not want, it will go away," when what really happens is that the more you push against it, the bigger it becomes and the more often it manifests in your experience.

It is helpful to remember that every subject is really two subjects: *what is wanted* and *the absence of what is wanted.* It often seems like a fine line between focusing upon the problem and focusing upon the solution, but that line is not a fine line at all, because the Vibrational frequencies of the problem and of the solution are vastly different. *The best way to identify which side of the equation*

491

you are focused upon is by paying attention to how you are feeling. Your emotions will always indicate whether you are focused in the direction of your Broader knowing and your solution, or in the opposite direction toward the problem.

Abraham, Speak to Us of Love

Jerry: *Love* is a predominant word in our culture. How do you see humankind, in general, in relation to the word *love?*

Abraham: Being in the state of *love* means being in the state of complete alignment with the Vibration of the Source within you. When you are in the state of love, there is no active Vibration of resistance within you. For example, if a parent were focused upon the absolute Well-Being of his child, that parent would be in complete harmony with the way the Source within him views the subject of his child, and therefore there would be no resistant Vibration present—and the parent would feel "love." But if a parent is focused upon what he considers to be the bad behavior of the child, or if a parent is worrying about something unwanted happening to the child, those thoughts are completely disharmonious with the way the Source within him views the subject of his child, and therefore there is resistance present within the parent's Vibration—and he would feel anger or worry.

So, in the same way that the "problem" and the "solution" are very different Vibrations, the subject of "love" can be discussed from the state of being aligned with *who-you-really-are,* or from the state of being out of alignment with *who-you-really-are.* A mother who shouts at her child, "Don't you know how much I love you!" from her place of trauma or worry or anger is doing so from her state of misalignment. And so, even though she is offering the word *love,* her Vibration could not be more opposite.

One of the most confusing things that children encounter as they begin to understand language is the dichotomy between the words their parents offer and the accompanying Vibration. It is of such value to a child when a parent expresses, with words, what he is actually *feeling*. And of even more value when the parent works to be in alignment with the truest of his feelings *(love)* before he expresses anything at all toward his child.

When Is It Time to Quit Trying?

Jerry: Why do people often continue to cling to relationships that bring them pain?

Abraham: Often people believe that having a relationship, even if it is not a good-feeling one, is better than having no relationship at all. And so, they stay because it seems less painful to be angry than to be lonely, or to be continually aggravated than to be insecure.

Jerry: And what degree of discomfort or pain should a person reach before you would recommend seeking a separation from the negative relationship?

Abraham: Walking away from exposure to unpleasant or un-wanted things does give you the relief of not being continually confronted with those things, and you may find it easier to find more pleasant thoughts and to be more often in alignment with your Broader Perspective. But while there is often temporary relief following an abrupt departure, if you have left without actually achieving Vibrational alignment with the Source within you, the relief does not last—and the next relationship you attract feels, often, very much like the last.

Of course, if someone is experiencing physical or even verbal abuse, we would encourage a physical separation as quickly as pos-sible. However, just removing yourself from the current situation will not stop your feeling of abuse if you continue to think about it, resent it, and use it as your reason for leaving.

You cannot continue to focus upon unpleasant thoughts without keeping the thoughts active within you and therefore holding yourself out of alignment with the solutions and relationships that you really do desire. In short, you just cannot get to where you want to be by pointing at the evidence of that which is unwanted. It defies Law.

Often people are surprised to discover that by physically remaining in a relationship (by not moving out) but at the same time deliberately deactivating the *unwanted* aspects of their relationship by activating more *wanted* aspects, their relationship improves so much that they no longer want to leave. We are not suggesting that, in all cases, it is possible to suddenly focus so positively that you cause personality or behavior changes in those who live with you—but we do know that nothing can come into your experience unless it is active in your Vibration.

Many argue that unpleasant things would not be active in their Vibration if other people had not behaved in a way that caused the activation. And while we acknowledge that it is certainly easier to feel good when you are around good-feeling people, *we would never go so far as to say that the behavior of others is responsible for the way you feel, because you have the power to focus, and therefore attract, despite the behavior of others in your environment.*

If, every time you see something unwanted, you merely move to a place where, for the moment, you do not see the unwanted behavior, in time you will have yourself backed into an impossible corner of complete isolation. But if, every time you see something *unwanted,* you realize that, in the same moment, your awareness of something *wanted* is keener—and you quickly turn your attention in the direction of the newly emphasized *wanted*—everything in your experience will continue to improve.

Instead of physically removing yourself from the unpleasant relationship, and instead of asking your partner to behave differently so that you could feel better by merely observing, if you would ride each new rocket of desire that is born out of the continual conflicts, your physical Vibrational patterns of thoughts (or new chronic beliefs) would be such that the *Law of Attraction* would have to match you up with different experiences. . . . *It is always true that whatever you are living always matches your chronic Vibrational patterns, or beliefs. And it does not matter even if you have an excellent excuse for your negative thoughts and negative emotions—they still equal your point of attraction. What is manifesting on every subject in your life is an indicator of the beliefs you hold and your chronic patterns of thought.*

It is very empowering to discover that your patterns of thought do not have to follow your current situation, and therefore your current situation (on all subjects) can change. . . . We do not recommend taking the physical action of leaving a relationship without deliberately coming into thought alignment with the new desires that have been born out of your current relationship. And then— whether you stay in this relationship or move on to another—you can have exactly what you desire.

ᘓ⑫ᘔ ᘓ⑫ᘔ

PART II

Mating, and the
Law of Attraction:
The Perfect Mate—
Getting One, Being One,
Attracting One

Why Haven't I Yet Attracted My Mate?

Jerry: As humans, we seem to be driven toward the idea of coupling, or mating, even from rather early in our experience. You have called it "co-creation," but it seems that many people, or even most people, struggle with this subject of *mating*. Many worry about finding the right mate or worry that they may not find a mate at all, while many others are already involved, but in rather unpleasant relationships. So what would you say to the large mass of people who are single, who haven't found a mate (and want to), or to the large percentage of people who do currently have mates but who find their relationships unsatisfactory?

Abraham: You intended to interact and co-create with other humans when you made the decision to focus here in this physical time-space reality because you understood that all joyful motion forward requires a variety of viewpoints from which to expand. *You knew that by interacting with others, new ideas would be born from the mix; and you knew that as the new ideas or desires were hatched from these co-creative experiences, the potential for joy was a sure thing whenever you individually or collectively focused in the direction of those new ideas.*

When you want to be joyful and you remember that your joy is not dependent upon the behavior of others—and you consistently look for good-feeling subjects to use as your chronic point of focus—all desires on all subjects will be satisfied. But, from your place of not feeling good—as you worry about not finding a mate, or notice that you are unhappy with the one you have—your desire

499

for a good relationship cannot come to you because you are not a Vibrational Match to your own desire.

Whether you are without a mate and trying to find one or un-happy with the mate you currently have, your work is the same: *you must find thoughts about your relationship that harmonize with the thoughts your Inner Being has about your relationship.*

If the strongest Vibration you are offering about relationships is about the *absence* of the relationship that you desire, then it is not possible for the *presence* of the relationship that you desire to come into your experience. The Vibrations are too far apart. You cannot find the *solution* to any problem when the *problem* is the most active Vibration within you.

I'll Focus on What I *Want* in a Relationship

What it comes down to is, you must find a way of offering a Vibration that matches the relationship that you *want* instead of the relationship that you *have*. You have to ignore the *absence* of the relationship you are seeking, or ignore the *presence* of the unwanted relationship that you have, before you can get to the relationship that you want. And that is the tricky part. *You must make what you want a more dominant part of your Vibration than what you have; and once you are consistently doing that, what you want and what you have will intertwine, and you will be living your desire. In other words, until you have tended to the relationship between what you desire and the chronic thoughts you think—until you have tended to the relationship between the Non-Physical You and the physical you—no other relationship can be satisfying.*

When someone holds you as their object of attention and they are approving of, or appreciating, what they see, it feels very good to you because, in their appreciation of you, they are in alignment with their Broader Perspective. And as they hold you as their object of attention, you are flooded with the good-feeling Source Energy Perspective. But then if they look away, tending to something else, or lose their alignment by seeing a flaw or a fault, you may feel like the puppet whose strings have been dropped, no longer buoyed up by the behavior of another.

While it does, and should, feel good to be appreciated by another person, if you are dependent upon their appreciation to feel good, you will not be able to consistently feel good, because no other person has the ability, or a responsibility, to hold you as their singular, positive object of attention. Your Inner Being, however, the Source within you, always holds you, with no exceptions, as a constant object of appreciation. So if you will tune your thoughts and actions to that consistent Vibration of Well-Being flowing forth from your Inner Being—you will thrive under any and all conditions.

Most people, from an early age, develop an expectation that, at some point in their lives, they will find a mate. Whether male or female, they often hold a romantic image of walking off into the sunset, hand in hand. But they also often refer to that kind of relationship as "settling down," which indicates a somewhat negative expectation of giving up some freedom and some fun for the more serious experience of a permanent relationship. In fact, as they observe the majority of the relationships that surround them, they do not see those relationships as providing joy and satisfaction and freedom (which is at the very basis of *who-they-are* and what they want), but instead, they see *loss* of joy and satisfaction and freedom. And so, there is tremendous discord around the subject of mating, or permanent relationships, because while most people do come to expect that they will eventually mate with another, they often do not look forward to the loss of freedom they have also come to expect.

Sometimes people feel that they are not really "complete" until they find another person to share their life experience, but that is not a good basis for beginning a new relationship. It is another example of "you cannot get there from there." In other words, if you are feeling inadequate and are therefore looking for another to "complete" you, so to speak, the *Law of Attraction* must find another person who *also* feels inadequate. *Now, when two who are feeling inadequate come together, they do not suddenly begin to feel adequate. The basis of a really good relationship is two people who are already feeling very good about who they individually are. Then when they come together, they are a couple who feels good.*

Asking your relationship with any other to be the basis of buoying you up is never a good idea, because the *Law of Attraction* cannot bring to you something different from the way you feel. If you are consistently feeling bad about yourself or about your life and you enter into a relationship with another to make it better, it never gets better. *The Law of Attraction cannot bring you a well-balanced, happy person if you are not yourself already that. The Law of Attraction, no matter what you do or say, will bring to you those who predominantly match the person who you predominantly are. Everything that everyone desires is for one reason only: they believe they will feel better in the having of it. We just want you to understand that you must feel better before it can come to you.*

A woman, who was annoyed at our suggestion that she get happy and then look for a mate, said to us, "You want me to make myself happy by imagining my mate is here, even though he is not here. I don't think you care if he ever actually comes." She was right, in this sense: we knew that if she could consistently be happy, then not only would what she desires have to come about (it is *Law*), but she would be happy, in the meantime, along the way.

It is amusing to us that people often seem to protest that happiness is a very big price to pay for successful outcomes. That is especially amusing to us because we know that the reason for every success they seek is because they believe they will be happier in the achievement of it.

When you discover that your happiness is not depending upon outcomes of others, but that it is simply the result of your *deliberate* focus, you will finally find the freedom that is your most intense desire. And with that understanding will also come everything else you have ever wanted or will ever want. Control over the way you feel—over your response to things, over your response to others or your response to situations—is not only the key to your consistent happiness, but to everything you desire as well. *It really is worth practicing.*

In simple terms, if you are not happy with yourself, or with your life, the attraction of a partner will only exaggerate the discord, because any action taken from a place of lack is always counterproductive.

If you do not currently have a mate, you are in the perfect position of bringing yourself into alignment first, before attracting another person who will surely amplify the way you feel. But even if you are in the midst of a relationship that is often unpleasant, you can still begin moving toward a satisfying relationship anyway, because you really *can* get to wherever you want to be from wherever you are.

People are often eager to find their mate immediately, even though they are not currently feeling good about themselves. They even believe that finding a mate is the path to feeling better about themselves. However, the *Law of Attraction* cannot bring them someone who will appreciate them when they are not already appreciating themselves. It defies *Law*.

Therefore, if you are currently without the mate you want, it is much better to make peace with where you now are by beginning to accentuate any and all other positive things that are currently happening in your life right now, trying to soothe your discomfort about the absence of your wanted mate, making the very best of your life as it is, making lists of the good things, and coming into greater appreciation of yourself. It is our promise to you that as soon as you begin to really like yourself and you cease your incessant awareness of, and subsequent discomfort about, the absence of your mate, your mate will come. That, too, is *Law*.

If you are in the midst of an unpleasant relationship, you must find a way of distracting yourself from the negative aspects of the relationship. Some say it is more difficult to be alone and wanting a mate, while others complain that it is more difficult when you feel you are with the *wrong* mate, but we want you to understand that it really does not matter where you are currently standing or what you are currently experiencing.

You can get to where you want to be from wherever you are—but you must stop spending so much time noticing and talking about what you do not like about where you are. Be a more selective sifter, and make lists of the positive things you are living. Look forward to where you want to be, and spend no time complaining about where you are. The responsive Universe makes no distinction between the thoughts you think about your current reality and the thoughts you think as you dream of your improved life. You are creating by virtue of what you are thinking about, and so there is no advantage whatsoever to pondering, or remembering,

or observing, or speaking of things you do not want. <u>Make your active</u>
<u>Vibration be about what you do want and notice how quickly your life</u>
<u>changes to match your Vibration.</u>

Haven't You Observed Many Disharmonious Relationships?

Jerry: As a child, I remember observing many relationships, but I don't remember any that were happy ones. Most of those relationships were enduring relationships; they survived, but not in joy. I used to say that the majority of relationships I observed were experiencing a sort of "quiet desperation." I didn't hear a great deal of complaining, but I also didn't see much joy.

Abraham: Your childhood observation of predominantly joyless adults surrounding you is not uncommon even with children in your current time. It is much more common for children to observe their parents complaining about their relationships with employers, other drivers, the government, neighbors, and so on than it is for them to hear appreciation.

Most children do not have the advantage of observing parents who are in chronic states of appreciation and alignment, and so most children are developing unhealthy patterns of thoughts or beliefs about their relationships with others. But beneath those newly acquired unhealthy beliefs that they are picking up along their physical trail (as they observe the discontent of the adults who surround them) pulses a powerful desire for Connection, love, and harmony. In other words, even though, like you, children rarely see truly happy relationships, most are still hopeful that *they* will be able to find one.

We want you to understand that even if everyone you know is experiencing an unhappy relationship, there is a deep understanding within you that harmonious relationships are possible—and, in fact, every time something unpleasant occurs within a relationship, an equal desire is born out of it. . . . *The more unpleasant things you experience within relationships, the more specific your desire becomes about what you would prefer instead.*

The reason why the subject of relationships is such a big subject, and the reason why so many people feel overwhelmed by the prospect of improving their relationships, is because the more you experience what you *do not* want, the more you ask for what you *do* want, but your observation of what you *do not* want prevents you from moving toward what you *do* want. So you hold yourself, without knowing it, in the impossible tug-of-war of reaching for expansion while holding yourself back from the very expansion you seek.

There is one easy-to-achieve understanding that would put every relationship you have into alignment: *I can be happy regardless of what anyone else does. . . . By using my own personal ability to focus my thoughts, I can achieve Vibrational alignment with my Source (my Source of happiness), and I will feel good regardless of what others are doing.*

But What If My Relationship Doesn't Last?

Jerry: I traveled a great deal in my life, and I was single a great deal of my life—so, as a result, I experienced a multitude of relationships. It seemed easy to begin them, but difficult to bring them to an end. And I notice that in our general culture as well, the going into a relationship seems to be fairly easy, but coming out of one is much more difficult. In the dissolution of relationships, in the settling of property, and so forth, there is often anger, violence, or revenge.

It seems like we observe so many relationships not working out and then really getting worse when they try to come to an end. Doesn't that also add to our guardedness or negative expectations regarding relationships?

Abraham: It seems, from the observations that you have offered here, that there are really no good reasons *to* enter into relationships. "If people stay together, often they are not happy; and when they attempt to end the relationships, things often really get bad." The most important thing that you are emphasizing with your questions is that most people enter into most relationships with negative beliefs about relationships; and those beliefs (or thoughts they continue to think) make it unlikely that their relationship will be a happy, successful one.

While you have, deep within you, a desire for harmonious relationships, there is an even stronger, deeper tenet, or basis, of your very Beingness: your desire to be free. And at the basis of your desire to be free is your desire to feel good—and at the basis of your desire to feel good is an unhindered relationship between you and You.

Whenever, for any reason, you feel less than good, you know something is wrong, and it is your natural instinct to identify the reason for the discord. Often you relate your not feeling good to another person who is present, or involved, while you are not feeling good. So then, as you do not feel good, and therefore are not in alignment, you believe that the person needs to do something different from what he or she is willing or may be able to do. And as you see that you are powerless to effect the change you believe is necessary, you do not feel free. So the most important desire at the very basis of *who-you-are* feels challenged, and your relationship breaks down.

But we want you to understand that it was a relationship that was based on a flawed premise to begin with, because it is never possible for another person to behave sufficiently, or consistently enough, to keep you in balance. That is your job. If you can accept, when you do not feel good, that it is no one else's responsibility to bring you back to feeling good, you will discover the freedom that is essential to your maintenance of personal joy. And if you do not, you just move from unsatisfying relationship to unsatisfying relationship.

Your sense of <u>who-you-really-are</u> pulses so powerfully within you that you always continue to reach for satisfying relationships, because you understand, at very deep levels, the potential for joy contained in relationships with others. And once you decide that your happiness depends on the intentions, beliefs, or behaviors of no other, but only upon your own alignment—over which you have complete control—then your relationships will not only no longer be uncomfortable, but they will be deeply satisfying.

In the absence of a personal Connection with Source, there is a feeling of insecurity that people often try to fill through their relationships with other people, but no other can sustain the Connection you need by giving you their attention. Many relationships feel good to you in the beginning stages because you are giving each other your undivided attention, but in time it is natural that your attention does begin to turn back to other aspects of your life; and if you were counting on the attention of the other, it is likely that, without his or her undivided attention, you will return to feelings of insecurity.

A consistently good-feeling relationship occurs when each of the parties involved is maintaining his or her own Connection with Source. There is no substitute for that relationship. There just is not another person who can love you enough to compensate for your lack of alignment with Source.

Why Does the Relationship with Abraham Feel So Right?

Jerry: I know that there are many forms of, and reasons for, mating. There are marriages of convenience; arranged marriages; and marriages resulting from physical attraction or sexual lust, with high emotions exploding . . . and some people find mates because they just don't want to be alone.

But Abraham, I've been thinking about the absolutely perfect relationship that I have with you. Is it possible for those of us who are, right now, focused in our physical bodies to see others who are physical in the way I see you? In other words, can we get past the specific details, somehow, and get to the *essence* of a physical Being so that we can have the harmonious relationship with one another that I feel with you?

Abraham: You could not have asked a better question at this point in our conversation because what you are describing in your appreciation for what you are calling "Abraham" is the alignment between *you* and *You* that we have been talking about.

Your appreciation for us is not because we are behaving in pleasing ways for you, for there are many people who do not feel appreciation for, or alignment with, us. Some are not pleased with us when they realize that we will not *do* for them. (From their feeling of shortage or lack, they could plead for miracles or help from us that they would not find.) Others find us annoying because we are very clear about who we are and about what we want—and we are unyielding. We are not willing to set aside our intentions—which we have established over all that we have lived—to satisfy a whimsical desire of someone who is asking in this moment. We will not pretend that the *Laws of the Universe* do not exist as they do for the sake of entertaining you in this moment. And so, there are many who, as they interact with us, find negative aspects within us. And, as a result of their looking for and finding lack, our relationships are not satisfying.

The reason you feel that you have a perfect relationship with us is because you are currently focused upon the aspects of us that resonate with *who-you-really-are*. But you have the ability to hold anyone as your object of attention and do the same thing. It is *your* focus that is responsible for the way you feel about us, not something we are projecting to you.

When you are interacting with any others, it is always to your advantage to look for their positive aspects. By activating the Vibration of wanted things, more of those wanted things will flow into your experience. *When you discover the art of looking for, and finding, positive aspects in others—so much so that you develop an expectation for positive things from others—only positive things can come to you.*

Jerry: So, what I'm hearing from you is that the relationship I have with you, from my perspective, is a sort of self-love?

Abraham: Perfectly stated. By your appreciation of that which *we* are, you have come into alignment with *who-you-really-are*. And that is what love is: alignment with Source, alignment with self, alignment with love.

Jerry: So, in other words, from what I want in life, I have attracted you or am attracting from you that which fulfills me? And would you call that a form of codependency?

Abraham: *Dependency* indicates that "I am not whole, in and of myself," and that "I am needing another in order to be whole"; and that is not the case with you or with us. In fact, this question really points us toward a very important premise, or basis, for good relationships: When people feel insecure in their singularity, and so seek a companion to shore them up, the relationship is never stable, because it is on an unstable footing. But when two people who are independently secure and in alignment with their respective *Inner Beings* join together, now their relationship has a solid footing. In other words, they are not dependent upon each other for resources. They are getting those resources from Source, and now they can interact and co-create from that solid basis.

When two or more minds come together that are positively focused upon a subject, those two minds are many times more powerful than one-plus-one. And so, the attraction of ideas and solutions goes beyond the sum total of the two individuals. It is truly exhilarating. And it is really what co-creating is all about.

Something that is very basic to productive co-creating is that the individual creators who are coming together must be in a place of positive attraction before they come together, or nothing positive can come out of the co-creation. *If you are negatively focused and therefore not feeling good, you can only attract others who are in the same state of negative attraction. That is why looking for a mate from a place of insecurity, or lack of anything, can never bring you the mate you really want, but instead brings one who amplifies your current lack.*

People are often confused because they think their discomfort is about not having a mate. So then when they achieve the physical action of finding a mate, they do not understand why their discomfort does not subside or why it gets bigger. *The physical action of mating, or moving in together, or marriage, cannot fill the void that exists when you are Vibrationally out of alignment with <u>who-you-really-are.</u> But if you have tended to that alignment first, then the physical action of co-creating can be sublime. In other words, do not take the action in order to fix misalignment. Fix misalignment and then find a mate.*

Shouldn't a *Soul Mate's* Mind Be Beautiful?

Jerry: I hear people refer to "Soul Mates." When two people who are very positive in their thought attract one another, is that a form of what people call *Soul Mating?*

Abraham: Often when people speak of finding their Soul Mate, they infer that there is one specific person that they are meant to be with—a sort of soul alliance that they formed before they came forth into this physical body in this time-space reality. And while it is true that you do have intentions to rendezvous with others for the purpose of specific co-creating (and rediscovering those relationships can be tremendously satisfying), you were not looking to those physical rendezvous as the source of your alignment. Instead, you intended to accomplish a consistent alignment first, understanding that then you could attract those relationships into your life.

You could be in the presence of a person with whom you had a Non-Physical alliance, and if you were disconnected from your Source, you would not recognize the relationship. Often the people with whom you feel the greatest annoyance or disharmony are actually your Soul Mates, but, in your lack of alignment with *who-you-really-are,* you do not recognize them.

The best way to approach the idea of a Soul Mate is to seek alignment with the pure, positive Vibration of the Soul, or Source, within you; and then, by the allowing of that alignment, you will recognize every opportunity for these wonderful rendezvous, just as you have intended. The simple intention to find things to appreciate would put you in continual alignment with your Source and in the perfect position to attract your Soul Mates on myriad subjects.

Remember that even though you are new to this physical body, you are actually a very old Being who has experienced a tremendous number of life experiences, and through the living of all of that life, you have come to powerful conclusions. Your *Inner Being* now stands in the knowledge of all of those conclusions; and through your alignment with your *Inner Being*, you, too, have access to that knowledge—and anything less than that is out of balance and will not feel good to you.

Nothing Is More Important Than Feeling Good

Jerry: And so, what would you say to young people who are just out of school, beginning their lives, seeking their first mate or between mates? How would you guide them regarding their relationships?

Abraham:

— First, we would remind them that nothing is more important than that they feel good, because unless they feel good, they are not in alignment with all that they have become, and anything less than that alignment will always feel lacking.

— Next we would encourage the continual setting of an intention to find good-feeling subjects to focus upon, and if a not-good-feeling subject should be activated within them for any reason, to do their best to distract themselves from that by looking for relief by focusing upon a better-feeling subject.

- For example, let us say that you observe an unpleasant relationship in progress, and you hear the negative conversation of this unhappy couple. Your desire for harmony, and even your more specific desire for a harmonious relationship, causes your involvement (by your listening) in this unpleasant experience. The negative emotion that you would be feeling is your *indicator* that this focus is not helpful to you. If you have in place an active intention to feel good, you would easily move yourself out of earshot of this conversation. You would deliberately turn your attention to other, good-feeling objects of attention.

— We would remind them that creating occurs from the inside out. *In other words, the thoughts you think and the way you feel are at the center of what you attract. Rather than looking for things outside of you that cause you to feel better, it is much easier to decide to feel better first and then attract, from the outside, things that do.*

— We would encourage a time of focusing upon what is wanted before jumping into any action. *When you take action as you focus upon what you do not want, you only get more of what you do not want. But if you take the time to focus upon what you do want before you take the action, then the action that is inspired will enhance your desire.*

— We would also advise them:

- As you move through your day into the variety of changing segments that make it up, stop often and restate to yourself your intention to feel good and to stay in alignment with your *Inner Being* or Source.

- Let your desire to feel good be the dominant intention that is present no matter what else is occurring in that segment. And remind yourself, often, that it is up to *you* to make that Connection and to feel good, and that no other person has a responsibility or the ability to make that important Connection for you.

- Look to your relationships with others as a way of enhancing the alignment you have already achieved, but not as a means of accomplishing the alignment.

- Independently, by your own focus with Source, reach the consistent place of loving yourself. Do not ask others to love you first. They cannot.

The dominance of your thoughts is what brings everything to you and is what is behind the action that you offer. By seeking good-feeling thoughts that align you with your Source—your action will then always feel good. You cannot muster enough action to compensate for misaligned thought, but action that is inspired from aligned thought is always pleasurable action.

She Wants Someone, but Not *That* One

Jerry: Okay, so what would you say about a woman who seems to feel good about herself, who continues to express her desire for a mate, but who disqualifies them, one by one, as the parade of men moves through her experience?

Abraham: Her *desire* for a mate keeps the men coming, but her *belief* in bad relationships causes her to push them away. And her attention to unwanted characteristics makes it impossible for the characteristics that she desires to come to her.

If she is continually focusing upon what she does not like in the men coming to her, her chronic attention to the lack in others is keeping her from being in alignment with *who-she-really-is*. And under those conditions, she cannot be feeling good about herself or about anyone.

Finding lack in others is not the path to liking what you see in yourself. *If you are a person who has trained yourself to look for positive aspects, you will find them in yourself as well as in others. If you are a person who has trained yourself to look for negative aspects, you will find them in yourself as well as in others. Therefore, it is always accurate to say that no one who is critical of others really likes themselves. It defies Law. Whenever you see those who are very critical of others, you are actually seeing people who do not like themselves.*

The appearance of a superior attitude you sometimes see, which causes you to think that people really like themselves, is often their way of covering up the insecurity or lack of alignment they are feeling. *When you really like yourself, you are in harmony with the Source within you; and when that is the case, your appreciation of others flows abundantly—and when that is the case, wonderful things flow steadily to you.*

When you are in alignment with your Source, the *Law of Attraction* can then only match you up with others who are also in alignment with their Source, and the ensuing relationship is then one of satisfaction and delight. But when you are out of alignment and feeling bad, the *Law of Attraction* then can only match you up with others who also feel bad, and those relationships are unpleasant and uncomfortable.

You want to co-create with one another, but if you are not tending to your own personal alignment, then co-creating with others only exaggerates your misalignment. Interacting with others adds immeasurably to the expansion of your planet and to *All-That-Is,* and yet, most people deny themselves the pleasure of co-creating because of their attention to the unwanted aspects of those around them. In other words, for the most part, you are focused upon the worst in one another rather than the best of one another. And the reason for that is, you have not found your centered place before you came together, and so when you come together, you perpetuate the imbalance in one another.

Relationships, and the *List-of-Positive-Aspects Process*

Whether you are currently without the relationship that you desire or in the middle of a relationship that does not please you, there is nothing that you could do that would be of greater value in moving you in the direction of the relationship that you want than to take a notebook and spend time every day writing the positive aspects of the people in your life.

Make lists of positive aspects about the people around you, the people from your past, and yourself. And, in a very short period of time, you can demonstrate to yourself the power of your aligned thought and the cooperative nature of the *Law of Attraction.* By releasing all effort toward the futile control of the behavior of others and, instead, focusing the power of your positive thoughts, you will find the delicious relationships that you have been dreaming about.

You are the thinking, vibrating attractor of your experience; and the thoughts you think determine everything about the life that you live. As you turn your attention toward the positive aspects of the personalities and behaviors of others with whom you share your planet, you will train your point of attraction in the direction of only what you desire.

The relationships that you desire are not only possible, not merely probable—they are certain. But you must train the frequency of your thought-Vibration into alignment with those desired relationships if you are to experience them in the tactile, physical, "real life" ways that you desire. *Not only does the power of your thought determine which people make their way into your life, but the power of your thought determines how they behave once they get there.*

By Virtue of My Vibration, I'm Attracting

Jerry: In my early experience, I remember observing a common pattern where it seemed like most people were not interested in having a relationship with the people who wanted to have a relationship with them. It seemed like every boy was interested in a girl who didn't want him, and every girl wanted to be with a boy who didn't want to be with her.

Abraham: Well, the best part about your observation is that the contrast of their experiences was helping them to more clearly identify what it was that they each did want. This rather common scenario occurs because most people believe that in their search for the "perfect mate," they must root out the imperfections. They believe that by identifying what they do not want, and then by keeping a list of those unwanted characteristics, if they sort long enough, they will arrive at their desired destination of the "perfect mate." But the *Law of Attraction* does not allow that.

When the list of what you do not want in a mate is the dominant Vibration that you are offering regarding mating, the *Law of Attraction* will bring you a continuing string of unwanted partners. It is necessary to use your own self-discipline in directing your thoughts to the positive aspects of your current relationships before more of what you do want can come to you.

Over time, through your interaction with a variety of relationships, you have certainly identified many characteristics that you do not want in a partner. And each time your experience has helped you to identify what you do not want, you have been emitting a Vibrational request for what you prefer instead. As a result of all of those relationships, both those you have personally lived and even those that you have observed that others are living, you have created a Vibrational version of your "perfect mate." And if you could then give your undivided attention to *that* version, the *Law of Attraction* would bring to you only those who match that version. But if you continue to focus on the flaws or unwanted character-istics of those people, you will hold yourself apart from what you really want.

When we explain that the fastest way to get to the relationship you really want is by finding appreciation right where you stand (you may be in a temporary relationship, or you may be currently without any relationship), people often resist because they believe that if they say nice things about where they are, somehow they will get stuck right where they are. But that is not how it works.

When you look for, and find, positive aspects in your current situation, you are actually using your current situation as your reason to be a Vibrational Match to your own Vibrational Escrow, to *who-you-really-are,* to your *Inner Being,* and to everything you really desire. Feeling good about where you are is the fastest path to even greater improvement. But when you find fault with what is going on in your current life experience, the negative emotion you feel is your indication that your current thought and current Vibration is holding you apart from your own Vibrational Escrow, from *who-you-really-are,* from your *Inner Being,* and from everything you really desire.

The reason why "the grass always looks greener on the other side of the fence" is because many people have developed very strong tendencies toward complaining about what is on their "side of the fence."

But What about When Others Choose Our Mates for Us?

Jerry: I'd also like to hear your comments on the cultural as-pects of mating. There are many cultures where the parents, or the adults in the communities, choose the mates for their children; whereas, in our culture, we believe more in romantic love, where we fall in love with someone and choose our mates because we have fallen in love with them.

Abraham: Of course, it feels better to you, and therefore feels right to you, for you to be the one to choose your mate—or anything else, for that matter. But even in your culture or society, where you believe that you are freer to choose your mates, you are still very much bound by the beliefs of those who surround you. In other words, there are many within your freer-seeming culture who would not dare to marry outside of the wishes of their parents, religion, or culture. But we do agree that your society does allow more leeway than some others.

But there is an even more important thing we would like you to consider regarding the "choosing" of a mate. You are not making your choices with your words, but instead, with your Vibrational offering. And so, sometimes, without realizing it, you are actually "choosing" the exact opposite of what you really want. For example, people "choose" cancer—not because they want to experience the disease of cancer, but because they "choose" to give their attention to resistant thoughts that disallow the Well-Being that would be there otherwise. And so, in a similar way, people choose unpleasant partners because of their chronic attention to what they *do not* want, or their chronic attention to the absence of what they *do* want. In other words, a person who often feels lonely is a person "choosing" the absence of something very much wanted.

Finding, Evoking, or Being the Perfect Mate

Jerry: So how would you recommend that someone find the "perfect mate"?

Abraham: In order to *find* what you are calling the "perfect mate," you must first *be* the perfect mate. In other words, you must consistently emit a Vibrational signal that matches the mate you desire. The not-so-perfect relationships that you have observed, or lived, have given you wonderful opportunities to decide and fine-tune the kind of relationship you would like to have. And so, you have only to think about those *wanted* characteristics of a relationship in order to train your own Vibration into one that matches your desire.

When you point out what you do not like in relationships, or remember unpleasant events from past relationships, or even watch movies where people are mistreating one another, you are unwittingly training your Vibration away from your *desired* relationship. And you simply cannot get there from there.

You cannot get the relationship of your dreams when your chronic thoughts about relationships feel lonely or angry or worried or disappointed. But as you look for things you appreciate in yourself and others—as you make lists of positive aspects of past and present relationships—you train your Vibrational offering to match the Vibration of your desires, and your "perfect mate" must then come. It is <u>Law.</u>

Wanting a Mate, or *Needing* a Mate

[The following are examples of audience members' questions at an Abraham-Hicks workshop.]

Questioner: So it seems like my wanting someone pushes them away, but my not wanting them brings them to me. Why does that happen?

Abraham: When you *want* someone but the dominant thought within you is about the *lack* of that person—then your most active Vibration holds him or her away from you. When you do not want someone, but the dominant thought within you is about this unwanted person pursuing you—then he or she is drawn closer to you, by you. . . . *You are getting the essence of what you are thinking about, whether you want it or not.*

Questioner: Is this similar to the distinction between *wanting* and *needing?*

Abraham: Yes, and that is a good way of thinking about this. When you *want* something and are thinking about how wonderful it will be to have it, your current emotion feels good because your current thought is a Vibrational Match to your true desire. But when you *want* something but are currently thinking about not having it, about the absence or lack of it, your current emotion feels bad because your current thought is a Vibrational mismatch to your true desire.

The difference between *wanting* and *needing* is not just speaking different words. A pure state of *desire* or *wanting* always feels good because you are a Vibrational Match to what is in your own Vibrational Reality. A state of *need* always feels bad because you are a Vibrational Match to the absence of your desire and are therefore a mismatch to your Vibrational Reality.

Is There a Way of Staying Positive Around "Lackful" Others?

Questioner: How can I remain positively focused when my mate is predominantly focused on lack and makes no effort to be positive? And it gets to me—it's hard not to also feel lack.

Abraham: We know that it is easier to feel good when you are seeing or hearing something that causes you to feel good, but it is extremely liberating to show yourself that you have the ability to feel good in any situation even when those close to you do not.

You will discover that it is far easier to learn to direct your own mind than to arrange, through action, the people with whom you spend your time. Even if there is only one person who is with you often whom you need to train, you could not train him or her sufficiently. And, of course, there are many more persons than one to whom you are having an emotional response. *When you do become adept at directing your thoughts to things that are pleasing, the unpleasing people (or unpleasing aspects of those people) will leave your experience. It is your attention to the unwanted that holds it in your experience.*

Many people disagree about that when they first hear it, because they believe that negative things are in their lives because someone else is putting them there: "My abusive husband asserts himself negatively into my experience." But we want you to understand that if you use your power of focus to withdraw your attention from the negativity or abuse, and put your attention upon positive aspects, instead—the abuse cannot remain in your experience. *It is empowering to discover that any and all negative aspects stay in your experience only because of your attention to, and therefore continuing invitation of, them.*

We acknowledge that holding positive thoughts in the midst of negative conditions is not easy. Especially in the beginning. The best time to begin to make the effort to direct your thoughts really is not when you are the middle of a negative situation. It will be easier for you to reach for better-feeling thoughts when you are alone: *Begin by trying to remember when you did easily feel good about this person. And if you cannot find that beginning place, then choose another topic altogether. The first thing that is necessary to break a negative trend and start it in a more positive direction is the acceptance that your thoughts do create the reality that you live. Next you must accept that you do have the power to direct your own thoughts. And then, what is required is a willingness to direct your thoughts in the direction of what feels better until that pattern is established within you.*

One of the most exciting things about beginning the process of deliberately focused thought is that the Law of Attraction *will bring you evidence of your improved thought immediately. And while old patterns may be hard to break, and you may slip back into those old patterns from time to time, the evidence of your effort will be undeniable to you.* And, before long—with much less effort than you spend trying to dodge negative conversations, or train another into better behavior—all of your relationships will improve.

A Brief Bedtime Exercise That Transforms Relationships

As you lie in your bed before sleeping, if you will think of good-feeling things from your past or present, or even speculate into your future, you will set the tone of the Vibration in which you will awaken in the morning. In the morning, when you first return to Consciousness, try to remember what you were thinking about in the evening, and make an effort to reestablish that positive trend of thought. This one small exercise will change the way everyone you meet responds to you in this new day. And as you do that—night after night, and then morning after morning—new patterns will emerge, and your relationships will transform.

What Am I Expecting from a Relationship?

You have the power to evoke from others the relationships that you desire. But you cannot get to a new-and-improved situation by giving your attention to the current situation. The Universe, and all physical and Non-Physical players in it, is responding to the Vibrations that you are offering; and there is no distinction made between the Vibrations that you offer as you *observe,* and the Vibrations that you offer as you *imagine.* . . . *If you will simply imagine your life as you want it to be, all cooperative components will be summoned. And even more important, all components that are summoned will cooperate. It is* Law.

You have the power to evoke from others a relationship that is in harmony with the freedom, and the growth, and the joy that you seek, because within each of the others are those probabilities. Within each of them is the probability of someone being very understanding—or not. Of someone being very pleasant—or not. Of someone being very open-minded—or not. Of someone being very positive—or negative. *The experience that you have with others is about what you evoke from them.*

Have you had the experience of behaving with someone in a way that you had not intended? It just sort of came out of you suddenly. That was you experiencing the power of influence from another's *expectation.* Have you noticed the personality of a child changing depending on which adult it is interacting with? Cooperative and pleasant with one person, and obstinate and cranky with another? You were witnessing the power of influence from another's *expectation.*

When you train yourself into steady alignment with your own Broader Perspective, you will tap into the Energy that creates worlds, and you will be pleased by the positive response that you receive from those around you. No longer blame others with whom you share relationships; and instead, acknowledge that you are the attractor of your experience. True freedom comes from that understanding.

As you tend to your relationship between you (in your physical focus) and the Broader Perspective of your *Inner Being,* as you train yourself into the good-feeling thoughts of your Source, as you come into alignment with *who-you-really-are,* as you learn to love yourself—the others with whom you interact will not be able to buck that current of Well-Being. They will either love you back—or they will gravitate out of your experience.

What Are the Desired Characteristics of a Perfect Mate?

Jerry: Is it possible for one person, the same mate, to continue to be our perfect mate even though we are growing and changing and evolving? I mean, there was a time in my life when I was an acrobat, and I had to be able to throw my partner high and catch her, and so she had to be under five feet tall and weigh under 98 pounds. And when I met Esther, many years later, none of that was relevant anymore. Other things attracted me to Esther. And so, she was the perfect mate at the time she came into my life. So it seems like monogamy, or being with one person forever, could be pretty challenging.

Abraham: As you are moving through the details of your life experience, you are continually generating new preferences from the details of your new, current experiences. That process never stops. Those rockets of desire are received and held by your *Inner Being,* in your Vibrational Reality. In other words, every new experience causes you to amend, in small and large ways, your new version of the life you desire; and your *Inner Being* never ceases to keep up with the new version.

As you, through the power of your focus, hold yourself predominantly in an attitude of feeling good, you stay up to speed with your own Vibrational Reality, and so it continues to unfold and present itself to you in natural and comfortable ways. In other words, you have a continuing feeling of *This is the next logical step* as you *allow* the perfect unfolding of your own life experience. And so, it is possible that a new partner is "the next logical step" for who you have become, but if that is the case, the releasing of one mate and the receiving of another would not be an uncomfortable or unpleasant situation.

It is a rather illogical and impossible standard that your culture seems to want to hold you to when you make the statement: "I will stay together with you, in sickness . . . [no matter the situation] until death do us part." A much better intention or vow would be: *"It is my dominant intent to focus my thoughts in a positive direction so that I maintain my Connection with the Source and the Love that is really who I am. And in doing so, I will always present the best of myself to you. It is my desire that you ask the same for yourself. And it is my expectation that as each of us works to maintain our individual alignment with <u>who-we-really-are,</u> our relationship with one another will be one of continual and joyful expansion."*

Do Nature's Laws Not Govern Our Mating?

Jerry: For much of my life I have been trying to determine what is the natural and right way for humans to approach relationships. I looked at the other beasts that roam the planet and have noticed that, for the most part, they are not much for monogamy. The elephant runs off all of the other male elephants, and the rooster will fight to the death any rooster that interferes with his flock of hens. I've wondered, *If humans were to behave more like the animals in regard to mating, would the human species become stronger and more powerful, like in "the survival of the fittest" with the animals?* From the perspective of the Non-Physical, is there a right and wrong approach to relationships? *So, my question is, what is natural?*

Abraham: There are enough natural forces at work to assure the sustaining of the human species: enough variation, enough diversity, enough balance. In the same way that your natural impulses to satisfy hunger and thirst assure your survival, your sexual impulses and mating impulses also assure your survival. *Our interest in the subject of human relationships is not because you need to adjust your behavior to ensure your survival, because the survival of your species is not in jeopardy. Our interest in human relationships is about your survival in joy.*

We have the benefit of being in full view of the Vibrational Escrows you have created from the contrasting experiences and relationships that you have lived, and it is our desire to help you find a way of achieving your own Vibrational alignment with those expanded creations so that you can live them, fully and joyously, now. *When something that you have lived has caused you to ask for an improved aspect, you must allow yourself the fullness of that desire or your joy is diminished. In simple terms, you have to keep up with what life has caused you to become or you cannot feel joy.*

These are the most correct, truthful, accurate, *natural* things that we know about you as you are expressing through your physical form:

- You are extensions of Source Energy.

- You are physically focused for the purpose of experiencing contrast.

- You are choosing to experience contrast for the purpose of new ideas and decisions about life.

- Those new ideas and decisions about life equal the expansion of the Universe.

- The expansion of the Universe is the inevitable consequence of life.

- When your physical life causes the Non-Physical part of you to expand, you must go with the expansion if you are to experience joy.

- Joy is the most natural tenet of that which you and we are.

- Relationships are the basis of your contrast.

- Therefore, relationships are the basis of all expansion.

- Therefore, relationships are the basis of your joy.

- If you do not find the thoughts that allow the joy, you are holding yourself back from *who-you-have-become.*

- Your relationships are your reason for your expansion.

- Your relationships are often your reason for disallowing your expansion.

- It is natural to be in a state of joy.

- It is natural to be in a state of growth.

- It is natural to be in a state of freedom.

- These are the most important things for you to understand about relationships.

What Is Natural for Mating Humans?

Jerry: But which is more natural, having one mate or several? Should men have more than one wife at a time, or should women have more than one husband at a time? Even today, our cultures disagree about these things.

Abraham: Your question points directly at another very large, very flawed premise:

Flawed Premise #13: There are right ways and wrong ways to live. And all people should discover and agree on what the right way of living is, and then that right way should be enforced.

This flawed belief that there is only one right decision about any topic is at the heart of tremendous discord and upheaval. It is fortunate that you have no way of enforcing this flawed concept, for if you could, it would surely lead to the end of Beingness. In other words, since all expansion is born from the new intentions and ideas that are born from the contrast—elimination of the contrast would stop the expansion.

Do not worry, for that will never be the case, for the perfect balance of diversity has been very well established and flows with the *Laws of the Universe*. We are not discussing these things with you to preserve mankind or Eternity, because none of that is in jeopardy. We do discuss it with you, however, because your *joyful* survival is predicated upon your understanding of these things.

When your life causes you to radiate a request into your Vibrational Escrow, your Emotional Guidance System will help you find Vibrational alignment with it. And finding that alignment is necessary to your joyful fulfillment and expansion. And no laws that are apart from that have any bearing on you.

The majority of the laws that surround you, both religious and secular, were written by those not in alignment with the Broader Perspective of Source. Your laws are usually written from the perspective of what is *not* wanted. And so, many people spend a tremendous amount of time in argument about which laws are right and which laws are wrong, and, in doing so, hold themselves apart from their expanded perspectives. And then they use the negative emotion that they feel (which exists because of their separation from Source) as their justification for their arguments.

When you no longer seek the final word on the rightness of your behaviors and instead seek alignment with the Source within you by finding thoughts, words, and deeds that fill you with love while you participate, you will understand that it is possible to live upon this planet with large numbers of other Beings—who believe and behave in a variety of ways—in peace.

When you are able to focus in such a way as to allow your alignment with Source, even though others are choosing to behave differently than you are choosing, then you will truly be free from the bondage of attempting the impossible task of getting everyone to agree on one right way. One right way would lead to endedness. Many right ways allow Eternal expansion.

The reason why people believe that they need laws to control others around them is that they believe that the behavior of others can negatively impact them. But when you come to understand that nothing can come into your experience unless you invite it through thought, then you understand that you can release the impossible task of trying to control the behavior of others and replace it with the much simpler task of controlling the direction of your own thoughts.

We have come to remind you about the *Art of Allowing:* the *Art of Allowing* your Vibrational alignment with all that you have come to be and to desire. There is enough room in this very large, very diverse physical world for all that you are wanting. And every awful or abhorrent thing that you see exists only because someone is *disallowing* the Well-Being that would be there otherwise. The *Law of Attraction* is the *Law* that manages all things that are Vibrational. (And all things are Vibration.) You do not have to work at that *Law*—it just is. If you will put your attention toward understanding and applying the *Art of Allowing,* you will live in joy regardless of what others are doing. Just remember, during the time you are giving your attention to those who are not joyful, you are not practicing the *Art of Allowing.*

Will Feeling Good Always Attract Good-Feelers?

Questioner: Is it a good idea for me to look for a mate who makes me feel good about myself?

Abraham: Of course. When others hold you as their object of attention and feel appreciation at the same time, it would feel very good to you, because they are in alignment with their own Source and are flooding that aligned Energy in your direction. That always feels good to both the flow-er of the appreciation and the recipient of the appreciation. But do not let your feeling good be dependent upon someone's positive attention shining on you. Show yourself that you can connect to the Non-Physical Stream whether you are being held in someone's positive flow or not. You have your own Connection, and when you practice it often, you will always be able to maintain your balance; whereas, if you wait for another to be in alignment and focused upon you, then your good feeling is dependent upon what someone else does, and that person may not always be in alignment, or you may not always be his or her only point of focus.

The reason why most relationships are much better feeling when they are new is because in the beginning, both partners are more inclined to look for the positive aspects in one another. Since your relationship is new, you are not yet aware of one another's flaws, but as time goes on, it is common to begin seeing more flaws and to be making less effort to be optimistic in your expectation.

When you are dependent upon no other for your Connection to Source, you will discover true freedom—freedom from the only thing that can ever bind you: resistance to *who-you-really-are.*

Couldn't Anyone Become My Perfect Mate?

Jerry: If there were only two people on the earth, no matter who that other person was, couldn't we create out of that what we want? Couldn't we find within that one person, the perfect mate?

Abraham: First you must understand that if there were only two people on the earth, the experiences of contrast that you would have lived would be so limited that your desires would not be very evolved. However, under those limited conditions, your desire would also be limited, and so you would very likely be rather happy with that limited Being. But that is not the point you are getting at with your implausible hypothesis. Your point is, "If there is that which is wanted and that which is unwanted in every particle of the Universe, then can I not find *wanted* in *all* things? And if I focus upon wanted, won't the *Law of Attraction* bring me more wanted?" And the answer to that is *yes.*

Looking for positive aspects wherever you are always leads to an improved future. So even if you were enduring a mostly terrible relationship, out of that contrast would be born desires for improvement, which the Source within you would be holding as the object of its undivided attention. By deliberately focusing upon any small positive aspect you can find, you would then *allow* your alignment with the greater desires that had been born out of the contrast. And a consistent offering of that positive Vibration would deliver to you the physically manifested version. And, if (in your extreme hypothesis) there were only one other person on the planet, that desire would then have to be satisfied from that one person. Fortunately, you have a much larger, more cooperative playing field to draw from.

Questioner: When asked about what a perfect mate would be, someone whom I consider to be very wise said, "A perfect mate is someone who brings out the best in you, and also brings out the worst in you." What do you think about that?

Abraham: This person would be a bit like the contrasting world in general. In other words, whenever you know what you do not want, you always know more clearly what you do want. So he definitely would be helping you with the *Step One* part of the equation: *the asking.* Your success at making this a successful, and therefore happy, relationship would depend upon your ability to then focus upon the desire that this rascal helped you to launch. If your mate is evoking a steady stream of *I know what I don't want* awareness, and so you are launching steady rockets of desire about what you *do* want—and if you are then able to focus predominantly on what you *do* want—then, in your aligned state, your power of influence would be strong, and he would stop the negative prodding. But if his negative prodding was strong enough to stand in the face of your continuing *Allowing* state, then he could not remain in your experience. The *Law of Attraction* would put you in different places.

☙ ❧ ☙ ❧

PART III

Sexuality, and the *Law of Attraction:* Sexuality, Sensuality, and the Opinions of Others

The Topics Are Sex, Sexuality, and Sensuality

Jerry: Sex, or sexuality, seems to be a sensitive topic in that it evokes guardedness and strong opinions from many who contemplate it. My first experience with anything remotely related to sexuality turned out very badly when a little girl and I were playing in a wooden box when we were about two years old. We got caught with our panties off, and we were both severely punished.

Also, as a child, I remember hearing my mother arguing with my father about sex. She told him that she had her three children, she was not interested in having sex with him, and he should find some other woman if it was important to him. Then later, I remember, as still very young children, the little boys and girls I knew and I were all having different sorts of sexual experiences with one another, but by the time I reached the age of actual sexual maturity, I guess because of the powerful stigma around the topic of sex, my concerns and fears and inhibitions were so strong that I would do just about anything to avoid the topic. It was a long time, for me, before my sexual barriers went down or were resolved and I was able to move into happy sexual experiences.

I would like to hear your perspective about the sexual aspects of physical human Beings to, perhaps, clarify the subject and leave people feeling better about it.

Abraham: As children, you are often met with adults who have lost Connection with their own sense of value, of Well-Being, and of worthiness; and from that lackful, disconnected state, they pass their guardedness on to you.

Over time, humans evaluate the subject of sexuality endlessly, passing new laws; amending old laws; struggling futilely to come to agreement with others about the correct attitude and approach to the subject and, even more futilely, to enforce the laws they create from their lackful positions. Your rules or laws about sexuality diverge from culture to culture, generation to generation, society to society, and religion to religion, but in nearly every case, your laws about this and every other subject tend to hinge on the economic impact of the time. And, most important, your sexual laws and rules, like all laws and rules, are made by those who are out of alignment with their Broader Perspective.

If humans were to understand that you are all Vibrational Beings and that the *Law of Attraction* is bringing to each of you only what you are a Vibrational Match to, you would not be so concerned about the behavior of others, for you would not fear their behavior negatively impacting you. But in your ignorance about how you *do* attract what comes, and in your fear that unwanted things *will* come, you make decisions and laws and rules that are not only impossible to enforce, but that foster even more of the behavior you seek to eliminate. *It is always true that the harder you push against what you do not want—the more of what you do not want comes into your experience.*

By far, the largest amount of pushing against the subject of sexuality comes from people of various religious groups who believe that *God* has spoken to humans and has given specific instructions regarding the topic. The inconsistency of the message man believes he has received accentuates the impossibility of receiving answers from the pure love of Source when the receiver is standing in a place of blame or guardedness. The very idea that "what I have received is correct, and what you or others have received is wrong" holds you in the place of resistance to the very Source from which you claim to have received it. Which leads us to the most important flawed premise of all:

Flawed Premise #14: *There is a God Who, having considered all things, has come to a final and correct conclusion about everything.*

This belief, or flawed premise, is at the root of man's continual assault on humanity. It is at the basis of your wars, your prejudices, your hatred, and your feelings of unworthiness; and it is your primary reason for disallowing your own Well-Being. This flawed premise is so important, and the ramifications of it are so immense, that we could write an entire book speaking only about man's distorted view of himself, of others, and of that which he calls *God*. This inaccurate conclusion—that Source (no matter what name you want to give it) is no longer expanding but instead stands at a place of completion, or perfection, demanding your physical compliance with its narrow rules—not only defies the *Laws of the Universe*, but then requires another flawed premise, and then another and another, to try to prop it up. From *outside* the Vibration of the love of his Source, man stands guarded and blameful and guilty and fearful, and then assigns those same lackful characteristics to that which he calls *God*.

Humanity continues to argue about the laws passed down from God as it bends and twists them to suit individual economic desires or needs. Often humans are informed by their religious leaders of the value, or necessity, of keeping these rules. You are told that the keeping of some rules will bring blessings, while the breaking of others will bring punishment; but when you notice that those who are breaking the laws seem to be thriving while those who strive to keep them most are often suffering greatly, you are told one of the greatest flawed premises of all:

Flawed Premise #15: *You cannot know,*
while you are still in your physical body, the true
reward or punishment for your physical actions. Your reward
or punishment will be shown to you after your physical death.

The loving *Laws* that support *All-That-Exists* are *Laws* that are Universal and therefore always apply. And alignment with them is evident in every moment of alignment, just as misalignment with them is evident in every moment. What feels like love, *is*—and what feels like hate is not love.

There are many who want to live in the appropriate way, but sorting out proper behavior from the enormous lists of diversity leaves most people uncertain of the rightness of their path. Which leads to yet another flawed premise:

Flawed Premise #16: By gathering data about the manifestations or results of the way the people of the earth have lived and are living, we can effectively sort them into absolute piles of right and wrong. And once those determinations have been made, we then have only to enforce those conclusions. And once we get everyone to agree with our determinations—and, more important, once we get them to comply with them—we will then have harmony on Earth.

And so, more people die every day in the struggle to defend, or prove, which way of life is the correct way, with each group claiming to have the absolute approval and support of God. And, in not one bit of any of that is any true Connection to God.

You did not come into this physical body with the intention of taking all of the ideas that exist and whittling them down to a handful of agreed-upon ideas. In fact, that is the very opposite of your prebirth intention. Instead, you knew that you would be coming into an environment of extreme variety, and that from that platform of difference and choices would be born more new-and-improved ideas. You understood that the Eternal nature of that which humans call *God* would be enhanced by your participation. You knew that this platform of enormous contrast would be the foundation of the Eternal expansion that exists within that which humans call Eternity. *There is no ending to the expansion of God, and physical humans' participation cannot be separated from that expansion.*

The most destructive part of humans' confusion about their Connection with God or Source is that in their need to find and defend their values, they must push against the values of others. And the very nature of focusing upon and pushing against unwanted aspects of others prevents their alignment with the very *goodness* and *Source* that they seek. And then they blame the differences in others for the emptiness they feel. Which leads us to another flawed premise:

Flawed Premise #17: Only very special people, like the founder of <u>our</u> group, can receive the right message from God. And all other messages from all other messengers are therefore incorrect.

It is interesting that in the midst of a conversation about sexuality, we would not only uncover one of the biggest flawed premises of all, but that the subject of sexuality is also the avenue through which the existence of humans hinges. A basic feeling of unworthiness, due to the lack of Connection with *Source,* is at the root of the confusion around the subject of sexuality.

It is a rare human who has found what he believes to be the appropriate way to behave, who has then also mustered the self-discipline to behave that way, because the natural instincts that are inspired from a much Broader knowing run counter to the restricted behavior assigned by human Beings.

Are Our Sexual Laws Decreed
by Non-Physical Dimensions?

Jerry: So what is *natural* for me? I remember, as years went by, that I always wanted to understand not only what is *natural,* but what might go against the higher laws. For instance, as I observed or read about cultures around the world, it seemed like every one, no matter how primitive or how supposedly advanced, had taboos and rules—which controlled the newer people coming in—regarding sex. And so, I wondered if we bring any of that from our higher knowing or from our *Inner Beings.*

Abraham: No taboos or rules are coming from your *Inner Being* or from your higher knowing or from Non-Physical, but instead, they are the product of your physical vulnerability. Without exception, every law—religious or secular—comes from a perspective of lack, from a position of trying to protect or guard someone from something. If you were really paying attention to what is happening regarding these laws, you would realize that the laws do not deter the lawbreakers. They only hinder those who would not break the laws anyway, restrict freedom, and add confusion to the lives of those who seek approval from others through conformity.

Can you hear the birds? [Abraham is commenting on sounds of nature that are audible from inside the house.] That is a very *sexual* call. A moment ago, the rooster was crowing so loudly that you considered not continuing with the recording. In other words, your world is filled with Beings who are all receiving direction from Non-Physical. And yet, it is only the humans who are guarded and resistant regarding the subject of sexuality; it is only the humans who are coming from this extreme place of lack regarding the subject of sexuality. And, from your perspective of lack, from your concern that you may be doing something wrong, from your concern that has been fostered within you from those who have gone before, you are, most of you, in a place of great confusion and not very much joy.

Sexuality Is Guided by Impulses, Not Laws

Jerry: Okay. So there are no rules from the Non-Physical dimension telling us how to behave sexually here in physical form, and so when we are born into our physical bodies, we didn't come knowing any rules because we weren't sent with them. Is that why children are so unguarded and behave in ways that adults see as too loose or too careless? And is that why adults then feel a need to rein them in or control them?

Abraham: You were not born into your physical body holding the memory of lists of right and wrong because those lists do not exist, but you were born with an effective *Guidance System. The emotions that you feel, without exception, are indicators of the Vibrational alignment—or variance—between the thought your human* *brain is focused upon and the perspective of your Broader Non-Physical Perspective regarding the same subject.*

Since the Source within you is Eternally expanding, your understanding, perspective, intentions, and the knowledge of that part of you is Eternally expanding as well. That is the reason there cannot be a static list of right and wrong or good and evil for you to measure your experience against. Instead, you have personal, individual, loving, accurate feedback, thought by thought, moment by moment, to help you know when you are in alignment with that Broader Perspective or when you are not. *There is not only one guidance list handed down from Source for all, but individual Guidance for all physical Beings, in all points in time and space, and regarding all situations.*

If, in your desire to socialize the new arrivals into your society, you are unaware of your own *Guidance System,* and therefore unaware of theirs, then you embark upon the impossible task of determining which actions are the right actions. You also have the even more impossible task of enforcing those decisions.

The reason why so many people feel a need to control the behavior of others is because they believe that others have the power to assert themselves into their experience. When you remember that nothing can come into your experience without your Vibrational invitation of it, then you do the simple work of paying attention to your own Vibrational offering, and you save yourself the enormous and impossible task of controlling the behavior of others. *When you remember that the varied behavior of others adds to the balance and the Well-Being of your planet even if they offer behavior that you do not approve of; and that you do not have to participate in the unwanted behavior, and will not—unless you give your attention to it—you become more willing to allow others to live as they choose.*

The need to control others always stems from a basic misunderstanding of the *Laws of the Universe* and of the role that you have intended to play with others with whom you share your planet. But there is another very big flawed premise that arises here:

Flawed Premise #18: *By ferreting out the undesirable elements in our society, we can eliminate them. And in their absence, we will be freer.*

True freedom is the absence of resistance; true freedom is the presence of alignment—true freedom is the way you feel when you are no longer disallowing your complete alignment, or blending, with the Broader Non-Physical part of you. Therefore, it is not possible to be in the act of pushing against something unwanted and be blended with *who-you-really-are* and what you want at the same time. *You cannot be in the state of pushing against what you <u>do not</u> want and be in harmony with what you <u>do</u> want at the same time. And so, you will never get to a better-feeling state by trying to control others, no matter how well-meaning you believe your motives to be.*

You did not come knowing rules of correct behavior, but you certainly came feeling impulses. In other words, just as you have the impulse to drink when you are thirsty in order to keep your body replenished or to eat when you are hungry to keep your body fueled, so the sensation, or the urging, of sexuality comes forth naturally for the perpetuation of the species upon your planet.

What If Humans Behaved, Sexually, Like the Wild Animals?

Jerry: So, getting back to the animals, who do seem to behave from their Non-Physical Guidance or *instinct,* as we have come to call it . . . our rooster and his hens have no written laws, or rules, that they are conforming to; it's just what comes from within them. And so, if we could be born into this planet and start fresh like that, without rules, it seems like we, too, should be able to operate from our *Inner Being* without the need of outside restrictions. But, instead, we are born into societies and cultures that already have rules and controls that they insist we conform to.

Abraham: What we most want you to understand is that, as humans, you, too, do have Guidance that is coming forth from within. And your Guidance, your innate knowing, your sense of self—indeed, the Eternal nature of *who-you-are*—is what is dominant within you. And while you do believe that you are hindered by the controls set forth by other humans, we want you to know that this control is not as large or as hindering as you believe, because your innate Non-Physical impulses are even stronger.

Even though your societies have imposed endless rules or laws regarding your sexual behavior, many more of you break those rules—and always have broken those rules—than keep them. That is because your Non-Physical impulses are so strong. If your government, or some controlling agency, were to tell you that you were no longer allowed to eat food—your natural impulses of survival would prevail, and you would find a way to eat.

You and your world do not need this book in order to free your behavior from the binding laws and rules and misunderstandings about sexuality, because your natural impulses are so strong that you really are not behaving as if you feel bound by them. In other words, your natural instincts and impulses are so strong that they do lead your behavior. But then you suffer emotional discord as you then measure your behavior against those unrealistic rules that have been created from your place of attempting to control behaviors. In other words, you behave naturally, but then you feel bad about it.

Your societies will never find the happiness they seek—or know the deliciousness of true freedom—as long as they believe in controlling the behavior of one another. It is the control of your thought, and the alignment with your Broader Perspective, that you are really seeking.

What about When Society Disapproves of Sexual Individuality?

Jerry: So what if you feel good when you think about a specific action, but when you consider what others think about your action, you don't feel good? Then what would you suggest?

Abraham: We would say that now you are off track because you are attempting to guide your actions by the opinions of others outside of you, when the only guidance that counts is the Guidance that you feel as your thought, in the moment, harmonizes—or does not harmonize—with the Broader Perspective of your Source.

No other human really knows the intentions you held as you came forth from Non-Physical. They have not walked in your shoes through the thousands of interactions you have experienced, and they were not a part of the rockets of desire that you have launched as you have lived your life. They are not privy to the Vibrational Reality that you have created through the living of life, and they cannot feel the harmony or discord—the allowing or resisting—that you feel through your own emotions.

Your question is an important one because through it you are trying to understand which of your emotions to trust or follow: the good-feeling emotion that came in response to your personal thoughts about your personal experience, or the bad-feeling emotion that came in response to your awareness of the disapproval of another.

Nothing could be more important than coming to recognize the existence of your *Emotional Guidance System* and how it works, for without it you have no consistent guidance. The emotions you feel, in any moment, are pointing out to you the agreement or disagreement between you and your Source regarding the thought that is active in you at the moment of the emotion. If you can understand that through life, before you entered this body and since, your *Inner Being* has become the Vibrational summation of all that you have lived and now stands as the Vibrational equivalent to all that is good—and if you can then understand that your emotions are giving you feedback about how your current thought blends with that all-knowing, Pure, Positive Energy viewpoint of Source—then and only then can you fully appreciate your emotions.

So when you feel negative emotion, it always means that your currently active thought is out of alignment with the knowledge of Source. In other words, when you find fault with yourself, when you decide that you are inappropriate or unworthy, you will always feel negative emotion—because the Source within you only feels love toward you. When you disapprove of others, you will always feel negative emotion—because the Source within you only loves others. If you will remember that whenever you feel negative emotion, it always means you are in disagreement with Source, then you can deliberately reframe your thoughts until you come into alignment. That is the way to effectively utilize your *Guidance System.*

When people replace this very personal Guidance by attempting to modify their behavior to please other people, they very soon discover the inconsistency of that guidance and soon find themselves confused about what to do. Many people have lost conscious Connection with their own *Guidance Systems,* and so instead of deliberately focusing their thoughts into harmony and alignment with their Source and their power—instead of making sure that they are steadily tuned to the Vibration of their clarity and love and power— they turn their attention to the results of what they and the people around them have been thinking. In other words, they examine and catalog and pigeonhole and evaluate and judge the results of the Vibrational creating that is happening around them, putting those results into categories of *good* and *bad, right* and *wrong.* And in all of that data, they lose their way.

There are so many differing opinions and so many extenuating circumstances and so many motives that make it impossible to sort out the rightness or wrongness of interpersonal behavior in your societies. And even when you come to, more or less, general consensus of what you agree upon as a society as the appropriate ways to live, you have no way of convincing all others of the rightness of your opinion. And even when you come together and pronounce laws against "inappropriate" behavior, you have no way of enforcing those laws. . . . *While your societies continue to try to dictate and enforce human behavior to please the majority—because of your diversity, it continues to be an uncomfortable struggle that, again and again, falls of its economic weight. There simply is not enough money in the world to buck the natural currents of individual freedom and independence of thought.*

When people have forgotten that this is an inclusion-based Universe, and that the *Law of Attraction* is the manager who is arranging every detail of every rendezvous that occurs, they fear something that can never be: *they fear that unwanted things can assert themselves into their experience.* But when you remember that nothing uninvited ever comes into your experience, and that every invitation of both wanted and unwanted comes because you have given considerable thought to the essence of it, then you can begin to utilize your own powerful *Emotional Guidance System* with the assurance that you *do* create your own reality.

If people would simply pay attention to the harmony or disharmony within themselves—which is offered to them in the form of positive or negative emotion—they would be able to eliminate the arduous and impossible task of trying to control the behavior of others.

By deliberately focusing your thoughts in the direction of your Broader understanding, and no longer wasting time and money on things you cannot control, you will not only come into alignment with Source and feel the relief of that in your emotions—but all things wanted can then come to you.

So getting back to your powerful question . . . your thought about a behavior or action that brought you pleasure—regardless of the opinions of others who stand upon their endless opinions and rules and disapproving platforms—is a thought that the Source within you agrees with. And your thought of your own inappropriateness that made you feel bad, because of your assumed disapproval of others (whether real or imagined) is a thought that the Source within you does not agree with.

To sort out all of the behaviors of your societies, past and present; to sort out all of the opinions of people around your world; to review all of the laws; to understand how the laws came about; to evaluate the evolution of the laws; to try to live up to all of them, or enforce them . . . is confusing and overwhelming and impossible.

To know if <u>Source, Infinite Intelligence, Inner Being, God</u> agrees or disagrees with the thought, word, or action you are involved in—you have only to notice if it feels good or bad.

To find your peace regarding anything, it is necessary for you to set aside your desire to find approval from others and to seek approval from self. And you do that by starting from the inside out—by acknowledging that you want to feel good, and that you want to have a life experience that is in harmony with what is good. And if you start there, it is our absolute promise to you that you will never find yourself in a situation where the action that you are experiencing, or even contemplating, will put you in a position of feeling that you have betrayed your greater sense of right and wrong.

Who Gets to Set Humans' Sexual Hierarchy?

Jerry: It seems to me, as I have evaluated sexuality within our culture, that we have what might be called the high priest, who *doesn't* engage in sex; then there are the common folks, who *do* engage in sex (but only for the purpose of creating children); and then, on the lower end of the hierarchy, there would be those who would engage in sex for pleasure. But it seems to me that we all have some of all of that—

Abraham: We have to interrupt you here because all of those ideas come from a perspective of lack, from humans believing in their unworthiness.

Your physical life experience is a life of sensuality. You come forth into this physical realm with the sensual eyes with which to see, the sensual ears with which to hear, the sensual nose with which to smell, the sensual skin with which to feel, and the sensual tongue with which to taste. This Leading Edge time-space reality is about the intricate Vibrational interpretations that your physical senses provide, and all of that is for the enhancement of your physical experience.

If you will pay attention to your emotions, they will help you find the appropriateness of your behavior, and you will come to understand the worthiness that is at the core of you. It is not necessary, or even possible, to pinpoint the turning point when humans stopped believing in their value and worthiness. It has been a gradual erosion caused by the disallowance of Connection with Source because of the comparison of human experience in search of the one "right" answer or the one "right" behavior. And now, a feeling of unworthiness runs rampant on your planet, and much of human thought is directed toward lack, which only promotes more disallowance of alignment with Source and with love and with Well-Being.

You are here in your physical bodies as extensions of Source Energy, experiencing specific contrast and coming to specific new decisions about the goodness of life, and every time your experience poses a question to you—an equivalent answer is born in the experience of Source. Every time your experience poses a problem to you—an equivalent solution is born in the experience of Source. And so, because of your willingness to live and explore and experience contrast, you are giving birth to constant new rockets of desire—and *All-That-Is* expands because of what you are living.

When it becomes your dominant intention to find good-feeling thoughts, then you become one who is most often a Vibrational Match to the Source within you, and the good feeling that will then be usually present within you is your indication that you are fulfilling your reason for being and that you are continuing to keep up with the expansion of your own Being.

Every experience causes you to expand, and your positive emotion is your indication that you are keeping up with that new expansion. Negative emotion is your indication that the greater part of you has moved to an expanded place—but you are holding back. And so, by paying attention to the way you feel, and by continually reaching for the best-feeling thoughts you can find, you will establish a rhythm of alignment that will help you immediately realize when you are straying from the goodness that you have become.

It is our absolute promise to you that you will never be able to take action that is contrary to the joyful, loving, God-Source Being within you without feeling very strong negative emotion. . . . There are many people who are completely out of alignment with the Source within them, who stand in condemnation of others while asserting their claim on righteousness. But the anger that burns within them is evidence of their disallowance of the very rightness they are making claim to. *Anger and hatred and condemnation are not symbols of alignment with God—but indicators of misalignment with that which you call God.*

Some would say, "Then the feeling of guilt that I have must mean that I am doing something evil or wrong." But we want you to understand that your negative emotion simply means that the thought that is vibrating within you does not match the Vibration of your Source. Source continues to love you. When *you* do not love you, you feel the discord.

If we were standing in your physical shoes and we were contemplating an action that caused negative emotion, we would not proceed with the action until we had resolved the negative emotion. We would make sure that we had come into alignment with Source before proceeding. *By feeling for the improved thought, in time, and usually in a short time, you will feel the harmony of your Source; and you will know the appropriateness of your behavior. We would not look for the long lists of right and wrong, but instead, we would feel for the emotion of alignment with Source.*

Negative emotion does not mean that you are not good. It means that your currently active thought does not harmonize with the currently active thoughts of Source on the same subject. If you have come to believe that sexual interaction is wrong and you are about to engage in sexual interaction, your negative emotion is not confirming that sexual interaction is wrong. It is confirming that your opinion of your behavior and of yourself in this moment does not harmonize with how Source feels about you. Stop and reach for loving, approving thoughts about yourself and feel the discord disappear.

Usually, by the time you have spent 50 or 60 or 70 years in your body, you come to the very clear awareness that you cannot please them all. In fact, you usually understand that you cannot please very many of them, because each of them wants something different from you. Attempting to guide yourself through the approval of others is futile and painful. But you may trust your inner Guidance. In fact, it is really the only thing that you *can* trust, because it holds the complete understanding of *who-you-really-are, who-you-have-become,* and where you stand in Vibrational relationship with that expanded Being.

When you understand your relationship with the Source within you and you are aware of your own *Emotional Guidance System*—which continually indicates your Vibrational relationship with Source—it will not be possible for you to stray from the wholeness and goodness and the worthiness that is you.

How Can We Coordinate Our Sexual Co-creations?

Jerry: It seems to me that humans have, within them, an innate urge to procreate, as well as an innate desire to enjoy sensuality. And I believe we also have an innate desire to create through thought, but the subject of sexuality really points to the idea of co-creation, where the desires and beliefs and intentions of two people are now involved. How can two different people who are moving through time and experiences continue to co-create in harmony? How can I coordinate my desires with the desires of my mate, since both of us are changing?

Abraham: As we discussed in the last question, it is important that your desire for harmony with your mate not become a desire to seek approval from that person. There is no more destructive force to relationships than the feeling of the loss of freedom in the effort to find agreement. Which leads us to another flawed premise:

*Flawed Premise #19: A good relationship is
one in which the dominant intention of each person
involved is to find agreement and harmony with the other.*

How could two people looking to find harmony with each other possibly be the wrong basis for a good relationship and a happy life? Both people have created their own Vibrational Escrow (Vibrational Reality) to which they must seek harmony if they are to be happy. When finding harmony with your mate takes precedence over finding harmony with your Inner Self, there is a strong probability that discord between you and Source will occur. That feeling of discord is then translated as a feeling of loss of freedom; and then your partner, with whom you truly want to find harmony, begins to feel less good. Your loss of connection to your own Source feels off to you, and *is* off, and so then (without wanting to) you begin to resent the partner whom you are trying to please. In short, there is no substitution for alignment with Source.

Again, you are looking for love in all the wrong places. We are not suggesting that you should not want to get along well with your mate. But we are strongly suggesting the powerful benefit of seeking, first, alignment with Source. *When you find alignment with the Source within you, you also find alignment with your furthermost expansion. And when you are in alignment with who-you-really-are and all that you have become, you are then automatically in harmony with the best of your relationship with your partner.*

Couples, or anyone involved in co-creating of any kind, who attempt harmony by trying first to please each other always discover the flaw in that premise. *If you are not selfish enough to seek and find harmony with your Source, you have nothing to give your partner anyway.*

If you see it as your job to keep your partner happy, and so you work hard and behave in ways that please your mate, you are actually setting your mate up for ultimate unhappiness because you are training that person to look to you and your behavior in order to feel good rather than seeking personal alignment with Source. And no matter how good you are at pleasing, and no matter how hard you try, you do not make a good substitute for your partner's alignment with Source.

The message that you want to convey to the others with whom you are co-creating is this: "I will never hold you responsible for the way I feel. I have the power to focus myself into alignment with my Source, and therefore I have the power to keep myself feeling good." If that is your true intention, then you have discovered the path, the *only* path, to true freedom and true happiness. But if your happiness is dependent upon the intentions or beliefs or behaviors of any other, you are trapped, for you cannot control any of that.

Fear of Sex Spoils the Pleasure of Being Touched

Jerry: Abraham, I would like to read to you some questions that people have asked you. These are real-life examples that are happening with people, and I'd like to hear your responses relative to the *Laws* and processes that you've been teaching us.

A young woman says: "My mother and I are both uncomfortable with sex. We don't like hearing about it, reading about it, seeing it on television, or participating in it. I guess, as a result of my mother's strong negative feelings about sex, I now have fear anytime my mate even touches me that it might turn to having sex. I want a good marriage, but how can I enjoy the sensual part, or the touching part, without this fear that it will push on into the sexual part?"

Abraham: Most anyone reading or hearing the perspective of this woman would have a strong reaction to her words. Some would feel sorry for her husband to have a wife who is so repulsed by the idea of sexual interaction, while others would identify with her feeling about it. If this woman is married to someone who feels differently about the sexual experience than she does, then one of them will always be uncomfortable regarding the subject.

The most important thing that we want you to understand (and it is usually the most difficult thing for most people to understand) is that this conversation, and ultimately this solution, is not about the *action* of sexuality, for there is no rule about right and wrong sexual behavior. A strong pattern of negative emotion attached to a specific subject means that the thoughts you have chronically activated about that subject strongly disagree with the perspective of your Source.

For example, if, as a young girl (age is irrelevant, but these things usually begin when you are very young), you felt strong disapproval projected toward you in response to your words or behavior regarding the subject, you most likely have concluded that you were inappropriate to be offering those words or that behavior, or even those thoughts. You called the empty feeling *guilt,* and you accepted it as evidence of your wrongdoing or wrong speaking or wrong thinking. But the guidance that your *Emotional Guidance System* was offering was very different from that: Your feeling of guilt was, instead, a simple indicator that your conclusion about your inappropriateness was a very different opinion from the Source within you. In other words, you were condemning you—and your Source was not.

There is nothing that you innately want more than to recognize your own value and goodness, and when you harbor chronic thoughts that disallow that, you feel bad. If you have decided that a particular behavior is wrong—you will always feel worse if you perform it. If you have decided that a particular behavior is good—you will always feel better if you perform it. But your life becomes very complicated as you try to sort that out through putting behaviors in categories of *right* and *wrong,* of *good* or *bad.*

For example, if you believe that a good wife is one who tries to cooperate with her husband, you would feel bad by not yielding to his sexual desires. If you believe that sexual interaction is wrong, then yielding to your husband's sexual desires would also feel bad, so whether you say *yes* or *no* to his request, you feel bad. It is an impossible thing for you to sort out. And so, in time, you decide that his sexual desires are inappropriate.

But we want you to understand that none of these emotions that you have been feeling have anything to do with the rightness or the wrongness of his request or behavior. Your emotions are always, and only, about whether your thoughts about a subject align with the thoughts of your *Inner Being.* And when you decide you are inappropriate, you are always out of alignment with your Source. When you decide that your husband is inappropriate, you are always out of alignment with your Source. If you decide that your mother was wrong to influence you on the subject of sexuality, you are out of alignment with Source.

Let us say that, through the life experience that you have lived, you have decided that you do not want to participate in a particular activity, sexual or otherwise. And let us also say that you spend no time thinking about what you do not want regarding the subject, so there is no active Vibration within you about it. Under those conditions, the powerful *Law of Attraction* would bring to you a partner who is in complete agreement with you, and you would have no struggle in living your compatible life.

Now, let us say that, through the life that you have lived, you have decided that you do not want to participate in a particular activity. You made that decision when you were young. In fact, you learned it from your mother, whom you trusted. This feels like an important decision to you. You read books about it. You seek counsel about it. You are very, very clear about what you do not want; and you justify that decision often. In this situation it would not be possible for the *Law of Attraction* to bring you a partner who agrees with you because the Vibration that you predominantly offer on this topic does not agree with your own decision. So you would attract partners who ask or demand of you the exact opposite of what you have decided that you want.

It is not our desire to guide you toward or away from sexual activity, but we do want you to understand that this is another case where "you cannot get there from there." You cannot continue to offer a Vibration that consists mostly of what you *do not* want and get what you *do* want. And we also would like you to understand that when you pay attention to the way you feel, and deliberately choose more thoughts that feel good while you think them, you will begin to recognize the nature of your Broader Non-Physical desires. *The majority of negative emotions that you feel are not because the subject of your thought is wrong, but instead, because you are condemning something that your Source does not condemn. Your Source is one of love, not one of condemnation.*

And so, over time, as you come more into alignment with the Vibration of the Source within you, it is our promise to you that your feelings of sensuality will return. For you have come forth into this physical body wanting to explore and enjoy the delicious nature of your physical beingness. We have never seen a physical human who was in *alignment* with Source who was repulsed by physical interaction. Repulsion is an indication of *disconnection*.

We Can Always Have a Fresh Start

Jerry: Abraham, before meeting you, I described life as like moving along a path that had many possible branches that forked this way and that way. I could choose this branch of the path or that one; and if I ever found myself at a point where life didn't feel right, I could just backtrack to the last fork in the road and then, perhaps, choose a better path. But it seems like you are saying that I don't have to double back, and that I could just start fresh at any time.

Abraham: The thing that your analogy does not factor in is that during the time on your trail that you were not having a good time, as it was not feeling right, you were sending out Vibrational rockets of desire for the equivalent improvement or solutions—and in doing so, you added to your Vibrational Escrow your newly amended desires. Further, the Non-Physical part of you became that expanded Being living that better experience. It is neither necessary nor possible for you to backtrack to a former physical perspective. Life has caused you to move on. And, most important, that expanded version of you is calling you; and if you will listen, a well-lighted and easy-to-navigate path will appear before you.

How Does One Regain the Frequency of Pleasurable Sexuality?

Jerry: On the other side of the question posed by the young woman we just discussed, there is a gentleman who says: "For the first three months of our marriage, my wife and I had sex three or four times every day. But now, after a few years, it has actually reached the point that the activity of sex is distasteful to my wife. And so, if I don't make it happen, it just doesn't happen. She is not interested in any form of mental stimulation, like words, films, or books. She won't allow anything that would shift her focus in that direction. I don't want to have sex with her if she doesn't enjoy it, because if it's not pleasurable for her, it's not pleasurable for me. *What thoughts must I change in order to change the experience that I am having?*"

Abraham: Many people find themselves in troubling situations where there seem to be no viable solutions: "Since my wife doesn't want sexual interaction, then my choices are: (1) I could go along with not having sex . . . which doesn't feel good to me; (2) I could leave my wife and find another partner who is more compatible on the subject, like we were in the beginning . . . but I don't want to leave her; (3) I could stay in the marriage but find another sexual partner . . . but I don't want to betray or deceive my mate, and I am certain she would not condone my doing that; (4) I could try to convince her or even assert pressure to move her in the direction of my desires . . . but that is uncomfortable and suppresses my own sexual desire."

The reason none of the choices just mentioned afford any viable solution is because none of them are addressing the real problem. When two people are in love (like so many people describe at the beginning of their relationships), their positive attention to each other, and their positive expectation about their relationship, is often a catalyst that causes them both to align with their respective *Inner Beings.* So you could say that they are each using each other as their excuse to be in alignment with *who-they-really-are.* And that alignment translates as harmony. *There is no greater symbol of co-creative harmony than the physical blending of two people in sexual interaction.*

Of course, it is possible to interact physically without one or both of the parties involved being in alignment with Source, but when that physical/Source alignment is in place, then the physical intertwining is divine.

Of course, you would want your mate to be in alignment with her Source for many more reasons than because she would be more likely to be willing to engage in sexual interaction with you, but, in any case, her connection to Source is what we would focus upon.

You do not have the power to align others with their *Inner Being.* You only have the power to align yourself with your own. You cannot focus upon your sexual incompatibility and be in alignment with your *Inner Being* at the same time. You cannot notice that your mate is not in alignment with her *Inner Being* and be in alignment with your *Inner Being* the same time. You cannot focus upon the absence of something that you desire and be in alignment with your *Inner Being* at the same time. Your solution hinges upon your ability to find thoughts about sexuality with your mate while at the same time being in alignment with your Source.

In short, as you often find thoughts about sexual interaction with your mate that feel good to you while you think them, you will be in alignment with the Source within you and with your desires. When you think about sexual interaction with your mate and you feel guilty or blameful or disappointed, you are not in alignment with your Source or with your desires. When you think about sexual interaction with your mate and you feel eager or happy or sensual, you are in alignment with your Source and with your desire. So, over time, as you are able to focus upon the subject and remain in alignment with your Source, the powerful *Law of Attraction* will find more and more compatible rendezvous points, and you will rediscover your early passion with your mate.

It is possible that your mate could remain resistant to her own alignment, and if that is the case, then the *Law of Attraction* will bring to you another mate who matches the Vibration that you have developed. However, once you are consistently holding your mate as your positive object of attention while you are in complete alignment with your *Inner Being*, it is much more likely that she will return to her natural alignment.

Engaging in sexual interaction, as inspired from Connection with your *Inner Being*, is a delicious physical experience, while engaging in sexual interaction out of a feeling of commitment or responsibility is not.

In short, if you do not allow yourself to get into a feeling of shortage or lack because of something that another does, and you are able to maintain your alignment with the Source within you, what you desire must come to you. And, in this situation, where it is clear that this man cares about the feelings of his mate, his alignment will most likely inspire hers.

So this conversation is not about how to get yourself into a position where you can get from another something that you desire. Instead, it is about how to align yourself with Source regardless of what another is doing. And then, by your own consistent alignment with Source, you *may* inspire the alignment of your mate. And the by-product of all of that alignment is—as the man discovered in the early days of his relationship—a desire to become one with the positive object of your attention.

Sex, Religion, and Mental-Hospital Incarcerations?

Jerry: Some years ago I was visiting a group of friends who were psychiatrists and psychologists who told me, in essence, that the majority of people who were incarcerated in a mental hospital where they worked, near Spokane, Washington, were there as a result of their confusion either about religion or sex. And I'm sure it was not only their confusion that put them there, but also their behavior.

Abraham: That is not surprising, because both the subject of religion and the subject of sexuality point toward the origin of human Beings. Many people look to religion to help them understand why they are here. They want to understand their purpose for being here, and they want to fulfill that purpose. And the subject of sexuality is the means through which they came forth into their physical bodies.

Most religions offer tremendous patterns of "pushing against" as they scrutinize human behavior looking for evidence of wrongdoing and sin. And often that perceived wrongdoing is pointed toward sexual behavior. Every thought that devalues self, even if it is spoken from a religious platform, causes separation between the human physical self and the Non-Physical *Inner Being.* And that is, in fact, what *confusion* is. Only people severely separated from Source would offer an act of hostility, violence, or sexual aggression. There is a powerful connection there: *since they are focused upon lack, they take the subjects that are of greatest importance to them and focus upon the lack side of it.*

Why Do People Use *God* and *Sex* in Vain?

Jerry: And another thing I have noticed is that, for some reason, in our society when people are really angry or violent or threatening, or are really trying to hurt someone's feelings, they use words that are related to sex or religion as curse words. It seems like the worse they feel, the more they use sexual or religious words in a derogatory way to get their point across.

Abraham: That is because when they are focused upon lack—and therefore disconnected from Source—they choose the subjects that are the most meaningful or important and find the lack side of them.

Why Does the Media Broadcast Pain,
but Censor Pleasure?

Jerry: I also notice that in our culture it seems perfectly appropriate for television and movies to depict the maiming of people, and destruction and gore—anything horrible as far as destroying the human body—while it seems inappropriate to show human sexuality and pleasure. I've never understood why our culture has come to the place where it can stand hate and anger and pain, but doesn't want to see pleasure.

Abraham: It is not a matter of their wanting to see hate, anger, and pain, and not wanting to see pleasure. In fact, the opposite of that is true: people really *do* want to feel good, and they want to see things that are successful and beautiful and pleasurable.

Many people are attracting to themselves unwanted things by virtue of their attention to those unwanted things. A misunderstanding of the *Laws of the Universe* is at the heart of this conversation as the people of your society wage wars against the things they do not want: war against terror, war against AIDS, war against teenage pregnancy, war against violence, war against cancer—and every one of those things is getting bigger because attention to unwanted creates more unwanted.

Your moviemakers, whether they understand the *Law of Attraction* or not, understand that people do gravitate more toward viewing unwanted things than wanted. And we submit that the reason that is true is because there are strong active Vibrations in most people about what they do not want. If you were to engage the average person in conversation about what is going on with his life, you would find him much more articulate in expressing the things that are not working well—things that are unjust and things that need to be changed—than he would be able to express the beauty of his life and world.

Also, once you have decided that the world is leaning toward anger and hate, you are no longer a Vibrational Match to the beauty of the world—and the world, as you attract, then leans in the direction of your belief. Anyone who begins to make lists of the positive aspects of the world around them will train their Vibration and therefore their own point of attraction to more of that. Meanwhile, the people who make movies will continue to make the movies that people are attracting from them.

We would like to help you remember that if you are waiting around for your society to get straightened out before you have a happy life experience, you will have a very long wait. If you are waiting for anybody else in your experience to get straightened out before you have a happy experience, you will have a very long wait.

You are not here to *discover* that which is perfect. You are here to *create* or to *attract* that which is perfect. As the contrast of your life, and even of what you are calling unpleasant movies, helps you know what you *do not* want, you also understand more clearly what you *do* want. *Focus upon what you do want, become a Vibrational Match to what you do want, train your point of attraction to what you do want—and watch your personal world become that.*

Monogamy: Is It Natural or Unnatural?

Questioner: Where I'm stuck is on the whole issue of *monogamy.* That is the way I was raised, and so I assume that that's a value of mine, but I've noticed a lot of pain and fear associated with it. First of all, you have to find someone who wants the same thing, and then you have to control the person's wanting, which is not fun by itself, and . . .

Abraham: Not only is it not fun to attempt control over another, it is not possible. People often believe that what they really want is just some final ruling on the rightness or wrongness of monogamy so that they could then keep the rule or break the rule, but at least they would know what the rule is. And so, in your societies that rule has moved back and forth many times. It varies today depending upon what part of the world you are living in. But we want you to understand that it was never your intention as you came into the physical from Non-Physical to find one way of living and convince or coerce all others to abide. You understood that the world is big enough to accommodate vast differences in desires, beliefs, and the creation of lifestyles.

Which brings us to the first point of this question: *I need to find someone who wants what I want.* Coming together with another who is in agreement with the desires that you hold does make for good relationships. And, surely it is obvious that there are enough people with whom you share your planet that it should not be too difficult to find someone who is a match to you and what you want. But the thing that hinders most people—as they are looking to find that other person who matches the things that they desire—is that they cannot find that person unless they themselves are a match to their own desires.

People who worry about finding someone who will remain true to them cannot find such a person because the most active thoughts within them are worrisome thoughts of betrayal. People are finding it difficult to find the mate of their dreams not because that person is not out there, but because of their own contradiction to their own desire in the thoughts they offer about the subject every day.

When you consistently offer thoughts about your future relationship that feel good while you think them, that means you are consistently matching the desires that you have discovered as you have lived life. And under those conditions, only someone in agreement with your desires could come to you. Under those conditions, no need for control is necessary.

Questioner: So is it our "natural" nature to have only one relationship over a lifetime? Or is that something that was imposed on us by culture or religion?

Abraham: It was your intent to interact with many others on many subjects. And whether you choose the subject of sexuality to be something that you experience with only one, or whether it is something that you want to experience with more than one, or with many, it is an individual thing. And your ideas about it are continually changing.

It is worth noting, however, that the rules and laws that are meant to restrict behavior are always born out of the disconnection from Source. In other words, as your officials or leaders or rulers legislate laws or rules in an effort to eliminate something from society, their attention is usually upon the aspect of society that they do *not* want. And so, even though they make laws and attempt to enforce them, they have but minuscule control, because they are fighting the natural laws of nature. *The most powerful force inherent in all who exist is the acknowledgment of personal freedom.*

It is not possible for you to form your ideas about what a wonderful relationship really is if you have no exposure to things that are not wonderful. The best relationships that exist on your planet today are those that have erupted from a series of not-wonderful relationships. *Through each exposure to interacting with others, you launch continuous rockets of desires of what you prefer. And when, and only when, you are a Vibrational Match to the culmination of those desires, you will allow your rendezvous with someone who matches those intentions that you have gathered along your physical trail.*

Sex, Art, Religion, and Monogamy

Questioner: I want to expand on what Jerry was saying earlier about the people in mental institutions being there because of their confusion about sex and religion. I am an artist, and I have heard it said that all great art is inspired from sex and religion; and during this discussion about sex, I realize that, from my perspective, the ultimate relationship involves a perfect fusion of creative and sexual Energy. So, regardless of what society says I should or shouldn't do in terms of my sexual choices, it feels to me that this fusion of Energies is more intense and more delicious with one person.

Abraham: It is true of everything. When you are positively focused in a moment, giving your attention to some positive object of attention and therefore in complete alignment with the Source within you, your Energies are aligned and your experience must be wonderful. But this is a conversation about coming into alignment with Source first, by virtue of your positive attention, not a conversation about the merits of one lover versus many.

For the most part, those who are seeking many sexual experiences are those who have not completely defined what they want. They are still collecting data, and there is nothing wrong with that.

Questioner: In my own mind I use the term *life partner* instead of *monogamy* to describe what I am looking for.

Abraham: *Life partner, for this moment,* can be a good idea. But since the details of the life you are living will always produce more clarity about what you desire, you will always be sending out new rockets of desire. The most productive and sustaining commitment that you could ever make would be to the continual aligning with the expansion that life causes you to discover.

In other words, as you live life, in all of its detail—including the person you are in love with and living with, or married to— you are still sending out rockets of desires of improvement, and the Non-Physical Source Energy part of you receives each request and melds it into the Vibrational becoming that is truly *who-you-are.* Your intention to keep up with that expansion is your true path to happiness.

Of course, those who are consistently in alignment with the Source within them would continue to inspire harmony and love from their partner. So we are not suggesting that you should not or cannot sustain a wonderful lifelong relationship with another. But we are saying that your relationship between *you* and *You* must come first, before any other relationship can remain satisfying.

Many people who are worried about the loss of love enter into marital agreements, "till death do us part" agreements, as they try to protect themselves from unwanted things. That is the opposite of what we are explaining here.

What Is the Ultimate Sensual/Sexual Experience?

Questioner: What is the *sexual force?* For me, the ultimate sexual experience involves a perfect fusion with another person, communicating on all possible levels of sensual and Spiritual and emotional harmony. I feel an expansion of myself in that, like a lessening of my boundaries.

Abraham: Whether the sexual experience is the reason for your positive focus and therefore alignment with Source, or whether you were already in alignment with Source as you were coming into the sexual experience—it is the alignment with Source that is important.

Have you noticed that you cannot have that sort of experience if you are in the middle of an argument? You cannot be noticing flaws in your mate, or feeling insecure and incomplete in and of yourself, and have that experience.

As physical Beings, you are extensions of Source Energy, of the Energy that creates worlds; and when you take the time to consistently tune to the frequency of that Pure, Positive Energy, and then you turn your attention to your art, or to your lovemaking—you experience the Energy that creates worlds flowing through you. That is that *sexual force* that you are trying to define. . . . *A wonderful sexual experience is much more about being in alignment with your true Creative Energy Stream than it is about the actual physical interaction.*

Questioner: My current mate is very aware of the Non-Physical aspects of his Being. He meditates and wants to be Spiritually focused, but he says that when he engages in sexual activity, it is as if he has to become this one small physical personality and don his ego; and that, for him, he then loses that sense of the larger psychic, Non-Physical experience.

Abraham: In that case, he is having trouble with all aspects of physical, not just the physical sexual part. This leads us to an explanation of another flawed premise:

***Flawed Premise #20:** When I focus upon
things of a physical nature, I am less Spiritual.*

Since you are creators who have come forth from Source, you are literal extensions of Source. As you focus into this physical world, you are focusing upon creations of Source, and you are continuing to add to the creation of Source by your willingness to explore contrast and ask for continuing improvements. *Being physical does not separate you from Source, and having sex does not diminish your Spiritual connection. It is pushing against unwanted, and learning patterns of Vibration that are different from the Vibration of Source, that disconnects you from Source.*

There is nothing more Spiritual than to allow the true spirit that is you to flow through you into your physical life. The absence of Spirituality is not about the subject or the activity. It is about the Vibrational choices that you are making.

Source loves you, and when you do not, you are not Spiritual. Source loves the others with whom you share your planet, and when you do not, you are not Spiritual. Source understands the expanding nature of you and of *All-That-Is,* and when you think you should stand in completed perfection on every subject, you are not Spiritual. When you feel unworthy, you are not in alignment with Source.

But, as we have been discussing here, your Connection to Source must not depend upon your mate's Connection to Source. You must use you own power of focus to keep yourself in alignment with *who-you-really-are.* Your very discussion about your mate's feeling of loss of expansiveness causes the temporary loss of it within you as well.

You really cannot sort these issues out from the outside by trying to determine the rightness or wrongness of behavior. Your determination to tend to your own Connection with your own Spirituality will put you in the best position of inspiring the same in your mate. And if he continues to believe that the act of sexuality moves him away from the Spiritual person he strives to be—the *Law of Attraction* will move him out of your experience. And if you continue to remain focused upon the things that allow your alignment with your

Source—the *Law of Attraction* will bring to you another who is not only in alignment with Source as well, but who shares your values and desires regarding the subject of sexuality.

Each Marriage Was Different but Not Better

Questioner: I've been married four times to two different husbands. In each case, we remarried thinking it would be better. It was different; it was not better. In each case, I can see now from what you were saying about freedom that these marriages just reinforced my desire to be free.

One of my husbands said to me, "You're really just interested in romance." And, in a sense, that was true. I thought maybe I'd rather be his mistress than his wife, because in marriage we are talking about two different things: *Sexuality* is one thing; *marriage* is another. In marriage you've got children, in-laws, property, responsibilities, duties. . . .

Abraham: It turns out it is not possible to separate anything from anything, though, because at the core of all of those things is you and the way you feel. As you focus upon one unpleasant or unwanted aspect of life, it bleeds over into all other aspects.

Questioner: That's right. And so, finally, my desire for freedom dominated so much that in each case, I left. I like the premise of life that you identify, of freedom and growth and joy, but my marriages were bringing no joy.

Abraham: Can you see, in looking back, that there were opportunities to look for positive aspects, but because you were fixated upon negative aspects, those became your dominant experience?

Questioner: Yes, but I so disliked the feeling of being hemmed in and pinned down and having to perform certain duties all the time that even though I did them, and did them well, what I wanted was to be free, to be my own person. . . .

Abraham: *The actual "freedom" you were seeking was freedom from negative emotion, freedom from feeling bad, freedom from not feeling good, freedom from not being <u>who-you-really-are.</u>*

We want you to understand that, in every moment, even those over which you feel you have no control, you have the freedom to ponder them in a way that feels better or in a way that feels worse. You have the freedom to focus upon them through the eyes of your Source or from the perspective that pinches you off from Source. Your pinned-in, not-free feelings were about your Vibrational discord, not about the subject you were focusing upon, which brought about the Vibrational discord; and that is such an important distinction.

You are not seeking freedom from experiences that cause your desires to expand, but you *are* seeking freedom from the hindering thoughts that keep you from allowing your expansion. The feeling that you are describing as being pinned in or not free is actually the feeling of not keeping up with your own expansion—the expansion, in fact, made possible by your relationship.

Have you noticed that, in terms of physical activity, you are as busy now as you have ever been? [**Questioner:** I am actually busier.] And yet you feel freer because you are no longer focused upon lack.

We are not suggesting that you should have done something differently. We are not suggesting that it was right that you stay and wrong that you go, or the other way around. But we do want you to realize that, in every moment, the way you feel is because of one thing and one thing only: the thoughts you are thinking and the Vibrational relationship with your opinion and that of the Source within you. And there is no other person, no matter how hard he tries to be a good companion, who can stand on his head in enough ways to make up for the thoughts that *you* think.

We know that some people seem to be much easier to live with than others, but, even so, we do not encourage anyone to try to guide their own behavior by trying to make others happy. *A well-meaning person who does everything in his power to make you feel better is actually making it less likely that you will direct your thoughts into harmony with your Broader Perspective. And since your feeling of freedom and joy and growth are contingent upon your Non-Physical Connection, then anything that distracts you from that important work does not help you.*

Abraham Offers Some "Coming Together" Vows

Questioner: Abraham, I was involved in a religion for three years that taught that Spiritual Beings do not have physical contact, do not make love. They likened the body to a battery, and they said that by having sexual contact with another, in effect, you discharge and waste energy.

Abraham: The only way that you "discharge and waste energy" is by focusing upon the lack of what you desire. Since the Source within you is focused upon *who-you-really-are,* all that you have become, and all that you desire—when you focus otherwise, you lose your Connection. It is your *belief* that you are inappropriate that is causing the disharmony, not your physical behavior.

If you are having a sexual experience and you are feeling extremely guilty about it, for whatever reason, then the experience is not of value to you. Then you *are* draining your Energy. But if you are having a sexual experience and you are feeling very good about it, then the power of the Universe is behind you.

Questioner: Well, if only I had known 25 years ago what I have just learned here today. . . . I came from a situation where everything is a "no-no," right down to the fact that your only responsibility in life is to get married, have kids, and obey your husband. And that is even what my marriage vows said: you will love, honor, and obey this man for the rest of your life. Boy, if I had known then what I know now, I'd have run so fast.

Abraham: Let us offer you the perfect coming-together vows, whether you are calling them marriage or something else:

Hello, friend. We are here as co-creators. And it is my expectation as we move forward in this marriage [or in this relationship] that both of us will find ourselves satisfied in every way that is possible. It is my desire to discover who I am and who you are. But most important to me is that I be happy so that I may inspire happiness in you.

I do not take your life as my responsibility. I take my life as my responsibility. And I am looking forward to a very good time here. I am anticipating that as we move forward in this life together, we will have the ultimate of all positive experiences—because that is what I intend to look for. As long as we are having a good time, let us stay together. And if we should stop having a good time, let us separate—either in thought or in physicalness—until negative do us part.

We are not encouraging you to disassemble your marriages or your existing relationships. But we are encouraging you to tend to the relationship that matters most of all—the relationship between *you* and *You.* When you reach for thoughts about everything and everyone that harmonize with the perspective of the Source within you, you will feel the true alignment of your Being; and then, and only then, will you have something to offer another. *You must be selfish enough to be in alignment with your true self before you have anything to give.*

෴ ෴

PART IV

Parenting, and the *Law of Attraction:* Creating Positive Parent/Child Relationships in a World of Contrast

What Is the Supervising Adult's Role
in the Child's Behavior?

If small children were allowed to interact with one another without the supervision and Vibrational interference of misaligned adults, they would naturally align to their own Broader Perspective, and they would positively interact with each other. They would observe the differences they would find in each other, but those differences would not become focal points to which they found opposition. And so, positive, effective, and pleasurable co-creation would occur. But when an adult who is not in alignment with Broader Perspective enters the picture, the positive dynamics disappear.

Many adults believe that if children are left to themselves, they will stray away from the path of rightness. And so, the adults inject themselves into the equation, watching for evidence of what they believe is wrong behavior, trying to guide the children away from what is unwanted; but children who are encouraged to focus upon "wrong" behavior, or who merely observe the adult who is now looking at them with disapproval, feel strong discord within themselves, as they are being influenced away from their loving, approving *Inner Being.*

When adults, or anyone, expect or demand that you adjust *your* behavior to something that is more pleasing to *them,* they are attempting to lure you away from the benefit of your personal *Emotional Guidance System.* And the breakdown of every relationship, the reason for every dissatisfaction, the cause of every illness or failure, stems directly from this incredible misunderstanding: *you never intended to be guided by the approval or disapproval of others, but by the harmony or disharmony of the Energies between you and your Source.*

If this group of children were to be joined by an adult who is already in alignment with her own *Source,* who is not dependent upon *their* good behavior for *her* good feeling, they would not be negatively impacted by her presence, for she would be encouraging—through the power of her example—their own personal alignment. . . . *When two or more people interact who are personally in alignment with their own Broader Perspective, the physical rendezvousing is pleasant, productive, and life-giving.*

Suddenly removing worrisome adult supervision from the experience of the children would not immediately restore them to their natural state of Well-Being, because the children have learned their Vibrational patterns from the adults, and now they are behaving with each other through the framework of those patterns. But everyone, from the oldest to the youngest among you, wants to feel good because the Non-Physical part of you, your *Inner Being, does* feel good. So, in any moment that you feel less than good, there is something very much out of alignment. . . . Because children have practiced their resistant thoughts for a shorter time than the adults who surround them, it is easier for them to return to, and maintain, their state of alignment.

What Is a Child's Relationship with Other Children, Without Adults?

Let us remove all worrisome, guarded, controlling, resistant influences, which adults often add to the mix, from a group of children and consider what their interaction with each other would be like:

Using their physical senses, they would observe and consider one another carefully. They would see the variety of personalities and beliefs and intentions, much as you see the variety of choices at a food buffet. You do not feel threatened by the things you see that you personally do not want to eat or experience, but instead, you simply choose what you *do* prefer and put *it* on your plate.

In a similar manner, children who have not been taught to push away *unwanted* components would simply gravitate toward *wanted* components. *Children with like interests or desires, in any given point in time, would gravitate together, providing meaningful and satisfying interaction. Children with differences simply would not gravitate together—and so, a harmonious environment would result.*

Many people would argue that they have never seen such an environment, and they would be right. Others would argue that such an environment is highly unlikely, and we would agree with them, also, because it is an extremely rare child who is afforded the freedom to make his or her own choices without the deliberate influence from the adults who have fostered them into their life experience. But it is possible that once you understand your own personal *Guidance System* and how it works (that you are actually a physical extension of Non-Physical Consciousness; that your Non-Physical perspective exists even at the same time that your physical perspective exists; and that you are seeking, first and foremost, alignment with your own *Guidance System*), it is possible for you to find harmony in whatever physical environment, classroom, situation, or relationship you find yourself involved in.

By practicing your own alignment first, you could become as the children we were describing. You could interact with them, feeling no need or compulsion to push the unwanted aspects of them away. You could be (like your *Inner Being* within you) inclined to see only the best in others, as well as in yourself, therefore allowing the powerful *Law of Attraction* to match you up with only wanted things.

What Are the Natural Father/Mother Roles?

Jerry: From your perspective, what is the primary, or the natural, role of a father in the progression of the lifetime of his child?

Abraham: The primary role of both the father and the mother is to provide an avenue for the Non-Physical Source Energy of the child to come forth into the physical experience.

Jerry: You don't see different roles for the father and the mother?

Abraham: Not different in any sense that is really important. The differences are evident when you think in terms of influences that would be offered, but parental influences are not as important as your society believes that they are. At its best, parenting provides a stable environment in the early days of adapting to this new life in this new environment and this new body. At its worst, parenting hinders the child's ability to make choices and know freedom. And so, often, parental influence is not of advantage to the child. Parents often have developed negative expectations about life, and so the influence that they offer to the child is negative, also.

A Perspective of a Perfect Parent

Jerry: What is your perspective of a perfect parent?

Abraham: The best thing that a parent could do for a child is to understand that this child, while very small and dependent-seeming at first, is really a powerful creator who has come into this physical environment with great eagerness, purpose, and ability. The best thing a parent could do for a child is to watch for evidence of brilliance, taking note only of the positive aspects of the child. The most important benefit that any parent could offer to any child would be that of influencing the child to his own inner *Guidance System*.

We know that your intention in presenting these questions is to help guide parents to satisfying relationships with their children, and we are eager to have this discussion. But we would also like you to understand that it was not the intention of the children, coming into this time-space reality, to be born into the feathered nests of perfect parents. Once you are here, interacting with one another, experiencing the discord that often comes from interpersonal relationships, you often blame others for the way you feel or for the way your life is going. But from your Non-Physical perspective, you understand completely that the influence of those around you need not negatively impact your experience; and, in fact, not one of you, before your birth, was seeking a perfect environment in which to be born.

Most parents do want the very best for their children, and you have many varying opinions about what is the best thing to provide for your children. From our perspective, and from the perspective of your child before coming forth into this physical body, the best thing that you can offer your child is a clear example of someone who strives to align with the Source within you and to demonstrate, through the clarity of your own personal example, your effective utilization of your own *Emotional Guidance System*.

The thing that causes the most discomfort, for both parent and child, is the parent's misunderstanding of the internal wisdom and purpose of the child. And the reason why the parent misunderstands that in his child is because he misunderstands it in himself. In other words, if a parent sees a world filled with threatening, dangerous, unpleasant things and feels protective and guarded in the face of those things, he is then out of alignment with his true understanding and power. And under those conditions, he guides his child into the same guardedness.

But a parent who recognizes the value of his own *Emotional Guidance System;* who seeks alignment with his own Broader Perspective first; who understands the nature of the creative Vortex of Energy, swirling on his behalf; and whose first priority is to be in alignment with *who-he-really-is*—that parent can influence his child to seek his own Guidance.

The reason why so many people blame their parents for their failures or unhappiness is because they were trained by their parents to look to them for guidance and support. Even the most well-meaning parent cannot begin to replace the guidance and support that comes forth from within. But it is even more than that. *As each of you lives the details of the contrast that surrounds you and sends forth the constant Vibrational rockets of expansion, you must follow those rockets and allow yourself the full evolution of that expansion—or you cannot be happy.* When a parent interferes with that natural process by convincing you that what you feel is unimportant, that what your emotions are telling you should be disregarded, and that what really matters is that you comply with the opinions and rules and beliefs that are being set forth by your parents, it is no wonder that an inner rebellion occurs. And that inner rebellion will continue until the moment you deliberately and consciously come into alignment with *who-you-really-are*.

So, the best thing that a parent could do for a child is to relinquish attempted control over the child's behavior and thoughts; and to encourage the child's awareness of his own Vibrational Escrow, his Vortex of Creation, and his *Emotional Guidance System*. And the only way that a parent could influence a child's understanding of those things is by fully understanding them himself.

When a child, or a parent, feels the emptiness of *fear* or *anger* or *disappointment* or *resentment,* it is only because he is Vibrationally disallowing his Connection to the expanded Being that he has become. Those negative emotions are symptoms of his perceived loss of freedom, and the feeling of not being free is only and always about disallowing the fullness of *who-you-have-become* to be active within you in the moment.

It is interesting that the parental approach that most parents take—of observing the world, evaluating the components, deciphering the rightness and wrongness of it, sorting that into piles, and then working to guide the child away from the unwanted—is exactly contrary to the intention of both parent and child when coming into the physical experience.

And so, our perspective of a most joyous, valuable parental approach is this:

> *I understand that my child is a powerful creator who has come into this physical environment, not unlike myself, to carve out a wonderful experience. My child will have the benefit of sifting through the contrast of life in order to determine his preferences. Each time my child has an experience that amplifies his awareness of what he does not want, a Vibrational request for the improved opposite will emanate from him, and will be held for him, in his Vibrational Reality, in his Vortex of Creation. And as he pays attention to the <u>Emotional Guidance System</u>*

within him and seeks the best-feeling thoughts he can find, he will gravitate into alignment with <u>who-he-has-become</u> and will know the fullness of <u>who-he-is.</u> And, in all of that process, he will feel the satisfaction of being the creator of his own reality. And, as his parent, I will support him completely in his becoming.

What Are the Familial *Inner Beings* of Parents and Children?

Jerry: I'd like to back up just a little bit to before we were born into this physical reality. What are the relationships between the *Inner Beings* of the parents and the child?

Abraham: Everyone who comes forth into the physical is an extension of Source Energy, so, in that sense, everyone is connected to everyone. And all relationships are Eternal. Once a relationship has been established, it never ceases to be. You come forth from Non-Physical in what you might call clusters of Energy or Families of Consciousness, and, without exception, you have long Vibrational Non-Physical roots with the members of your physical families.

The primary intention that you held regarding your co-creation with other people was not one of dependency at all. You knew that through the variety of interpersonal relationships, more wonderful ideas of creation would be born, and you reveled in anticipation of the new ideas that would be born from those relationships. Before the birth of the child, and even before the birth of the parent, you all anticipated your future interaction and knew the value that would come forth from it. And while you understood your Non-Physical Connection, your attention was primarily upon your expansion, and so you were not looking back, tracing roots, looking for stability and security. You were stable and secure.

Jerry: Is there any value to giving conscious consideration to the connection we had with our parents before we were born?

Abraham: There is not a great deal of value in attempting to look back at your Non-Physical origins because it is not tangible enough for you to really understand it from your physical format, and since you cannot make any real sense of it, it proves to be a distraction from what you have intended in your physical now. But, even more important, through the interactions that you have experienced together in this physical time-space reality, you have set forth powerful requests, and you are dynamic catalysts for expansion for one another. As you make an effort to align with the expanded version of yourself, you will also align with the expanded version of your parents—and the satisfaction that will come from that alignment is enormous. And you can accomplish all of that through the simple process of looking for the positive aspects of each other and finding as many reasons as possible to appreciate.

Do Families Have Specific Prebirth Mutual Intentions?

Jerry: So, since our relationships are Eternal, do we have specific intentions regarding our interaction with our parents or our children after we are born? Or is it all just kind of general?

Abraham: In most cases, your intentions are of a general nature in the sense that you understood your creative power and the *Laws of the Universe;* and you felt eager to jump in and stir things up, experience contrast, and create. You saw your parents as a wonderful avenue into physical experience and providers of early stability while you found your creative sea legs, so to speak. Your dominant intention was to come into your physical body and immerse yourself in the contrast, which you knew would cause you to take thought and life beyond anything that it had been before. You expected your relationships with your parents, and with all other people, to provide a wonderful basis for contrast, and therefore a wonderful basis for asking, and a wonderful basis for expansions. And you knew that the details would occur through the living of life. You did not try to figure it all out in advance.

To Whom Are We Most Responsible?

Jerry: Are you saying that we have no different responsibility from parent to child and child to parent than we do to any other human on the planet?

Abraham: We are saying that. You have come forth into this physical experience as co-creators with *everyone* upon your planet.

What Could Parents Learn from Children?

Jerry: In the way that a teacher often learns from the student while the student is learning from the teacher, is it the same with parents? Do they learn from their children?

Abraham: When a question is born within you, the equivalent answer immediately forms in your Vibrational Reality. While you are churning in the midst of a problem, an equivalent solution forms in your Vibrational Reality. And so, it is natural that, in your interactions with one another—parent/child, teacher/student, person to person—you are discovering questions and problems that are creating answers and solutions. And so, learning (or what we prefer to call *expansion*) is the result of all co-creative experience.

Jerry: So, we're learning, even though we don't realize that we are?

Abraham: Unless you are a Vibrational Match to *who-you-really-are*—unless you are in Vibrational alignment with the expanded version of you that exists in your Vibrational Vortex—you cannot be aware of your expansion. Your expansion is constant. Keeping up with it is optional. The better you feel, the more you are keeping up with your expansion and the more you recognize that expansion. In other words, *who-you-really-are* has learned. But unless you are in the Vortex, you cannot recognize the learning. Every experience is giving you more knowledge, whether you are consciously aware of it or not.

Why Do Siblings Respond Differently to Similar Influences?

Jerry: I've noticed that even though siblings are from the same set of parents, often they do not grow up as carbon copies of one another. In other words, one child can grow up to be healthy and happy and what I call a successful Being, while a brother or sister out of the same family can experience a very painful life. Does that mean that parental influence, which is similar with each child, is not a significant factor in how children turn out?

Abraham: It is not possible to maintain the consistent success that you refer to as *happiness* without a conscious striving for alignment with your Broader Non-Physical Being. Sometimes a parent or teacher can be a catalyst for influencing you in that direction. And everyone is born wanting to feel good and has natural instinctual tendencies toward finding that alignment. It is the influence that hinders that natural alignment that is really at the center of this discussion, because children naturally gravitate to feeling good and to their alignment with Source. In other words, if left to their own natural instincts, children would make their way more quickly into alignment. But well-meaning, guarded parents often stifle those natural impulses by worrying about what could happen, and by influencing their children away from their own *Guidance System.*

Contrary to what most parents believe, the less concern they feel for the welfare of their child, the better off their child will be, because in the absence of the negative speculation and worry, the child is more likely to gravitate to his own alignment.

And so, getting back to the specifics of your question . . . often the first child born to well-meaning but overprotective parents is the object of more fussing and worrying and negative influence than the children born later.

There are many factors that influence the way children, or people in general, feel, but there is only one factor of importance to consider: *does the thought being offered by this person, in this moment, harmonize with the thought of the Source within?* That is the influence you want to tune in to. All other influences are secondary. Just as a cork, when it is held down under the water, will take the most direct route back to the surface when it is released, when you release the resistance caused by your contradictory-to-Source thoughts, you will return to clarity, happiness, success, and the knowledge of your Source.

Must Children "Take After" Their Parents?

Jerry: My mother used to say to me, "Well, Jerry, you know, you take after Daddy," or "You take after my father," or "your uncle," and I remember feeling strong disagreement with her.

Abraham: Why do you think you disagreed?

Jerry: I didn't necessarily think I took after anyone, but, also, it seems like when she was pointing that sort of thing out to me, it was usually because she was expressing disapproval of me at the time.

Abraham: That's really what we wanted you to realize. The discord you felt was because your mother's disapproving opinion activated within you a thought that was in complete disagreement with your *Inner Being*. In other words, as your mother was pointing out some flaw in you and likening it to some flaw in someone else, in a sense trying to control you by threatening you with the prospect of an unhappy outcome, your *Inner Being* was offering a very different opinion of you, to you. And your negative emotion was your indication of the disparity. That is how your *Guidance System* works. Whenever you feel negative emotion, it means that your active thought (no matter how you came upon it) does not match what your *Inner Being* knows about the subject.

Jerry: Even today, from time to time, something will come up that will take me back to my mother pointing out some of those flaws.

Abraham: And you still feel negative emotion when that happens, which means your *Inner Being* still does not agree with the words of your mother.

Must Inherited Traits Determine My Future Experience?

Jerry: But aren't there traits that we pass on to our children? In the same way that physical characteristics are passed on, don't we also pass on other traits?

Abraham: What, specifically, are you thinking about?

Jerry: Like capability of mind, capability of body, abilities, health. . . . How much control does that have over me now?

Abraham: You need not be negatively affected by anything, but when you *are* negatively influenced, it is because you are allowing your active thought to be one that disallows what you really want.

It is quite common to pass negative *expectations* on from generation to generation, but at any point, a person who recognizes the discord of that negative thought, who recognizes that the negative emotion means that his *Inner Being* does not agree, can gradually omit those resistant thoughts, which are at the core of all illnesses, diseases, and negative experiences.

Shouldn't Children Be Taken from "Abusive" Parents?

Jerry: If the current rules and regulations had been around when I was a child, and having the life that I had, I would have been taken away from my parents and put in a foster home. But at that time, I guess it was just kind of accepted as the way we were all living. And so, once I grew up and left it, I didn't look back on it as such a negative thing. I think even then I saw it more as an adventure—a way of life, with excitement and variety. And so, I never looked back and blamed my parents for how terribly I was treated. It was just the way we were all co-creating. In other words, I knew my part in it, and I assume they knew their part in it. But today, we're living in a different era, and child abuse is a big issue.

It seems to me that there are many people who deliberately expose themselves to what I would consider to be *abuse* as they play hockey or football, or face a challenger in boxing. . . . Is it possible that we are all *choosing,* and that I, in some way, chose that abusive treatment from my parents?

Abraham: We are appreciating your question because many people would take issue with the idea of similarity between people being beaten up by the sports they are choosing to play and children who are being beaten by their parents—but you are right about the similarity.

What people do not understand is that you do not choose something by looking at it and shouting "Yes, I would like some of that!" You make your choices by your attention to things. In this Universe that is based on attraction, when you look at an unwanted thing, your attention to it causes an activation of the Vibration within you, and then the Law of Attraction brings more like it into your experience.

Of course, it is a terrible thing when a child is abused, but it is also a terrible thing when a child is disallowed the freedom to be *who-he-really-is.* And we want you to understand that, in every case, those who are offering abuse—no matter how severe it is on your scale of things unwanted—are suffering their own disconnection from Source while offering the abuse. In other words, it is not only the child suffering the abuse from the parent that is the problem, but the adult suffering the abuse of disconnection.

Removing a child from physical abuse has to be seen as the best thing to do in that circumstance, but that action in no way solves the problem. In fact, the discord that was at the root of the abuse is only exacerbated by the physical removal of the child. Now, an unworthy-feeling parent feels more unworthy and, in an effort to feel better, usually moves to more abuse. And, often the child, who is worn down by the whole experience, feels even less secure, as he is now disallowed interaction with someone he truly loves.

The issue of child abuse will not come to an end until people understand the emotions that they feel and are able to control the direction of their thoughts. Until the self-inflicted abuse—of denying themselves Connection to *who-they-have-become,* to their *Inner Being*—subsides, violence, in all forms, will remain.

Children are resilient and return to the Connection of the Source more easily than adults do. In the absence of a social worker pointing out to you how mistreated you were, you survived the abuse, set off rockets of desire into your Vibrational Reality—and benefited from the experience. And that is the most difficult thing for people to understand. "Why would a child willingly come forth into an abusive home? Why would a loving God allow such a thing?"

So, we remind you that you were not looking for a feathered nest, where the only thing present for you to observe was something perfect. You wanted diversity and variety, and even discord. You wanted an opportunity to define an even better experience. You knew that you were a creator, and you wanted experiences to help you to choose. You are learning and expanding all of the days of your life. Not only when you are children.

Without Discipline, Would Children Perform Household Chores?

Jerry: Abraham, where does discipline fit into the equation between parents and children? For a harmonious flow of the execution of the details of physical life—like cleaning the house, hauling out the trash, and so forth—how do you see *discipline?*

Abraham: We are not proponents of *discipline* because that is a component of trying to *motivate* another to action, and we never see that work out well. In other words, if a parent has a desire for a well-ordered home environment, and envisions the children living in the home as harmonious helpers, then there is no Vibrational separation within this parent, because his desires and his expectations Vibrationally match. And, under those conditions, he would *inspire* the willing cooperation from his children. We would encourage that kind of *inspiration* rather than *motivation*.

Motivation works more like this: A parent recognizes that there is much to be done, focuses upon children who are not helping; his observation does not match his desire, and so he experiences Vibrational discord, which feels like negative emotion. In his frustration, or anger, he issues an ultimatum about discipline that will be offered if the cooperation does not occur. The child is motivated to action because he does not want the negative consequences of his inaction. But in his lack of connection to Source, he is listless, not focused; does not do a good job; resents having to do the job; and on it goes. This is another perfect example of not being able to get there from there.

If we were a parent, or anyone wanting to inspire positive behavior from another, we would do our personal Vibrational work first. We would align with our Source Energy by envisioning the outcome we seek and by holding those involved as positive objects of our attention. We would not allow any current unwanted behavior to be the reason for our attention to them.

Another way of saying it is: Do not let your uncooperative children distract you from the vision of the helpful, happy children that are in your Vibrational Escrow. If you are able to hold to your vision of cooperation and not give your attention to their inaction, which disconnects you from your power, they will eventually feel the pull of your powerful influence of Connection. Your children will become very creative, actually looking for ways that they can be of benefit, rather than begrudging every little thing that they have to do because you have convinced them that if they do not do it, there will be negative consequences.

Must "Family Harmony" Inhibit Personal Freedom?

Jerry: When a family is living together, whether it's a small family with one parent and one child or a larger group of 14—parents, grandparents, and children, all living in one family household—how

585

would you suggest that they come together in an attitude of respect for one another, without losing their individual freedom? Doesn't someone have to be in charge, or can everyone be free and make their own decisions and still live in harmony as one family unit?

Abraham: It is possible for a group of any size to live or play or work in harmony if the individuals involved are first in alignment with *who-they-really-are.* And, it is not necessary for everyone in the group to be in alignment with their *Inner Beings* before you can experience a harmonious experience within the group. The harmony that everyone in this group dynamic is seeking is the alignment with their own *Inner Beings;* and when that is achieved, then, and only then, can harmony with other people occur. *A person who is consistently inside his own Vortex will find harmony with other people even when they are not finding harmony with him.*

Everything that everyone desires—whether it is a material object, a physical condition, a financial situation, or a harmonious relationship— is wanted for only one reason: they believe they will feel better in having it. Once you show yourself—through practicing increasingly better-feeling thoughts, through making lists of positive aspects, by indulging in <u>Rampages of Appreciation</u>—that you can maintain your alignment with your own <u>Inner Being</u> and predominantly stay inside your Vortex of Creation, you will find harmony in the world around you, also.

And who will be in charge? A better way of stating it is: Who will *lead* this group? And the answer to that question is: *One who is in alignment with Source is more powerful than millions who are not. And so, the person most aligned with his <u>Inner Being,</u> his Vortex of Creation, and the power that creates worlds will emerge as the leader. People naturally gravitate to clear-minded, stable, happy people.*

If no one in the household is in that sort of alignment, then the leadership usually falls to the biggest one or the strongest one or the loudest one. But in a group where no one is in alignment with Source, we see no real leadership.

Many people approach life and leadership in a very backward manner. They want people to behave in ways that please them so that in their observation of what pleases them, they will be pleased. We are encouraging you to focus your attention upon *thoughts* that please you, even when there is no pleasing *evidence* to observe, because a consistent absence of resistance, and of negative emotion, will cause you to align with all that is inside your Vortex. And a happy and harmonious family is in your Vortex.

Which Family Member Should Be in Charge?

Jerry: So, in this family that we're discussing, isn't anyone in charge?

Abraham: That is like asking who is in control of the others, and the only actual control you have is over the direction of your own thought. The answer that most people would give is: "The biggest ones or the more powerful ones are in charge, or control," but your history does not bear that out, because that defies the *Law of Attraction*. One who is connected to *who-he-really-is*—in other words, one who is inside his own Vibrational Vortex—is more powerful than millions who are not.

It is not control of your family's behavior or beliefs that you seek, but control of your ability to see them as you want them to be. And when you gain control of your thoughts and are consistently in alignment with your ever-evolving, expanding version of their happy, successful lives, your power of influence will be such that others watching you will wonder what your magic is.

Our encouragement to you is that you no longer worry about what others are doing, and that you seek thoughts and words and actions that feel good to you. Train yourself into Vibrational alignment with all of the wonderful experiences and relationships that you have projected into your Vortex of Creation, and notice the harmony that will surround you as a result of your Vibrational work.

Parents and Children, and Harmonizing vs. Traumatizing

Jerry: I can't help but notice how the family dynamics have changed since I was a child. My parents clearly believed that it was their responsibility to be in charge of me. I believe my mother did much of what she did out of her belief that she was doing the best thing for me, but it's obvious to me now, from what I've learned from you and because of the beatings she gave me, that she was not in alignment with her own *Inner Being* much of the time.

A short while ago, I was walking down the corridor here, and I noticed a mother and her daughter. The little girl was standing back and shouting, "No!"

And her mother said, "Oh?"

And the little girl said, "No!"

And then the mother said, "Oh, *you* want to be the leader?"

And the little girl said, "Yes." So then the pouting little girl came down the stairs while her mother waited, and proceeded to lead her mother to wherever she wanted to take her.

And I thought, *The pendulum has swung all the way in the opposite direction of when I was a child.* Today, it is not an uncommon thing to see little children making demands of their parents and to see their parents yielding to their demands. Would you discuss that, please?

Abraham: When neither, or none, of the people involved in a co-creative situation have taken the time to align with the power of their own Vortex so that everyone involved is outside of their Vortex, usually the one most disconnected—the one feeling the very worst—is the one who takes charge of the situation. But measuring the power of powerless people is a bit like asking a confused person for clarity. Nothing productive happens, and everyone is unhappy.

From our perspective, effective leadership or parenting or mentoring can only be offered by people who are consistently inside their creative Vortices. If you have not taken the time to align yourself with the power and clarity and knowledge of Source, you have no leadership to offer.

Children learn their tantrums from disconnected, out-of-alignment adults.

Children learn their stability and clarity from adults who are in alignment with Source.

Must Children Be Imprinted with Their Parents' Beliefs?

Questioner: We often become very young parents who haven't yet learned the things that we will know later in life. How can we teach our children if *we* haven't yet learned?

Abraham: Often your children are still remembering things that you have forgotten: They still remember that they are good. They still expect things to turn out well for them. They are still in Vibrational alignment with their own *Inner Beings*. In other words, your children are still in their Vortices. That is one of the reasons why they are often unwilling to listen to you, or to agree with you, as you are pronouncing them inappropriate in some way. There is another important flawed premise surfacing here:

Flawed Premise #21: It is my job as a parent to have all the answers so that I can teach those answers to my children.

You will never have all of the answers because you will never have asked all of the questions. You will Eternally discover a new platform of contrast that will produce more questions to be answered. That, in fact, is the joy of your Eternal life . . . the joy of Eternal evolution and expansion and discovery. *Words do not teach. It is life experience that teaches. Your children did not come forth to learn from your words, but instead, they came forth to learn from their own life experiences.*

The greatest value that you can be to your children is to understand the relationship between the physical aspect of you and the Non-Physical aspect of you; to effectively utilize your own *Emotional Guidance System;* and to work, every day, to be as close as you can to your own Vortex.

If you are not inside your Vortex, and are therefore not feeling very good, do not pretend that you *do* feel good. Be real. Let your children know that you are aware that you are not in alignment with *who-you-really-are,* and demonstrate to them your desire to find that alignment. Show them the processes you have learned that cause you to feel better; and apply them often, and openly, until you are very adept at moving inside your Vortex whenever you choose.

If you pretend to be happy when you are not, or confident when you are afraid, you only cause confusion in your children. Show them, through the clarity of your deliberate example, how well your life goes when you deliberately manage the Vibrational gap between the two Vibrational aspects of you. Let them know that you *want* to feel good, and demonstrate to them that you *can* feel good whenever you choose, regardless of what is occurring around you.

And, most important of all, let your children understand that you do not hold them, or their behavior, responsible for the way you feel. Free them of the impossible bondage of needing to please you—and, in doing so, release them to their own wonderful *Guidance System.*

Who's to Blame for This Dysfunctional Family?

Questioner: My childhood experience was that my parents screamed and yelled and fought, and the children were hit. I grew up with a core belief that the world was not a safe place and that really bad things could happen. And then I went into therapy for five years, and from that I came to the belief that I was not responsible for what had happened to me, but that I was a victim of two parents who were out of control.

Abraham: While the therapist did not want you to feel blame for what happened to you, it is really of no greater value to you to put the blame upon your parents, because whether you are feeling *blame* or *guilt,* you are still outside of your Vortex; you are still not in alignment with *who-you-are. There is no more destructive conclusion to come to than the belief that you are a victim and that others have the power to inflict pain and suffering upon you.*

Now, we know that it is difficult to understand what we are getting at when you, in fact, were the receiver of pain and suffering as a direct result of something that someone else did. And there are important factors that must be explained before this can make sense to you: Your parents did not hit you because you were bad. And your parents did not hit you because they were bad. Your parents hit you because they were out of alignment, and because they felt power-less. It is not illogical—in fact, it is extremely logical—for a person to go from a feeling of powerlessness to a feeling of *revenge* or *anger,* because that is a step toward alignment on the Vibrational Scale.

In other words, a feeling of *powerlessness* is the emotion that indicates the greatest distance from the Vortex of *who-you-really-are.* *Revenge* is closer, *anger* is closer still, *overwhelment* is closer to *who-you-really-are,* and *frustration* is much closer to *who-you-really-are.* *Hope* is a great deal closer to *who-you-really-are,* and now you are almost there; you are almost inside the Vortex. *Belief* in Well-Being and *knowledge* of Well-Being are inside the Vortex, along with *appreciation* and *love* and *passion* and *eagerness* and all good-feeling emotions.

As you found yourself in the middle of a terrible and uncontrol-lable situation, your response was to be afraid. And as you cowered and cried (an absolutely understandable response), you evoked more of what you did not want from your parents. It may be hard to understand, but if you could have mentally removed yourself from the drama of those battles, focusing upon your toys, staying in your room, not becoming a part of the Vibrational mix of it, your parents would have left you out of the drama. But it is not an easy thing not to notice what is going on or have an emotional response to it.

The same thing was true of your parents. Undoubtedly there were unwanted things going on in their lives that they had a difficult time ignoring, which caused them to be pulled into more and more unwanted situations. It is a sort of chain-of-pain that develops as someone is unhappy (and often justifiably so), so he or she lashes out at another, who lashes out at another, who lashes out at another. . . .

Most people involved in the chain-of-pain, whether they are children or adults, come to the conclusion, from the uncomfortable life that they are living, that they are not worthy and that good things do not come to them. And because they feel that way—that is what happens.

And then, most, even those in therapy, spend a great deal of time trying to sort out the rightness or the wrongness of the behaviors of the parties involved. Children blame themselves, children blame their parents, parents blame themselves, parents blame their children, and on and on the chain-of-pain goes.

Only when you are willing to find a thought, any thought, that brings you a feeling of relief can you begin your trek up the *Emotional Scale* in the direction of the *love* and *appreciation* that represents *who-you-really-are*. And only from inside the Vortex can you fully appreciate the experience and the expansion, and the understanding, that it has given you.

Most people believe that what they are looking for is someone to love them, and they also believe that it is the responsibility of their parents to love them. But parents in *despair,* far from their Vortices of Well-Being, have no love to give. And so, the child assumes he is not loved because something is wrong with him, rather than understanding he is not being loved by his parents because they are out of alignment with love.

Again, we must say that humans are looking for love in all the wrong places. Look to your Vortex; look to the expanded you; look to your Source; look to the resource of Love. It is always there for you, but you must find Vibrational alignment with it, within you. You must tune your Vibrational frequency to that of love—and your Vortex will envelop you—and you will be surrounded by love.

But How Could Babies "Attract" Unwanted Experiences?

Questioner: But how do you attract terrible experiences when you are only nine months old?

Abraham: Even though you are only nine months old in your physical body, you are a very old and wise creator focused in that baby's body. And you came with powerful intentions to experience contrast and to launch clear rockets of desire into your Vibrational Reality for the purpose of expansion.

People often assume that because a child is not yet offering words, the child could not be the creator of its own experience, but it is our promise to you that no one else is creating your experience. Children emanate Vibrations—which are the reason for what they attract—even from their time of birth.

Most children are born into situations that do not challenge their natural tendency to remain aligned with their own Vortices. Most children are not influenced out of their Vortices by those who surround them in the early days of their physical experience. But sometimes, when you have come into the physical experience with a powerful intention to teach Well-Being, you intended, even before your birth, to have early exposure to contrast that would stimulate your desire early on in your physical experience, because you understood the power of the asking that would come out of that experience. When you really know what you *do not* want, you ask with greater clarity for what you *do* want—and your Vortex expands more rapidly as a result.

You also understand, from your Non-Physical perspective before your birth, that the true source of discomfort or negative emotion or sickness or all things unwanted, is misalignment with your Vortex, misalignment with *who-you-really-are*. And so, there is actually an eagerness on the part of all Beings coming into physical bodies to have early contrasting experiences in order to project rockets of desire to their Vortices of Creation, because the more powerfully the Vortex spins, the louder the call of Source. *All Non-Physical Beings understand that when wanting is higher, awareness of resistance is greater; and so, since resistance is the only thing that ever thwarts joyous creation, then the greater the awareness, the better.*

We understand that if you are still standing outside of your Vortex, disconnected from the powerful Being that has emerged from the contrast that you have lived, none of this explanation will be satisfying. But it is our promise to you that as you look for more reasons to feel good; as you try to give your parents, or anyone who has hurt you or betrayed you, the benefit of the doubt; as you move into your Vortex, you will then understand. For when you merge with the evolved, expanded part of you, surrounded by the

Vibrational equivalent of everything that you have been asking for and that you have Vibrationally become—you will harbor no ill will toward anyone who helped you achieve that. In fact, you will stand in appreciation for the part they played in your joyous expansion.

Why Are Some Children Born Autistic?

Jerry: What would cause a child to be born with an unwanted physical condition? For instance, there seems to be an almost epidemic number of children being born with the condition called *autism*. At what point before its birth could a baby be thinking thoughts of lack?

Abraham: From your physical perspective, you often do not remember the immense value of contrast and difference, while from your Non-Physical perspective before your birth, it is often a very big factor in the choices that you make. Many parents and teachers who have forgotten the value of contrast and differences have a powerful desire that their children "fit in," which has resulted in a truly troubling epidemic of conformity. And so, many Beings come into the physical experience with an express intention of being different enough that they cannot be controlled into conformity. All Non-Physical Beings coming forth into the physical experience are clear and eager and sure, and they never come from a position of lack. No exceptions.

❦❦ ❦❦

PART V

Self-Appreciation, and the *Law of Attraction:* Appreciation, the "Magical" Key to Your Vortex

Appreciation, Your Key to the Vortex

We have very much enjoyed our interaction with you in presenting our knowledge of the Universe, of the *Laws of the Universe,* and of the important part that you play. Always, our primary intention as we interact with our physical human friends is to help you remember who you actually are so that you may experience the fullness of the appreciation for your part in this joyous, Eternal, Universal creation.

It is an important dance that we dance with one another as we dialogue back and forth between physical perspective and Non-Physical perspective, because both perspectives are integral to the whole. Both the perspectives of physical and of Non-Physical are essential to our Eternal expansion, but the most significant understanding that we are presenting in this book, and the most important knowledge that you will ever acquire, is about the integration of those two Vibrational vantage points.

Your physical viewpoint is spectacularly compelling to you as you explore it and observe it through the detailed deciphering of your physical senses. The contrast of your tactile, sensuous, fragrant Earth environment, in all of its detail and vividness, causes you to pronounce your world "reality." Indeed, your attention to your physical world is serving you and *All-That-Is* extremely well, but there is more to the picture and more to the story of reality than what you are discovering with your physical senses here on your amazing planet, in your amazing galaxy, in your amazing time-space reality. For all of this, all that you see, is a precursor to that which is to come: a bouncing-off place to more joyous reality and more joyous becoming.

When people observe the wonder of their galaxy and planet and speculate that it was somehow set into motion by Non-Physical forces, while their understanding and explanations are scanty, they are essentially accurate: *Your physical world is an extension of Non-Physical Energy and creation. Everything that you now behold was created from the conscious attention of Source Energy.*

The story of the creation of you and your world is not a story of something that happened—but a story of something that *is* happening. The Source Energy that created your world continues to flow forth to you and through you for the continuation of creation and for the expansion of the Universe.

Often, humans, in their humility, refuse to accept their important role in the continuing expansion of *All-That-Is,* and that is the reason why we are offering this book. It is our desire to awaken within you the memory of *who-you-really-are* and of why you are here. We want to help you return to the knowledge of your creative ability; we want you to reap the benefits of the important work you are doing in your physical bodies; we want you to return to the Vortex.

Your physical exposure to your physical world is providing the contrast that is necessary for you to form your opinions and desires about how life could be improved. And even though you cannot see them, and are often unaware of them, your desires for improvement shoot out from you as Vibrational rockets, or messengers of request. They shoot out into the Vibrational atmosphere in the same way that the original rockets that created your planet were sent; and they are received by the Source of the Energy that creates worlds, the same Source Energy that is the origin of *All-That-Is.* And those ideas, requests, and desires are understood; and—in the moment of their launch—they are answered.

Most people have neither an awareness of the launching of the rockets nor of the receiving and answering by Source, but even so, powerful new creation is begun. Some people, as they contemplate these words, can understand the logic in the Eternal nature of creation. Many can accept that creative forces still exist, and that expansion still continues. But the part that is most often misunderstood, or overlooked, by our human friends is that, in the living of physical life and in the launching of those rockets of desired expansion, it is not only an expanded world you are creating—it is an expanded you.

As you observe sickness, in yourself or in another, you set forth a new Vibrational request for wellness that is received and answered by Source. When the contrast of your physical world reveals to you corruption or injustice, you set forth a new Vibrational request for fairness and justice. When someone is rude to you, your rocket asks for nicer experiences. When you do not have enough financial resources, your rocket asks for more. And with each request offered all day, every day, a Vibrational Escrow, or Vibration Reality, is forming. The Broader Non-Physical part of you, the part of you that existed even before your birth, the part of you that exists in the Non-Physical even while you are focused in physical—the Source within you (your *Inner Being*)—not only answers your request for improvement, but becomes it.

People often have a difficult time conceptualizing a creator, or a force, or the process through which something as amazing as your planet, spinning in its orbit in perfect proximity to other planets, could have come to be. And yet, even though you do not understand it, and cannot begin to explain it, you are—every one of you—continuing to add to the expansion of all of that through your living of life and the launching of rockets into the Vibrational Reality that will someday be fully realized by physical inhabitants.

We have written this book because we want to call your attention to the Vibrational Reality that you are in the process of creating. We want you to be aware of your Vortex of Creation; and most important of all, we want you to find a way, by the deliberate directing of your own conscious thought, to become a Vibrational Match to the contents of your swirling Vibrational Vortex of Creation, because every desire that has been born within you thus far exists there, just as you have dreamed it to be, waiting for your alignment.

Everything that you see that is now physical, tangible, visible, audible *reality* was previously swirling in a Vibrational Vortex of Creation; for first there is *thought,* then *thought-form,* then *reality* as you know it in your physical world. Your dreams and desires and ideas of improvement have been received by the Broader part of you; and as that older, larger, wiser part of you focuses purely upon your requests, holding no resistance whatsoever, the powerful *Law of Attraction* responds. And then, all cooperative components (all components with same Vibrational frequency) are drawn into this swirling Vibrational Reality, this precursor to the physical reality that is now available to you. Only one thing is necessary for this Vibrational Reality to become real in a physical sense, manifested into things and experiences that you can see and hear and smell and taste and touch: *you have to go into the Vortex!*

When your husband, in his frustration, yells at you, and you are reeling in the absence of love that he is currently showing you, you launch a rocket of desire to be respected, to be loved; for a mate who feels better, for a mate who loves you. And *click, click, click, click,* those requests are received and integrated into your Vibrational Vortex of Creation. And now, the *Law of Attraction* responds to this swirling creation, drawing in all cooperative components—and your newly amended creative Vortex expands. But there is a very important question that you may want to consider: *Are you, right now, a cooperative component? Are you in the Vortex?*

- If you are still reeling in discomfort from your mate's verbal abuse—you are not in the Vortex.

- If you are telling your girlfriend about what happened, defending your innocence in the whole affair—you are not in the Vortex.

- If you are longing for the time when he treated you better—you are not in the Vortex.

- If you are letting it go and remembering how you felt when you decided to marry him—you are in the Vortex.

- If you are not taking his outburst personally and are focused upon other positive aspects of your experience—you are in the Vortex.

- If you feel terrible—you are not in the Vortex.

- If you feel better—you are closer to the Vortex.

A simple way to understand the Vortex is this:

- Before your birth into this physical body, you were in the Vortex (no resistant thought resides there).

- A part of the Consciousness that was you is now focused into the physical you that you know as *you*.

- The contrast of your life causes you to send rockets of expansion into your Vortex, where the larger Non-Physical part of you exists.

- The Vortex, which holds only your positive requests for improvement and expansion, holds no thoughts that contradict improvement and expansion.

- The *Law of Attraction* responds to the pure, nonresistant Vibration of your Vortex and gathers all cooperative, Vibrational-matching components that are necessary for the completion of the creation.

- You are one of the components of your creation.

- In fact, *you are the creation.*

- So the only question is: *Are you, from your physical format, right now, a Vibrational Match to your creation?* Or not?

- And the way you feel, right now, as you focus upon the subject of creation is your answer.

- If you are angry—you are not a Vibrational Match—and you are not in the Vortex.

- If you are feeling appreciation—you are a Vibrational Match—and you are in the Vortex.

The key to getting inside your Vibrational Vortex of Creation, of experiencing the absolute absence of resistance, of achieving complete alignment with all that you have become and all that you desire, and of bringing to your physical experience everything that you desire—is being in the state of appreciation. And there is no more important object of attention to which you must flow your appreciation than that of self.

The habit of thought, or belief, that holds most people outside of their Vortex of Creation, more than all other thoughts put together, is the lack of appreciation of self.

Why Would Someone Lose Self-Confidence?

Jerry: Well, I guess I usually talk about my own experiences because they are the ones where I'm surest about what happened and how I felt. I remember that, as a little child, I had such self-confidence. I didn't know a stranger. I felt capable of accomplishing just about anything. But then, as the years went by, I began to accept the criticism of others, I began to feel criticism toward myself, and I lost that self-confidence. I became almost introverted.

Today, when I see little children coming in with that bravado and high self-confidence, I remember feeling that way. But then, little by little, I see them get what I call "chopped down" as their self-confidence diminishes. Would you clarify why we experience this erosion of self-appreciation and how we can prevent it? And how can we uplift others to a higher degree of self-appreciation?

Abraham: You are right—it is really only through your own experiences that you can understand anything, for this reason: Your life has caused you to expand, to launch rockets into your Vibrational Vortex of Creation; but true knowledge, or understanding, is experienced only when you allow yourself to catch up with and merge with those rockets. No knowledge is ever experienced by your trying to catch up with rockets that have been launched by others. That is why words do not teach. It is only your own life experience that teaches.

That is why you are so fiercely independent in the beginning: not wanting to take other people's word for things, wanting your own experience, wanting to make your own decisions, wanting your own freedom to choose. None of that wanting ever recedes or becomes less. In fact, it becomes more! *The reason why the bravado that you are born with usually fades is because you allow yourself to become distracted from your Vortex. In other words, you allow others to convince you that it is more important to you to pay attention to how they feel than how you feel.*

Every emotion that you feel is an indication of your relationship with your Vortex. When you feel confident, that means that your current thought is a perfect match to the way the Source within you, from inside your Vortex of Creation, is feeling about you. When you feel embarrassed, that means that your current thought does not match the way the Source within you is feeling about you. So, when parents or teachers or friends project an attitude of disapproval toward you (in an effort to evoke a more-pleasing-to-them behavior from you), if you respond to their disapproval by modifying your thoughts, words, or behavior to please them, you have distracted yourself from your own true Guidance and from your own true Source of confidence.

And so, it is not that your self-confidence *erodes,* but rather that you are disallowing the continual replenishment of it. As you seek approval from them, you are distracted from your fountain of Source Energy renewal. Again, "looking for love in all the wrong places."

For you to uplift others, you must direct them to their own fountain of replenishment. You do not help them by asking them to respond to your approval or disapproval. Many of you think that the way to uplift others is by showering them with your own approval. But if they are looking to you for the refreshment of their being and you have other things to which you want to give your attention, they will be in trouble. Or if they are looking to you and you yourself are not connected to your own Stream of replenishment, so you have nothing to give them, they are again in trouble. But if you help them understand that they have a Source of refreshment that is independent of all other humans, and that they have only to understand the nature of their own Vortex of Creation and align with it often, now you have offered them true upliftment that will serve them, independently, all of the days of their lives.

What Is a First Step Toward Self-Appreciation?

Jerry: I recall the negatives that were directed at me, criticizing me and causing me to feel really bad about myself, but then I remember my grandfather, who uplifted me tremendously. There were teachers who deflated me and tried to humble me and embarrass me and belittle me, but then I remember my speech teacher, Mr. Hanley, who uplifted me and made me feel good about myself. I remember the people in the gymnasium who made fun of me, but then Mr. Piers, the gym coach, uplifted me tremendously. I remember enjoying participating in the teenage programs at the church and in the choir and the Scouts, but then there was so much criticism in the church directed at all other churches and toward the rest of the world that I just wanted to get away from it. I wanted to take my physical body away.

But now, what I am hearing from you is that it's not an action kind of thing—that we need to leave what we don't want. We don't need to look to those other teachers or family members to uplift us or give us self-confidence, although it does help. We can find it directly in ourselves, no matter what's going on around us, right?

Abraham: You have just pointed out, through the examples in your own life, the problem with looking to others for your upliftment. Those who were in a state of appreciation—and therefore were in alignment with Source; with their Vortex; with the Pure, Positive Energy that creates worlds—as *they* held you as your object of attention, you felt the *advantage* of their gaze. But when those not in their Vortex, not in alignment with Source, held you as the object of their lackful attention, you felt the *disadvantage* of their gaze. It is the inconsistency of the responses that you garner from others that eventually erodes your confidence.

Your Vortex of Creation, the Source within you (your *Inner Being*), is undeviating and dependable. When you make your way to your Vortex of Creation through the thoughts that you choose— you will always be replenished. A balanced, good-feeling life requires that you return often to drink from the Source.

How Does the *Law of Attraction* Affect Competition?

Jerry: Do you see competition as helpful or unhelpful? When I was a teenager, whenever I saw someone doing a spectacular dive on a diving board, I felt inspired to come up with something even better. Or if I'd see a juggler who could outdo me in some way, then I'd try to develop juggling routines that no one else had done. It seemed to me that I was constantly evaluating myself in comparison with someone else's talent and ability. But then, as an adult, I tried to pull myself away from anything that felt competitive, because I didn't like the idea that in order for someone to win, someone else had to lose. I liked winning, but I didn't like losing; and I didn't really enjoy others' losing, even when I was winning.

Abraham: You have deliberately positioned yourself in this time-space reality filled with variety and contrast because you enjoy the stimulation of thought that it provides. The key to effectively utilizing the variety or competition of ideas and experiences that surrounds you is to use it to stimulate your desire, but then once your desire has been formulated and your rockets have been launched into your Vortex, to now turn your undivided attention to you and your thought-by-thought relationship with your own Vortex. Once your rockets have been launched, the physical competition has served its purpose for you. In other words, competition is a tremendous impetus to *Step One* of your Creative Process, but it is a tremendous hindrance to *Step Three* of your Creative Process.

Jerry: Aren't you speaking more of comparison than competition?

Abraham: Competition is just an advanced version of comparison. And it is important to remember that there is never an ending to the game, for there will always be another combination of contrast that will cause you to launch another rocket of desire. Therefore, you will always have the fun of moving toward your Vortex; of closing the Vibrational gap; and of experiencing, in detail, your newly launched expansion.

What about Comparing Ourselves Unfavorably to Others?

Jerry: Long after I was able to afford a more luxurious car, I continued to drive more conservative cars because I remembered being critical of people who drove luxury cars. Then once I left my criticism of luxury-car owners behind, I drove the most expensive car that was made. But, in both cases, I was influenced by the response that I would attract from other people. Would you call that an unhealthy game?

Abraham: Anytime what someone else thinks about you becomes more important than your own balance with self, you are in a less-than-healthy position. Anytime you take action to try to manipulate or affect others' opinions or attitudes toward you, you are in a less-than-healthy position, because you are replacing your own *Guidance System* with their *opinion.*

What If We're Fearing a Worldwide Financial Crisis?

Most people are so distracted by what others are doing and what others are thinking that they forget to tune themselves to their own expansion. And when the resulting empty feeling comes, they incorrectly assume that it has something to do with the behavior or opinions of the others. But it is never about that. *Every emotion that you feel, good or bad, is about the relationship between your current thought and the understanding of the Source within you on the same topic.*

Some people are feeling acute fear or anxiety because they are personally, right now, without work or income. But the fear that *most* people are feeling today is because of their negative speculation about how bad conditions may yet become and the negative impact that those future, unwanted conditions may have on their personal lives.

By giving attention to the financial trauma that some people are experiencing, and by adding to that trauma with their own anticipation of how much worse it *could* become—without meaning to, and certainly without wanting to, people are adding massively to an even worsening economic situation. Their worried thoughts are not a driving negative force that is somehow destroying businesses and employment and resources, but those thoughts are holding *them* apart from the financial well-being that they so much desire.

When you see others experiencing hardship and become fearful that similar hardship will befall you, you hold yourself in a Vibrational tension that disallows your natural Well-Being from flowing. *As more people observe hardship and strike a tense, resistant pose—and therefore disallow their own Well-Being—others use them as their reason to do the same. And, in a very short time, a very negative pattern of resistance can sweep through your population. The good news in this scenario is that, in every moment that every person is feeling negative emotion about the economic state, Vibrational requests for more abundance are launched—and those requests are heard clearly, and responded to immediately, by Source. And a Non-Physical, Vibrational Vortex of Creation begins to swirl in powerful response to that powerful asking—and all compatible components are drawn into the Vortex for the discovery and relief of those who allow themselves to be drawn inside.*

Although there is a great deal of confusion about what to do about the economic situation of your nation, or of your world, your solution does not lie in the action you take, but in the Vibrational stance that you discover that allows you to see clearly the path to the solutions that you seek. In simple terms, since the solutions you seek have already been assembled by the powerful *Law of Attraction* inside the Vibrational Vortex of Creation, you have only to stop harboring the thoughts that hold you outside of the Vortex, for by often offering thoughts upon a subject that are Vibrationally opposite in nature, you prevent yourself from finding the solutions you seek.

The personal and collective *contradictions* in thoughts regarding abundance and financial well-being are running rampant in your society, in your government, in the minds of those who propose to resolve the situation, and in the general public at large. In other words, you cannot have it both ways: Your businesses acknowledge that they want people to buy their products and services, and to spend money to stimulate the economy; and they acknowledge that many thriving businesses make for a general thriving economy. But then a contradictory assertion also rings out that says it is arrogant and improper to display your opulence by spending too much money or living too well.

Many people want to experience more personal wealth at the same time that they are criticizing those who are already experiencing personal wealth:

- "We need you to spend/Your spending makes us uncomfortable."

- "I want to be wealthy/Wealthy people are somehow immoral."

- "I would like to be rich/Rich people are depriving poor people of resources."

- "Spending stimulates the economy/Spending is wasteful."

- "Spend, and stimulate the economy/Save and sacrifice for the sake of the economy."

- "I want to thrive/There is not enough to go around."

It is natural that you thrive, and the resources are there for all to thrive. But chronic thoughts of shortage, or chronic thoughts of pushing against those who are thriving, hold you in contradiction to your own desires and, more important, to what you have put into your Vortex of Creation for yourself.

The negative emotion that you feel when you believe that others are depriving you of something is not about what *they have* and therefore what *you do not have.* Your negative emotion, in every case, is about what you are, in the moment of your negative emotion, depriving yourself of receiving. And, even more important, if you had not already called forth the abundance by virtue of what you have been living, and if the abundance you have asked for were not already swirling in your Vortex in anticipation of your receipt of it, you would not feel negative emotion as you deprive yourself of it.

If you seek financial well-being for yourself—you must praise it wherever you see it.

If you would like more abundance for yourself, personally, or for others you care about—you must not criticize those who are experiencing abundance. When you criticize or condemn or push against anything, you activate an opposing Vibration to what you seek. Every time. No exceptions. Which leads us to another flawed premise:

Flawed Premise #22: *I can criticize successful
people and still achieve my own success.*

Whenever you criticize, or push against, anything, you hold yourself outside of your Vortex. Your own success can only be realized when you are inside your Vortex. Flawed premises hold people outside of their Vortices of abundance and prevent them from the ease and Well-Being that they deserve. You cannot "criticize yourself" to success. You cannot "condemn yourself" to Well-Being. The negative emotion you feel, in your disappointment, anger, and condemnation, is the indication of the opposing thoughts within you. You are opposing your success. You are opposing your abundance. You are opposing your alignment with Source. You are opposing the Vortex that holds all that you seek.

Selfishness, and the *Law of Attraction?*

Some offer criticism because we place such emphasis on the value of your feeling good, accusing us of teaching *selfishness.* And we acknowledge that true selfishness is at the very core of our teaching, because if you are not selfish enough, if you do not care how you feel, if you are not willing to continually redirect your thoughts in the direction of feeling good, you cannot come into alignment with the Source within you. And unless you are in alignment with the Source within you, you have nothing to give another. Alignment with Source—being inside your Vortex of Creation, becoming one with the true expanded version of you—is the ultimate selfishness.

And yes, in that state of alignment, all good things must come to you. Every rocket of desire that you have launched will be fulfilled.

True success is not the attainment of things, or the achievement of tasks, or the achievement of financial abundance. True success is the coming into alignment with You. Yes, selfishly aligning with your desires, your clarity, your confidence, your knowledge, your love—with Yourself!

Must We Be Guided by the Intentions of Others?

Jerry: If each of us felt totally at one with ourselves, if we were consistently inside the Vortex, would there be any need for leaders or people in the world to control us or to tell us what to do?

Abraham: Your alignment with Source is so much more than any guidance you could ever receive from any other place. Sometimes, as an individual or as a culture, you have the benefit of a leader who is leading from *inside* the Vortex. And when that happens, you feel the power of the individual, and you often receive clarity and insight when you listen. But, more often, as a leader begins to lead, as he focuses upon the problems to be solved, he moves *outside* the Vortex and then attempts to lead from his vastly weakened position. If we were standing in your physical shoes, we would not seek a leader, asking him to go into the Vortex in order to lead you. We would find our own way in, and we would work to consistently stay there, and we would discover the power that creates worlds flowing through our own fingertips.

Most often, you gather together in numbers out of your feeling of weakness. From your places of insecurity, you try to make it better. But a large gathering of people who are not in their Vortices never offers clarity or strength or solutions. *One person consistently inside the Vortex is more powerful than millions who are not.*

How Can I Feel More Self-Appreciation?

Jerry: Well, this philosophy clearly is about the value of our feeling good. Can you guide us on how to feel good? Can you give us a process or a technique to feel good about ourselves? In other words, speak to us about how we can deliberately acquire self-appreciation.

Abraham: The ultimate in self-appreciation is the allowing of yourself to be in Vibrational alignment with Source, with the expanded you inside your Vortex, and it is not necessary that you focus upon yourself in order to do that. In fact, for most people, especially in the beginning, it is easier for you to find alignment while focusing on many other things, other than you.

Over time, you have developed many opinions and attitudes, and habits of thoughts—or beliefs about yourself—that when activated hold you outside the Vortex. And so, it is easier to get inside the Vortex by focusing upon other subjects that are easier for you to feel good about.

For example, you could think about your favorite pet, and in your appreciation of that pet, you may move right into the Vortex because you do not hold resistant thoughts of envy or blame or guilt toward your pet. We would really like you to see that when you are thinking about your cat—or anything that holds no resistance to your Vortex, and so you flow easily inside—you are then joined (or better stated, you have *allowed* yourself to merge) with the whole of that which you are. We would call that the ultimate self-appreciation, even though you were not thinking about *you* in order to accomplish it. If we were standing in your physical shoes, we would choose the subjects that we easily feel good about as our focal points for getting into the Vortex.

Your physical orientation has trained you to be objective, to weigh the pros and the cons of every subject, but you will discover, as you play the game, that the pros of a subject may very well put you right inside the Vortex; while, as you focus upon the cons, the Vortex will spit you right out. *You cannot focus upon unwanted and be in the Vortex at the same time. . . .* By often making the statement "Nothing is more important than that I feel good," you will make yourself more aware of your proximity to your Vortex.

THE ESSENTIAL LAW OF ATTRACTION COLLECTION

What Is My Purpose for Life?

As people stand amidst the contrast of their physical lives, they often wonder, *What is my purpose for life? Why am I here?* And we want you to know that you deliberately came to enjoy your exploration of the contrast of your time-space reality because you knew that it would inspire new ideas and desires, and that it was, in fact, the foundation for expansion.

It is our expectation that, through the reading of this book, you now have a clearer understanding of how you, in your physical body, fit into the larger picture of creation and the important role you play, from your physical format, in that larger picture.

We are most eager about helping you remember that even though you are powerfully focused into your physical body, in your physical reality at this time, you—and we—are creating a Vibrational Reality that holds the promise of your future manifestations. And the amount of time that will expire before *you* begin to see and experience those desired manifestations is only the amount of time that it takes you to get into your Vortex. In other words, your moods and attitudes and emotions are your indicators of your proximity to your Vortex, to your Vibrational Reality, to everything that you desire, and to all that you have become.

If you have been a student of our teachings for any length of time, or have read the series of books that have preceded this one, you have discovered that we are prolific spewers of processes, and we want you to know that every process that we offer is done so with the intention of helping you release any resistance that is holding you outside of your Vortex.

As we conclude this book, we are going to offer a handful of very simple processes that, if consistently applied, will help you achieve a gradual but steady alignment with the *Energy-that-is-really-you,* and will assure your entry into your Vortex; and once you are consistently there—your physical life will be transformed.

Some Processes to Get into the Vortex

It is not necessary to deliberately apply these, or any, processes in order to raise your Vibration and get into the Vortex. Many people move easily into the Vortex simply because they like feeling good and consistently offer thoughts that do feel good. You could know nothing about what we are offering here in this book; you could be completely unaware of the *Law of Attraction,* know nothing about the Three-Step Creative Process, be unaware that you are an extension of Source Energy . . . and still be consistently inside the Vortex—simply because you like feeling good, and so you direct your thoughts to what does feel good. Your grandmother could have offered an example of a cheerful person who looks for the best in everyone and everything, and since you felt the power of her influence of Connection, you may very well be doing the same thing. But if you are like most people who are observing the world around you, you have probably developed patterns of thought that do not serve you, and that hold you—while you may be unaware of it—outside the Vortex.

When you have a belief about something (a belief is only a thought you keep thinking) and you think about it often, and therefore keep it active in your Vibration, the *Law of Attraction* simply brings you evidence to support it (because you get what you think about, whether it is something that you want or something that you do not want). And without making a decision to do something about changing the pattern of Vibration that is contained within those beliefs, nothing can change in your experience, and you will have no deliberate control of your proximity to your Vortex or to *who-you-have-become* and what you desire.

And so, the following processes are offered to help you release resistance and to provide an inevitable path into your Vortex:

A *Bedtime-Visualization Process*

Tonight, as you lie in your bed, focus your attention on the best-feeling things you can find. Draw your thoughts inward, away from any overwhelming details of your day, and feel the ease that occurs when you focus up close to where you are. Think, in detail, about your bed: its comfort, the feel of the bedding. Think about the relationship of your body to the mattress, and imagine the mattress floating or your body being absorbed into it. . . . Relax and breathe, and enjoy the comfort of your bed. Say things such as: *I like this. This is a good thing. I have a good life.* And sleep.

When You Find Yourself Awake

When you awaken in the morning, deliberately stay in your bed with your eyes closed for five minutes or so, with the intention of basking in the most pleasant things you can bring to mind. . . . During your slumber, you have released all resistance, and if you do not activate it now, it will not come up. So this extra five minutes in bed is for the purpose of allowing your naturally higher Vibration to get a strong foothold. . . . Find pleasure in your thoughts, and hold them in that pleasant place as long as possible. And, in the moment that the slightest uneasiness surfaces, breathe deeply, focus back upon the comfort of your bed, find something to appreciate— and then get up to begin your day.

The *Focus-Wheel Process*

Once you have eaten your breakfast and refreshed your body, sit in a comfortable place with the intention of doing one or two *Focus Wheels,* a process that has been designed specifically to help you release resistance and focus you into your Vortex. And, in fact, the process itself mimics a swirling, attracting Vortex, which gathers momentum as it swirls.

Have you seen the hand-pushed merry-go-rounds that are often in school or park playgrounds? It is common to see children piling on and then making the merry-go-round go faster and faster. It is easy to get onto it when it is stopped or going slowly, but when it is really going fast, it is harder, or impossible, to jump on. And if you try, the momentum of the wheel tosses you off in the bushes. Considering this merry-go-round will help you understand the *Focus-Wheel Process.*

During the course of your normal day, you will come across many things that, as you see them or remember them, will cause an activation of resistance within you. It may be some unpleasant thing you read about in the newspaper, or something that someone says to you; but when resistance occurs, you will always feel the pang of negative emotion. Often you cannot stop what you are doing right then to deal with newly activated resistant thought, but we do encourage you to make a mental—or better still, written—note about it: *My employer's attitude toward me makes me uncomfortable. He doesn't appreciate the contribution that I make here.* Now you have a subject for tomorrow's *Focus Wheel* segment.

So yesterday, while lying in bed, you released resistance before sleeping. During the night, you released all resistance. And when you awakened, you deliberately kept the resistance-free zone going by basking for a while. You had breakfast and showered and brushed your teeth, and now you plan to sit for 15 or 20 minutes to clean up any pieces of resistance that are lurking in your thought processes. And the very best time to do that is while you are feeling good.

As you read your note about your perception of your employer's attitude toward you, you will reactivate the resistant thought. So, take a large sheet of paper and write at the top of it: *My employer's attitude toward me makes me uncomfortable. He doesn't appreciate the contribution that I make to his business.*

Now draw a large circle on the page, as large as the page will allow. Then draw a small circle in the center of that large circle, and then draw 12 small circles around the perimeter of the large circle, positioning them like the numbers on the face of a clock.

Whenever something happens in life that points out to you, with great clarity, something that you do not want, an equally clear awareness of what you do want hatches within your awareness at the same time. By focusing upon your belief that your employer does not appreciate the contribution that you make, an equal *desire* is born: *I like it when my employer understands the depth of my interest and the contribution I make to the success we are all having here.* Write a version of that inside the circle in the center of the wheel.

Now, like the merry-go-round in the playground, you must find a way to get on the wheel. If your resistant thoughts are spinning too fast, you will not be able to get on. The wheel will just toss you off in the bushes. So try to find something that you already believe that matches, in some ways, what you felt when you wrote the words in the center circle.

You may think:

- *My boss does appreciate me.* (Off in the bushes.) You really do not believe that—not right now, anyway.

- *My boss doesn't deserve me.* (Now you are not even trying.)

Keep focusing back on the words in the center of your *Focus Wheel.* It will help you to feel the activation of beliefs that you already hold that match that sentiment.

- *My boss wants his company to succeed.* (You are on the wheel.) Write that at the 12 o'clock spot on your wheel.

- *His company was well under way when I joined.* (You have not solved any problem here, but this statement is something that you believe, and it does somehow make you feel better.) Write that at the 1 o'clock spot on your wheel.

- *There are aspects of this work that I really enjoy.* (That is true, too, and now you are gaining a bit of momentum.) Write that at the 2 o'clock spot on your wheel.

- *I really enjoy it when my boss and I are clicking.* (That is true, and it feels good.) 3 o'clock spot.

- *We both can feel the synergy of our collaboration.* (More momentum . . . now you're rolling.) Write that at the 4 o'clock spot.

- *I have felt my boss inspire a new idea in me.* (Now you are off and running. Your resistance is gone.) 5 o'clock spot.

- *I am certain my boss has felt me inspire a new idea in him.* 6 o'clock spot.

- *I think we all realize that we are all in this together.* 7 o'clock spot.

- *I would not want to be without this job.* 8 o'clock spot.

- *My boss often asks me to lead projects and direct others.* 9 o'clock spot.

- *It is obvious that he has trust in me.* 10 o'clock spot.

- *I am happy to work with him.* 11 o'clock spot.

And then, in the center of the wheel—right over the top of what you had written before, around the edge of it, or all across the page—in bold, confirming letters, write: *I know my boss sees my value.*

You have moved your Vibration to a new place on this topic, and therefore your point of attraction has shifted and your relationship to your Vortex has shifted. That is Deliberate Creation at its best. In this one short process, you have released resistance, improved your relationship with your boss, brought yourself back into alignment with *who-you-really-are*—and you have entered your Vortex. And now that you are inside the Vortex—you are looking at your world through the eyes of Source.

The *List-of-Positive-Aspects Process*

Now that you have released your resistance about your employer and established a higher, resistance-free Vibration about this topic, it can be of tremendous value for you to keep this resistance-free ball rolling for the purpose of really establishing your new Vibrational base and point of attraction. In other words, let us milk it for a while and get all of the value we can from the momentum you have going.

So now that you are in alignment with your *Inner Being,* make a list of the positive aspects of your employer and your work from the perspective of Source. From inside the Vortex, this is an easy process to do. And the reason we encourage you to do it is because there is great value in being inside the Vortex. And so, the longer you can stay here, the better.

Now, turn your paper over and write, as a heading at the top of the page: THE POSITIVE ASPECTS OF MY EMPLOYER:

- *He cares about his business.*

- *He is deliberate about who he hires.*

- *He often jumps in to help with a project.*

- *He smiles easily.*

- *People like him.*

- *His business is financially sound.*

- *He got the ball rolling before he hired any of us.*

- *He always makes payroll, and on time.*

- *His business steadily grows.*

- *I'm glad that I work here.*

- *I like what I do.*

- *I really like this man.*

This list may go on even longer, because in your alignment, you are very clear-minded. And so, you will feel the words flowing easily onto your page. You may later be surprised by your flowing compliments of someone who is often annoying, but remember: *in this moment, you are seeing your employer through the eyes of Source.*

The *Rampage-of-Appreciation Process*

Now if you are really wanting to firmly stake your claim on your newly acquired higher Vibration about this topic, move on to this final process: the *Rampage of Appreciation*. Move to another, clean sheet of paper and begin writing and/or speaking your appreciation for your employer:

I appreciate . . .

> . . . *his beautiful car.*
> . . . *that he puts money back into his business.*
> . . . *that he often buys our lunch.*
> . . . *our beautiful work space.*
> . . . *the scope of this business.*
> . . . *where it is going.*
> . . . *the potential we all have in working here.*
> . . . *the contribution this business offers to the world.*
> . . . *the flexibility I have here.*
> . . . *his eagerness to learn.*
> . . . *how he loves good ideas.*
> . . . *his wonderful laugh.*
> . . . *his dedication to his business.*
> . . . *the stability of his business.*
> . . . *the work he offers me.*
> . . . *the thrill of adventure.*
> . . . *the opportunity to expand.*
> . . . *the contrast that helps me expand.*
> . . . *my <u>Guidance System</u> that helps me keep up with my expansion.*
> . . . *this world.*
> . . . *this wonderful time of technology.*
> . . . *my life!*

What Life Is Like, from Inside the Vortex

This book is offered to you to assist you in accepting the existence of your Vibrational Reality Vortex and to inspire within you a desire to go there often, because we have the benefit of existing inside this Vortex that you are creating. From inside your Vortex, we focus upon all that you have asked for and therefore upon that which you have become. As you pay attention to your emotions, and reach steadily for the best-feeling thoughts you can find, you will move into your Vortex whenever you desire; and the more often you are there, the more often you will want to return—because life from inside the Vortex is sublime.

Your point of attraction will be such that only things that are wanted will flow into your path. The people you encounter will be perfect matches to your highest interests, and you will not rendezvous with those not up to speed with who you are. You will feel vital and alive and clear-minded and sure.

You will find the best in others, whether they see it or not. And your appreciation for life will ripple through your body in the form of thrilling sensations as you focus upon the objects of specific appreciation.

But occasionally, even often, you will remember or observe something not up to speed—and your Vortex will spit you out. But do not be alarmed, for you have deliberately emerged into an environment of contrast for the value of the new idea that is always born from the contrast. It is normal to have those *Step One* (asking) moments where you know, so very well, exactly what it is that you do not want. Just remember that, in those moments, you are launching specific rockets of desire into your Vibrational Escrow; and that later, after you have worked the bugs out of your resistance, you can find your way easily back into your Vortex, where you will again reap the benefit of your earlier contrasting moment.

Now that you understand the whole picture, you will find confidence and ease in the Three-Step Process of Creation. When something occurs that causes you to ask (since you now understand the Vortex, and how to get in), you will no longer writhe in the discomfort of powerlessness. No matter what unpleasant problems you may encounter along your way, an improved desire or request will emanate from you, and its solution will amass as all cooperative components assemble, waiting for you to enter the Vortex.

You do not have to explain this to anyone else; and, in fact, even if you try, they may not understand your words. But it is our promise to you that, through the reading of this book, you now do understand your relationship with the Vortex—and through the power of the example of your joyous life experience, others may be inspired to want to know, also.

We have enjoyed this interaction immensely.

There is great love here for you, and we remain joyously incomplete.

— Abraham

Flawed Premises

1. I am either physical or Non-Physical, either dead or alive.

2. My parents, because they were here long before I was born, and because they are my parents, know better than I do what is right or wrong for me.

3. If I push hard enough against unwanted things, they will go away.

4. I have come here to live the right way of life and to influence others to the same right way of living. . . .

5. Because I am older than you, I am wiser than you; and therefore you should allow me to guide you.

6. Who I am began the day I was born into my physical body. . . .

7. With enough effort, or hard work, I can accomplish anything.

8. To be in harmony with another, we have to want and believe the same things.

9. The path to my joy is through my action. . . .

10. I cannot have everything that I desire, so I have to give up some things that are important to me in order to get others.

11. If I leave an unwanted situation, I will find what I am looking for.

12. There is a finite container of resources that we are all dipping into with our requests. . . .

13. There are right ways and wrong ways to live. . . .

14. There is a God Who, having considered all things, has come to a final and correct conclusion about everything.

15. You cannot know, while you are still in your physical body, the true reward or punishment for your physical actions. . . .

16. By gathering data about the manifestations or results of the way the people of the earth have lived and are living, we can effectively sort them into absolute piles of right and wrong. . . .

17. Only very special people, like the founder of *our* group, can receive the right message from God. . . .

18. By ferreting out the undesirable elements in our society, we can eliminate them. . . .

19. A good relationship is one in which the dominant intention of each person involved is to find agreement and harmony with the other.

20. When I focus upon things of a physical nature, I am less Spiritual.

21. It is my job as a parent to have all the answers so that I can teach those answers to my children.

22. I can criticize successful people and still achieve my own success.

ABOUT THE AUTHORS

Excited about the clarity and practicality of the translated word from the Beings who call themselves Abraham, **Esther** and **Jerry Hicks** began disclosing their amazing Abraham experience to a handful of close business associates in 1986.

Recognizing the practical results being received by themselves and by those people who were asking practical questions and then applying Abraham's answers to their own situations, Esther and Jerry made a deliberate decision to allow the teachings of Abraham to become available to an ever-widening circle of seekers of how to live a happier life.

Using their San Antonio, Texas, conference center as their base, Jerry and Esther have traveled to approximately 50 cities a year since 1989, presenting interactive *Law of Attraction* workshops to those leaders who gather to participate in this expanding stream of progressive thought. And although worldwide attention has been given to this philosophy of Well-Being by Leading Edge thinkers and teachers who have, in turn, incorporated many of Abraham's *Law of Attraction* concepts into their best-selling books, scripts, lectures, and so forth, the primary spread of this material has been from person to person—as individuals begin to discover the value of this form of spiritual practicality in their personal life experiences.

In November 2011, Jerry made his transition into Non-Physical, and now Esther continues to conduct the Abraham workshops with the help of her physical friends and co-workers and, of course, with the Non-Physical help of Abraham and Jerry.

People are able to access Abraham directly by attending the seminars in person or by participating in the online live streaming of most events. There is also an extensive YouTube library of Abraham videos.

Abraham—a group of uplifting Non-Physical teachers—present their Broader Perspective through Esther Hicks. And as they speak to our level of comprehension through a series of loving, allowing, brilliant, yet comprehensively simple essays in print and in sound, they guide us to a clear connection with our loving *Inner Being,* and to uplifting self-empowerment from our Total Self.

Abraham-Hicks Publications may be contacted through the extensive interactive website: **www.abraham-hicks.com;** or by mail at Abraham-Hicks Publications, P.O. Box 690070, San Antonio, TX 78269.

We hope you enjoyed this Hay House book. If you'd like to receive
our online catalog featuring additional information on Hay House books
and products, or if you'd like to find out more about the
Hay Foundation, please contact:

Hay House, Inc., P.O. Box 5100, Carlsbad, CA 92018-5100
(760) 431-7695 or (800) 654-5126
(760) 431-6948 (fax) or (800) 650-5115 (fax)
www.hayhouse.com® • www.hayfoundation.org

▲▼▲

Published and distributed in Australia by: Hay House Australia Pty. Ltd., 18/36
Ralph St., Alexandria NSW 2015 • *Phone:* 612-9669-4299
Fax: 612-9669-4144 • www.hayhouse.com.au

Published and distributed in the United Kingdom by: Hay House UK, Ltd.,
Astley House, 33 Notting Hill Gate, London W11 3JQ • *Phone:* 44-20-3675-2450
Fax: 44-20-3675-2451 • www.hayhouse.co.uk

Published and distributed in the Republic of South Africa by: Hay House SA
(Pty), Ltd., P.O. Box 990, Witkoppen 2068 • *Phone/Fax:* 27-11-467-8904
www.hayhouse.co.za

Published in India by: Hay House Publishers India, Muskaan Complex, Plot No.
3, B-2, Vasant Kunj, New Delhi 110 070 • *Phone:* 91-11-4176-1620
Fax: 91-11-4176-1630 • www.hayhouse.co.in

Distributed in Canada by: Raincoast, 9050 Shaughnessy St.,
Vancouver, B.C. V6P 6E5 • *Phone:* (604) 323-7100 • *Fax:* (604) 323-2600
www.raincoast.com

▲▼▲

Take Your Soul on a Vacation

Visit www.HealYourLife.com® to regroup, recharge,
and reconnect with your own magnificence.
Featuring blogs, mind-body-spirit news, and
life-changing wisdom from Louise Hay and friends.

Visit www.HealYourLife.com today!